Also by Bob Woodward

The Agenda

The Commanders

Veil: The Secret Wars of the CIA 1981–1987

Wired: The Short Life and Fast Times of John Belushi

The Brethren
(with Scott Armstrong)

The Final Days
(with Carl Bernstein)

All the President's Men
(with Carl Bernstein)

THE CHOICE

How Clinton Won

BOB WOODWARD

A TOUCHSTONE BOOK
Published by Simon & Schuster

 TOUCHSTONE
Rockefeller Center
1230 Avenue of the Americas
New York, NY 10020

Copyright © 1996 by Bob Woodward
Afterword copyright © 1997 by Bob Woodward
All rights reserved,
including the right of reproduction
in whole or in part in any form.
First Touchstone Edition 1997
TOUCHSTONE and colophon are
registered trademarks of Simon & Schuster Inc.
Designed by Amy Hill
Manufactured in the United States of America

10 9 8 7 6 5 4 3 2 1

The Library of Congress has cataloged the
Simon & Schuster edition as follows:
Woodward, Bob.
   The choice / Bob Woodward.
       p.   cm.
   Includes index.
   1. Presidents—United States—Election—
1996.   2. Presidential candidates—United
States.   3. Clinton, Bill, 1946– . 4. Dole,
Robert J., 1923–   .   5. United States—Politics
and government—1993– .   I. Title.
E888.W66   1996
324.973'0929—dc20   96-26120
                                                  CIP

ISBN 0-684-81308-4
      0-684-82616-x (Pbk)

AUTHOR'S NOTE

Karen Alexander, a 1993 graduate of Yale University, has been with me every step of the way on this project. Attempting to write a book about an ongoing presidential campaign is both an endurance contest and a high-speed chase. She brought unmatched intellect, grace and doggedness and an ingrained sense of fairness to this book. Karen was my collaborator on the reporting, writing, editing and thinking. She spent weeks in the home states of candidates, gathering research and doing vast amounts of original reporting. Each day she enriched both the project and the lives of myself and my wife, Elsa Walsh. We were able to confide in her and rely on her in every way. This book could not have been done without Karen, and it is hers as much as mine. As she leaves to pursue her own writing career, she falls into that rare category of "friend for life."

To Elsa's parents,
Mary and Redmond Walsh,
and to my father,
Alfred E. Woodward,
and to Alice Woodward

A NOTE TO READERS

Work on this book began just weeks before the Republicans gained control of Congress in the November 1994 elections. In the 19 months that followed, I interviewed hundreds of people who were directly involved in the Republican presidential primary campaigns, the Senate Majority Leader's Office, the White House and the Clinton-Gore reelection campaign. Dozens of these people were interviewed repeatedly, many of the key sources between five and ten times. Most of them permitted me to tape-record the interviews; otherwise I took detailed notes. Many also provided me with their fresh recollections of events just days or even hours old. Some gave me access to memoranda, meeting notes, speech drafts, transcripts, schedules, polling data, videotapes or other documentation.

The interviews with the presidential candidates were on the record. For example, Bob Dole was interviewed for more than 12 hours and the typed transcripts run over 200 pages. President Clinton declined to be interviewed, though key members of his administration, White House staff and campaign were interviewed. Nearly all of the interviews with others were conducted under the journalistic ground rules of "background" or "deep background," which means that I could use the information but would not identify the sources of the information. Without such a stipulation, people generally would not candidly discuss their conversations or interactions with the president, candidates or other high-level officials. I took great care to compare and verify various sources' accounts of the same events. Extensive research, documentation and the willingness of key sources to allow me to review with them important meetings, discussions and decisions many times have provided a highly unusual look at the candidates for president in 1996 and the evolution of their campaigns. Each major scene, decision or event presented in this book has been reviewed with the candidates, firsthand sources or spokesmen for those people depicted.

Dialogue and quotations in this book come from at least one participant, from memos or from contemporaneous notes or diaries of a participant in the discussion. When someone is said to have "thought" or "felt" something, that description comes from the individual or from someone to whom he said it directly. I have tried to preserve the participants' own language as much as possible, even when they are not directly quoted, in order to capture the flavor of their speech and their fundamental attitudes. Quotation marks were used only when the memories of sources or the documentation was precise about wording.

Every major declared and potential presidential candidate was given serious attention and evaluation by myself and my assistant, Karen Alexander. Their political and personal backgrounds were researched carefully. For example, we spent weeks researching Senator Phil Gramm of Texas, California Governor Pete Wilson and former Tennessee Governor Lamar Alexander, though the stories of their candidacies are much compressed in the book because their efforts to win the Republican nomination failed.

The decision to seek the presidency is audacious. A candidate is declaring himself both fit and worthy. It is an act at once somewhat arrogant and selfless. I have attempted to capture the important moments in the lives of the candidates and their words and actions over the last two years.

This is a contemporaneous account, more than a newspaper or magazine could provide but not the whole story of this presidential race by any means. By virtue of its immediacy, I was able to sit with many of the candidates and key players and ask about the questions of the day as the campaign unfolded. Recollections were fresh, and issues could be examined before the possible outcome or meaning was at all clear or the possible consequences were weighed. So this book—reported in the heat of the battle—may have captured some events and emotional day-by-day reactions that would otherwise have been lost to the public record. At the same time, this account lacks the perspective of history. The more I learn about any subject or person, the more apparent it becomes to me as a reporter how much I do not know. Yet this is the best version of the story I could write based on the information available to me.

Presidential elections are defining moments that go way beyond legislative programs or the role of the government. They are measuring points for the country that call forth a range of questions which each candidate must try to address. Who are we? What matters? Where are we going? In the private and public actions of the candidates are embedded their best answers. Action is character, I believe, and when all is said and sifted, character is what matters most.

Bob Woodward
Washington, D.C.

PROLOGUE

President Bill Clinton insisted that one item on his weekly schedule remain inviolate. His private lunch with his vice president, Al Gore, could not be dropped unless there was a crisis or one of them was out of town. Though there was no doubt about who was the senior partner in the relationship, Clinton had come to rely on Gore as his indispensable chief adviser. Just as Clinton had mastered campaigning over the course of his lifetime in politics, Gore had mastered government, bureaucracy and even Washington.

At their lunches, in a small room off the Oval Office, discussion inevitably focused on the Clinton presidency. There were no two people who had more to lose if it failed, and by the spring of 1996 Clinton and Gore were heavily involved in overseeing their reelection campaign. The lunches sometimes did not start until 3 P.M. because of other business. Clinton, who had a notorious appetite, tried to eat lighter food. They began lunch with one or the other of them saying a short prayer.

Each week Gore had a formal agenda, but no subject was more sensitive or more important than the discussion of Clinton himself and his development and experiences as president. Clinton and Gore talked about it at length. Understanding the immediate past was central to figuring out a way to win in 1996.

The first two years of his presidency had been more than difficult, and Clinton often acknowledged to Gore that the administration did not have its bearings. The crown jewel of his domestic program, health care reform, had gone down to a crushing defeat at the hands of Congress and the Republicans. He had not yet gained mastery of foreign affairs, though a United States peace initiative had at least temporarily halted the slaughter and ethnic cleansing of the war in Bosnia. And an independent counsel was investigating the 1978 Whitewater land investment that Clinton and his wife Hillary had made in Arkansas.

But Clinton also thought a lot of the criticism he received was unfair. He had expected that his presidency would be defined by how he handled big issues, like Russian President Boris Yeltsin. Instead, incidents like an expensive haircut he had received on Air Force One in Los Angeles and the inaccurate reports that it had delayed air traffic received much attention, becoming a metaphor for his presidency. He had acquired a reputation for indecisiveness, but Clinton felt people were projecting their own anxieties and uncertainties onto him. He believed he was unusually decisive for a president.

Gore had some advice. Clinton always had found excess reserve within himself. He would just have to find more, Gore said. The president was everyone's target—as were his past, his habits, his staff, his wife. There were no boundaries any more. Nothing was off limits. The world's troubles were his, as were everyone's personal grievances. There was only one way to succeed: Clinton would have to absorb the searing experience of the presidency itself, and then step beyond that experience and even beyond himself.

He had, Clinton said. He knew he would have to transcend himself. Bill Clinton the person generally said what was on his mind. His conversation was expansive, though his remarks often tentative, and he thought out loud. He was an experimental person, always reaching out for new ideas and people. He realized that he was going to have to shut down this side of himself, and create more distance.

Gore agreed. The hallmark of 1996 would be self-discipline. In his remarks, ideas and behavior.

Yes, Clinton said. He would have to use the office, use the presidency. He could not just be Bill Clinton. He couldn't take what was happening that personally, even though he had taken his whole life personally. He had to think of himself as a man of history, not a man experiencing history. It was hard.

On big decisions Clinton frequently told Gore, "I'm risking my presidency on this." He used the line so often it became a kind of cliché between the two. Risk was the nature of the job, more than either had appreciated. Often, their discussion would turn to the larger consequences of Clinton's decisions, and one or the other of them would note, well, there goes the presidency again.

"Time to throw the long ball," Clinton said once. It was a football metaphor for the long, strategically risky pass when you needed to score, and they returned to it time and time again in their discussions. Often it seemed they had several balls in the air at once hurtling through to the end zone.

Gore developed a different but extended metaphor to frame the 1996 race against Senate Majority Leader Bob Dole, who was going to be the Republican nominee for president. Clinton would be 50 at election time, Dole would be 73. Clinton and Gore would probably never say it out loud, but it would be the driving image and contrast they would try to create. It was not just about the age or generational difference, but about something more fundamental.

In Gore's metaphor, there was a patriarch who had built an institution the way he wanted it. Satisfied, the patriarch finally had decided his generation should turn leadership over to the son. This son was full of energy, but he made mistakes, some large, some small. But the son had given it his whole heart and developed a seriousness of purpose. Then the patriarch, because of the mistakes the son had made, says, I'm not satisfied and I want to take it back.

Dole's World War II generation had already produced six presidents while most generations had only three, and Dole, the old survivor, was the patriarch. The point, Gore said, was the argument they would have to make in the campaign: "It's not fair to take back the reins."

Clinton liked Dole and found him a worthy advocate, but he harbored two resentments against him. First, he felt that Dole had waited only about three hours and 15 minutes into Clinton's presidency before telling him that the Republicans wouldn't provide any votes for Clinton's initial 1993 economic plan. That plan included substantial tax increases, mostly on the wealthy, and Dole had said forthrightly that if it didn't work, they could then blame Clinton.

"I didn't run for president to be a bare-fanged partisan," Clinton said. But the Republican refusal had helped make Clinton into one, and his economic plan did not get a single Republican vote in either the House or Senate. Though Dole's candor helped him realize that the 1996 presidential campaign began the day he became president, Clinton still felt Dole should have been more flexible and at least tried to work for a bipartisan compromise of some sort.

Clinton's second resentment was very personal. In early 1994, Clinton's mother Virginia Kelley died, and less than eight hours after her death Dole had gone on three network morning television shows. He had been very sympathetic and praised her as a strong, dynamic woman. At first when asked about the Whitewater scandal, Dole said, "I even hate to discuss these things today." But then he did. He lashed out at the White House, saying the behavior was "unbelievable" and "mind-boggling," and "big, big news," adding, "It cries out more than ever now for an independent counsel."

Dole's criticism continued for two days, even as Clinton was burying his mother. Gore realized that Clinton was in inconsolable grief. Clinton's father had died before his birth, and now his mother was gone. Recognizing the deep emotional dimensions for Clinton, Gore had finally gone on television to try to plead for some civility. "Now doesn't it bother you a little bit to have the president attending the funeral service of his mother and to have members of the political opposition, as the service is going on, on the airwaves making these attacks?" Gore asked.

Dole issued a statement saying he was "saddened" that Gore had "stooped" to invoke the death of Clinton's mother to try to stifle criticism. Damage control wouldn't obscure the facts, Dole said.

Clinton was thunderstruck by Dole's behavior. For that man to attack me on the day of my mother's death and the day of her funeral, Clinton said, is just unforgivable.

1

The fall of 1994 was a disquieting time for President Clinton. He felt isolated, lonely and angry. The first two years of his presidency had been grueling, leaving him off balance. He had not yet conquered the presidency.

Though he offered many explanations for his situation as president, Clinton frequently railed against people in his own inner circle who he felt had betrayed him and presented the media with a false portrait of him and the way he made decisions. "Traitors on my staff," he called them to more than one intimate. Polls showed his approval ratings had dipped dangerously low, jeopardizing his reelection. Clinton reached outside for help.

He turned to Dick Morris, a Connecticut-based political consultant he had first used 17 years earlier in his initial run for governor of Arkansas but who now worked almost exclusively for Republican candidates. Clinton had talked intermittently with Morris throughout his presidency, but now the conversations became more frequent.

Clinton and Morris had shared a stormy, on-again and off-again relationship for much of the past two decades. Morris, 47, represented a side of Clinton that the president disliked in himself—the pragmatist who knew that a candidate needed to jockey and reposition himself to gain approval and win elections. But Clinton was always eager to be liked, and the attraction between Clinton and Morris was almost magnetic.

They knew and understood each other so well they could finish each other's sentences.

The coming 1994 congressional elections will be a calamity for you, Morris told Clinton. He expected the Democrats were going to suffer huge losses. Even on the phone Morris conveyed his intensity, his voice like a spring about to pop in your ear. He spoke aggressively and with total confidence, in a clipped New York accent.

The reason for the trouble was simple and powerful, Morris said. The public did not identify Clinton with any clear, visible accomplishment. Clinton's biggest achievement had been to substantially reduce the federal deficit, but Morris said he had conducted some polls that showed most voters didn't believe it. Deficit reduction was a Republican issue, and voters just didn't believe a Democrat like Clinton would really reduce the debt. They did believe that Clinton had increased taxes as part of the deficit reduction package, because Democrats did raise taxes. Likewise they didn't believe Clinton had led the charge on the crime bill, again a traditionally Republican issue. Clinton's accomplishments kind of fell into a black hole, Morris said.

At the same time, voters did give Clinton credit for the family and medical leave legislation that guaranteed workers time off for childbirth and illness. Though small, it was believable. Morris said people were distrustful of large claims. They were in the mood to receive news of small accomplishments.

Morris also reminded Clinton that the 1994 congressional races were not his fight. Clinton should minimize his role in the various Senate and House races. His popularity was down, so he wouldn't be able to help the Democratic candidates, much less himself.

The Republicans were trying to nationalize the elections, particularly through the so-called Contract With America that the House Republicans, led by Newt Gingrich, had put forth in September promising a new conservative agenda. Morris said the Republicans were trying to run under one banner. Don't let them, he advised. If Clinton was dragged into the debate, they would make him out to be the pro-government liberal. Morris told the president he not only thought the Democrats would surely lose the Senate, as many expected, but that the Democrats were in such trouble they would also lose control of the House.

Clinton disagreed vehemently that the results would be that bad, especially in the House, which the Democrats had controlled for 40 years, including most of Eisenhower's presidency and all of Reagan's and Bush's.

Get out of the way, Mr. President, Morris implored. Be less visible. The Republican wave is coming, he insisted.

Clinton mentioned that he was planning a four-day trip to the Middle East to sign the Middle East Peace Treaty at the end of October.

The peace was a Promethean accomplishment, Morris said, a huge accomplishment. Though by no means solely attributable to Clinton, the treaty was being signed on his watch. He should not take himself down from that pedestal to campaign. The Middle East peace was important, a giant symbol. A president could have no bigger role than that of peace-maker. Retain control of the large symbols, Morris advised.

Clinton's sense of loneliness, the feeling that the presidency was a solitary undertaking, had grown as he observed the behavior of those in his inner circle. Even many closest to him seemed to chafe at the way he spent so much time making decisions, consulting and weighing alterna-tives, going back and forth. His thinking and debating had been taken for indecisiveness. Many of those close to him had rebelled and turned him in, providing the media with unflattering accounts of his decision making. In front of staff and cabinet members, Hillary, though sympathetic to her husband, had decried the administration's failure to think and plan strategically to sell its economic program in 1993. "Mechanic-in-chief," she had called the president. When asked for advice about how to get the budget plan passed, Vice President Gore had said tersely to Clinton one day in the Oval Office, "You can get with the goddamn program!" His first Treasury Secretary, Lloyd Bentsen, had criticized Clinton to his face for not delegating properly and not separating the important decisions from the unimportant ones.

It was one thing for this advice to be given in private. It was quite another for it to appear in print, as these unflattering accounts and too many others had. In fact, the most severe and authoritative critique of his administration had often been provided not by his opponents or the Republicans. It had come from the inner circle, even his wife and vice president at times. Clinton told a friend he was paying a terrible price because of the frustration of others who had their own ideas about how to do his job. Who could he trust? Who could he depend on? he asked friends with increasing regularity. Clinton was speaking about trust more and more, and wondering aloud where he could find it.

He was confident he was a new kind of Democrat, that he could fashion a new governing philosophy. Yes, it incorporated some normally traditional Republican ideas—free trade, deficit reduction, an eye toward the bond market to get consumer interest rates down, a small and more efficient government, lower taxes for the middle class. It also incorporated some traditional Democratic ideas—spending for education and worker training, a strong safety net of social programs for the truly needy and a government with a heart, not a handout.

George Stephanopoulos, Clinton's 33-year-old senior White House political aide and one of the chief strategists and spokesmen for the 1992 campaign, had identified these warring factions within Clinton as the "unbridgeable chasm."

Clinton was determined to fashion that bridge.

At the end of October 1994, Clinton made the high-profile trip to the Middle East. Upon his return he found he had been scheduled on a whirlwind tour of non-stop campaigning. Clinton half-maintained to Morris that these trips were contrary to his wishes. But the upcoming elections were where the action was. He loved campaigning, and being out of Washington. He knew he was a master campaigner.

Morris argued again that interjecting himself in the local campaigns was a mistake. It would backfire if he tried to assist Democrats in key states. "If you want to help in Pennsylvania," he urged Clinton, "go back to the Middle East."

But Clinton began stumping the country for Democrats in Pennsylvania, Michigan, Ohio, Rhode Island, New York, Iowa, Minnesota, California, Washington State and Delaware. In addition, he made 17 radio and television appearances in the local markets and was interviewed extensively about the elections on the Black Entertainment Television network and by CNN's Larry King.

On Tuesday, November 8, 1994, midterm election day, President Clinton was up, dressed, and in the Oval Office by 7:12 A.M. He hated the early mornings, but he wanted to complete a final round of three short radio interviews to wrap up his effort. First up was John Gambling's *Rambling with Gambling* on WOR Radio in New York City.

"A lot of our candidates asked me to get out there and campaign," Clinton said, "including Governor Cuomo, so I tried to do all I could to make the best argument for why we're moving our country in the right direction and we don't want to go back to the policies that failed us in the 1980s."

But the president had never offered a fully satisfactory argument that laid out the positive reasons why his party should retain control of both the House and Senate.

"We don't want to go back," he repeated to Philadelphia radio station WWDB that morning. He went through a laundry list of legislative accomplishments, but he still sounded no compelling theme, nor did he give a clear definition of what was next for his presidency.

Clinton sensed the emptiness. Though he could muster the passion and emotional engagement for the fight, he knew this was nothing like 1992 when he had won the presidency on his pledge to fix the economy.

Election days mean waiting, and Clinton had extra time on his hands. He and his foreign policy advisers met with the president of Iceland. Clinton was charming, mentioning a TV documentary he had recently seen about Iceland and a stopover he had made there as a student. But his mind was clearly on the future of his presidency.

"Reagan really understood the symbolic importance of the presidency," Clinton said later to several members of his staff. "We've got to do better."

At an afternoon reception on the South Lawn for the volunteers who worked at the White House, Clinton again referred to the midterm elections. "There are clear choices between going forward and going back," he said.

He finally returned to the White House residency, where he and Hillary stayed for most of the rest of the day as early exit polling began to forecast an unthinkable disaster for Democrats. Incredibly the Republicans seemed to be winning control of both the Senate and the House. Most of the Democrats that Clinton had campaigned for were losing. It would soon be clear that not a single Republican incumbent in any race for the Senate, House or governor had lost. It was apparently an historic rout.

Clinton and Hillary raced through various responses. What could Clinton say? How could he get on top of this? He finally decided to say nothing publicly that night. As the night wore on, he retreated into himself. His White House staff saw it as a kind of withdrawal into an isolation chamber. Some took it personally. But Clinton and his wife were contemplating what was happening. To what extent was it a referendum on him? That was inevitable because he was the president, they agreed, but unfair. Why was he getting so little credit for the positive things he had done? Why was there no reward for their hard work? Was Dick Morris right? What had been the mistakes?

Clinton said that he probably had spent too much of his time as president in the legislative trenches. He had done what he knew from Arkansas, worked with the legislature passing laws, doing what he knew how to do best. Working with Congress had inevitably led to compromise and had prevented him from setting a definite direction.

Hillary was sympathetic. The health care reform task force she had headed had been shredded by the Congress, and she herself subjected to pounding attacks.

"I was a prime minister," Clinton said, "not a president. I got caught up in the parliamentary aspect of the presidency and missed the leadership, bully pulpit function which is so critical."

Hillary could see he was worried that the public was telling him he was not cutting it as president.

As the list of big Democrats who had been defeated grew, the shock increased. Mario Cuomo, the New York governor, was going down. So was Ann Richards, the governor of Texas. In the last 40 years, the party of a sitting president on average lost one Senate seat and about a dozen House seats in the off years. Now the Democrats were losing eight Senate seats and an incredible 52 House seats at a time of peace and economic growth.

Clinton finally became angry that night. One of his targets was himself. He had let the agenda get out of control, he had blown it. Then he got angry at the White House staff. They had misdirected him, misunderstood him, wasted his time. Next, he turned to the Republicans. They were at fault, not giving him a single vote on his economic plan, savaging them both on health care. No, he said, the congressional Democrats were at fault, the ones who persisted in their conventional liberalism. They had trapped him, let their internal differences prolong debate in a way that had hurt him—allowing the crime bill, for example, to be hijacked and disparaged, tagging on pork barrel and social projects that looked totally ridiculous in the face of violent crime.

Clinton spoke with Vice President Gore, who also was astounded at the election. Tennessee politics were being turned upside down. Republicans were taking both Senate seats, including the one Gore had held until

1992. It had been a kind of family seat since his father, Albert Gore, Sr., had held it before him. The Democratic governor was being replaced by a Republican, and the Tennessee congressional delegation lost two House Democratic seats, leaving the state 5–4 Republican. That was incredible and depressing, but the national dimensions were a genuine body blow.

After hours of talk, fury, disappointment and systematic consideration of the alternative villains, Clinton settled down to feel sorry for himself. But he was accustomed to converting bad news to good, and he eventually began talking about the loss of the Congress differently. Could it be an opportunity? Free him of the restraints? Give him a foil?

"Possibly liberating," Clinton finally declared amidst the despair and pain. He got very little sleep that night.

The next afternoon, the president appeared at a press conference in the East Room of the White House. He pledged cooperation with the new Republican Congress and its leaders.

"With the Democrats in control of both the White House and the Congress, we were held accountable yesterday," he said. "I accept my share of the responsibility in the result of the elections," he added. Voters had selected change in 1992 by electing him, and now in 1994 they were seeking more change. His fault, he said, was that there had not been enough change. Of the voters, Clinton said, "They looked at us, and they said, 'We want some more changes, and we're going to try this and see if this works.'

"And what I think they told us was, 'Look, two years ago we made one change, now we made another change. We want you to keep on moving this country forward, and we want you to accelerate the pace of change.' " Clinton separated himself from the Democrats, as if he were a non-partisan agent of change hovering over the process. Reporters asked him if that was what he really meant. "Are you essentially saying that the electorate yesterday was agreeing with you?" one incredulous reporter inquired.

"I think they were agreeing with me," he said, "but they don't think we produced them. In other words—let me say it in another way. I'm saying that I agree with much of what the electorate said yesterday."

It was a stunning but little noted performance because the media spotlights had instantly shifted to Newt Gingrich, the likely new House Speaker, and the new Republican Congress.

Gore was sympathetic. Clinton's comments did not reflect a complete internal analysis, but a president often had to give answers to the public before he had worked them out in his own mind.

In the days that followed Clinton talked with many people, conducting a kind of running seminar for himself. His emotions ran from shock to denial. He wondered how he might capitalize on the situation. And he had one basic question. What the hell did that earthquake mean?

Privately, the president complained that he had not meant to let the voting become a referendum on himself. For a while, he was a combination of depressed and defensive. The seminar phase of his inquiry continued, and he turned to the more important question: What was to be done? There were more phone calls, more meetings, more talk and endless late-night rehashes with Hillary, Gore and close friends. Clinton loved politics. It was his entire life, the single thread that connected each stage, from Arkansas to Washington. Politics was all he had, professionally. The defeat was a wound.

He seemed to take a kind of perverse delight in talking about his latest wound. It was at once a huge analytical problem and a problem in practical politics. He was, after all, still president and only 48 years old, presumably at the height of his personal powers. But the questions persisted. What had he failed to do both as president and as leader of the party? What had others failed to do? Who had let him down? What was the source of the miscalculation? Had he not listened? The calls and meetings continued with Dick Morris. He was the one who had been right about 1994.

Morris claimed that once, when he had been fired by Governor Clinton in 1980, Clinton had said to him, "You are an assault to my vanity. Politics is what I do best and you do it as well as I do." Clinton had lost his 1980 bid for reelection. But Morris was later rehired and had helped lay the foundation for Clinton's comeback to the governorship in 1982 by persuading him to apologize to the voters.

As president, Clinton was not looking for a new route of contrition. Clinton valued Morris not just for their long personal history together, or for Morris's tactical acumen or his notorious willingness to do just about anything to win. Morris was a *Republican* consultant. He had worked almost exclusively for the other side in recent years, and Clinton now had to understand the enemy better than ever. At the same time, he knew Morris was frequently wrong, misguided or even crazy. His ideas and proposals needed filtering; but Clinton could do that himself and act as the necessary check.

Clinton asked Morris to make an assessment, help reposition the administration and develop a message that would enable him to win reelection in 1996.

Morris told the president first that there had been too much people-pleasing and pandering in the Clinton White House—acquiescence to positions a cabinet officer or a powerful White House staff member was pushing. Second, Clinton had drawn too many ideas and staff from the orthodox wing of the Democratic Party. Third, the political consultants and young staffers like George Stephanopoulos seemed to regard Clinton as the Dauphin, a child king, and the administration as a regency government that had to be held together by the court—his staff.

"Your allies have become your jailers," Morris told the president.

In further discussions with Hillary and Gore, Clinton concluded he had three problems. He agreed with Morris that he had been marching too much in lockstep with some Democrats who had pushed him too far to the left. Rather than leading his party in the direction of the New Democrats, he had allowed the congressional Democrats to dictate.

Clinton also agreed that on the social and cultural issues his administration looked too leftish. The symbolism of the young, hip, inexperienced staff, embodied by Stephanopoulos, had been a public relations fiasco, particularly at the beginning of the administration.

But Clinton added an important third consideration. He had been too much out of touch with the middle class, especially on real wages, which were still declining—an issue he had identified and made much of in 1992. He had discovered the middle class in his presidential campaign and forsaken them as president. These were the swing voters. He needed to address their declining standard of living and honor their more traditional values.

Because Morris's presence could cause an uproar, Clinton was having him work outside the White House staff as a consultant. Only Hillary and Gore knew the full extent of Morris's charter. Gore supported the Republican adviser, but with apprehension. In his formal but still largely secret role, Morris expanded on his theories and worked on repositioning Clinton.

Lots of names would be applied to Morris's strategy. The most common was "triangulation," an alternative to the rigid orthodoxy of either conservatism or liberalism. The political spectrum was conventionally thought of as a line running from left to right, and political figures fell somewhere along that straight line. Morris argued that an innovative leader had to move out of the linear dimension to a point at the center but also above the conventional spectrum. That point then formed a triangle with the left and right.

The idea appealed to Clinton, who had always thought of himself as above orthodoxy. He was a New Democrat, incorporating some liberal elements and some conservative elements.

Clinton sought a deeper understanding of the core issues that had been successful for Republicans over the years. Success was what counted. What worked? As outlined by Morris, Republicans from Reagan to Gingrich had essentially four issues that resonated with voters: taxes, crime, welfare and the federal budget.

Clinton had to take these issues off the table, neutralize them by diminishing the differences between himself and the Republicans. Then, Morris said, Clinton could run and win on *his* issues—education, the environment, maybe even abortion, and some other social issues that reflected traditional Democratic humanitarianism and compassion.

Clinton and Morris agreed they needed new blood in the White House to help.

In late November, Clinton phoned William E. Curry, Jr., who two weeks earlier had lost his bid to become governor of Connecticut. Clinton and Hillary had met Curry in the 1992 campaign and had been very impressed with him. Curry, an articulate and verbose 42-year-old state comptroller, had been so taken with the Clintons that his friends thought he had acted as if he had joined a cult. Now Curry was licking his wounds after his defeat.

Clinton said he wanted Curry to come work in the White House on domestic policy and communications. He asked him to meet with Morris. Over a three-hour lunch in Waterbury, Connecticut, Morris and Curry discussed how they would engineer a remake of the Clinton administration.

Later, Morris made his pitch to Clinton about the importance of television advertising. Since a campaign was a communications exercise, Clinton, even as president, would need to raise money for massive TV advertising buys to get his message out, he argued. Advertising changed and molded attitudes. Advertising moved poll numbers. Most voters lived their lives outside the realm of political discourse, but prime-time television was part of their daily fare and it could be used to pierce their world.

2

Early Saturday morning, December 3, 1994, Senator Bob Dole walked briskly through the glass doors of his office, room 141, on the first floor of the modern Hart Senate Office Building. Dole, 71, appreciated Saturdays. There was much less pressure, fewer people standing in line to see him, he could wear casual sports clothes. He headed for his large private office in the back, a modern, well-lit room with tall windows and none of the dark-paneled look of the older Senate. Even the carpet was white. He had three important appointments scheduled. The first was at 9 A.M. with his wife, Elizabeth.

Elizabeth Dole wanted to discuss, systematically and at length, the possibility that he was going to run for president. For nearly two decades it had been an issue in their lives. He had run unsuccessfully twice before. "Okay, Bob," she had said several days before, "let's set aside a few quiet hours and let's just look at some of this in more detail."

In three days, he and Elizabeth, 58, would celebrate their 19th wedding anniversary. The résumé woman with a Harvard Law degree, she had held separate cabinet posts in the Reagan and Bush administrations, and was currently president of the American Red Cross. On the surface she seemed to be a soft southern woman, courteous and welcoming, with auburn hair sprayed firmly in place, vibrant eyes and a red-lipped, warm smile. Underneath, Elizabeth drove herself and others obsessively. She mastered the briefing books, and her husband recalled many a night when he could hear her in the upstairs of their town-house apartment practicing speeches aloud days in advance. Dole himself would appear for a major speech with a few scribbled notes on a scrap of paper, if that.

Dole had just been elected Senate majority leader, and Elizabeth was pressing him on whether he was going to run for president a third time. The Doles lived in a small, two-bedroom apartment at the Watergate complex, and she liked to keep their home as an oasis away from the noise and rush of their very public professional lives. By the time they were at home together at night, they usually had both been through 12-hour days and wanted dinner, perhaps an old movie and their shoes off. Rather than say to him in his own home, okay, you're on the firing line, 20 questions, Elizabeth had arranged an appointment. She wanted a Saturday morning meeting away from the swirl of people running in and out, phones and staff.

Elizabeth brought to the meeting one of their closest friends, Mari Will, a longtime political and media adviser, and speechwriter for both Doles since his unsuccessful 1980 presidential campaign. Mari, 40, was a six-foot, blond-haired version of Elizabeth. She had started in politics as a campaign press secretary to Senator Strom Thurmond, the conservative South Carolina Republican, in 1978, and was married to conservative columnist George Will. Elizabeth had explained to Mari that Dole was close to throwing the switch to run for president again. It was crucial, Elizabeth said, that he get a cold, objective view of what would be required were he to run. As his wife, she wanted to make sure that he was willing and enthusiastic and that he understood clearly what might happen to him in the process. They were going to give him a look at everything in the harsh light of day.

Personally, Will was going to be a reluctant warrior if Dole ran again. Most of the people and staff in political campaigns were not very serious people, but she considered both Dole and Elizabeth serious. She had prepared a memo that she was going to use as an outline for the points she wanted to make directly to Dole.

Campaigning in the 1990s was completely different than it was in the 1960s or even the 1970s, Will said. The media environment was wild and chaotic. It could be powerful when harnessed and incredibly destructive when left to its own course. That meant message discipline was absolutely essential. Dole would have to find the themes of his campaign, and repeat them again and again, not drifting or sliding off. No more winging it. Was he willing?

Dole said he understood that he had to change his style of communicating, which was undisciplined, chaotic and marked by a tendency to free-associate, often speaking in a series of cryptic sentences. He was prepared to improve, he said.

At one point, Will said that he had to be careful about his humor and jokes. Reporters would treat him differently. "They laugh at your jokes when you're majority leader," Will said; "when you're running for president, they write them down."

Turning to one of the most sensitive topics, Will said she knew he was worried about his age. In her opinion, she said, it would absolutely not be a factor. In fact Dole's age, which would be 73 in the fall of 1996, would be an asset if he wound up running against Clinton. The reaction against Clinton was so strong that people wanted someone steady, someone who had been there, someone with experience. People wouldn't care about age unless he became sick or acted senile, she said.

On this matter Dole just listened and nodded.

Some of the negatives from his unsuccessful campaigns for president in 1980 and 1988 would linger, Will continued. But within the party Dole had largely cleansed himself of the negatives from the 1988 campaign by supporting Bush, being a loyal Republican leader, and then after 1992 emerging as the effective leader of the party when Bush was defeated by Clinton. Now respected by both Republicans and Democrats as a kind of statesman, Dole was going to go down in history anyway. All that would be thrown into play if he decided to run for president.

Directly proportional to the upsides this time were the downsides. The toughest part for Dole, Will felt, would be to get the nomination. With the nomination, she said, beating Clinton would be comparatively easier. Yet a campaign against Clinton would be very negative. "The only way to emerge from that with your reputation intact is to win." His entire lifetime of achievement would be on the line in that single contest. Succeed, and he would be remembered for that. Fail, and he would be remembered for that.

Will went through the likely competitors for the Republican nomination, listing the various skills some possessed that would likely make a difference. She came back to the centrality of message discipline. In addition, she said, she thought the 1996 Republican contest and the general election would be about values. A candidate would have to be willing to talk about values.

Dole seemed uncomfortable at the mention of values.

It is hard for you, Will said, because in Kansas people didn't talk openly about values or personal matters.

Dole indicated that he agreed.

It's like being asked to read poetry aloud or something that you have written yourself? Will asked.

"Yes," Dole replied.

Talking about values was essential, she said. It was what the country wanted to hear, and he would have to do it. It could be the crux of the election.

Will considered Dole a populist conservative, a Boy Scout from Kansas and the straightest of straight arrows, who reflected popular attitudes. He just needed to explain himself. The authenticity had to come through. After some back and forth, Dole said he was willing to do it, he agreed there was a need to do it.

A willingness and a recognition of the need were not enough, Will said. Would he actually do it?

Dole said he would do it.

Elizabeth was mostly quiet as Will went through her points. It was now her turn. Elizabeth had two central points. Did Dole understand the two very different roles—Senate majority leader and candidate for president? Beginning the next month, for the first time in 40 years the Republicans would control both the House and Senate. That meant big responsibilities and a big agenda just in the day-to-day mechanics of moving things through the Senate as majority leader. His time would be filled, 12 to 14 hours a day, with getting that all done, managing a very broad responsibility in the Senate, every issue imaginable, every amendment someone might offer.

Then, Elizabeth said in her gentle but very attention-getting southern accent, on the other hand he would have to go out and shift gears, turn that off, go out and run for president, talk big picture. She knew Bob was not good at turning things off, and his specialty was not the big picture. "That's very different. I mean, you try to do those two roles simultaneously," she said. "Are you certain, are you absolutely clear that those two can be done simultaneously, because it requires a very different approach?"

Yeah, yeah, Dole said.

"You've got an opportunity to serve right where you are, Bob," she said. "Okay, you're majority leader. You have an opportunity to serve there. Now let's think about whether you can serve better from the standpoint of being president than you can from where you are right now."

Yeah, Dole had thought about that plenty.

Mari Will amplified. The style of leading the Senate, being master of that process, meant talking legislative jargon, moving and nudging the other senators along, discussing subcommittee votes, conference and closure. Oh, he was great at it, but that was the very opposite of running for president. The message discipline would have to include a carefully crafted presidential message that was an explanation of what he would do, where he would take the country. He thoroughly enjoyed being leader, they all knew that, but if he took his eye off the presidential ball, he could damage himself in the race and then all the downsides could emerge.

Will and Elizabeth had an additional point: if he did this, it couldn't be like 1988. It would have to be different. There had to be organization, discipline, and Dole would have to delegate authority—no last-minute decisions that he wanted to visit certain cities instead of those the campaign staff had planned. No more turning his campaign plane around in midair on impulse. He had brought old campaign workers to the verge of tears with his seat-of-the-pants decision making. This campaign couldn't turn out like the rest, couldn't falter because old mistakes were repeated.

"How do you feel about that, Bob?" Elizabeth asked. "You realize what it's going to take to do this?"

Oh, yeah, Dole said. He understood exactly what they were saying.

"Let's hear you say, Bob," Elizabeth pressed, "how you do it simultaneously."

Dole said he knew what it would entail, he felt very comfortable.

Elizabeth said she wanted them to appreciate fully what it was like to govern these days in the case that he was elected. Federal spending would almost certainly be cut, and there wouldn't be as much money in the budget for spending that presidents previously had used to ensure popularity.

Dole listened, nodded his head, agreed.

The media tended to destroy people who popped their heads up above the herd, she said. They would try to break him.

"Is this what we really want to do with our lives?" Elizabeth asked her husband at one point. "Why do we want to do this? If we lose, we lose everything." Dole later recalled Elizabeth saying that. His reputation, all the years of hard work and service. The thing that would be left in people's minds would be the last negative advertisement they saw.

"I don't think we lose everything," Dole replied. The stakes were high. The highest. But would losing mean that everything would be gone? No, he didn't think so.

Later, Elizabeth did not remember putting this question about the stakes to him so starkly. She was sure she hadn't. His memory had to be absolutely wrong. There had to be some huge misunderstanding. They had a very happy marriage. They loved each other, and she wanted to be supportive.*

That Saturday morning, Dole said he hadn't made a final decision whether to run.

Will felt that he was just going through his version of the motions. The meeting was Dole's way of checking off all the boxes, but he was running.

Elizabeth wasn't sure. There was more to this.

Dole's discovery that 1988 wasn't his time had been very difficult. It had been the time for "Ronald Reagan, Jr."—Dole's sardonic name for George Bush. Reagan had picked Bush as his running mate, and in a sense created Bush. Bush was in many ways the opposite of Dole. He had been born to bounty, the East and Yale. Bush had his Navy airplane shot down in World War II and escaped without serious injury. Dole had been born in economic despair, Kansas and struggle. His right shoulder had been blown apart in the mountains of Italy during World War II. He had spent three years in hospitals often close to death, finally undertaking the long and painful process of rehabilitating his body.

Dole's right arm still hung wasted and atrophied, two inches shorter than his left, making it impossible even to shake hands. Instead, Dole clutched a pen in it all day long to help conceal his gnarled fingers, hoping the pen acted as a danger sign, reminding people not to grab his hand. As Elizabeth once said of her husband, "When you think about that guy, every single day, everything he does, it's like having one hand tied behind your back."

After the 1988 defeat, Dole had awakened in the night for a year saying to himself, "What did we do wrong?" It had been torture; the loss still haunted him. Any reference to 1988 triggered the memory and the whole awful experience would come flooding back.

But now Bush was gone, ousted from office by Bill Clinton and back in Texas, out of it. Dole could list all the former heavyweights from both parties who were out of office. Walter Mondale, a former senator, vice president and presidential candidate, he too was gone, the ambassador to Japan, his name rarely heard. Dole in particular didn't want to end up

---

* Senator Dole said he recalled that his wife made the specific comment. In two interviews Mrs. Dole insisted she did not.

the Walter Mondale of the Republican Party—a perennial candidate who Dole thought couldn't live without this thing, the presidency. Jimmy Carter was somewhere else. Former President Ford was somewhere else. Reagan retired. Nixon out, now dead. George Mitchell, the Democratic leader, had just retired. Bob Michel, the House Republican leader, had also retired. "Bob Dole is still here," Dole said at one point. "And you kind of wonder, why am I still hanging around? Somebody out there, something going to happen?"

Destiny? In 1988, he had proclaimed the year was his "time" in history and that he would not try again. Was he destined to be president? Was some special sense of his place in the future luring him back to the game he said he would not play again? Dole resisted any talk about a plan or destiny, and if anyone started in on it he felt people would say, that guy's off the deep end.

Yet his survival, out of an entire generation of leaders from the 1970s and 1980s, was a fact. Still he wasn't sure he should run, and he saw nothing inevitable. Maybe it wasn't his time, Dole thought. He once said, "Elizabeth has a strong religious belief that God has a plan for everybody, and you can't do this unless you've got him on your side, prayed about it and stuff." He would ever so slightly roll his eyes to the ceiling at such talk.

A strong evangelical Christian, Elizabeth believed, as she put it, that it was important that a person not be outside God's will. It didn't mean that God had a plan for Bob to be president. It meant that she prayed about it, asking: "As Bob makes up his mind what to do, that we do your will, whatever it is, whether we run, won't run, whether we run and win, run and lose, whatever, that it is your will." God had his way of speaking through his word, through others, through events, she believed. But she knew that she would never know God's will for sure. The challenge was to find what God was choosing to do through them. So she prayed and tried to take 30 minutes a day to read some sort of devotional material. Whatever the outcome she realized it was a personal decision for Bob, it would require so much of him. She vowed to support his decision, whatever it was.

Elizabeth also wondered about the impact another campaign would have on her. She had worked for six presidents, served in two cabinet offices as Secretary of Transportation and Secretary of Labor; she was regularly listed as a possible vice president or even president herself. She had twice resigned offices to campaign for Bob. What about her future? What about her job at the Red Cross, which she felt passionately about?

They could bring in another Red Cross president and that would be it for her. Finished.

Running for president was grueling. You almost ceased to exist. It was total immersion. And, as she liked to say, they would be "accompanied." Wherever they went, accompanied by the Secret Service, accompanied by the press, accompanied by the voters, the curious. There would be a crowd of people everywhere, people would come up. The crowds begot more crowds. She knew that there was never a minute alone. It would be a long hard road.

Dole too pondered some more. Earlier in the year, he had attended the 50th anniversary D-Day celebration in Europe. With his old 10th Mountain Division, he revisited the hills of Italy where he had been wounded in 1945 about three weeks before the end of the war in Europe. Dole, a 22-year-old lieutenant, had been hit in the right shoulder by German artillery while trying to rescue one of his men. Dole's shoulder, upper arm and part of his spine had been shattered. For the next three years he had hovered often on the edge of death, fighting infections, paralysis, fevers and blood clots. His right kidney was removed. The doctors were certain he would never walk, but Dole rehabilitated himself with painful exercises and therapy. He learned to walk again, but his right arm remained paralyzed, the fingers useless. Even on his good left hand, Dole's fingers were numb.

The nostalgic trip to Italy got him all jazzed up again. But when he returned, he began to fear the 1994 congressional and Senate elections coming up in November—feared the time because then he would have to make the decision about whether to run for president.

Still, with all the other likely national leaders out, and as one thing led to another with Clinton in trouble and then the Republicans winning Congress, Dole wondered, "Well, Jimminy, maybe I could try it one more time." On the other hand, Dole thought maybe people were getting too much of Bob Dole, steady, steady, steady. Here he is right after the November election, he's running for president. He worried about looking and acting opportunistic.

But Dole felt he knew the answer. "You got to try to make it happen," he said.

He wanted to get away to Florida where they had a condo, where the phone didn't ring and he could focus on the question, "Is this what I really want to do? Is this what I really want to do?"

Elizabeth, he knew, was very happy with their life together. Lots of nice acquaintances. Both in jobs they liked. Neither was struggling to find something to do. A presidential candidacy would alter everything. Several years of running. And all of this seemed to be starting very early, almost two years before the election, instead of the usual year.

The Saturday morning that Dole met with Elizabeth and Mari Will, William B. Lacy, a longtime Dole political adviser, drove in from his home in Annapolis, Maryland, to Dole's office. Lacy, 41, had been political director in the Reagan White House for several years, had worked on Dole's 1988 unsuccessful presidential campaign and a month ago had managed the campaign of Fred Thompson, the former movie actor, who had just won one of the Tennessee Senate seats with 60 percent of the vote.

Lacy, a small, calm man with a comfortable manner and large eye-glasses, hoped to be the chief strategist for the Dole campaign if it ever was launched. Lacy both looked and thought like a professor of political science. To preserve the option of running in 1996, Lacy had been urging Dole to start organizing immediately or all the Republican campaign operatives with experience would join other candidates. If Dole was going to run again and have any chance of success, a new approach would be absolutely necessary. Lacy wanted to lay the foundation for a Dole candidacy.

Eight months earlier, on March 31, 1994, Lacy had sent Dole an eight-page memo entitled "RUNNING FOR PRESIDENT." It was carefully designed to get all the questions of the "old Dole" out on the table, and separate what Lacy felt were the alleged problems from the real ones.

Lacy dismissed conventional charges that Dole was a "dinosaur," "too old," "mean," "can't organize" and was "a two-time loser." All of these could be managed, Lacy said, if Dole addressed what Lacy maintained were the real barriers to a successful campaign for the Republican nomination:

"1. *Lack of strategic discipline*. We must develop a strategy and plan and stick to them. . . . Presidential campaigns are won by designing a plan and sticking to it.

"Look at the last four competitive presidential campaigns: Carter ('76), Reagan ('80), Bush ('88) and Clinton ('92) had fairly obvious plans and stuck to them."

"2. *Lack of organizational discipline*. You must force the senior people in your campaign to get along and for this once to put winning ahead of personal agendas."

"3. *The campaign structure must reflect your style.* I have come reluctantly to the conclusion that a typical campaign structure simply doesn't match your style.

"At one time in 1987, I counted twelve 'power centers' in the campaign that I felt I had to consult before making major decisions."

Playing to Dole's interest in sports, Lacy wrote that the campaign team could not operate like a professional football team with a series of set plays and specific, clockwork assignments. "In professional basketball, however, players are rewarded for their ability to innovate and respond to unique situations." Dole's campaign team would have to operate like a basketball team—a small group with designated positions but flexible enough to overlap and move around. "A small number of key people who have assigned roles but also wide talents that allow them to work outside their roles as necessary," the memo said. "They also must have a strong personal commitment to you."

In essence the memo advised Dole that if he was going to run, he would have to radically change the way he did business.

Lacy was under some pressure from other Dole staffers to make himself available to be the campaign manager and run it on a day-to-day basis. But Lacy was ambivalent about the very prospect of a Dole campaign. At times, he wanted to have nothing to do with it. After much thought he decided he didn't want to run it, didn't want the public visibility, didn't want to get shot at every day. But he did want to be the chief strategist, the one who thought things through, because it was on that ground that a Dole campaign would likely flourish or falter.

About 10:30 A.M., Dole's meeting with Elizabeth and Mari Will concluded and Elizabeth left the office. Mari and Dole were then joined by Bill Lacy and two others.

First in seniority with Dole was Jo-Anne Coe, a large, brash woman who had started out with Dole 27 years ago transcribing dictation for constituent letters. She was part of a breed of congressional staff aides who devote their lives to the boss. Jo-Anne was an extension of Dole, and spoke openly of feeling like a member of his family. She had been the chief inside person running Dole's previous campaign fund-raising operations. She knew Dole's indirectness as well as anyone, and she could read his grunts, single-word reactions and body language. Some found it almost telepathic. She once called this the "unspoken meeting of the minds." When Jo-Anne said, "Senator says . . ." or, "Senator wants . . ."

others quickly learned she knew what she was saying. On the question of running again for president, she had concluded that Dole was saying maybe he shouldn't close the door. To her it was up in the air.

Tom Synhorst, 37, a tall, handsome political organizer from Iowa, also joined the meeting. Though Synhorst had light hair, his long, serious face resembled that of the younger Bob Dole. In 1988, Synhorst, a relentless workaholic, had almost singlehandedly put in place the organization that enabled Dole to trounce Bush, 37 percent to 19 percent, in the Iowa caucuses, Dole's only real victory over Bush.

Synhorst had no earthly idea that Dole would ever even consider running again, but he had stayed closely in touch with him. He felt that Dole was way too bitter about the final 1988 defeat, and it had seemed to linger too long. But after Bush's 1992 loss, the election of Clinton and the focus on Dole as leader of the Republican opposition, Synhorst had tried to help keep Dole's presidential prospects alive.

Lacy produced an agenda of four items for the people assembled in Dole's office.

Can Dole win in 1996?

Lacy told Dole that the others had all discussed this among themselves, and they all thought this was his year. The rise of Newt Gingrich to the House speakership as the new Republican firebrand, coupled with the deep troubles and uncertainties about President Clinton, gave Dole a new stature. Lacy talked only for two minutes. "Now is your best opportunity," he said. "You can easily get the money and you can get the best political talent and Clinton is weak."

Dole said nothing.

Lacy turned to the structure and personnel of a campaign.

Okay, Dole finally said, putting on his glasses and pointing to the agenda. He was offhanded and rushing. He seemed to want to move on. As they went through the items from discipline and decision making to junior personnel, Dole pushed them on, marching through the subitems. Synhorst had never seen Dole quite so detached and hurried.

Lacy said some decisions had to be made. He wanted to send a signal that Dole intended to set up a presidential exploratory committee to let the party and the activists know that Dole would be a candidate. They would not formally set up the committee before December 31, the end of the year, because they didn't want to have to file a report with the Federal Election Commission on fund-raising.

Dole didn't give his approval. He wasn't deciding.

Jo-Anne Coe began discussing the fund-raising plan.

Not strong enough at the staff level, Dole said, engaging the others directly for the first time that morning. "We need more experienced people to help make it happen," he said.

Next, Synhorst had a list of some 150 calls for Dole to make in 25 key states to line up endorsements and organizers. It was too many, Synhorst realized, and Dole did not indicate whether he approved, disapproved or would make any of the calls.

They turned to the critical question of Dole's message discipline. "Mari," Dole said, "this is something you were talking about earlier." But he let the others talk around him about the delicate subject and made no commitments.

Lacy at one point noted that Republicans normally nominated the front-runner and had done so since Nixon. Dole was very well positioned, Lacy said, as the "moderate."

"Oh, my gosh," Mari said, "don't use that word." It was dreaded in bedrock Republican circles—guaranteeing the kiss of indifference, if not death, from the conservative activists, which included herself.

"He didn't mean it that way, Mari," Dole said, "he means more moderate than Newt and certainly more conservative than Clinton."

At the end, Dole said they could put together lists—people for staff, people to contact in the future. He took copies of the lists and said if they didn't mind, he was going to show them to Elizabeth.

Dole thought some of his advisers were more eager for another presidential campaign than he was. The others realized that there was no decision. They would come back next Saturday.

When the group left, Senator Trent Lott, the Mississippi Republican who the day before had been elected majority whip, Dole's deputy, was waiting for the third appointment. Dole had not wanted Lott, a former House member close to Gingrich, to be his deputy. And more than enough Republican senators had looked Dole in the eye and promised to vote for Senator Alan Simpson, the whip for the last decade, to defeat Lott. But in a secret ballot among Republicans, Lott had won by one vote and Dole had been stunned. He was forced to one inescapable conclusion: some of his fellow Republican senators, the troops he was supposed to lead, had lied to him.

Lott and Sheila Burke, Dole's longtime chief of staff who was considered a liberal, were bitter enemies, posing an additional problem for Dole.

But when Lott came in, Dole reached out: good old Trent, part of the team, Trent my man. Great! We'll work together. Thumbs-up, new team, new future!

Dole knew, even at his age, that he was still growing up in the business of politics. There were always surprises, always defeats. He had learned to accept defeat and, above all, not to let it show. Letting defeat show had been his problem. Welcome, a new Bob Dole.

Even when Senator Phil Gramm, the conservative Texas Republican who was definitely running for president, came into the office lately, Dole was all pleasantness and charity. Months ago, Gramm had arrived, saying with his confident bluster, "I know you're going to run. I'm going to run. If it can't be me, I want it to be you."

"Oh, that's great, Phil!" Dole had said.

Even when Gramm was agitating in public, going for the sound bite or the headline, which was often, he came again to see Dole. "Am I going too far?" Gramm asked.

"No!" Dole said. He welcomed all ideas, all candidates.

"Am I causing you problems?" Gramm asked, both needling and inquiring.

"No!" Dole said, even though Gramm was a giant pain. This was the new Bob Dole, which meant, Don't show the anger. Don't let anyone get on the other side of you. Just stay in neutral. Yeah, he liked being the new Bob Dole. Didn't know how long it would last, though.

3

Three days later, Tuesday, December 6, Colin Powell, the retired chairman of the Joint Chiefs of Staff, was waiting at his new home, a large chateaulike structure, in McLean, Virginia. An intense, nearly hysterical surge of speculation and drama was building about whether Powell would capitalize on his status as the most popular and respected figure in the country and run for president. Was he a Republican or a Democrat or an independent? What was his precise stand on the issues of the day?

Powell, 57, had been largely sheltered from partisan politics in his 35 years in the Army, and he was carefully testing the waters. What was really going on in the country? At the same time he was trying to dig deeply into himself and take his own pulse. What did he want?

People were declaring themselves supporters for his possible candidacy, calling, writing—new friends, old friends. Powell was listening hard and welcoming those who might have useful advice.

At 8:30 A.M. that day Powell's visitor was Thomas Griscom, who had been White House communications director during much of 1987, the next-to-last year of the Reagan administration. During that year Powell had been the deputy national security adviser to Reagan. Working together on speeches and Moscow summits, Powell and Griscom had become very close.

He and Griscom sat in the formal study that was filled with Powell's medals and pictures with the presidents he had directly served—Reagan, Bush and Clinton. Powell explained that Alma, his wife, was truly enjoying the freedom of private life. Being out of the Army was liberating, and he was enjoying watching her enjoy it. Despite the constant drumbeat of political speculation, Powell said he had been focusing on writing his memoirs, which would be out in less than a year.

"The book is close to being finished," Powell said, "and I'll start this book tour in September. So it clearly doesn't hurt anything to have a lot of speculation going on, because it will dovetail behind the book tour." At the same time, people were giving him plans and drafts of plans, and ideas and issues for his political future.

"You've got an aura," Griscom said. "A very strong aura."

Powell laughed and said when he went out to give speeches, sometimes at places a black man would not have been allowed as recently as 20 years ago, people came up promising him their undying support. He would come home with a handful of business cards from people who had pledged to help.

Griscom said that many people were self-promoters and others wanted to be kingmakers. Too many people were probably blowing in his ear out of their own self-interest, not his.

Powell agreed fully.

Politics would make Powell's life an open book, Griscom added. "Everything becomes fair game. There are a lot of things, right or wrong —sometimes unfortunately it doesn't matter—that somebody may dredge up here or there. I'm not saying there's anything out there. There doesn't necessarily have to be anything."

Powell felt he had been scrutinized completely, but agreed that a presidential campaign would be more intense.

Griscom also said that any black person would have problems running for president, especially in the South. "You are black, and at some point that will kick in," Griscom said, "and it may kick in in a very unseemly way because if it ever really took off—and this is the seedy side of politics—there will be some things that are said, implied or whatever, that will clearly play up that issue."

Powell had no illusions about race.

"Colin, I can't think of anybody that I would rather see break down the racial barriers than you. At the same time, I don't want to see you broken down in that process."

"There are a lot of these people out there who really don't know me," Powell said, "don't know who I am."

Griscom reminded Powell that he would be on everybody's short list for vice president.

"I understand that," Powell said. "It doesn't necessarily mean that I'm going to do that."

"Right," Griscom said half-facetiously. "You never want to sit here and say, 'I'm glad I'm being considered for vice president.' "

They both laughed.

After Griscom left, Powell realized it was a clear warning. Lots of friends were waving him off. Richard Armitage, a former Assistant Secretary of Defense who was probably Powell's best friend, had been telling Powell not to run. "It's not worth it," Armitage had said. "Don't do it."

And Alma very strongly opposed a run.

Around this time, I called Powell and spoke with him by phone. I had come to know him well when I worked on *The Commanders,* my 1991 book on the Gulf War and the Pentagon. Over several years we had talked and sparred dozens of times in interviews on the phone and in person. Powell could be hard and tough if he didn't want to talk, but when I had specific information he generally would respond. Most significantly, I found that on important matters he had not misled me. This time I explained that I was writing a book about the 1996 race for president and I wanted to discuss what he was doing.

"Your book can be complete without me," he said emphatically. The strong suggestion was that he would not be running, but I couldn't be sure.

Warren Rudman, 64, a turbulent, confident attorney and former senator from the key primary state of New Hampshire, was one of Dole's closest friends. He had been deeply involved in Dole's crucial 1988 New Hampshire primary campaign, which Dole had lost, eventually sending him out of the race. Rudman saw that after losing, Dole was a haunted man. He repeatedly found Dole sitting around his Senate office after that, not doing much of importance. Rudman would come down to sit with him over coffee and try to boost his spirits.

If Dole were going to run in 1996, Rudman believed he had to face up to and forthrightly address his largest handicap: his age. Dole was probably too old to run. He had been described as last generation's candidate in 1988, and he was 23 years older than President Clinton. So Rudman decided he would try to find Dole a young running mate who was fully qualified to govern the country—someone with a proven record, someone distinguished, someone who immediately would be considered presidential. He wanted someone who could run with Dole and not leave the country worried about the guy next in line, someone with almost instant moral authority.

In the spring of 1994, Rudman had arranged to have lunch with Colin Powell. Rudman, a former Army infantry officer during the Korean War, had known Powell since Powell had been a junior Army general who attended Senate hearings with Secretary of Defense Caspar Weinberger some ten years earlier.

"Colin," Rudman said over lunch on the patio at Powell's home, "I want nothing from you and I'm not trying to sell you anything. I'm your friend." Then Rudman proceeded to both ask and sell. "There are two ways for you to become president." First, Powell could run in either party —the Republican, Rudman hoped—or as an independent, which would be difficult, almost impossible. Second, there was an easier way. Become Dole's running mate, and Dole would pledge to run only for one term.

Rudman described Dole's dilemma. "What are you, 14 years younger than Bob?" If the Dole-Powell ticket won, the presidency would likely be Powell's then for two full terms. If something happened to Dole, it would be Powell's sooner. Rudman said he had done some research. As vice president, Powell could also serve as Secretary of State. He just couldn't receive two salaries.

Powell didn't respond directly. He was used to offers, people making soundings, speaking without authority, promoting themselves. Why didn't Rudman run? Powell asked. Then the two of them could run together.

"A black and a Jew on the Republican ticket?" Rudman asked.

"Who said anything about the Republican ticket?" Powell shot back, ending the discussion with a big laugh. Powell had never stated his membership in either political party, a subject of mounting speculation.

In Rudman's eyes, Powell certainly had not said yes. But he also had not said no.

On a Saturday soon after, Dole and Rudman met for breakfast at the Palladin restaurant in the Watergate. Rudman reported on his discussion with Powell.

Dole said he hadn't made a final decision about running himself, so a discussion of a possible running mate was premature.

Do you want straight talk? Rudman asked.

Yes, of course, Dole replied.

"Bob, it's hard to be the last of anything," Rudman said, noting that

Dole was the last political leader of the World War II generation. But because Clinton didn't serve in the military and had clearly worked to dodge the draft during Vietnam, the contrast could all be used to Dole's advantage. "I don't think we have to be defensive about the age issue," Rudman said, believing it was Dole's chief hesitation and doubt.

"It's interesting, Bob," Rudman said, "that you have the reputation of a hard-bitten son of a bitch. I've known you for 15 years and I've not seen it." Rudman said that the view of Dole came largely from the two famous public outbursts: Dole's declaration in the 1976 vice-presidential debates about "Democrat wars" causing millions of deaths, and in 1988 when Dole told then Vice President Bush via national television, "Stop lying about my record." Rudman said, "You said it in a very threatening way." So there could be no more public outbursts, he warned.

The rise of Newt Gingrich to Speaker of the House was helping Dole. "To be honest with you, Bob, Newt has a way of making you look warm and fuzzy." But Dole had to keep his cool.

"You're right," Dole said. "I think I'm going to run, but I don't have to be president. It's different this year. I want to win, but I don't have to."

"I'm going to be a constant pain in the ass, Bob, reminding you of these things. Is that what you want?"

"Yes," Dole said, "that's fine."

Dole hadn't decided yet, but the Powell idea was worth pursuing. He wanted to talk directly to Powell. Not to get Powell as vice president specifically, not to make a deal. That would be impossible. He wanted to see who Powell was. Sit down, get it out of the way. Dole liked to clear the clutter before moving to the next thing. He and Powell, just the two of them, had not really ever sat down to talk. In 1993 when Powell was about to leave the chairmanship of the Joint Chiefs of Staff, he was to have come by for breakfast with Dole and some other Senate Republicans. But Powell had called to cancel. "Can I beg off?" he had said. "I've got so many of these things."

"Sure," Dole replied, "forget it. Just owe me one, owe me a cup of coffee." So whenever they'd run into each other, they'd renew the promise, banter back and forth. But it never happened. When you sat with a man eye-to-eye, coffee, alone, relaxed, you might get the measure of him, or at least get started. Dole had promised himself he would do it. Appointments were set but Dole had to have a hernia operation, and then he had a tooth that needed work, causing postponements.

• • •

On Saturday morning, December 10, Dole had most of his prospective campaign team back in his Hart office. They had a six-pager of names from the top down. National chairmen, staff, Iowa and New Hampshire names. It was important in New Hampshire, they all knew, to have as many people play as possible so no one would feel left out.

Dole was pretty active, commenting on who would likely be with them.

California Governor Pete Wilson would be someone good to have at the top as a national chair of the Dole for President organization. There had been some communications with Wilson's staff. Though speculation was high, they all felt Wilson wouldn't run, and believed they would have a good chance of getting his endorsement.

The wish list of possible supporters was big. Honorary chairs on the list were the Reagans, the Bushes, the Fords—the former presidents and first ladies. Governor after governor, all the important names, seven regional chairs across the nation. Lock it up.

Dole held back. "I don't want people to think I just got elected leader," he said, "and I'm already running for president."

Tom Synhorst had a plane to catch. "I'm going to have to leave," he said, "but this is what I'd like to do in Iowa." He knew the thousands of precincts, the 99 counties. He flashed his list of names and responsibilities. "I'd like to ask these guys to do these things."

"No," Dole said, "I want you to wait."

What?

"No," Dole said again, "I want to wait a week or two, but then I'll let you know."

What? A week or two, still indecision? Lacy worried about the old Dole. Synhorst was dejected.

As Clinton continued to thrash around in the weeks after the 1994 November elections, he told Dick Morris he wanted to give a speech that would begin the repositioning process, and, without telling the White House staff, he asked Morris and Bill Curry to work on a draft. Clinton wanted to raise the flag about his renewed concern for what the voters were saying. Morris had conducted polling that showed that people wanted tax cuts, economic recovery, more education and programs that addressed the real needs of families.

The White House speechwriters also received instructions to begin drafting a speech. One speechwriter was asked to draft an assessment of the American spirit, an attempt to take the public temperature, define it and embrace the uncertainty and anxiety. This was later rejected as dangerously close to President Jimmy Carter's celebrated speech diagnosing a kind of public malaise. Another idea given serious consideration was that Clinton deliver a speech from the library in the White House and at the end of his remarks, get up and put a Christmas tree ornament on the tree to celebrate the season. Also proposed was a speech that would be a statement of Clinton's beliefs and convictions, because there had been some public confusion about what they were. Clinton hated this idea because he said he knew the answer. Still another plan called for a speech on "New Democrat" themes rejecting standard liberalism, helping business, reducing government and cutting taxes. The wandering and aimlessness in this project were apparent.

The television networks had agreed to give Clinton time at 9 P.M. December 15, 1994. Early that day there was still no text ready, and no one in the White House knew exactly what was happening.

Part of the explanation was that Clinton was working on a speech by himself, and secretly had been exchanging ideas over the phone for several days with Morris, who was vacationing in Paris with his wife. They had agreed that the theme would be built around tax cuts to expand educational opportunity, help the economy and assist families.

Curry also weighed in, suggesting that the proposed tax cut be about one third the amount of the Republican proposal. He felt it was important that Clinton not present something extravagant. Clinton agreed.

Working over the transatlantic phone, the president and Morris devised what they called a "middle-class bill of rights." Gore saw the idea as an attempt to redeem the 1992 Clinton-Gore campaign pledge to give a tax cut to the middle class. In several more calls back and forth they put together a draft.

The morning of the speech, Clinton called in the speechwriters and dictated a draft. He did not indicate where the ideas had come from, and he spoke as if the text were coming to him from some other universe. He said that he would propose the new Congress pass a "middle-class bill of rights." Using some policy ideas that had been worked over by the White House staff, he decided to propose a $500-a-child tax cut for families; making college tuition tax-deductible; and allowing tax-free Individual Retirement Accounts to be used for medical expenses, education or the purchase of a first home.

"This holiday season," he began at 9 P.M. from the Oval Office, "everybody knows that all is not well with America, that millions of Americans are hurting, frustrated, disappointed, even angry." The question, he asked, was what could be done about what matters to most people? "Tonight, I propose a middle class bill of rights." The president laid out his plan and explained how he was cutting federal spending and the payroll. "I want a leaner, not a meaner Government, that's back on the side of hardworking Americans, a new Government for the new economy—creative, flexible, high quality, low cost, service oriented—just like our most innovative private companies."

Clinton spoke for ten minutes. The proposals drew a good deal of criticism. "Gingrich lite," one commentator called it. Republicans charged Clinton with flip-flopping, pointing out that Clinton had promised a middle-class tax cut in the 1992 campaign, abandoned it in his first two years as president, and had now returned to it. In contrast, Gingrich and the Republicans claimed they were going to do something unusual in American politics. They were going to do exactly what they had promised in their Contract With America the first time, and pass their own larger tax cut.

Clinton was furious in private when it was suggested that he was pandering to the right and trying to upstage the Republican revolution. It drove him crazy that his public political persona was that of a waffler. "I find it amazing that anybody could question whether I have core beliefs," he declared in an interview with *Newsweek*. "This idea that there's some battle for my soul is the biggest bunch of hooey I ever saw. I know who I am. I know what I believe!"

After the December 15 speech, Bill Curry, one of its unacknowledged authors, went to see White House chief of staff Leon Panetta about the job in domestic policy and communications that Curry had discussed with the president.

Panetta, outgoing and even mirthful, was welcoming. He and Curry laughed together and had a wonderful time. Curry explained that he wanted a staff position advising the president on domestic policy and communications strategy on a daily basis.

"Great!" Panetta said.

Curry left convinced that Morris was absolutely right, that Panetta and the White House team were mired in daily events and had failed to formulate an overall long-term issue and communications strategy for the president.

Several days later, one of Panetta's deputies called and offered Curry a job as one of the assistant secretaries in the Department of Housing and Urban Development.

Curry called Nancy Henreich, the director of Oval Office operations for Clinton, to explain that the president's wishes weren't getting through. Curry then spoke with Clinton. Soon Panetta's deputy called with a new offer: presidential counselor for domestic affairs. Curry would formally take the position early in 1995 and in the meantime work with Morris outside the White House.

In the following weeks, the president watched with frustration as the media and the attention increasingly, even obsessively it seemed to him, focused on Newt Gingrich and the Republicans. Clinton's middle-class tax proposals were very nearly brushed off, while each statement by Gingrich was charted in great detail. It was as if an empire were being built, a revolution under way, and Clinton was the old regime. The Republicans were calling the shots and occupying much of the national political stage. The president himself would have to find a way to work himself onto that stage.

Clinton's most important discussions about what to do were with Gore. In the intense competition of politics a form of adult sibling rivalry still marked their relationship. Clinton frequently joked to his staff about the good press that Gore received. But the president and vice president, only 20 months apart in age, had grown increasingly close and trusting of each other. Both tried not to make a major move without consulting the other. The weekly private lunches were their primary opportunity. They opened up to each other about personnel, legislation, family, even rumors, and the expectations they had for themselves.

One topic, however, had never come up between them. They had not discussed whether Gore would remain on the ticket. His remaining was just assumed and incorporated into their discussions. Gore had fleetingly entertained some private doubts about whether he wanted to be vice president for another four years—to stay as the understudy and in the shadows. But his doubts were not serious, and they had receded. Most modern sitting vice presidents had at one time or another been subjected to the often cruel political debate and speculation about whether they should be ejected from the ticket. But "Dump Gore" was a phrase that could not be found in the most thorough computer search of articles or columns in print.

Clinton and Gore agreed the administration was adrift. What had they wrought? They needed an edge, and they would have to begin a formal reelection campaign for 1996.

Gore, frequently an advocate of bold action, said that the administration and Clinton himself too often tried to please too many people or groups instead of taking a firm direction and sticking to it. The question, he said, had to be what Clinton wanted—not what other staffers or cabinet members or interest groups were seeking. What direction did Clinton want to take? That was the proper question. What did Clinton want?

Clinton said he wanted his presidency back.

Before Christmas, Secretary of State Warren Christopher came to see Clinton in private to say he wanted to quit. He was tired, foreign policy had not gone particularly well, his wife was not entirely happy in Washington, and he missed the rest of his family who lived in California. "I'm going to think over the holiday," Christopher told the president. He offered a list of possible replacements.

Instead of urging or even requesting that Christopher reconsider, Clinton accepted his senior cabinet officer's wishes.

"Jesus Christ," he said afterwards in a rage, "with all I got to worry about, and now I've got to pick a new goddamn Secretary of State!"

Clinton met secretly with Colin Powell to see if Powell was interested in the job. Clinton was aware of Powell's soaring popularity. Bringing him into the administration could serve two purposes—fill State with a proven leader and eliminate a possible opponent in 1996. Powell said he had to honor the contract to finish his memoirs and could not consider the appointment. He didn't say how uncomfortable he was with the way Clinton made foreign policy. Clinton also sounded out Senator Sam Nunn, the Georgia Democrat, who was going to lose his position as chairman of the Senate Armed Services Committee in the Republican takeover of Congress. Nunn too declined.

After the holidays, Christopher returned and announced he would stay if the president wanted. Foreign policy was steadying out, the problems could be fixed, and they would do better, Christopher said.

Clinton was deeply relieved because he hadn't found anyone to take the job.

4

Before Christmas, Elizabeth Dole had to undergo surgery at Massachusetts General Hospital in Boston to clear a blocked artery in her neck. Dole was very scared and worried. He went to Boston and stayed in the Holiday Inn across from the hospital. Elizabeth thought it would provide him what she called "quiet, quality think time." She wanted him to think through whether he was going to run. Generally he would go campaigning for any Republican running for sheriff if he had any down time, and she hoped this interlude in the Boston Holiday Inn would give him several days away from the hurly-burly to think. She suspected he might be sitting over there making phone calls, but she hoped it would be an opportunity to be sure he had the fire in the belly to run, to sort out the pluses and minuses.

But in Boston, Dole didn't spend a lot of time thinking about running as Elizabeth had hoped. Massachusetts Governor William Weld, a Republican who had won reelection with a spectacular 71 percent of the vote a month earlier and was considering whether to run for president himself, invited Dole to visit him on December 20. They did not know each other well. Weld indicated that as a governor little known outside his state, if he wanted to run for president he would have to begin now. But Dole was in a better position as the well-known Republican leader. "You can afford to wait," Weld said.

Dole didn't wait. He told a Boston reporter, "The next logical step for us is to have an exploratory committee, which doesn't commit you but it gets you in position where you start raising money. . . . We haven't made a final decision, but I think it's pretty close to that." The story made the news wires.

So much for quality think time at the Holiday Inn.

Clarkson Hine, Dole's Senate press secretary, called Jo-Anne Coe. "You ought to know what the senator has said," Hine said, reading her the story.

Well, Coe thought, nothing like hearing there's going to be a campaign from the wires. Coe called Bill Lacy. "Just calling to give you a heads-up," she said. "What we were asking him to do, well, he said it." She also called Synhorst, who contacted some of his people. A broadcast fax was dispatched to about 600 people.

Harold Ickes, the White House deputy chief of staff, oversaw the political account for Clinton inside the administration. Ickes, 55, an intense New York lawyer and Old Democrat liberal, had a friendship with Clinton that went back to the anti–Vietnam War protest movement. As the chief political operative in the White House, Ickes knew the immediate problem was to deter, if not foreclose, any possible challenge to Clinton in the Democratic primaries for 1996. Back in 1980, Ickes had helped Senator Edward M. Kennedy launch his challenge against the sitting president, Jimmy Carter. Carter had defeated Kennedy in the primaries, but the challenge had crippled Carter, perhaps permanently. Ickes knew the importance of campaign money—not just as an instrument but as a symbol. Money could scare off a challenge, which many thought was almost inevitable. After the 1994 loss to the Republicans, Clinton appeared weak. Money could make him strong.

Ickes was determined to solve the campaign money problem early. He dispatched his secret weapon.

The morning of Tuesday, December 27, 1994, Terrence McAuliffe headed for a one-on-one breakfast with President Clinton in the White House residence. McAuliffe, 37, a handsome, wealthy real estate entrepreneur, was the full-time volunteer finance chairman of the Democratic Party. Despite the catastrophic setbacks in the 1994 elections, he had broken all party fund-raising records. Tall, well dressed, with modish long hair, McAuliffe was a wizard at rounding up campaign money for the Democrats. Since big campaign fund-raising was normally the province of Republicans, people joked that McAuliffe was so good he must be a Republican.

The White House residence was as quiet as a graveyard that morning two days after Christmas. Clinton and McAuliffe sat at a table after 9 A.M., and both ordered just toast.

"Let's talk about the fund-raising for a second for the campaign," McAuliffe began. He felt he might be the most optimistic person around Clinton, and he wanted to allay any concerns that Clinton might have. Political debacles were often followed by a drying up of contributions. "The money base is out there," McAuliffe said. "They support you. They are with you no matter what happened in the '94 election, and I will sit here and tell you today, sir, that we will raise your Clinton-Gore money faster than it's ever been done before. We will get it done. Don't give it another thought. We'll put the plan together, we will execute it, and the money will not be a concern for your campaign."

Clinton seemed to stop to think for a few seconds. "Terry," he finally said, "that is great." He knew that McAuliffe had delivered over the last two years on everything he'd promised. This meant raising possibly $25 million.

"Sir, I've never given a number or a budget that I've never met in 16 years," McAuliffe added. He had started fund-raising for Jimmy Carter back in 1976.

"Is there anything I need to do?" Clinton asked.

"Sir," McAuliffe said, "I need to get people to see you." He hoped to be able to run 20 to 25 people through—the key organizers and donors just so they could spend a few minutes with the president. By starting the fund-raising very early, some time in 1995, they would make it much harder for a possible primary challenger to get going. "Sir," McAuliffe added, "I'll put the whole plan together. As I sit here I'll guarantee you that the finances for the campaign will be a non-issue. Don't worry about it, and don't give it a second thought."

Clinton knew that McAuliffe traveled the country and was plugged into the party mood as much as anyone. What do people really think out there? the president asked.

The people he spoke with did not think the '94 election was a referendum on Bill Clinton, McAuliffe said. Government didn't seem to be serving them well. They were worried about their own personal incomes, their standard of living had gone down. There had been a huge frustration vote.

• • •

With Clinton's popularity down and his relevance publicly debated in the news media, Ickes continued to worry about a Democratic challenger. It would be too easy for someone, almost a free shot. Pat Buchanan, the former Nixon and Reagan aide who was a radio and television commentator, had challenged Bush in the 1992 New Hampshire primary and after a six-week campaign had won 37 percent of the vote. Though Bush won New Hampshire with 53 percent, the skirmish had wounded him considerably. A primary challenge to an incumbent president was the nightmare scenario in the media age. Reporters covered challengers with relish.

High on most lists of possible challengers to Clinton was Senator Bob Kerrey, the Nebraska Democrat and Vietnam War hero who had won a Congressional Medal of Honor. Kerrey had run unsuccessfully in 1992. After Clinton became president Kerrey was outspoken in his criticism, maintaining that Clinton was not asking the American people to sacrifice enough, especially to balance the federal budget. Kerrey felt Clinton had fallen short both thematically and specifically, and often said so, most vocally in the summer of 1993 when he had reluctantly provided the 51st and last Senate vote needed to pass Clinton's economic plan.

Ickes was right to be worried. As his name kept circulating, Kerrey envisioned his phone call to Clinton to announce that he would run in the primaries in 1996. Kerrey loved Jack Nicholson's performance in the movie *Hoffa* about the Teamster labor leader Jimmy Hoffa. When the goons came after Nicholson-as-Hoffa, he got off what Kerrey considered one of his favorite political lines: "I ain't afraid of you cocksuckers." If Clinton's position declined some more and there was enough prompting, Kerrey imagined he would make a phone call to Clinton with the equivalent message:

"Mr. President, you've got a bunch of teenagers down there running your shop. There's all this Clearasil on desks. They don't appear to be as serious as you and I are. I can only take so much of this stuff, and so here's the deal. They've been telling me I'm going to run, so I'll see you in New Hampshire."

Someone who had once run for president, no matter how big the loss, kept the possibility in the back of his mind. "Anybody like myself who has once made the decision that they want to give a State of the Union address and take the country in a different direction never ever permanently surrenders that," he had said. But there was no immediate longing or hunger, necessary elements before he would do it again. In the end

Kerrey agreed to take over the Democratic Senate campaign committee, and he informed Clinton personally that he would not run.

Senator Christopher J. Dodd, the affable Connecticut Democrat, was trying to figure out that December what had happened to the party. Dodd, 50, had just lost the minority leader's post to Senator Tom Daschle of South Dakota by a single vote, 24 to 23. He was a longtime Clinton watcher.

Back in 1981, some six months after Clinton had lost his reelection bid as Arkansas governor, Dodd had a long session with him. Clinton was then obsessed with talking about his loss. As Clinton barreled on blaming others for his defeat, Dodd, who had just been elected for his first term in the Senate, decided to stay on to hear Clinton utter the words, "I screwed this up," or, "I fucked this up," or some version of self-blame. Dodd had stayed past 3 A.M. with Clinton and never heard the words or anything approximating them. Everyone else was to blame, according to Clinton. Was it the same now?

At the White House one night in December 1994 during a three-hour discussion with Dodd, Clinton attributed much of the Democrats' 1994 setback to failed communications. They needed a means to get their message out. He wanted Dodd to take over as chairman of the Democratic Party. Dodd argued that he had little interest in the party organization, or "plumbing," as he called it. He would be more helpful from the Senate. Initially Dodd felt he had talked Clinton out of it, but Clinton said he wanted him as the general chairman and official spokesman for the party. They eventually would bring in Donald Fowler of South Carolina to be the day-to-day operating officer and Dodd would be the traveling spokesman.

Dodd finally agreed. He felt he knew the president's flaws, but he liked Clinton and thought him the best retail politician in the business, capable of mesmerizing people in small and large groups. He literally had to be dragged from the room once he got into that mode. The overall wholesale package was the problem. In Dodd's opinion, Clinton needed to keep more distance. People needed to feel a sense of mystery about the president, and Clinton wasn't allowing that to develop. He concluded that Clinton would probably need a genuine crisis to fully demonstrate his leadership. But Dodd had an idea for a 1996 victory: make Newt Gingrich the issue. That was the way back.

Dodd soon began to receive phone calls from Clinton, who wanted reports from Dodd's appearances around the country before Democratic groups. Some of the calls came late at night. One was after midnight. As they talked at about 12:30, Dodd heard an occasional snapping noise in the background. The sound perplexed him at first as he recounted one trip, reporting in detail the good news that Clinton had genuine support among the party faithful. Finally Dodd recognized the distinctive sound of playing cards being shuffled and slowly turned. The president was playing solitaire. Jesus, Dodd thought, at least he ought to be able to get Clinton's full attention at that hour. The memory of the young president playing solitaire, on the phone late at night, seeking ideas and comfort, remained with Dodd.

Clinton and Hillary had invited a group of communications and popular self-help authors to Camp David to help them dissect what had happened in the first two years of the presidency and to search for a way back. They met the weekend beginning Friday, December 30. Three of the attendees were well-known authors: Anthony Robbins, the author of *Awaken the Giant Within,* who calls himself a "peak performance coach"; Marianne Williamson, the love guru who presided at Elizabeth Taylor's 1991 wedding and the author of *A Return to Love;* and Stephen R. Covey, the author of *The Seven Habits of Highly Effective People.* Their names leaked out to the public, but all three later refused to discuss the substance of the meetings.

The identities of the other two in attendance did not leak, and they were the ones who played a significant role over the weekend and in the year that followed.

The first was Jean Houston, co-director of the Foundation for Mind Research, which studies psychic experience and altered and expanded consciousness. Houston, 55, the author of 14 books, was one of the most high-energy and aggressive conference and seminar leaders in the country. She was a believer in spirits, mythic and historic connections to the past and other worlds. Houston believed that her personal archetypal predecessor was Athena, the Greek goddess of wisdom. She conducted extensive dialogues with Athena on her computer that she called "docking with one's angel." Houston, an attractive woman with long, dark hair and a large, generous smile, wore an ancient Hellenistic coin of Athena set in a medallion around her neck all the time.

The second was Mary Catherine Bateson, Houston's colleague, an anthropology professor at George Mason University in nearby Virginia and the daughter of the celebrated anthropologist Margaret Mead. Bateson, a respected academic, was the author of *Composing A Life*, the story of the struggles and frustrations of five women on non-traditional life paths. Hillary said *Composing A Life* was one of her favorite books.

As the five authors sat with the president and the First Lady for hours at Camp David, they asked Clinton to describe his best qualities.

"I have a good heart," Clinton said, "I really do. I hope I have a decent mind." He said that he wanted to do the best that he could for the American people.

Clinton explained that he wanted to look very deeply at the presidency. He acknowledged that he was feeling pretty beaten down. As both Clinton and Hillary described their lives and the White House, Jean Houston felt their deep torment. But she saw possibilities in their extraordinary openness about their pain.

The president said he was looking for ways to see his office and to speak to the public from another perspective. He needed to talk to different people, and he was exploring all avenues.

There is a "field," Houston said, that comes with being president. The job brought a whole historical procession of previous presidents, of the greatness of the office and the country and the struggle. She advised that Clinton, as a student of history and biography, take the fact of the unique historical circumstances of his presidency, go back to his predecessors and try to harvest their learning. From that the president could construct a vision of a better society, what she called "the possible society."

Hillary and Houston clicked, especially during a discussion of how to use the office for the betterment of society. Houston said that Hillary was carrying the burden of 5,000 years of history when women were subservient. The rising of women to equal partnership with men was the biggest event in history. Hillary represented the "new story," Houston said. Hillary was reversing thousands of years of expectation, and was there on the front line, probably more than virtually any woman in human history—apart from Joan of Arc. Hillary was a stand-in for all women, and as such had an historic opportunity.

Houston saw some bitterness, but more sorrow, in Hillary over the health care debacle and the constant personal attacks she endured, which had forced her to the sidelines of the policy and public issue debates. Houston felt at one point that being Hillary was like being Mozart with his hands cut off, unable to play.

Though Houston did not articulate the image, she felt that Hillary was going through a female crucifixion. She had perhaps never seen such a vulnerable person, but also one who was so available to new ideas and solutions.

Houston told Hillary she would prevail. Hillary was creating a new pattern of possibility for women. She had to hang in there, not give up. Her time would come, a time when she would be in the place and the role in which she could really express the fullness of what she was.

The last day of the year, Saturday morning, December 31, Dole gathered most of his potential campaign group again at his Senate office.

"Okay," Dole said. "If I'm going to get into this thing, I want to make sure there is water in the pool. I'm not going to jump into the water if it's not very deep. I want to know what's out there first."

Synhorst realized it was still sort of up in the air in never-never-land. If those already on the team did not rise to the occasion and tell him what was there, take control of what Dole was about to do, then he might balk.

Lacy was more laidback. This was how Dole made decisions.

"Let's put some meat on it," Dole said. "Let's go state by state." Iowa was first, always the first. The caucuses, the scene of Dole's 37-to-19 victory over Bush in 1988.

"Well, in Iowa," Synhorst said, "this is what I think we have." The old tens of thousands of names. He was very specific. It was real meat. "This is what I think we can get," Synhorst said. The governor, senators, congressmen—all kinds of support. He explained how he would organize it—grass roots, state of the art. Just like before.

They turned to New Hampshire, scene of the last disaster. They had thousands of names there, too, and would duplicate the intense precinct organization.

"Just like Iowa," Dole said. He wanted to know about New Hampshire Governor Stephen E. Merrill, who was a very conservative Republican, the senators, all the players at the top. They had to find a role for anyone they could get. No one's involvement could be diluted.

Next came Arizona, which was trying to crowd New Hampshire with an early primary. Of Governor Fife Symington III, Dole said, "Boy, he told me he was with me." But Symington had just let Dole know he was going with Senator Gramm. Dole was very disappointed.

As they went through the key states, it looked like Dole had or could get 25 percent of the key elected officials in most of the states; another 10 percent were with other possible candidates; and the rest seemed undecided or up for grabs.

"Okay, now we're doing it!" Dole remarked with unusual lift to his voice after one state looked particularly good for him. To the campaign staff, it was as if he were making them jump through the hoops. Dole said that he was flooded with invitations to speak and travel, but he wasn't going to do them all, only the important ones. Bob Dole wasn't going to show up at every dogfight or fish fry this time. In 1988 he'd been a bulldog, too hungry perhaps. If someone was supposed to do five events, Dole would do eight, or on a day off he would go to a campaign rally. Dole had finally given up on the idea of meeting all 260 million Americans.

Synhorst said that they were going to have to be much smarter about how they used his time, get the most value from it.

"Yeah, I know," Dole said.

"I've got to leave now," Synhorst said about noon. "Just so I'm straight on this, then: we're going to go out and ask for leadership, ask people to take leadership roles and find out where people are in the key states?"

"Yes," said Dole.

"Then in terms of the first tier, then I can start to ask people to take specific roles?"

"Yes."

Golfing and relaxing in semi-retirement at his home in the California desert, Stuart Spencer, one of the enduring and profane godfathers of Republican politics, was looking for a presidential candidate. Spencer, 67, had been a player for decades, acting as adviser, manager, friend and the hovering voice of realism to presidents. He once frankly told President Ford, "Mr. President, as a campaigner, you're no fucking good." In the 1980s he was political consigliere and close personal friend to both President Reagan and his wife Nancy, acting as an outside sounding board and dinner and phone buddy.

In the aftermath of the Republican takeover of Congress, it seemed to Spencer that 1996 could be a very big Republican year. His party just needed the right presidential candidate.

Spencer's first choice for the Republican nomination was Dick

Cheney, who had served as Bush's Secretary of Defense from 1989 to 1993. Spencer had known Cheney for 20 years and had closely watched him working under pressure, beginning as the 34-year-old White House chief of staff to President Ford in the 1970s, through his time as a congressman from Wyoming (rising to the number-two Republican leadership position in the House), to his management of the Pentagon and the successful 1991 Gulf War against Iraq. Spencer's only concern was whether Cheney, cool and clear-eyed nearly all the time, had the fire in the belly to run for president. Cheney was tough, but would he be willing to grub for it? He had spent the last two years traveling the Republican circuit helping the party and candidates in 47 states. Cheney was debating whether to run but holding his cards very close, too close, in Spencer's view.

"When the fuck are you going to get off the pot?" Spencer said in a call to Cheney before Christmas. Cheney was at his home in Jackson Hole, Wyoming. "You know I'm putting the screws on you," Spencer continued. "I'm getting these phone calls and I'm sounding like a dummy." Spencer hated nothing more than to sound out of the loop, particularly about the future political plans of his friends.

"The family's gathering," Cheney replied. "We'll be here for Christmas and New Year's. We'll talk the whole thing over, and we'll make a decision. I'll let you know."

For Cheney, there were two pieces to the decision. First was the political part. Could he raise the money? Would he generate the support? Would his candidacy pass the laugh test? Would people feel he was overreaching? On this side, he felt he had a shot. The second was the personal side. Was he prepared to sacrifice everything during the next two years for that one goal and objective? Cheney wasn't sure.

There was another factor, not definitive but important to him and his family. A relative was gay. Cheney worried that this would make the newspapers, become part of the endless scrutiny. It seemed unfair that his whole family tree would become subject to an in-depth examination and discussion in the media. Some no doubt would contrast this with his own opposition to gays in the military.

Spencer warned Cheney that it would likely be made public. There was a thin line between the public and private lives of presidential candidates. The line was so thin that it had virtually ceased to exist. "You've got to realize," Spencer said, "you'll go to the grocery store and see your face plastered on the *National Enquirer*." Spencer wanted to make certain

Cheney understood how the political game was played in this era. Members of the Christian right, where Cheney drew lots of support, might quote biblical passages that seem to argue against homosexuality.

"Is it worth it?" Cheney asked. He decided it wasn't. He did not want to go through the process, have to be on continuously for two years. On Tuesday, January 3, 1995, Cheney announced that he would not run. A number of old friends and close associates told him he might have made the best president.

"When have we elected the best?" Cheney had asked bluntly and somewhat bitterly. The grueling process had put it out of reach for him.

He spoke with Spencer.

"You probably made the right decision," Spencer told him. Spencer realized that Cheney was at peace with himself, proving that he had lost a little of his edge. Cheney liked the free time—to fish, to make money, even to take a nap.

Cheney was most immediately concerned about the people who seemed to be counting on him to run. Several staffers and those waiting to sign up were now left high and dry.

"Don't worry about those bastards," Spencer said. "They'll find another horse."

5

At lunchtime on Monday, January 2, 1995, the New Year's holiday, Scott Reed—casually dressed and youthful-looking, with clear blue eyes, thick dark hair, and a mustache—hopped out of his car and walked briskly into the Red, Hot and Blue, a Memphis-style barbecue restaurant outside of Annapolis near the Chesapeake Bay Bridge. Dashing, with the jaunty self-confidence and command presence of a seasoned sailboat skipper, Reed lived in Annapolis and regularly sailed his 34-foot *Tartan*. He had been executive director of the Republican National Committee under chairman Haley Barbour for the last several years.

He sat down with Bill Lacy, a longtime political friend who was trying to get the Dole campaign launched. Reed had worked for the Reagan-Bush campaign in 1984 and then under Lacy as the northeast regional political director for the party. Reed had joined the 1988 unsuccessful presidential campaign of Jack Kemp, the conservative former New York congressman, and later for three years was Kemp's chief of staff when Kemp was Secretary of Housing and Urban Development in the Bush administration.

Lacy thought Reed would be a perfect number one as the Dole campaign manager. A calm and steady behind-the-scenes organization man, Reed could provide the cool edge necessary to impose discipline on a new Dole campaign operation, and on Dole. Reed's vast national party connections would no doubt help, and bringing in a Kemp protégé would be good politics.

Synhorst had already approached Reed several months earlier about the possibility of becoming the Dole campaign manager. Reed had said, "No. I'm flattered, but I like what I'm doing."

Now, over at the Red, Hot and Blue, Lacy knew he had to make a strong sales pitch. Operating with Dole's authority, he offered Reed the manager's job outright. Dole could win, and an iron will at the top would be essential. Dole would require a very strong manager; the execution of decisions would be critical. The campaign had to be workmanlike and efficient. They didn't need any brilliant, bold, gambling strategy, Lacy said. Lacy hoped to be the strategist, think long term and oversee the polling and the campaign advertising. As an old Dole hand, Lacy would also deal with the countless people who considered themselves old Dole friends and advisers. Lacy promised to keep these "assholes" at bay— listen to them, keep them informed, but keep them away from the decisions, the actual campaign apparatus, and as much as possible, away from Dole—and Reed.

Lacy said that he had found Dole to be honest, at times too honest. He often said what was on his mind without measuring the political consequences. A lot of the campaign message would have to be the leadership component, ultimately Dole's strong point, Lacy said. There was no way they could claim in a campaign that Dole was an outsider—his 34-year career as congressman and senator in Washington spoke for itself. Also they couldn't try to pass Dole off as the most conservative candidate because he clearly wasn't. He was a known compromiser and dealmaker. Yet Lacy found Dole to be an intuitive conservative, not an intellectual conservative. He would generally come to a conservative solution, but not always.

One key to understanding Dole, Lacy said, was this: "Dole's strength is what you see is what you get. Dole's weakness is what you see is what you get." Lacy also reviewed the points he had made in his campaign memo to Dole from the previous year, the central need being strategic and organizational discipline.

If Dole had confidence in those running his operation, Lacy said, he could be managed. "He is not a micromanager," Lacy said, "he is a meddler." By proving themselves, they could reduce Dole's tendency and his opportunities to intrude.

Reed said he saw real obstacles, but clearly things had changed since he had talked with Synhorst before the Republican takeover of Congress. Reed was very interested in the job, but he would have to reach a very explicit understanding with Dole. They agreed that Reed would speak directly to Dole and Lacy encouraged him to be frank. The more they spoke with one voice, the better chance they had of getting and holding Dole's attention.

Several days later, Reed met alone with Dole at the Senate. He wanted to be direct about the obstacles he saw to an effective campaign, Reed said. The Majority Leader's Office needed to be tamed. From where Reed sat at the Republican National Committee for the last couple of years, Dole's staff seemed too liberal. They had led Dole down a number of stupid political roads. So the leader's office and the campaign would have to work in sync. Reed didn't pretend to know the ins and outs of legislation being managed out of the Majority Leader's Office, but a campaign manager would have to know what was going on so he could prepare politically. Every action would have an impact on the campaign.

Second, Dole would have to coordinate with Gingrich, Reed said. Dole's success would, to a certain extent, be tied to Newt's and the progress of legislation on the items in the ambitious and highly visible Contract With America, the list of ten legislative goals set by the House Republicans in the 1994 congressional campaigns.

Third, Reed said, Dole needed a campaign with a structured decision-making process, and the manager would have to be at the top. Dole would have to have confidence in that manager. There couldn't be three or four orbits of decision making out there floating and in competition. Two or three little separate campaigns being run within one campaign was impossible. Reed said he didn't want to manage such a campaign. He didn't like gray areas of responsibility in an organization. He liked to have the organization humming with clear, vivid lines of authority.

Dole described how they did the campaign in 1988 with a chairman, the big foot, and then others with specific responsibilities.

That's probably why you had a problem, Reed said. He had just been an outside observer, but it was well known that Dole's 1988 campaign had too many centers of power. It was essential to have a process in place so responsibilities were known, and a hierarchy so that everything was properly approved or disapproved. If that didn't exist, as they both knew, not making a decision in the business of politics could often become a decision. For example, in 1988 the Dole campaign's inability to get a stupid television ad on the air before the New Hampshire primary to respond to Bush's last-minute attack labeling Dole "Senator Straddle" on tax increases was inexcusable. Reed said that wouldn't happen if he were managing the campaign.

Dole offered a number of additional references to the past, how it had been done before, and Reed countered with his own ideas about how he would handle similar situations. A sense of diffusion and randomness wouldn't work. Making seat-of-the-pants, airborne decisions was not the way he operated. Such a loose style makes it harder on the candidate. His approach, Reed indicated, would make it easier.

Reed reminded Dole that in 1988 he had been with Jack Kemp, whose campaign had been the yapping dog trying to get in the picture. Dole's 1988 organization in the field had been damned good, but the problem had been at Washington headquarters with no one really in charge.

Fourth, Dole needed a coherent and understandable message on which to run, Reed said. Deep down, he added, he knew Dole knew what he wanted to say, but he probably needed some help putting it together and delivering it.

Reed sensed Dole's enthusiasm, though it was not boundless enthusiasm. Dole seemed eager to change if it meant winning. Reed felt he had hit the right weaknesses. Clearly Dole was not going to capitulate on everything. He was still Dole.

After about an hour, Reed said he thought he could manage the problems they had discussed. "I'm going to go away for a while and I'd like to talk to you about it when I come back," he said.

Dole wanted Reed to say yes. Reed was obviously top quality and very strong. It was pretty clear to Dole that two things couldn't happen. No more Bob Dole running the campaign, and no more 50 people running the campaign.

But Dole saw the other side. He had always been of the view that if a candidate had 50 people running his campaign and he won, he would be considered a genius. So would all 50 people. Winners were always geniuses. James Carville, Clinton's 1992 campaign strategist, might look bad now in 1995, but he'd been a certified genius in 1992.

Before leaving on a week-long junket to Israel, Reed told his boss Haley Barbour that he was considering leaving to manage the Dole campaign. "You know what you're getting into?" asked Barbour, who didn't want to lose his executive director to anyone, especially Dole. "This guy's unstructured. He's got a bunch of liberals around."

• • •

On Saturday, January 7, Clinton held a secret strategy session in the White House with Hillary, Vice President Gore, Panetta, Ickes and several cabinet secretaries. Clinton asked everyone to keep the discussion private. He said he wanted to recapture the winning themes of his 1992 victory, with emphasis on the middle class and traditional party groups such as labor. But it was a mushy meeting, and because some details soon leaked to the media no more such large sessions were held. This was not the way back.

As Clinton continued his search, he lamented that he could not see a big, clear task before him. Part of him yearned for an obvious call to action or even a crisis. He was looking for that extraordinary challenge which he could define and then rally people to the cause. He wanted to find that galvanizing moment.

"I would have much preferred being president during World War II," he said one night in January 1995. *I'm a person out of my time."*

In Dole's Majority Leader Office in the Senate on the second floor of the Capitol, Sheila Burke, his chief of staff for the last ten years and an aide for eight years before that, was watching as Dole moved with studied indirectness toward running. She wasn't surprised. She knew as well as anyone that Dole rarely made a definitive decision. In her 18 years with him, she had never once heard Dole say, "Here's what we're doing." He never, never, never made a commitment until first taking little steps and dropping hints about where he was heading. The signals would mount: grunts, half sentences, a growl of displeasure, a thumb-up of approval. Eventually he created a foregone conclusion. The cumulative effect— putting a structure in place, having meetings and discussion go on around him, asking important questions, watching others, warily testing the wa- ters—eventually equaled a decision. But he never would come right out and say it. Dole had an inability to reach out fully or lay out completely what was on his mind. He held things so close. He didn't systematically vet things with her or even regularly delegate to her. Burke was his closest aide but never his alter ego. She had grown used to living in a state of imbalance, never sure where things were heading or even precisely where she stood. A handsome woman, Burke had been a nurse for four years and then come to work for Dole as a legislative assistant on health care in 1977. She was pregnant with the first of her three children during Dole's 1988 campaign so she had stayed on the sidelines.

Burke's youngest child now often called her at the office three or four times a day, and she felt guilty a lot of the time for being at work so much. Burke was the resident liberal, a former Democrat who was hated by many of the conservative senators. She even jokingly called herself a "lunatic liberal," one of the "squishees" who had infiltrated Dole's office to keep him soft. But Dole kept her on, she believed, because he wanted a moderate counterweight to all the conservative true believers around the Senate. In his heart, she believed that Dole was a moderate with an undying streak of compassion for the weak, the ill, the helpless and those at the bottom of the ladder.

Still there was this enduring mystery about Dole. For example, she was never sure why he picked people to be on his staff or campaign. There was no theme and she didn't have a clue about the qualities he was seeking or whether someone would survive or not. Some of the best didn't, some of the worst did. She saw that Dole was alone, walled off. That was also a strength. He was no one's puppet, certainly not hers, as some conservatives alleged.

There had been one moment when he had reached out to her. On Christmas morning 1991, Dole called Burke from Walter Reed Hospital where he was a patient. A week earlier he had undergone a radical prostatectomy for cancer. He was uncomfortable, and the operation would probably make him impotent.

"You thought of coming by?" Dole asked on the phone. "Today might be a good day."

Burke had just had a baby two weeks earlier. She was breast-feeding. It was Christmas morning. It couldn't have been a worse time.

"Yes, Senator," she had said. She never called him "Bob," never thought of calling him "Bob" or anything else. Elizabeth and Robin, Dole's daughter from his first marriage, were there in the senator's hospital room. They all had cookies and talked for a couple of hours. Finally, Burke got a phone call saying the new baby needed to be fed, so she left.

In the second week of January 1995, Elizabeth Dole called Burke. Elizabeth was very worried. Bob was preparing his forms, the Statement of Organization and Statement of Candidacy, setting up his presidential exploratory committee. This was the formal registration required by the Federal Election Commission before a potential candidate could raise money. But instead of filling out the one-page form and signing it, he had drafted a supplemental letter, saying that this registration did not mean he would be a candidate. Elizabeth had not seen the letter but Mari Will had just told her about its existence.

Such a statement would send entirely the wrong signal, Elizabeth said. It would reinforce the view that Dole couldn't make up his mind. The exploratory committee was just that—an exploration of the possibility, a legal requirement to prevent someone from raising and spending money under the shadow of a non-candidacy. Bob wanted to register, but with an additional qualification on what was already qualified and exploratory. He still wanted it both ways. She had to get through to Bob, Elizabeth said in exasperation, and hadn't been able to reach him.

Burke quickly tracked Dole down to inform him that Elizabeth disagreed with the supplemental letter.

Dole said he liked the idea of sending a signal that he had made no final decision. He was still uncomfortable declaring for president just a month after becoming majority leader. He made it clear it was one last chance for him to protect all flanks—he was running but maybe not running.

Jo-Anne Coe called Bill Lacy, who was vacationing in Hawaii. She explained about the letter. They were all worried that this double-mindedness in Dole would be seen as halfheartedness. Lacy agreed the letter was unnecessary. It would indeed raise too many questions, and it didn't give Dole any more flexibility than he had anyway. Lacy said his vote, for what it was worth, was to drop the notion completely, but he was going to go back to the beach and not worry about it.

Elizabeth finally reached her husband.

"I'm sort of inching along," Dole told his wife.

Yes, she knew. Don't include that qualification, she said. That will raise the same questions. It will look like you haven't made up your mind, that you haven't decided. People are going to ask, Is he running or not running? People want an answer. They are entitled to an answer. They want to know, Where do I send the money? Things like that, Bob. If the letter is included, the story will be, Is Dole running? Kill the suspense, Bob. It had to be one way or the other.

Dole was really struggling with this decision. It was unsettled in his own mind. He almost got what he referred to as one of those Excedrin headaches—intense, powerful pain. From doubt. "Should I do this?" he said to himself. "Should I do this?" He also asked of himself, "Am I just doing this because I'm doing it?" Was the drive just momentum? Or habit? "Am I doing it because I should do this?"

He also wondered if there was something he had to prove. He felt he had given himself this test. It was reflected in his whole life. He wasn't perfect, he knew, but he hadn't gotten in any real trouble in four decades of public life. Yet he wondered if he'd graded the test properly. He was in good health, felt he understood things better, thought he might be able to stay above the fray, but couldn't forever be above it. As his mind bumped all over the subject, he recalled defeats. Even Ronald Reagan had his bitter losses—lost the Iowa primary in 1980 to George Bush of all people, before he went on to trounce Bush. All of them had had their defeats.

Dole knew all the players, all those who might run. They were all friends of his. Conventional political wisdom was floating around saying that Phil Gramm could win the Republican nomination but not the election against Clinton. Dole, others said, couldn't win the nomination, but if he did, he could beat Clinton. Dole wasn't sure. He asked himself who decided those things. Certainly not the political columnists. It was the voters.

And then there, big smack on the front page of *The Washington Post,* Friday, January 6, 1995, the day after he and Newt had gone to meet with Clinton at the White House for the first time as the new Republican leaders, was a picture of the three of them with big pie charts underneath showing their approval and disapproval ratings in a recent poll:

	Approve	Disapprove	Don't Know
Gingrich	35%	37%	28%
Clinton	45%	51%	4%
Dole	62%	25%	13%

Not bad—not bad at all! Some 17 points more approval than the sitting president and 27 points more than Gingrich.

With Dick Cheney out, Stu Spencer's other horse in the Republican race was Pete Wilson, the governor of California. Spencer went back 35 years with Wilson and knew him as a man who never ran from a fight, the perfect guy in a trench. With his slender, boyish appearance, Wilson, even at age 61, still looked like an Eagle Scout. Spencer thought Wilson was a tiger, all fire in the belly. No one was more focused on what he did —no one was as relentless. In 1990 when Wilson, then a U.S. senator, said he was thinking of running for governor, Spencer had warned him against it. "Pete, the state's not governable, too many problems, it's a Third World nation." Wilson of course had run and won.

Two months earlier Wilson had just won a second term as governor 55 percent to 40 percent. His chances of reelection had been widely thought almost nonexistent a year earlier, so his 15-point victory was remarkable, a near landslide. A governor of California, the largest state and one with 20 percent of the needed electoral votes to win the presidency, was automatically on any short list of likely presidential candidates.

On January 11, Spencer was in Sacramento for a private dinner Wilson and his wife Gayle were holding at the Hyatt Hotel across the street from the Capitol. Wilson had assembled ten of his key political advisers, including Spencer, to discuss the possibility of running for president in 1996. He pledged them all to secrecy. During his reelection bid for governor, he had publicly promised not to seek the presidency during his term. If he left the governorship, a Democratic lieutenant governor would take his office. An upcoming Republican state convention the next month could turn into a bloodbath if it got out that he was even considering breaking his pledge and running for president. He feared the party's conservatives would pass a resolution denouncing him if word leaked.

At the dinner, exhaustion was evident—nearly all had been heavily involved in the gubernatorial reelection campaign. But there was a congratulatory pat-on-the-back mood.

Donald L. Bren, the billionaire chairman of the Irvine Company, the largest private landowner in Orange County, and Wilson's chief fundraiser, led off the meeting. He said he hoped they would examine, attempt to understand and put on the table all the options for Wilson. And if one of the options was running for president, he said, "We can raise the money."

For Spencer, that was the answer to a big question. Spencer knew about $25 million would have to be raised, and he knew Bren could deliver.

Wilson had lots of questions but there was a seize-the-day, seize-the-initiative quality to him.

"What's the chances?" Wilson finally asked.

Spencer said the Republican presidential nomination in 1996 was worth having. He reminded Wilson of something Richard Nixon had said. "Hey, one of our mentors both you and I had, old R.N., used to say timing is everything. That's where you are, Pete. You really want to be president? There's no better time to do it."

But there is another route, Spencer said. There is the vice-presidential route. Because of the problem with breaking his pledge and leaving the state to a Democrat, it would be easier for Wilson politically to be drafted as vice president than to go out and start running for president tomorrow. "I'm not advocating it. I'm putting it on the table," Spencer explained.

"That's interesting," Wilson said.

"There is one other caveat to it," Spencer said. "Dole's going to run for this thing. I think it's important that Dole pick his running mate early." Because of Dole's age, Spencer said, his vice-presidential pick would be unusually important. "I will not be surprised if Bob Dole asks you to be his running mate," Spencer said. He thought Dole might do that at some point to keep Wilson from running, and also to help ensure winning California in the general election.

Dole does not have a message, Wilson said flatly.

Discussion turned to the question of whether there was a new Bob Dole. Most said no way. Dole had too much past.

Spencer, the old warhorse and the only one with real national experience, was the focus of much attention, and many of the questions were directed at him. Were there things they were not privy to in national elections? What were the pitfalls?

Spencer told Wilson, "You have a damn good team around you." But some important elements were missing. A national campaign wasn't like a California campaign. It was obviously on a larger stage, but it moved faster, the incoming fire was more intense, from every direction.

"Hey, you got to want it," Spencer said, adding his standard caveat. "That's a personal decision that you got to make, Pete. If you want to be president, that's something you've got to make. Nobody can make it for you."

Spencer looked right across the table into Wilson's eyes. He had seen the look before in a few others. This guy wanted to do it, and it was going to take a hell of a lot of people to get him out of it.

As the meeting recessed for a break, Spencer drifted over to a corner with Don Bren.

"This son of a bitch is running!" Spencer said.

"It sure looks like it," Bren said.

After the recess, the discussion turned to television. "Elections are now determined by Larry King type shows," Spencer said, noting that Ross Perot had launched his 1992 campaign on the CNN call-in show. You could be on a goddamn talk show in America every night, he added. "That's where people get their information today."

Wilson shrugged and laughed and said, "I love those things. I like those things. I can handle those things."

Spencer disagreed, so he shut up. In Spencer's view, Wilson was still fatally weak on TV. Wilson was an enormously disciplined person in so many areas, but he had not mastered message delivery. Having won so many elections, Wilson didn't think it was a real problem. And in some respects Wilson had become like George Bush, who would say to those who criticized him, if you're so smart how come I got elected?

The meeting degenerated into logistical questions about campaign finance laws and limits on contributions and how to qualify for federal matching funds. Spencer tuned out. It was the kind of small thinking that would deter them.

Finally the dinner was over. Wilson thanked everyone. He said he was thinking about it and would get back to them. He reminded them that none of this should be discussed elsewhere. The meeting, the subject of discussion, even the notion it was under consideration had to be secret.

In inching along, Dole realized, you sort of get to the point where you're just there, you're running. He had taken many small steps toward the line and suddenly he was upon it. He woke up one morning and he was running. He agreed not to include the supplemental letter with his routine exploratory committee and statement of candidacy papers. He signed his formal name, Robert J. Dole. Both were hand-delivered to the Federal Election Commission, arriving at 11:14 A.M. on Thursday, January 12.

Jo-Anne Coe had to find an office at once. None of the presidential campaigning or fund-raising could legally be conducted out of any Senate office or facility. They found a small suite of temporary offices ten blocks north of the Capitol.

Suite 120 at 220 Eye Street Northeast was like a storefront in Russell, Kansas, Dole's hometown. "Dole for President Exploratory Committee" was printed out by computer on a piece of paper and four pieces of transparent tape held it to the glass window by the door. Lacy had an office in the back that resembled a jail cell. There were bars on a small, basement-size window and the walls badly needed fresh paint. Instead of a cot, he had an old desk, a chair and a phone. But it was a start.

Synhorst recruited Jill Hanson, the former political director for the Bush 1992 presidential campaign, to play the same role for Dole. The political director was in charge of day-to-day field operations and contacts in the key states. Hanson, 42, a small, intense politico with short blond hair, knew the Republican state operations from the governors through to the important counties. Her job was the "ground game" of organization, as opposed to the "air war" of advertising and media strategy. She was hired without meeting Dole.

The Republican National Committee had its winter meeting in Washington the weekend beginning January 21. Hanson had four or five campaign workers speak personally to the 153 key state Republicans at the meeting to see who they might support for president. It was an utterly routine, do-it-in-your-sleep "whip check" or poll to measure early support in the states. Finally Dole was introduced to the woman who would fill one of the four or five central roles in his campaign. She reported that 37 of the 153 at the winter meeting—25 percent—would support Dole for president right away and another 30 people were leaning in his direction.

"Wow," Dole said. Good numbers. He had never had anyone do such a check in advance during his previous presidential campaigns.

On Sunday, Dole appeared on CBS's *Face the Nation,* one of the morning talk shows. Over the last dozen years Dole had appeared on the Sunday shows more than any other single guest. He loved the visibility. Near the end of the show he was asked, "You're running?"

"I think so," Dole replied. "Last time I checked."

"Yes?" one of the questioners asked.

The show ended in laughter.

Dole had still one other nagging piece of business. He bit his lip when talking about it. The visit with Colin Powell was finally set. He wanted to be at his very best for the sitdown with Powell. Right after the show Dole's driver took him out to Powell's McLean house. He didn't really know Powell, and Powell didn't really know him. Going to settle that this Sunday, Dole thought.

At his house Powell was anxiously awaiting Dole. He didn't want Dole to ask him anything, none of the questions about his future or whether he would run for president, questions that had been haunting Powell since his retirement. And if so, when. Or in which party. Or what he believed. Powell was pretty sure that Dole would know not to ask.

Because of electronic problems with the intercom and doorbell in Powell's house, he was kind of hovering in the foyer area expecting to notice the car arrive.

When Dole's car pulled up, Dole got out and went up to the door and rang the doorbell. Nothing happened. No one came to the door. Nothing. Tried again. Kept ringing. Nothing again. And again. "God, he didn't stand me up, did he?" Dole said to himself. He walked back to the car where he happened to have Powell's phone number and called. Powell answered. Been having trouble with that doorbell for some time, the general said.

"You've got to get that fixed," Dole said, thinking how close he had come to driving off, perhaps leaving Powell feeling stood up, insulted, mad at Bob Dole forever.

Dole was welcomed in and accepted a diet Coke. Powell gave him a tour of the house—six bedrooms, three-car garage, the large office in the basement. Dole lavished praise. What a house!

Powell pointed out that there were several vacant houses of the same size in the neighborhood. "Now," Powell said, "you could . . ."

"Well," Dole said, "I'm looking for another house right now."

They both laughed at the obvious reference to the White House. Dole could see that Powell was patient, not hurrying, not pushing anything, could wait him out. They sat by a fire in the fireplace.

"Well," Dole finally said, "I'd like to pick your brains from time to time. You know, I'm going to get into this thing. And I'm not asking you for any commitment, not asking for anything." Sliding off, Dole said he just wanted to talk occasionally about foreign policy.

Powell mentioned Dole's public assertiveness on Bosnia, pushing to lift the arms embargo. It was contrary to Powell's immense caution. Powell didn't like to use military force unless it could be used in a way virtually to guarantee success. Lifting the embargo could not happen instantly. Everything would not happen the same day. There would be a long period where that would give the already well-armed Serbs a free hand unconstrained because it would take time for weapons to reach the Muslims. And if that resulted in the Bosnian Muslims losing more ground and finding themselves in an even more horrible situation, there would be some finger-pointing. "If I were you, I'd be very careful," Powell said. "You don't want to be the guy blamed if something happens over there." Tragic as Bosnia was, Powell didn't believe that military force could do much without an overwhelming commitment of ground troops—something way beyond what would probably be supportable in Congress and with the public.

Powell noticed that Dole was listening patiently and with seriousness. So he went on. It was important to be careful, Powell said, about inserting yourself into conflicts where the current belligerents have a vital interest at stake. Especially where those fighting have declared they will make any commitment necessary to achieve their aims, even risk their lives and the survival of their country or heritage. And you as an outsider have no such vital interest.

Dole appreciated the advice. But that wasn't what was on his mind. Dole felt he couldn't just walk in and ask Powell if he was going to run for president. Powell might say, none of your damn business, meeting's over. But Dole had vaguely dropped the question by stating his intentions.

Powell got around to repeating what he had been saying in public. He was going to keep his options open. He wasn't sure he had a passion for politics. He had lots of other interests.

"Well," Dole said, "for somebody not interested in politics, your numbers look pretty good." Polls showed Powell with the highest approval ratings of any possible candidate, and in hypothetical face-offs showed him beating everyone—Clinton, Dole.

"I think I'm running behind you in New Hampshire," Powell said, making it clear he was up on the latest polls, and hoping the humor would get Dole off the subject. No such luck.

"Aagh!" Dole said, "I'll tell you, when I look at the polls I can't compete with a guy like General Powell." Dole noted that Powell was first, then somebody else, perhaps Clinton, then Dole.

The two men discussed Ross Perot, the Texas maverick billionaire, and whether he might run. Perot had won 19 percent of the vote in 1992, and his entry into the 1996 presidential race could throw everyone off. Powell had been bewildered by Perot's sub rosa smear campaign against Powell's closest friend Richard Armitage in the late 1980s that had denied Armitage the post of Army Secretary. Yet Powell kept in touch with Perot and talked to him, keeping a friendly relationship, but intentionally at a distance.

Powell preferred to talk about foreign and defense policy. On the subject of defense spending, Powell said that once the president and Congress had picked a military strategy, and approved it, they all had an obligation to fund it. If you don't like the strategy that is costing so much money, Powell said, you ought to change your strategy and accept whatever risk comes with that change.

As they discussed some of Powell's foreign and national security views, they never got to his views on social or domestic issues. Dole wondered why these issues never came up. He guessed correctly that Powell was pro-choice on abortion and that he felt very strongly about civil rights.

"I'm thinking about serving only one term," Dole said. It was just an idea he and his advisers were kicking around. If he won the presidency, he would consider pledging to step down after one term as president. Dole didn't need to say that this situation could put his vice president at the political helm.

Powell, who had already heard these ideas from Warren Rudman, didn't offer a view on this.

"I have a nightmare," Dole confided in a semi-humorous tone. That he and other Republicans would announce, run hard, beat their heads against each other for 17 months and no one would win. "And someone comes in on a white horse."

Powell didn't say anything. He just laughed. It seemed that Dole was just musing aloud.

It seemed to Dole that Powell was being truthful when he said he had no plan, was just keeping his options open. Of course, Dole said. Why not? He would have his autobiography coming out in the fall, hit a real high note, no doubt, be stronger than horseradish. Then in November, Dole said, Powell could even come in late. "Jimminy, you got the Iowa caucus." In February 1996. "Maybe you can still wipe everybody out," he added, sort of kidding.

Powell wagged his head noncommittally and laughed again.

At the close, Dole said they should visit again.

Powell said that Dole and Elizabeth ought to come out and have dinner alone with him and Alma.

Yeah, great.

Dole was back home about 3 P.M. The bottom line as he saw it was Powell probably wouldn't run, but he could be a running mate.

Powell told his friends that it had been an unexpectedly pleasant meeting. Dole was laidback, relaxed, funny, good company, candid and not racing like many politicians. And most importantly Dole had not really asked anything, especially if Powell wanted to be his running mate.

The next day, Monday, January 23, Scott Reed went to see Dole. Reed had concluded that it would be stupid for him not to seize the opportunity to manage the front-runner's campaign. It would be boring to watch the presidential campaign unfold from the Republican Committee, which would have to stay neutral in the primary contests for the party's nomination. The center of the political universe was moving to the presidential campaign, and he wanted to move with it. As Reed thought it through and realized what he was seeing, he knew another reason he was going to say yes. One of the immense attractions of managing Dole's campaign was the huge void that existed around Dole. Reed was amazed. Dole was lacking many of the simplest things—organization and ideas for starters. It was a vacuum that Reed thought he could help fill.

"Let's go," Reed told Dole. "I want to do this." He was very grateful for the opportunity, he said, and at one point in sealing the deal Reed put it more informally to the majority leader twice his age, "Let's rock 'n' roll."

6

Clinton's State of the Union speech to a nationally televised session of both houses of Congress was scheduled for Tuesday, January 24. It was his chance to get in the game. Clinton and his speechwriters had draft number 12 ready several days before, and it looked as if the process was going to be smooth for the 50-minute address. Clinton was determined to acknowledge publicly that he had made his share of mistakes, but he was going to take credit for the improved economy and a smaller streamlined government and at the same time lay out the case that government was still important and could be a partner in improving people's lives. Clinton also had his back channel open with Morris and Bill Curry, who were providing pages of text and ideas. The day of the speech, Clinton tried to synthesize it all. His basic solution was to include everything. He was still writing and sorting the text in the car on the way up to the Capitol. At the podium he added material extemporaneously. The speech lasted 82 minutes, nearly twice as long as planned.

Columnists and pundits savaged the speech. "A speech about everything, and therefore about nothing," wrote David Broder, the *Washington Post* columnist. Panetta was disgusted and sick with frustration. He had told reporters the speech would be only about 40 minutes. What a debacle, Panetta thought, and how embarrassing. The utter craziness of putting together a major speech this way. Order and process had collapsed. Later polls, however, showed that the speech actually helped Clinton a little.

Afterwards, Clinton told Panetta that they might have to let Gingrich, the Contract and the revolution sort of crest and wash up on the shore. Hate it as he might, he was going to have to give Gingrich the first 100 days of his revolution.

The next Sunday, Dole and Elizabeth were at a brunch when Colin and Alma Powell came up and asked to join them. That started tongues wagging. Lots of people flowed by to say hello.

"Aagh! What a ticket," Dole joked to someone who passed by. "God, what a ticket here."

"I'm going to be his vice president!" Dole said to another.

By the end of the week, Tom Johnson, the president of CNN, called Dole urgently. We're not going to go with this story now, it is too big, Johnson said. You're my friend; we need to talk because we have it from three sources that are friends of yours that you've made a deal with Colin Powell and he'll be your running mate and it will be announced when you declare officially for president.

"Tom, believe me," Dole said, "if that were the case, somebody would have known it by now." It wasn't true at all. CBS anchor Dan Rather also brought it up with Dole.

One late January afternoon at 4 P.M., Dole met with Senator Alfonse D'Amato, the boisterous, outspoken New York Republican, who had one of the most powerful state organizations. Dole and D'Amato had a close working relationship based on doing favors for each other. Dole wanted to win the New York presidential primary, the third richest in delegates after California and Texas, and D'Amato held the key. But D'Amato was holding out his support for a Dole presidential bid contingent on Dole's selecting his own campaign guru to run Dole's presidential race: Arthur J. Finkelstein. A Republican political consultant and polling specialist, Finkelstein, 49, was one of the most controversial political consultants in America, an attack specialist who had done three campaigns for Senator Jesse Helms, the ultra-conservative North Carolina Republican. A secretive, behind-the-scenes operative who avoided the press, Finkelstein loved raw, negative commercials.

D'Amato brought Finkelstein to the meeting and the consultant held forth on his campaign theories. He said that Dole had an appeal similar to Eisenhower on character and integrity. But it would be difficult for Dole to win in 1996 because the basic voting groups were more committed to their issues such as opposition to taxes, affirmative action, government spending, crime, welfare, illegal immigration. California Governor Pete Wilson might be the best candidate given the strong visible stands he had taken on these issues.

Finkelstein could run the Dole campaign, D'Amato said. It was the only way for Dole to win. Dole had to quit putting all these people on the campaign payroll. Arthur could do it all—polling, media consulting and campaign management. "He'd be by your desk," D'Amato explained, "and you wouldn't say *anything* unless Arthur tells you what to say."

Dole was very solicitous toward D'Amato and Finkelstein, but near the end of the meeting he turned and winked at Lacy and Synhorst, who were sitting off to the side.

In the old days, Dole would have caved instantly and said, yeah, come on in, given Finkelstein a big title, office. For the prospective new campaign team it was a critical test of discipline. Would Dole start setting up new and overlapping rings of authority?

Later D'Amato told Dole he would not support Dole's presidential bid unless he hired Finkelstein. Just can't do it without Arthur, D'Amato said. Dole called Mari Will to report D'Amato's threat. "I don't give people ultimatums," Will said, adding that she thought Finkelstein was the worst. "You have to do what you have to do, and you have to take New York, but this person is low."

After much discussion with D'Amato, Dole would only agree to offer Finkelstein a subordinate role. To save face, Finkelstein withdrew on his own, and D'Amato pledged to support Dole for president anyway.

Later that week, Reed, Lacy and Synhorst met with Dole. In ten months Dole had never commented on Lacy's long pre-campaign memo that outlined the need for strategic, organizational message and structural discipline. As they talked, Dole said for the first time that he had read it. His tone and body language suggested he agreed with it, but he stopped a mile short of actually endorsing the points. Yes, he would have to change the way he did business.

To be clear, Lacy said, this is the structure. Reed as the manager.

Number one. No big foot, no big-guy former cabinet officer or senator would be brought in to oversee.

Yeah.

These are the other people: Lacy himself as the deputy manager in charge of strategy; Jill Hanson as political director; Mari Will as communications director; Jo-Anne Coe on fund-raising; Synhorst for Iowa.

Fine, Dole said.

Lacy wanted more assurance. Is that acceptable to you?

"Yes," said Dole.

Lacy pushed for more.

"Let's do it that way," Dole finally said.

Just to make sure, Lacy took it a step beyond the nods, body language, so this was absolutely clear. He wanted more than Dole's passive consent. Dole had to have ownership of his campaign.

Finally Dole said, "I want to do it that way."

The next day, the campaign team was announced. Lacy's past with Reagan and Reed's with Kemp—the foremost conservatives of the 1980s —was headlined on the press release: "Former Reagan, Kemp Aides to Lead Dole Campaign."

On Monday, January 30, Jack Kemp, the former congressman and Secretary of Housing and Urban Development, formally announced that he was not going to run for president. Kemp didn't want to do the hundreds of necessary fund-raisers and didn't want himself or his family to live under the intense media spotlight. Despite his time in Congress and the Bush cabinet, Kemp realized he was a former physical education major who had spent 14 years as a professional football quarterback, and he acknowledged to close friends that he probably was not smart enough to be president.

But Kemp was a major force in Republican circles and was often considered the natural heir to the Reagan legacy. His formal statement of non-candidacy was major news in political circles. He would likely remain the sentimental favorite for an important core group of Reaganites whose support all the other candidates would seek.

Dole made sure he reached Kemp that night.

"Maybe it's sort of a relief to have made a decision," Dole said. "It's not easy. I've been struggling with this thing myself."

"I really appreciate the call," Kemp said.

"I'd like to have you come by whenever you think it's right," Dole said. "I'd like to talk to you. Everybody's going to want to talk to you." Dole then raised a delicate issue: clashes from the past in 1988 when they had both run unsuccessfully for the nomination. The two were opposites —Dole the legislative technician and Kemp the broad visionary capable of giving a stirring, rousing speech. "This myth out there that Bob Dole and Jack Kemp hate each other," Dole said.

"I agree with you," Kemp said.

"God!" Dole said. "We haven't seen each other for years."

Kemp promised to come by and talk.

Dole also knew he needed to sound out California Governor Wilson. They had served eight years in the Senate together and they liked to say they knew each other well, had even been fairly close. But their relationship was never personal; nearly all their encounters were through the unnatural haze of legislative maneuverings and in the context of each other's formidable ambition. At the end of January, Wilson was in Washington for the National Governors' Association gathering, and he arranged to go by to see Dole.

Wilson expected that if Dole won the Republican nomination, he would ask him to be his vice-presidential running mate. Rumors were circulating, and Wilson had heard some clear rumblings from Stu Spencer and Don Bren. It was an uncomfortable situation, and Wilson was not sure what he would say if asked. Perhaps he would just say, "I find that very flattering and let me think about it."

On Tuesday, January 31, Wilson went over to Dole's office, and the two sat down alone.

Dole wanted to find out if Wilson was going to run, and he felt he had found a way to ask, indirectly but in such a way as to smoke out Wilson's intentions.

"I'd like to clear the decks with you," Dole said, "because I want to come out and raise money in California." He added that he was in no great rush. Dole thought he wouldn't have been so straightforward in 1988. "But I want you to give me your blessing it's all right. If you're out there raising money, I don't want to be out there competing with you."

"I think we can work something out," Wilson replied enigmatically, and then suggested that Dole keep in touch with Wilson's chief of staff.

"Pete," Dole said, "if I can just talk to you as a friend, I think I may be the perceived front-runner, but if you had a Pete Wilson in the race, you could be the eventual front-runner. Big state, California. Big money."

Dole also said that D'Amato's chief political guru, Arthur Finkelstein, had said that Wilson would be a better candidate or have a better chance.

Wilson thought that Dole was at least being remarkably candid about that.

"We're friends in this thing," Dole said.

"I have great respect for you and Elizabeth," Wilson said. He didn't have any interest in supporting Phil Gramm, he indicated, and he didn't really know any of the others who might run or think much of them.

Dole tried to find out more about Wilson's eventual plans.

Concerning his own decision, Wilson finally said, he honestly couldn't tell Dole because he hadn't decided.

As the conversation proceeded, Wilson was struck by how tentative Dole was about everything. Here Dole was running for president. Wilson expected him to be very upbeat, ebullient and full of enthusiasm about running. Instead, Dole wasn't very focused, didn't even explain the rationale for his candidacy or what he wanted to do if elected president. Dole offered no plan, no program, not even a statement of philosophy. His conversation was rambling, with fits and starts of focus. He seemed ill at ease.

Dole told Wilson that he had recently met with Colin Powell, and what a great vice president Powell would make. He implied that Powell and Wilson were kind of on his short list.

Their conversation finally turned to a recent political column about a possible Dole-Wilson ticket.

"I don't think that ought to be out in the public domain," Wilson said. "Even if you're thinking of that I don't think you ought to be thinking about it publicly."

"You know," Dole replied carefully, "people speculate." All this was coming from the Republican fund-raisers, Dole's own finance people, Wilson's own finance people, he added, since a ticket of the Senate majority leader and the California governor would be potent, a ticket the money people would love.

After about 40 minutes, Wilson left.

Dole concluded that Wilson hadn't quite decided but his guess was that Wilson wouldn't run.

Later that afternoon in Washington, Wilson met at the California state office on North Capitol Street with two of his most trusted advisers. The first was Bob White, a fast-talking lifelong bachelor who had devoted his entire life to Wilson, serving as top aide, alter ego and chief of staff for 26 years of Wilson's political career.

The second close Wilson adviser was Don Sipple, a 44-year-old political media specialist who had worked in the 1992 Bush campaign and whose clients included the governors of such key states as Illinois and Texas. A tall, slender man with blond hair and a good tan, Sipple resembled the actor Paul Hogan who played Crocodile Dundee in the movies. Sipple liked to sit his candidates before the camera and push them to the limit, a kind of cinema verité, probing into their childhoods and core motivations. He wanted to get through to the real self. In Wilson's first race for governor in 1990, he had driven at Wilson very hard before a camera in private. "What are we trying to get at?" Wilson had finally asked. "I'm trying to get at your guts," Sipple replied. He never got there.

The meeting with Dole had been strange and disquieting, Wilson reported to White and Sipple. The rumor circulating that Dole was looking for some deal with Wilson to take the vice-presidency had not come up directly in their discussion. Oblique discussion was the norm with Dole, but it had even been more so. The prospect of being vice president was not appealing, even if Dole ran and served as president for only one term. "Hell," Wilson said, "I'd rather be governor of California than vice president."

Sipple felt this was a soft no, probably not categorical. It was possible that Wilson might change his mind if Dole asked.

"How many people back their way into the presidency?" Wilson asked rhetorically. "Bush," he answered his own question. "And look at what happened to him."

They discussed the news that Jack Kemp was not going to run. Kemp had excoriated Wilson for supporting California's Proposition 187, which would cut illegal immigrants off from government services, and Wilson was infuriated.

"That son of a bitch didn't have a shot anyway," he said tartly.

Wilson turned to his own presidential prospects—a "what if" discussion that had been going intensively for the three weeks since the Sacramento dinner.

Sipple told him that after that dinner half a dozen of his aides had met at Meadowwood, a posh resort in the Napa Valley, and secretly assessed the odds that Wilson could get the nomination. It came down to 1 in 3 on average, he told him. He added that he personally felt it was only about 1 in 5.

"I know about long odds," Wilson said, winking confidently. He didn't have to remind them that a year ago everyone was writing his political obituary.

The three got into a long talk about the nuts-and-bolts issues of getting on the ballot in the presidential primaries, raising money, delegate selection, and what might be done to expand Wilson's political organization beyond California, an essential step for a credible national candidacy.

Sipple said that California assumptions wouldn't work in a national campaign. "You can't take the approach of we'll raise the money, put the message on TV and win," he said.

They agreed that Dole was like Clinton, always talking process—the vote count, the mechanics, the legislative back and forth. Dole didn't get up and say, this is what I believe, this is what I want to do.

Yet Dole was the early front-runner, and the Republicans usually nominated the front-runner. Sipple said he personally thought Dole was on the B-team for winning the Republican nomination.

"No one wants to be on the first Dole team," Wilson said, referring to Dole's history of firing his first group of campaign advisers. "You want to be on the third Dole team."

Sipple and White chuckled.

Wilson reminded them that nothing could leak out publicly that he was considering a run for president.

"So what's your gut?" Wilson asked Sipple.

"There's a huge opening for somebody with the right message. I believe it will be a message year, not a credentials year. If you look at the front-runner," Sipple added, referring to Dole, "there is no message there."

Wilson sat quietly for a moment. "You're right," he declared with a characteristic head movement of determination, a kind of exclamation mark. In contrast, he pointed out that his own message—cracking down on crime, welfare and illegal immigration—was already out there, and clear.

Scott Reed began as Dole's campaign manager February 1. Immediately, he examined Dole's schedule. In his view, schedule was message. Who Dole saw, what he spent his time on, would define the man and his campaign. He quickly saw that Dole's schedule was too much a floating crap game—an assortment of drop-bys, informal talks at conventions and associations all over town, sometimes visits to three different groups in three different hotels on a single evening. Countless old friends had a clear call on Dole's time. Meetings on the schedule would often be described with a notation of the key staffer who had arranged the appointment—"Sheila" for Burke, or "Jo-Anne" for Coe. It was not always clear whether these meetings or events were to serve Dole or some staffer. But Dole kept tight personal control over the schedule and was ceding it to no one. Reed found he could get things added to it but not subtracted.

For February 2 the calendar showed an interview with *The Washington Times,* the conservative local newspaper that loved to snipe at Dole or worse. There was no plan for how Dole was going to handle this interview, in which he could get his head handed to him. The *Times* reporters would try to trip him up on questions about abortion or taxes. Reed dispatched Mari Will to see Dole the day before so they could review systematically what he wanted to accomplish, and what he did not want to say.

The next morning, after the interview, *The Washington Times* carried a big front-page story under a headline that was a kiss: "Dole Works at 'Reconnecting the Government to the People.' " The paper ran nearly 5,000 words of question and answer. Having absorbed his lesson, and as if he were driving it into his own head with a repetition that was occasionally comic, Dole was quoted saying, "the basic theme I'm going to talk about: reining in government, reining in government . . . it's government, government." Of his chief legislative goal, he remarked, "Balanced budget, balanced budget," adding, "and you say it over and over and over," as he did.

At Dole headquarters that morning they were walking around with heads high, couldn't have been better. "Wow, it works." Mari Will was excited and told Dole, "Ah, that's the message."

That morning, Dole appeared at the Loews Hotel, just ten blocks down from the Senate, for a brief talk to a conference. During the question period, Daniel Schorr, the hard-nosed former CBS reporter who had made Nixon's celebrated "Enemies List," stood up slowly in the front. At 78, Schorr, a senior reporter for National Public Radio, was seven years older than Dole. He was an experienced interrogator. In a deep, understated voice, conveying the lobbing of softballs, Schorr inquired, "Why do you want to be president?"

Dole smiled confidently. He was a powerful figure at the podium in a nicely tailored soft gray suit, perfectly tied necktie, and seemingly fresh from the shower, combed and scrubbed, looking almost boyish, certainly youthful. Dole knew, of course, that it was that simple question that

Roger Mudd had put to Senator Edward Kennedy in 1980. Kennedy's fumbling and incoherent response—praising the country's natural resources, technology and political system—had helped sink his presidential aspirations.

"I remember seeing that show," Dole said, referring to the Kennedy interview. "In fact, I went back and looked at it a couple of years ago." Mild laughter built even louder as the knowing Washington audience grasped that this was supposed to be a joke. Dole paused for effect. "But I guess if I just say it in a word, it seems to me that, whether it's me or anybody else, my view, it is time to reconnect the government with the American people," he continued, drawing on his session with *The Washington Times*. "I think that's my one broad theme, and secondly I think it's time to reestablish ourselves in the world as the leader."

Apparently realizing this might sound a little too forward-leaning, perhaps even imperialistic, Dole added, "Not in the sense that we have to, we're not after anything. But as I travel around, I see what's happening in foreign policy." He seemed about ready to pounce on President Clinton. "Again," he continued without pausing, "I didn't come here to be critical of President Clinton." So he put the criticism as mildly as imaginable. "I think there is a lot of work in that area that could be done. But there will be a lot of other issues, I mean, you know, once the race starts, which is probably going to be . . ." Catching himself, he noted at once, "Maybe it's already started, ah, but, ah there will be, ah, a lot of efforts by"—he slowed down and put the brakes on himself as it seemed he might name another candidate—"different candidates to position themselves." His voice slowed measurably and then dropped down somewhat dramatically. Shifting quickly, he said, "But I've been around here a while, you know, I've voted I don't know how many hundred thousand times. I assume there will be some votes that people will dig up from back in the 60s or 70s. I can't even remember how I voted in some of those kinds of things."

The audience responded with very mild, somewhat uneasy laughter, perhaps sensing that Dole's answer was not much better than Kennedy's, but this one was not recorded on national television. It was classic Dole —going for the laugh, somewhat hesitant, and always circling immediately back on what he had said, modifying, amplifying, and in the process often nullifying the impact of his own words. He did not have a declarative "I believe . . ." or "I want to be president *because* . . ."

Later that day, Dole flew to New York City for an appearance on the popular CBS *Late Show with David Letterman*.

Elizabeth was still on him about running.

"Have you decided?" she had asked the other night.

"I think so," he replied, noting that the full-blown public announcement had been set two months down the road, in April.

"I got to talk to you," she said. She wanted another review. Even though he had decided, Dole realized maybe his wife hadn't quite decided.

"Well," Dole said, "I'll be back from Letterman at eight o'clock." They taped the show earlier in the day.

On the Letterman show Dole appeared slightly uncomfortable and out of place, but made what he called his "informally official" declaration for the presidency. He read a scaled-down version of the "Top Ten"—his ways to balance the federal budget. In the spirit of frugality, cutting everything by 30 percent, he had only a "Top Seven." Under his seven ways to balance the budget, he read somewhat nervously, "No. 7. Stop paying Clinton's speechwriters by the word," to "No. 1. Arkansas? Sell it."

When Dole got back to Washington, Elizabeth had already left for Boston where she had a Harvard Board of Overseers meeting the next day. She was supposed to have left the next morning but a heavy snow was predicted and she had gone early to make sure she'd get to Boston.

Dole hadn't planned to stay up to watch himself on Letterman but he did so so that he could talk by phone to Elizabeth in Boston. He was also on a David Frost interview that aired on the Public Broadcasting System that night.

"Good job," Elizabeth told him. "I've been watching Bob Dole all evening."

Dole felt she wanted to make sure he had really made up his mind.

Elizabeth raised all the old questions. She sighed and laughed at the questions. The enormous commitment, the two years of running, their lives radically and perhaps permanently altered. And if he won, then he might be in for eight years. But if the presidency was the better place from which to serve, fine, she said, they would make the sacrifices in their personal lives.

Saturday morning, February 4, I went to interview Dole in his Hart office. Everyone, all the old Dole hands, new Dole hands, had predicted that he wouldn't sit still with me for very long. Up and out. And he certainly wouldn't talk introspectively or in paragraphs, they said. But he did. Maybe it was the heavy, unexpected snowstorm, making Washington deserted, quiet like Kansas in the winter, or even New Hampshire. The light was so bright, the air crisp and clean. Maybe it was because I was the last appointment of the day and the week. There was nothing to do afterwards, and Elizabeth was in Boston.

I saw him about noon. He was dressed casually in a handsome green wool shirt. For an hour and a half we reviewed Dole's decision to run, the why and how in detail, the steps as he inched into the race. He gave the long answers, and he didn't get up once. He would have talked longer, but I couldn't think of any more questions. I'd been summoned on short notice and had no time formally to prepare questions. My tape recorder sat on the arm of his chair, and his press secretary, Clarkson Hine, took copious notes.

After Dick Cheney had announced he would not run, Cheney had said to me, "When have we elected the best?" That was an important question for my book. Did Dole, I asked, think in 1988 that he was the best candidate?

"Thought I was," Dole said.

"You weren't elected," I asked, "so you have to come out of that period feeling the system doesn't elect the best?"

"I think it's true," Dole said. "I think Elizabeth raises that a lot, whether it's president, or Senate or whatever, that a lot of the best— somebody people would describe [as] the best—don't make it. That's the way the system works. You also come out of that, even though you lose, if you still have enough confidence in yourself, that you didn't lose because you weren't the best candidate. You lost for other reasons. You can always rationalize these things."

"Were you rationalizing that?"

"Yeah," Dole replied. "I think for a time I was rationalizing. We lost because, you know, up in the big snowstorm in New Hampshire the weekend before, Bush was out shoveling snow and doing things I couldn't. So. Wasn't his fault. I just couldn't do those things." Dole's war wound made shoveling impossible, and Bush had unleashed his "Senator Straddle" ad. "We could walk around in supermarkets. We didn't have a reaction to his stuff he was doing the last few days. *We were sort of paralyzed.* Like we were in the snowbank somewhere, and we had all these meetings but nobody could come to a judgment." Neither Dole nor his campaign had decided on a response ad or what to do—a now legendary story told many times in the campaign books.

I asked about the 1988 New Hampshire loss again. Dole had been quoted in one of those campaign books saying that he could have won "if I had been whole."

"I didn't quite mean it that way," Dole said. "But it goes back to the snowstorm. When I couldn't go out there and physically run the tractor. Bush got a lot of good press. He was dumping snow over there and shoveling snow. Pushing people's cars, and I don't know whether that makes any difference or not, but you just sort of look back. You know, why did you have a snowstorm? Why not next week? We were sitting around the motel with nothing to do, and Bush was out shoveling snow and helping the neighbors, and we were like I said, going through the supermarket. I doubt if that made that much difference, but everything could have lost it. You know what I mean. We were on sort of death watch or whatever it is, whether it's snowstorm or da-da-da-da . . ."

"Can't buy ads on TV," I interrupted.

"Can't buy ads," he agreed. "Nobody's made up their mind. We should have gone to Boston, did what Bush did [in his positive ads]. Had little groupies around ask the right questions, hit them out of the park. But that's why you wake up at night thinking of those things. I don't do it anymore but—"

"When did that stop?"

"I think it lasted about a year, maybe longer," Dole said. "But I think once you get into something, I mean, it wasn't just every night but you still," and he looked me dead square in the eye, leaning forward, his good, left arm up for emphasis, "you know some of these things in everybody's lifetime you never totally forget."

I believed him. He had not forgotten.

But, I later wondered, why had Dole not taken responsibility, seized the controls of his own campaign? He had reminisced, telling the story as an observer. In the 1988 campaign Dole was correctly accused of micromanaging, not letting go of the details, constantly fiddling with the small things. But on some of the large things he let events unfold around him. In some ways, the central feature of his personality was his passivity —particularly under pressure or at key moments. What might this mean during a Dole presidency?

That Saturday, February 4, Dan Quayle, the former vice president, picked up a confidential six-page memo from the fax machine at his home outside Indianapolis, Indiana. Quayle, 47, a figure of considerable

ridicule in the media—some fair, some unfair—was running a clear second after Dole in the public opinion polls of known Republicans who
might run in 1996. He had hired several aides for a possible campaign
and was almost universally expected to declare his formal candidacy later
in the month. He had traveled to key states and counties as vice president
to Bush, cultivating the local conservative party establishments in the
tradition of both Nixon and Bush when they had been vice presidents,
and made the grass-roots connections vital to winning the presidency.

The memo was from Mark Goodin, a senior Republican communications specialist who was organizing the nascent Quayle campaign.

"The Alternative Campaign," Quayle read. Goodin recounted that in
a meeting several months earlier, Quayle had proposed running a campaign openly attacking the federal deficit and questioning normally off-
limits entitlements, automatic Social Security retirement benefits and
Medicare health insurance for the elderly.

"More than ever, I am convinced that this so-called honest campaign
is not only in the best interest of Dan Quayle. More important, it is what
the nation desperately needs," Goodin had written.

Quayle, who was making a living giving paid speeches to business
and other groups, had been recently hospitalized with blood clots in his
lungs, and then a second time for removal of his appendix, which was
enlarged. The second hospitalization had created the stir and speculation,
but the first had been the far more serious. Unknown to the public,
Quayle had been told that he would die if another clot of blood in his leg
moved to his lungs. Each morning, he had to give a sample of blood that
would be taken to a lab for testing to make sure it was properly thinned.
He would then anxiously await the call telling him it was okay. Once the
doctors got his blood too thin and they were very worried. A daily blood
calibration was a constant reminder of his mortality.

"The Quayle Quandary," the first subhead of the memo read. Quayle
was behind in fund-raising and organization—slow off the mark as others
like Dole and Gramm were moving. Like a student who wouldn't do
his homework, Quayle had day after day resisted making the routine
fund-raising calls, delayed grabbing up money from longtime Indiana
supporters. This was the so-called low-hanging fruit that could be picked
up in a day of work on the phone. Quayle had a bad case of "call
reluctant." He'd been vice president, flying around the country and the
world on Air Force Two with dozens of staff to handle all the chores.
Now the smallest details needed his attention.

The Quayle organization, such as it was, had delayed payment to their travel agency. "Are we having cash flow problems?" Quayle had asked incredulously at one point. When some of his advisers were talking about a newly hired assistant fund-raiser, Quayle asked, "Who's she?" He wondered why old staffers were not doing more. The campaign gets its energy from the top, one friend replied.

"You've got to get out and call in the chips, twist some arms, make people remember all you've done for them," Goodin had argued at one time. "You've got to remind them they owe you."

"Shit," Quayle had snapped, "I'm not a candidate, I'm a banker." He didn't like to grub for money. At another point he asked, "When are we going to talk policy?"

In the memo, Quayle read, "I believe you are worse off now than you were six to eight weeks ago. . . . And within a few more weeks, it will become very clear [to the media] that you have no finance committee, no finance director, you've authorized few if any fundraisers and no direct mail, and that you have less than $100,000 in your exploratory account. The other candidates will post numbers in the millions. Add that to the fact that the media also knows that the big donors are quickly signing up with other candidates, and they won't be calling you a long shot. They'll be pronouncing you dead meat."

"Where can we go?" the memo continued.

"There are only three realistic options: 1) Run a low cost, low risk campaign that excites a few people, and get edged out early. . . . 2) . . . Surprise the world by announcing that you will not be a candidate for president. . . . 3) Run a lower-cost, high-risk alternative campaign. You become the conscience of the Republican party by traveling the primary states and telling the unvarnished truth about entitlements and cultural values. Tell the voters that this kind of campaign will undoubtedly hobble your chances to win, but that you care more about surfacing these issues and talking about possible solutions than getting to the Oval Office. . . .

"Any low-risk message does nothing to force that second look you acknowledge the public and the press need in order to force a reassessment about you."

Goodin recommended that Quayle strongly consider the alternative, high-risk campaign.

"I think you accomplish four crucial things by waging this alternative campaign: A) You pick up a bunch of dough from people who will like the brutal honesty of your message and you stun the country and the press into taking a second look at Dan Quayle. B) You totally outflank

Gramm, Dole and anyone else by becoming the one guy, the one candidate who is actually serious about the deficit in the future. . . . C) Not
inconsequently, you end up doing something really good for this country.
Something it is in desperate need of. Pop the bubble of doublespeak in
politics that is preventing us from attacking our problems. . . . You become the darling of the younger generation—a not insignificant voting
block, just ask Clinton—and the gutsiest guy on the block. The press
will love you. . . . Result: you become the trendsetter, not to mention the
ideological lead dog. . . . D) . . . Even if you go down in flames, you will
have done extraordinary things to enhance your image and your place in
history."

After finishing the memo, Quayle called Goodin.

"It's well written," Quayle said. "You give me an awful lot to think
about. Let me do that. I'll get back to you."

Quayle realized that as he was debating the question of whether to
run he could not outwardly show much hesitation, couldn't show *any*
hesitation, really. He had talked recently with Bush and had even left him
with the impression he was moving forward.

Five months earlier, on September 21, 1994, Quayle had spent 45
minutes with Dole alone in a little anteroom up in the Senate. There were
just two chairs in the room. Dole had said he hadn't made up his mind.
"My staff has," Dole joked, "but I haven't."

Quayle said he hadn't either.

They turned to a discussion of Clinton and how he was getting
pounded.

"Well, you know," Dole said, "Clinton probably deserves a lot of it,
but God, look what they're doing to him." Dole was amazed by the press,
the opposition. Dole himself was part of it, he realized. They try to break
you. "Look what they did to Bush?" Dole said. It was both a question
and an answer. "Look what they do to any president?"

Quayle agreed, and they discussed it. Then they looked at each other.
There wasn't much more to say, but the body language spoke volumes. It
was pretty rough out there. If they ran, they would be part of it.

Two days after reading Goodin's memo, Monday afternoon, February
6, Quayle went to Iowa. He had a bad cold, but his blood problem

prevented him from taking cold medicine. He asked to speed up the schedule. At a meeting of some 15 key members of the Christian Coalition, they asked him three times if he was viable, could he be nominated and elected? Quayle thought the questions were nasty and insulting. Next, Quayle went to Florida to speak and meet with other potential supporters. Flying back home Wednesday, February 8, he realized he had to make a decision.

He returned to his home, a sprawling modern upscale house with large rooms on four acres. A big "VICE PRESIDENT QUAYLE" was monogrammed on one of the carpets. A birdhouse replica of the White House was out by the pool. He was five minutes from the Crooked Stick Country Club, where he loved to play golf and where the staff called him "Dan," not "Mr. Vice President."

Quayle had already reached one conclusion about himself. "I'm not like Nixon," he said. "I don't have to be president." He knew he could emotionally walk away. He did not necessarily have to be president to have lived a full and successful life. He also did not have the clear-eyed— or was it irrational?—obsessiveness of those like Nixon. He'd been told he would have to conduct about 16 fund-raisers a month to raise the necessary money to run.

About 10 P.M. he walked up the stairs to find his wife, Marilyn. She had been urging him to make up his mind.

"Well, what is it?" she asked.

"I just don't think this is the right year for me to run for president."

"Are you sure?"

"That's my decision."

"Are you sure this is what you want to do?" Marilyn asked again.

"It's the best decision for now," he said. "I'm 47 and you're 45, and there's a lot of good things ahead of us." He calculated there would be six presidential elections before he was age 69.

Marilyn pressed him some more.

He held his ground. No more dancing around, no more second-guessing himself.

"Well, you know," she said, "it's your decision. . . . If that's your decision, that's the way it'll be. Who have you told?"

"No one."

"Well, don't you think you ought to tell the children?"

He walked down the hall to see his daughter Corinne, a junior at the nearby private Jesuit high school. Corinne, 16, knew the price political life had exacted from her father—time, emotion—and she knew that he had been beaten up severely in the past. She was adamantly opposed to his running, but she thought he was going to anyway. He explained that he had decided not to run.

Quayle would never forget her reaction. She threw her arms around him, and gave him a big hug.

"I love you," she said ecstatically. "You didn't do this because of me?"

"No," Quayle said.

His son Benjamin, 18, was in his first year of college at Duke University in North Carolina. He also had been opposed. He said, "I'm glad you're not."

Tucker, 20, a college junior at Lehigh University in Pennsylvania, had felt it wouldn't be so bad to have his father in the White House. But he said, "It's a pretty good choice, Dad."

In the morning Marilyn asked him, "How did you sleep?"

"Uh, so-so."

She wanted to go over it one last time before he started the ball rolling. "Are you sure you made the right decision?"

"Yes."

"Okay."

"It's all going to be momentum, polls, scandal of the day, sound bites, gaffes," he said. "Many of the irrelevancies."

About 6:30 A.M., he reached John W. Vardaman, Jr., a prominent Washington attorney, golfing buddy and close friend who was coordinating the staffing for the campaign as a kind of chairman of the board.

"I'm not going to go," Quayle explained. "I prayed about it."

"I wanted you to run," Vardaman said, "but I'm glad it's decided."

Quayle reached Mark Goodin.

"I've thought a lot about it," Quayle said. "I've thought a lot about everything. I just don't think it's the time." He thanked Goodin for his efforts, but returned to his own concerns. "I want a real life. I'm opting for that real life. Corinne is about to move out of the house. The boys are gone, and I want some time with her."

Goodin was disappointed. Quayle had been pushing others for evidence that a campaign would be credible. He was not pushing himself, and Goodin had previously reminded Quayle that in politics you make your own fate. Now Quayle had.

Quayle listed all the things he would not miss.

"This is a sick process," Goodin said. "You have to want it more than life itself. And there is something sick about just that." They didn't write the rules, Goodin added, and they knew if a candidate didn't obey them, the candidate would die. He suggested that Quayle hold a press conference to announce the decision.

"No," Quayle said, "you handle it." He didn't want it out until the afternoon. He had to inform many people, including his parents who were in Arizona.

"Congratulations, Dan Quayle, you're a sane guy," Goodin finally said. "You'll be a lot healthier and happier. You'll live to fight another day."

Quayle wasn't sure about the remaining Republican field. He had overlapped four years in the Senate with Phil Gramm, whom Quayle felt was a negative person. Negative people didn't get elected president, he believed. Dole shared a little bit of that problem himself. Clinton was an optimist, as were Reagan and Bush. Quayle felt he was an optimist.

Dole had additional problems in Quayle's view. His message would be about competence: I've been there, I've had the experience. That, Quayle worried, was too much like Michael Dukakis's theme in 1988—competence, not ideology, not passion.

Quayle reached former Bush White House chief of staff John Sununu. Sununu, the former New Hampshire governor, had helped deliver the crucial first primary state for Bush in 1988 and had promised to do the same for Quayle in 1996. The first time Quayle had been in New Hampshire to test the waters not long before, Sununu had taken Quayle to some guy's house for a two-hour dinner. "He was that important?" Quayle asked afterwards. "That was two hours well spent," Sununu had replied with absolute confidence.

Quayle explained his decision not to run.

"Who do we support now?" Sununu asked without missing a beat.

Quayle didn't have an answer.

Dole heard the news and called Quayle.

"Hey, what's this?" Dole asked. "You're not going?"

"Naw," Quayle replied.

Dole wanted to know when it was going to be announced officially. "What time?" He wanted to go out with a statement but, of course, make sure he did not preempt. Quayle said it would be at 3:30 P.M.

"Well," Dole added, "we've always been friends. Come see me sometime. I'd like to talk to you."

Quayle's written statement said, "We were convinced that a winning campaign could have been accomplished and the necessary funds could have been raised. However, we chose to put our family first, and to forgo the disruption to our lives."

7

At 9 A.M. Saturday, February 10, Dole, Reed, Lacy, Will, Coe and Synhorst met in the conference room of Dole's Hart office. They reviewed state by state the governors, senators and congressmen who were being recruited or had pledged to endorse him. Dole liked to hear what was going on, in detail. He was convinced that support in key state organizations would be critical in the accelerated and compressed primary schedule the next year when 70 percent of the delegates needed to win the nomination would be chosen in a six-week period.

On Iowa, Synhorst said that Phil Gramm had been courting the Christian Coalition. "Gramm's making it difficult out there throwing them all this red meat, and he's saying the things they want to hear," Synhorst explained. "Could we do that a little bit?"

"Aagh!" Dole snapped, "I'm not going to talk like Phil Gramm talks. I'm not going to say the things he's saying."

After Quayle's withdrawal two days earlier, Synhorst reminded them, Christian Coalition president Ralph Reed had declared that the situation was "the equivalent of a jump ball at the buzzer" in a basketball game. "The question is who will jump highest to get that vote," Ralph Reed had said.

"I'm not going to say these extreme things," Dole repeated. He didn't want to be in a contest with Phil Gramm to be the most conservative or shout the loudest. He didn't like Gramm's tone or style. It wasn't his. Dole felt he had stayed in the mainstream.

Dole's thoughts harkened back to 1988 when front-runner Bush had treated him like a fly to ignore. Whhhhhssstttt! he thought. Better to treat Gramm like a fly. Why make Phil Gramm the opponent?

New Hampshire was the horse that threw Dole in 1988, and the campaign decided to get him back on.

Synhorst prepared a schedule of nine town meetings, two press conferences and two speeches for Dole to do in New Hampshire over the upcoming three-day President's Day holiday weekend. "Do you think we can get all that done?" Dole asked when he saw the schedule.

"I'm going to do it like I did Iowa," Synhorst replied.

"Well, okay."

In New Hampshire, the local Republican activists said the trip was a terrible idea. A holiday weekend, the weather could be bad, many potential problems.

Synhorst called Scott Reed and explained why an aggressive schedule was essential. "Don't let this schedule be diluted one fucking bit!" Synhorst added.

"I agree," Reed said, but he noted that the New Hampshire people were nervous the meetings would not be successful.

"They'll be successful," Synhorst said. "I'm doing 'em. They'll be successful."

Reed figured the trip was a calculated risk, worth taking. It was important to show that the Dole campaign was not fucked up, and to demonstrate they had something to back up the good poll numbers, which they all knew didn't mean anything. Reed recognized that he had about 60 to 90 days to prove himself to Dole. He understood New Hampshire was an emotional hurdle. Dole had vividly shared with Reed his memory of the day before the 1988 New Hampshire primary, driving down the road and seeing Bush signs everywhere and not having a single Dole sign out. Reed concluded they all had to get over it or Dole wouldn't have any confidence in him or the rest of the team. He began micromanaging the whole weekend plan.

Dole wondered if they were biting off more than they could chew. No one mentioned the obvious point, that it would show Dole was vigorous and help put the age question to bed, at least for the moment.

• • •

Reed knew that Dole wanted him to be careful spending their campaign money. In 1988, seemingly millions had disappeared on big fat salaries for campaign staff and contracts months, even a year, before the first primary. Alex Castellanos, who had been the Dole media consultant in the 1988 presidential race and in 1992 for Dole's Senate reelection, wanted a huge contract for 1996. Over the summer, Castellanos had sent Dole a 19-page memo on message strategy, arguing that Dole had to become more conservative and more of a Washington outsider. In graphic terms, he said, "Change or die."

Reed decided to open up the media job to competitive bidding. The work would be limited in 1995 and he didn't want to start laying down a lot of money for reels of film and pretty pictures.

Castellanos took the open bidding personally. On February 13, he wrote Dole saying that he had accepted an offer to become Phil Gramm's media consultant.

Reed and the others wanted to hire Don Sipple, the media consultant for Pete Wilson, but Sipple said that out of loyalty he was waiting to see if Wilson would run.

Dole's weekend in New Hampshire went off without a single significant hitch.

Monday morning in Nashua 100 people attended the leadership meeting and then hundreds more the town meeting.

"Sure is different than '88," Dole commented to Warren Rudman, who was accompanying him.

"Sure is," Rudman said, joking. "I don't think it's you. It's Bill Clinton."

But by the end of the trip, Dole was complaining that the three-day schedule was too heavy, he didn't have time to think, didn't have time for anything.

Back in Washington the next day, Dole pulled Lacy aside after a fund-raising meeting. Dole reported that several friends and Senate colleagues had complained that his message of reining in the government was wrong.

"There's no magic in any of this," Lacy said. "You've got to have something that you're comfortable with, that you believe, that you can say consistently." The message just had to be coherent. It didn't have to fit into some 20-second or 40-second sound bite, Lacy said. It also didn't have to strike people as bold or innovative, or cause the media and intellectual establishment to stand up. That wasn't going to happen. There wasn't such a message and it wasn't Dole's style. "What you've got there will resonate with voters," Lacy added. "It may not be viewed by everybody as being brilliant or anything like that, but it will work and let's just stick to it."

Dole was going on the CNN *Larry King Live* television show in two nights to make the ritual pre-announcement announcement of his candidacy, and he had to be ready.

Senator William Cohen, a moderate Maine Republican, had watched Dole closely over the last 17 years in the Senate. In one respect he thought Dole was like a shark—he had to keep moving to stay alive. Cohen was going to endorse Dole for president, but not because Dole was a man of vision. He wasn't. However, he was a man of intuition, and his instincts were basically humane and moderate. Dole was not a man of words, either. He often just stopped in the middle of his sentences, but Cohen had come to detect what Dole generally meant. It would be in the body language or the grunts or what was unsaid. Or it would be in his eyes. Still, Cohen felt he never penetrated Dole's screen. Dole always kept some distance, but he was basically a good man who was approachable.

Dole had said publicly that he was going to review affirmative action programs—a clear shift from his previous support. Soon after, Cohen went to see him in private.

"I don't think you ought to get too far out on this," Cohen cautioned. "This is a codeword for lots of people." Ominously, Cohen said that it could be a long, hot summer if blacks felt more and more excluded.

"I only called for a review," Dole responded, blanching. "You can't disagree with that."

"No, I don't," Cohen said, "but you ought to be careful." It would appear as if the Republican Party didn't want minorities or women, he added. Cohen felt that Dole understood.

Thursday mid-afternoon, February 23, the day Dole was supposed to appear on the *Larry King Live* show, Cohen noticed that Dole looked exhausted. He could tell when Dole was strung out, and he was.

"Why don't you cancel out the rest of the day," Cohen recommended, "go home and get a nap. Don't run around. And then go do the Larry King show."

"Well, I'll try, I'll try," Dole promised, his voice trailing off. Dole went to a little hideaway office he occasionally used to take half-hour naps. He didn't sleep, but rested for an hour and a half. The phones didn't ring there and nobody bothered him, and he felt better.

Before the show, Reed, Lacy and Will reviewed with him the three broad themes in the message.

On the show, Dole tried six times to wade into the three points of his message. Once he actually said of his message—"whatever it is." Later he explained himself as the one to "do a lot of these things we want to do." When a caller asked how Dole would distinguish himself from the other Republicans, Dole said, "I decided with a message of reducing government, giving power back to people, less regulation, that somebody with experience might be the one." He radiated tentativeness.

Cohen thought Dole's performance was ridiculous. He told Dole the next day that he just couldn't say things like that. Dole replied that they were still working on the message.

Lacy thought that Dole had tried but that King had moved too quickly to other subjects and cut Dole off. At least the kinder, gentler Dole had shown through. But in broader terms Lacy was reminded how very different it was to run for president than to serve as president. He thought it was a shame that Dole had to go through a process of reducing himself to some "message." Lacy knew it ran close to being dishonest and stage-managed. To take something as complex as the presidency and say in 20 seconds what kind of a president you're going to be—and really have that bear a whole lot of resemblance to the huge scope of the job? Lacy had concluded this would be his last campaign. He wanted out of politics.

After two years as president Clinton still felt deep, even increasing, alienation from Washington. This isolation from his environment was one of the least understood aspects of Clinton's presidency. He expressed frequent contempt, at times even loathing, for the city's social life. Washington seemed to the president to be dominated by a permanent elite of former government officials from both parties who stayed to practice law or lobby, media executives and reporters who had been in the city for decades and wealthy hangers-on.

Because his first year as president had been difficult and contentious, Clinton had never really been able to partake of the goodwill that Washington—even the city's most entrenched establishment—extends to any president. He was rarely able to leverage this goodwill to his advantage and had not learned a basic truth: no group is more susceptible to presidential flattery than this Washington establishment.

"I'm not a Washington insider," Clinton remarked in private many times. But even to those alleged Washington insiders, Clinton's feeling of estrangement was not evident. He made occasional forays to key social events, schmoozing it up with all the people he claimed to disdain and displaying an endless penchant for talk which made him seem at home, a full and contented participant. He would stop in hallways to talk socially with people for 20 minutes or more. He was gracious, engaging and patient, masterfully making and holding eye contact. Unlike many politicians, his eyes did not dart around a room to see who else of more importance was there. He was always articulate, even gleeful. After all, he was the President of the United States bestowing his attention, and few people in the Washington establishment saw beyond that to sense his deep anger. But in private to his intimates it was "the Washington crowd" or "the fucking Washington crowd." He made scathing and graphically obscene references to individuals he thought embodied the city.

In spite of his outward gregariousness on social occasions, Clinton functioned as outsider in his own city. Not only was he not of his time, he was not of his place.

Hillary Clinton dramatically reinforced this sense of isolation and hostility. She felt that the Washington establishment looked down on them. "*The Washington Post* does it all the time," Hillary said privately to an associate. "They are so snotty about people who don't live in Georgetown, and I don't understand that. It's almost unconscious in a way and anybody who wants to play in their big league has to adopt that manner. And *The New York Times* does it, too. It infects the atmosphere."

For Clinton, it seemed as if an automatic cynicism was routinely applied to almost everything he or his administration did. "This cynicism is my enemy," he said. "Cynicism" was, in part, a codeword for media criticism. He felt he was being held to an impossible standard of perfection. His decision-making process had been held up to ridicule because he allowed an openness and breadth of debate. Details of his administration's often excruciating back and forth decisions had been reported in books and newspaper articles, making him look incompetent, he said. Of course there was debate and argument, and of course he shifted his position when stronger arguments were made and new information was presented. It was the way lots of large corporations made decisions, various chief executive officers had told him. "What do you think," he asked, "that I go up to Mount Olympus in the morning and we figure this stuff out and I come down?"

Clinton wanted to look at himself as the champion of the working person, the broad middle class, the poor and the destitute. He argued to his staff that it would be hard to redefine the Democratic Party as the party of the working person as long as the media was so removed and out of touch with real working people—let alone the destitute.

Clinton still had no formal reelection campaign set up. No campaign manager, no campaign chairman, no outside consultants, no media adviser, no pollster at this point. He wanted it that way for now, allowing him to remain presidential and above the day-to-day urgency of electoral politics.

Ickes wanted to get a formal campaign fund-raising plan approved, and arranged to have Terry McAuliffe come to meet with Clinton in mid-February. Gore, Hillary, Ickes and some of the presidential scheduling people attended the meeting in the residence.

McAuliffe handed out copies of a ten-page plan he had drafted. He wanted to schedule a dozen presidential galas for the rest of 1995—big formal dinners around the country. The dates would have to be locked into Clinton's schedule. The plan also said that about ten mass fund-raising mailings would be sent out.

McAuliffe called for an early start—three big fund-raisers in June. Clinton wanted to know why so early.

It was either start in June or September, McAuliffe said. You are blocked out of fund-raising in July, August and through the second week of September because nobody, at least not the big givers and donors, would be around and nobody cared during that period. Starting early would give McAuliffe all of April, May and June to put all the pieces together. If they waited until after the summer that would mean ten events in September—an impossible number in a single month for a sitting president. The other reason to start early, McAuliffe said, was that Ickes and he didn't want to have to fool around with a possible challenger in the party. That would give people a reason to hide and not give.

Others argued that perhaps June was too early. The climate might not be right. Suppose an early effort was put together and it didn't work out? Wouldn't that have the opposite impact and encourage a challenger?

McAuliffe said he felt good about Clinton's support. "From the time you give me the go, I can tie up every single major player in the country," McAuliffe said. The implication was clear that this was possible as long as no serious challenger emerged from among the Democrats.

The plan called for the gala events to begin in New Jersey, follow on to Little Rock and then to Chicago.

Clinton wanted to know why those cities?

McAuliffe said he believed they could collect $1 million or more in each of the first three gala dinners. He had a core of committed people in New Jersey where he had kept Democratic Party fund-raising to a minimum and the people there were itching to deliver, dying to be first off the bat. Same in Little Rock and Chicago, he said. McAuliffe could remember organizing $10,000 to $15,000 fund-raisers in 1988's presidential campaign when he had been finance chairman for Congressman Richard Gephardt. That had been 70 to 80 or more fund-raising events to raise $1 million—pathetic, no fun. It drove the schedule. But an incumbent president like Clinton could get more than 1,000 people out for a $1,000-a-plate dinner. It was all ego on the part of the givers—a presidential dinner, photograph and Christmas card were all most of them wanted.

After the three first cities, McAuliffe's plan called for ten additional events: Pennsylvania, Colorado, Texas, New York, Michigan and Tennessee, and two events each in Florida and California.

Hillary had some questions about the direct mail. How many letters were going out in each of the ten mailings? McAuliffe provided initial estimates. Who did he expect would give after receiving some of these? Why would they give to that piece? He answered those questions. She turned to a detailed questioning about the first mailing, scheduled for April. It was going to be a soft appeal, a two-page letter from Clinton announcing that he was running for reelection, underscoring the importance of his agenda over the Republican Contract With America. It wasn't even going to ask for money in a big way, only in a P.S. and in the response card.

Who would get the first mailing? Hillary asked.

They would target the Clinton-Gore donors from 1992, McAuliffe answered, plus the party base list run by the Democratic National Committee, a huge list of people that traditionally give to Democratic causes.

How many would get it?

When it was all duped out, McAuliffe said, about a million people.

Cost to print and mail it?

Perhaps $400,000.

Would people write checks on such a soft, indirect appeal? Hillary inquired.

McAuliffe said that his direct-mail consultant had said yes. "Listen, I got professionals who I hire to write these things, and they say it's going to work."

Hillary didn't have any more questions.

With Clinton's weakness in the polls and the array of naysayers, McAuliffe said he was going to make the fund-raising approach all positive. He wasn't going to have state finance chairmen, no real hierarchy under him in tiers, for example, which was normal in such a campaign. Instead, he was personally going to recruit 200 people to be on the Clinton-Gore Finance Board. Each would have equal status and each would have to agree to raise $50,000 from others, observing the $1,000 personal limit on individual contributions. That would total $10 million overall. And he would want $25,000 of each $50,000 pledge by the end of June, hopefully adding up to $5 million. The finance board would raise at least several million, plus the three large June fund-raisers, and the first mailing should give them a record quarter by the time the June 30 report was filed with the Federal Election Commission.

Clinton said he was in sync with the plan, and told McAuliffe to go ahead. Since all the mailings would go out under his name, he wanted to approve each letter personally.

At the end of the meeting, McAuliffe collected the copies of his plan, from everyone except Clinton.

On Tuesday, February 28, Dole was on the floor of the Senate until after 7 P.M., managing the vote on the balanced budget amendment to the Constitution. The amendment, requiring the federal government to balance its budget beginning in seven years and every year afterward, was a showcase issue in Gingrich's Contract With America. Clinton was strongly and vocally opposed.

But the amendment had already passed the House with 300 votes, ten more than the two-thirds vote required of constitutional amendments. The Senate had debated the amendment for more than 115 hours, and Dole had 66 votes—just one vote short of the two thirds also required in the Senate. The Senate was going to vote that night. The Washington buzz was intense: Was Dole a leader like Gingrich? Could he get it passed?

"I think we do stand at the crossroads in American history," Dole said, waving his good arm from the lectern on the floor. "I think this vote is one of the most important many of us will have cast in decades." He cited the polls showing that 75 to 80 percent of the public favored the amendment. He railed and assailed, especially against President Clinton, who opposed the amendment. Dole cited more numbers, and turned to quoting George Washington, "The basis of our political system is the right of the people to make and alter their institutions of government." Then Dole acknowledged that he was in search of another vote and abruptly moved to adjourn the Senate.

Senator Robert C. Byrd, the 77-year-old West Virginia Democrat who was leading the opposition, rose to denounce the delay of the vote as a sad spectacle, "a sleazy, tawdry effort" of back-room dealmaking "so that additional pressures can be made on some poor member in the effort to get this vote."

Dole rose in anger. He was tired, his body tight, his eyes intense. "To suggest that somehow this is unprecedented, tawdry, whatever, in my view, is out of bounds." He noted that the voters had just elected a Republican majority in both the House and Senate. "They sent us a loud and clear message last November, and as I said, nobody knows what the precise message was, but generally, it was to rein in the federal government. . . ."

Dole refused to yield to Byrd or anyone, and the Senate was adjourned at 7:41 P.M.

In New York City, Warren Rudman watched Dole blow up on television, and he placed an immediate call to him. By 9 P.M. Dole called back. Dole had begun jokingly to refer to Rudman as "The Oracle."

"Bob," Rudman said, "this is one of those calls where I promised to be a pain the ass. I watched you lose your temper with Byrd. Bob, you had a right to lose your temper, get angry. I understand. I would have done the same thing. But there is one difference: you're running for president." It had been his first slip in months. "You really looked nasty. Your head was down and you really bored in on Byrd." Dole had been on the edge of losing it. "Jesus, Bob!"

"You're right," Dole said. He wasn't sure how the performance was going to play.

"You looked tired," Rudman inquired.

"Yeah, I was," Dole replied. It had been three days of almost non-stop negotiations.

"There are two ways you reduce people to ashes," Rudman said.

"One is the way you did with Byrd, or you can do it with humor." He then noted that nobody was better with humor than Dole.

Dole didn't feel he had been that rough, but he didn't challenge Rudman's warning.

The delay on the balanced budget amendment vote didn't work and the next day Dole fell one vote short, failing to sway Senator Mark Hatfield, the Oregon Republican who chaired the Appropriations Committee, into voting for it.

Without consulting any of his political advisers—or anyone else—Dole had been floating the idea that if elected president, he might pledge to serve only one four-year term, not seek reelection. That way he could serve as president without worrying about running again. It would be a presidency, though short, without political deals. It was a sort of Ross Perot, populist idea, Dole thought. He wanted to prove that he would worry about solving the country's problems and making the tough presidential decisions, not becoming obsessed with his job ratings.

Lacy thought the idea was at least too radical and unconventional, if not crazy. It might be nice, but there was no way to put the presidency above politics. Everyone else who heard the idea linked it to Dole's age. Many interpreted it to be Dole's way of acknowledging that he might not be around or might not be up to the presidency before the end of his second term, when he would be 81.

On Saturday, March 4, Dole met with Reed, Lacy and Will. He was to appear the next day on CBS Television's *Face the Nation*. They went through a fairly detailed discussion of what he should try to accomplish. First, he had to put the one-term idea to bed. It just put the age issue in neon lights. Second, he had to shift the failure of the balanced budget amendment away from himself and back onto Clinton's shoulders. Clinton was the one who opposed it.

All three pushed pretty hard, emphasizing the need to figure out what he wanted his message to be and direct the interview that way, and not let the reporters dictate the agenda. It was a key part of the message discipline they were trying to impose.

At home in Annapolis Sunday morning, Reed settled in to watch the new message-disciplined Dole.

Put on the defensive right away about his inability to get Hatfield's vote, Dole—unprompted and unnecessarily—disclosed that Hatfield had volunteered to resign from the Senate, making it possible to win the balanced budget amendment with 66 of the 99 senators. Dole said that he had rejected Hatfield's offer. At the end of the interview, Dole said that if he won Iowa and New Hampshire, he'd have to take a hard look at the possibility of stepping down as majority leader in order to be a full-time presidential candidate.

Reed could not imagine a worse self-inflicted wound, stepping into Hatfield, keeping the focus on the Dole-Republican failure to win. His phone lit up. He went to his sailboat.

The Hatfield disclosure was the big news story the next day.

"What happened?" Reed asked when he spoke to Dole.

"Didn't get there, did I?" Dole replied. He thought the one-term idea coupled with the prospect of stepping down as majority leader would have an appeal. People would see he was being honest, candid. "A double feature," Dole called it. "A) one term; B) step down."

Reed pondered how he could make sure this did not happen again. He turned his attention to taxes. Being anti-tax was a virtual precondition for survival in the Republican Party, and Dole had not taken a strong enough stand.

"I'm managing this one myself," Reed told Dole. They had to be 100 percent committed to having Dole sign an anti-tax pledge. They had to do it in Dole's formal announcement in April. And it had to be done in New Hampshire, where in 1988 Dole had refused to sign a pledge not to raise taxes. The ghost had to be put to rest. It had to be the news of the announcement, and it had to be kept secret and sprung on the news media as a surprise. Big network news would be, "Dole Signs Tax Pledge." Had to be. "This is that important," Reed explained to Dole, "and I'm not leaving it to anyone else."

Dole opposed a formal across-the-board anti-tax pledge on the grounds that if the Congress closed some tax loopholes, that would technically be a tax increase for some.

Reed figured he just had to surround the problem and surround Dole. If Dole didn't lay the issue to rest, his whole campaign could collapse. All the Dole hands were brought in to make the case. Reed had a special anti-tax pledge drafted. Perhaps Dole would sign that?

Dole said that Phil Gramm was probably going to sign something stronger, so what was the point? And Dole's chief of staff Sheila Burke was opposed to a pledge.

Reed continued with a three-week campaign. He and Lacy had a private meeting with New Hampshire Governor Steve Merrill, the key

Republican in the state, who was remaining neutral in the presidential race so far. Merrill said he was for Dole signing an anti-tax pledge, and the word was passed to Dole.

Reed felt the campaign still lacked a comfortable center or clear direction. There were daily reminders. In an issue of *Newsweek* on the stands in late February, columnist George Will, husband to Mari Will, published a column about Dole's presidential candidacy headlined "Good Man . . . Wrong Job?" It argued strongly that Dole lacked the rhetorical skills and habits to be president. And here his wife was the chief rhetorician of the Dole campaign. Reed felt embarrassed for Mari. Was this a signal? Reinforcement for his wife? Or a warning of some sort? George Will had written of Dole, "His aversion to written texts reflects, among other things, the fact that he, like many legislators is comfortable only with the conversational, unstructured, almost cryptic discourse. . . . But before Dole can be president, he must be a candidate who has the steely will to stay 'on message.' "

8

In early 1995, no one was stirring the pot more actively in Republican presidential politics than Phil Gramm, the senior senator from Texas. "I'm going to run for president and I'm going to win this race," he had declared to his inner circle the year before. He was 52, but his own polls showed voters thought he was 65. An almost coy smile often rose on one side of his mouth, his head poking out and forward awkwardly like a turtle. Slightly wizened, his large, heavily lined forehead ran back to thinning white-gray hair. His eyes, deeply set behind his glasses, roamed his surroundings eagerly. Gramm had no apparent personal physical vanity, and from clothing to hairstyle he looked more like the former college economics Ph.D. professor he had been than a U.S. senator. He spoke with utter confidence. The tone was oddly soft at first, but he could be hard, even brutal, and certainly impatient, as he got wound up.

"One question is whether somebody as ugly as me can be elected president," he said. "Lincoln did it." He did not blush at the comparison.

As he surveyed the political landscape, one of Gramm's big problems was that a lot of people didn't like him. Even his wife Wendy freely admitted that her first impression of Gramm had been "Yuck!" He had a penchant for walking over people, including his natural allies, and he had alienated people who otherwise might be supporters.

Senator Orrin Hatch, the 18-year Senate conservative from Utah and an ideological soulmate of Gramm's, was among this group. As the head of the GOP Senate Campaign Committee in 1994, Gramm had refused to give Hatch, the chairman of the Senate Judiciary Committee, the $140,000 of committee money that Gramm earlier had pledged to his reelection campaign. Gramm had argued that incumbent senators like Hatch would have easy races, and the money should go to help Republican candidates who had close races so the party could win a majority in the Senate.

"I'm not going to give it to you," Gramm said at his most defiant.

"I could lose," Hatch explained. Strong Democrats were waiting to pounce.

"*Bull*shit!" Gramm said to Hatch, a practicing Mormon. He looked Hatch right in the face and could see Hatch was desperate, acting as if the world was coming to an end. As if saying no was not enough, Gramm forged on. "Orrin," Gramm said, "grow up! You don't need this money and I'm not going to take it away from somebody whose ability to win or lose depends on it."

Hatch persisted. This was contrary to all traditions of the Senate club, where looking after your colleagues, especially in the same party, was almost rule one.

"I *ain't* going to give it to you," Gramm said. "Forget it. Don't keep talking to me. I ain't going to give it to you."

Hatch sensed Gramm was trying to use humor to diffuse the disagreement, but he felt that Gramm had broken his word. Gramm had explicitly promised the money. Hatch believed senators should live up to their word. Gramm easily could have requested to be released from his pledge and Hatch would have let him off the hook.

He thought Gramm gave the impression that he would walk over his mother to become President of the United States. Gramm was too brusque, too hard-edged, trying to look big and tough.

In the raw political calculation, Gramm turned out to be right about the money. Hatch won reelection in 1994 with more than two thirds of the votes—69 percent to 28 percent. And the Republicans took over the Senate, in part because Gramm had raised millions for the marginal candidates. But in the human calculation, Gramm had paid a big price. Hatch did not endorse him.

The Hatch relationship was part of an unnerving pattern for Gramm. He displayed an impulse to conquer people.

In one interview, I asked Gramm why he was so driven to become president.

"Sort of the *zealot's zeal*," he replied.

He recalled what victory was like when he first won his Senate seat in 1984.

"At that moment there was a calmness that it was over," Gramm said. "It's like being an ancient warrior, and you're involved in this combat, and you suddenly look around the hilltop and you're the one left alive."

While many others involved in the Republican revolution of 1994 had taken some time off or basked in the victory, Gramm hit the money trail. In state after state, he personally gave a big-screen, multicolor slide presentation of his fund-raising Juggernaut with charts and graphs depicting stacks of greenbacks.

"In a campaign," Gramm said, "if you're down on your luck, but up on your money, you're okay."

Gramm essentially laid out his campaign theme as a lesson in economics. He described the big negative impact the federal deficit had on the overall economy—higher interest rates, less investment, fewer jobs, huge national debt. All else being equal, the elimination of the federal deficit could unleash an unparalleled economic boom that over years would benefit nearly everyone in the country. On the technical macroeconomic level, Gramm was dead right. But Gramm was framing his candidacy as if he were running for accountant-in-chief, not leader of a nation.

He formally began a national tour to announce his candidacy on Thursday evening, February 23, 1995, with a kickoff fund-raiser in Dallas that raised $4.1 million, the most ever raised in a single event by a candidate for national office. "I have the most reliable friend that you can have in American politics and that is ready cash," Gramm said that night.

Gramm was walking taller than ever, strutting around, almost bursting with energy and wondering if in fact the polls might have it wrong, that he, not Dole, was the *real* front-runner. He could feel it, people were for him, noticing him.

Charlie Black, one of the Republican Party's most enduring trench-warfare consultants, whose experience went back to Ronald Reagan's unsuccessful run for the presidency in 1976, had been tutoring Gramm for years. Though Black was now a lobbyist for major old-line corporate clients, he avidly mixed business and politics. Thin, with thick dark hair and a gentle North Carolina accent, Black had long been friends with Gramm, and he was the campaign's chief strategist.

"Number one," Black told Gramm in a strategy session, "you don't want to be the front-runner. You just want to have the threshold credibility to be taken seriously—and you've got that. I couldn't say that six months ago but I can say it now."

But Gramm could feel the support and attention building for him.

"Bob Dole is the front-runner, and your position is that Senator Dole is more popular than he's ever been and front-runners often win the Republican Party nomination. If he leaves an opening, you'll be there ready to move into it."

Gramm could feel openings all around.

Black, sensing Gramm's swelling confidence, cautioned, "Humility time is here."

James B. Francis, Jr., a Dallas businessman who had managed the successful campaign of Texas Governor George W. Bush, President Bush's son, was planning to manage Gramm's national campaign. In his conversations with Gramm, Francis gave what he called his "father-figure speech."

"The president," Francis said, "is sort of a father figure. It's a personal vote. It is not, 'I like his voting record,' when they elect a president. It is something bigger than that, it is something more encompassing than that and part of that has to do with"—there that word was again—"humility. Frankly, when Bill Clinton is at his best, it is when he is making fun of himself, that's when he is at his best, and all of these big, powerful politicians need to realize when they're running for president, and they are president, that people look at 'em as a human being and they want to see good human traits of not taking yourself too seriously and being able to take a punch and get up."

William Weld, the 49-year-old Massachusetts governor, had spent several months considering a run for president, asking himself questions. Am I the man? Is it my time? Could I embarrass myself? Would it be premature? His reelection victory in 1994 with an astounding 71 percent of the vote meant he could at least talk about the presidency without being laughed out of town.

But the 1994 victory was not the only reason Weld was considering the presidency. Dick Morris, who was now working for Clinton, had been Weld's consultant and had helped on polling in 1990 when Weld first ran and won the governorship. Then Morris was his strategic consultant in the 1994 reelection campaign. After the win, Morris had urged Weld to run for president in 1996. The 1996 presidential race was going to be about ethics, Morris said, Clinton's ethics. The Whitewater scandal would blow up, Morris said. He knew this from his longtime association with the Clintons back in Arkansas.

"Clinton is going to be indicted," Morris insisted one day in late 1994 to Weld and several of Weld's aides. It was typical overblown Morris rhetoric, but Morris insisted he knew the problems firsthand. The Rose Law Firm where Hillary had been partner was involved in all kinds of strange enterprises. It resembled the movie *The Firm,* based on John Grisham's legal thriller about a secretive and corrupt law firm, Morris said.

Weld was shocked when he learned later that Morris was working for Clinton. At first Morris denied up and down that he was advising the president, but later he had to acknowledge it.

Though Morris's advice could be dismissed, Weld was still weighing the possibility of running in 1996.

A Republican in the heavily Democratic state of John Kennedy and Michael Dukakis, Weld's gubernatorial campaign had been drawn from three themes: tough on crime, tough on welfare reform, and lower taxes. But he also argued that government had little or no role in personal decisions such as abortion and sexual orientation. So he was pro-choice on abortion and pro-gay rights. If he ran, his message would be "fiscal conservative, socially libertarian, pro-environment, tolerant, inclusive."

In mid-February, Weld asked Ray Howell, 34, his previous campaign manager, to put together a feasibility study. If he ran for president, he wanted Howell to run the campaign. "You can call me an asshole," Weld said.

"I can call you an asshole," Howell agreed, "you still need someone to run a campaign who knows what they are doing."

"Let's get something on paper so if it's a go, we're not caught flat-footed," Weld said. It might be a unique chance. He could not let the Republican Party be taken over by the Christian right if he could possibly stop it by offering an alternative. It would be a disaster for the party to nominate a right-winger who couldn't beat Clinton, Weld said.

Howell examined the national polling data, and found something that had to be treated very delicately. The strong conservatives controlled the Republican Party on the national level. Whatever nice labels might be put on the various groupings and factions in the conservative wing, it really got down to two, the polling showed. The first of those two were the Archie Bunkers—the so-called Angry White Males, who felt the economic squeeze acutely, hated affirmative action and were often intolerant of other races. The second faction was the Christian right. The pollsters said that no one could win the nomination who couldn't get at least one of those two factions, either the Archie Bunkers or the Christian right. Weld, Howell believed, could get neither. He was way too moderate.

Nonetheless, on February 24, Howell put together a seven-page memo for Weld called "What It Takes." Howell estimated that $17 million would have to be raised. Over the next ten months that would mean raising nearly $400,000 a week. In all it would require 168 fund-raisers, at least, or four a week.

Howell found five negatives for Weld in the Republican Party. Weld was pro-choice; pro–gay rights; a creature of the eastern establishment and its core institution, Harvard, where Weld had graduated and received his law degree; he had been born with a silver spoon and had money; and he was from Massachusetts, which most people would assume meant he must be a liberal. All five reinforced each other and all came back to Massachusetts, Howell wrote. The most effective way to handle the negatives was to meet them head-on and convert them to Weld's advantage. This could be done by building a message around Weld as the leader who changed the political culture of Massachusetts almost singlehandedly in four years. In the state known for high taxes (Tax-achusetts, as it was sometimes called) and liberal social engineering, he had produced nine tax cuts and started sweeping welfare reform. Who better to change the Washington political culture?

That Friday, February 24, Weld met with Howell and two other advisers for an hour and a half. The problem was that the first primary was going to be fund-raising, the first tangible measure. Weld would not be taken seriously if he failed to enter the money race. With the memo as an outline, Weld typically tried to poke holes in the arguments. Say he entered late or shunned fund-raising, and won New Hampshire and made the cover of *Time* magazine. What next? He wouldn't have the money for the next round, they all agreed. All their experience in Massachusetts was that you needed money to respond if the others were running negative advertising on television. It would be won or lost on television, Howell said.

Over the weekend, Weld discussed it with his wife, Susan, who was a great-granddaughter of President Theodore Roosevelt.

She had always been opposed. "I can't think of anything more horrible," she said. They had five children—four teenagers and one only 11— and all five had expressed considerable enthusiasm that their father not run. Weld concluded that his wife probably would go along and could play it either way. The kids couldn't. As he weighed all the factors, Weld realized that if he ran, he would have to say goodbye to his family and to his day job as governor.

On Monday, February 27, Weld declared in a press conference he would not be running for president in 1996. "I suppose it is possible to be a presidential candidate, governor and father of five teenagers all at the same time, but I think at least one of those roles would have suffered, probably all three would have suffered."

On the morning of Tuesday, February 28, in the East Tennessee mountain town of Merryville, a slender, plain but restless man in a red and black plaid shirt walked to a podium outside the local courthouse.

"I am announcing today that I am a candidate for the office of the presidency of the United States of America," said the former two-term Tennessee governor, Lamar Alexander.

Alexander, 55, had been laying the groundwork to run for president ever since Bush lost to Clinton more than three years earlier. Alexander knew Clinton and his wife from their overlapping years as governors and there sure was no magic about them. Alexander felt it was incredible that Clinton, six years younger, had made it to the presidency, a job that Alexander coveted for himself. And Al Gore was vice president, the former senator from Lamar's own state of Tennessee and seven years younger. If the Arkansas governor and the junior senator from Tennessee could do it, there was no question in Alexander's mind that he could do it.

When his political mentor, former Tennessee Senator Howard Baker, Jr., was considering a run for the presidency in 1988, Alexander had watched as Baker fumbled around at one private meeting listing all the obstacles. Alexander had grown exasperated and said, "Look, Howard, if you want to be president, no price is too high."

Alexander had started planning early. He was obscure and not as well known as the Washington-based figures. His wife, Honey, had been strongly opposed. "I don't want you running unless you can say clearly why you're running," Honey had said to him in 1992, "and what you hope to accomplish."

Alexander had been Secretary of Education in the Bush cabinet. The ink was barely dry on the newspaper political obituaries of Bush when Alexander and Honey spent the first weekend after Bush's defeat, November 6–8, 1992, at their cabin in the mountains for a three-day meeting with five of their closest political advisers to discuss and plan his run for the presidency. It was probably the earliest such meeting for any candidate who would seek the Republican nomination in 1996, and it hadn't been a great success. A number of Alexander's advisers felt that his rationale for the candidacy was simply his ambition and drive for the office. None of those advisers would wind up working full time in Alexander's campaign.

Alexander focused in the following two years to establish his credentials and develop a strong anti-Washington message. He hired one of the most promising Republican consultants, Mike Murphy, as his chief strategist. Murphy, a 32-year-old chunky wonder boy with long stringy blond hair and a mile-a-minute patter, was a conservative media wizard who had helped several Republicans win big governorships—including John Engler in Michigan and Christine Todd Whitman in New Jersey.

"The problem is to run a campaign that'll be successful," Murphy told Alexander, "you're going to have to do things that the political-journalistic smart-asses in Washington and New York are going to find highly unfashionable. The fact is unfashionable arguments win the Republican nomination."

Murphy was not bothered that Alexander was so unknown, or that his support was initially in the 3 to 5 percent range, the margin of error in any poll. "We, to the average primary voter, are going to have the most powerful thing in advertising," Murphy said, "We're *new. New* is good. Nothing beats *new.*" He had the feeling that the race was wide open, the situation incredibly fluid.

"What we're trying to do here is steal the nomination," Murphy had said to Alexander. The strategy was for Alexander to surface as the well-organized, well-financed alternative to Dole or Gramm, if the presumed front-runners failed to gain traction or faltered.

After Alexander's formal announcement at the end of February 1995, his red and black plaid flannel shirt became a symbol of the regular-guy populism he was trying to project. His campaign posters read simply: "Lamar!" He promised that as president he would move power out of Washington and back to the states. He decided he would walk across the state of New Hampshire to meet voters and get some attention.

Bill Lacy was mapping out the strategy in his new office at the Dole headquarters, which had moved to the third floor of a new building next to CNN just north of the Capitol. He wanted some detailed survey research first.

Lacy set out to discover what Dole believed. He sat down with Sheila Burke and some of the people from the Majority Leader's Office who really knew Dole's policy positions. He interviewed them extensively, posing a whole series of issues and ideas he knew would be politically very appealing. Dole was not consulted. Lacy was viewing it more as a crafting project. After considerable effort, Lacy had a seven-page catalogue of 83 short statements or positions that he hoped Dole would be comfortable with, reflecting his stand on issues from reining in the federal government and cleaning up Congress to immigration, foreign policy, crime, affirmative action and taxes.

On Wednesday, March 8, Lacy, Reed and Mari Will had a car and driver take them south of Washington about an hour and a half to Fredericksburg, Virginia, to witness firsthand two focus groups. The two small groups of Republican voters would be prodded for their opinions. It was a nasty night, rain turning to the last ugly snow of the season.

Each person in the focus groups was handed a nine-page questionnaire called "Issue Checklist." The first section listed Lacy's 83 ideas, posed as statements from a hypothetical presidential candidate. Each participant was to rate each issue on a scale of 0 to 10.

When the groups had finished filling out their surveys, moderators posed some questions. "If someone is 71, what would be the things that would be a concern to you about that person being sworn in for the first time as president?"

"I would want to know who the vice president is," a woman said.

The group of women laughed.

The men were next. "If Bob Dole were an animal, what kind of animal would he be and why?" After they had written down their answers, they were asked to explain.

"I think the question was ridiculous," a man named John said. "I just can't see the comparison as having any significance."

A participant named Rich said, "When you first asked this question, my immediate reaction was chameleon, so that was the animal I picked."

Mari Will thought all this was ridiculous. Dole couldn't stake out his positions based on polls—that was what Clinton did too often.

Lacy reached some broad conclusions. Voters were looking for three things: leadership ability, character and philosophy.

On the first two, Lacy believed, Dole was virtually unbeatable. The focus groups showed that people were sufficiently aware of or impressed with his previous work. They also knew he had character, was a war veteran, and had no scandal in his background. Which brought Lacy to the third area, Dole's true point of vulnerability. Dole was not identified with any specific idea or even philosophy. His scattered and sometimes confused message had to be brought under control and given definition. If the campaign could handle philosophy or message, then everything else would work for them, Lacy concluded.

Scott Reed wanted something dramatic, some meat. Listening to people describe what kind of car or animal they thought Dole most resembled was horseshit. But amazingly it had taken him weeks just to get copies of Dole's schedules in advance from the Senate office. Finally, Reed started getting them and he insisted on planning campaign events so Dole could give some newsmaking speeches. To explain in specific terms what reining in the federal government might mean, Mari Will drafted a speech for Dole to call for the abolition of four departments—Commerce, Energy, Education, and Housing and Urban Development (HUD). Not just cutting or trimming but closing. Of the 83 ideas they had presented to the focus groups in Fredericksburg, it had been one of the very least popular proposals. But it was the most concrete. Reed and Will did not consult Sheila Burke or anyone else on Dole's Senate staff. The ideological canyon between the campaign and the Burke Senate staff was too vast. Burke wanted Dole to run as a moderate. In the Senate, she was surrounded by mainstream Republicans and Democrats who basically held the balance of power. Accordingly, Reed felt she had come to believe that moderates had more influence in nominating their presidential candidates than they did.

Dole gave the speech Friday, March 10, before a newspaper group. He dropped some of the rhetorical flourishes, but stuck to the theme and called for the abolition of the four departments. The speech had good media pickup, putting Dole ahead of Gramm and Alexander. It was Reed's first clear victory, a successful end run around the Senate staff.

Burke first heard about Dole's proposal when the news of the speech came over the wires. She was angry and disheartened. Her staff person assigned to housing and urban development was apoplectic. Here he was spending his life on HUD issues and out of the blue with no notification the boss was calling for the abolition of the department? Burke was deeply concerned that Dole had made such a sweeping policy proposal without the necessary staff work to measure the impact, or consistency with his previous actions or statements. Her nightmare was that Dole would propose one thing and it would turn out that he had voted the opposite way. Dole had taken his share of federal pork over the years from these four departments. There were bodies buried everywhere, including a $6 million grant from the Education Department for the Bob Dole Hall at Kansas State University.

Burke and Will argued over the interpretation of some part of the speech in a meeting with Dole, who listened and laughed at the end.

Burke and Reed finally had a serious talk. They promised that they would not surprise each other. Lacy had set up a policy group of the key people from both the campaign and the Majority Leader's Office. They would meet Thursdays to examine the policy options that would be available to Dole, agreeing—in theory at least—that it would be both impossible and stupid to try to repackage him.

As if to prove the point, the next day, Saturday, March 11, Dole joined the weekly meeting of his top campaign aides. Someone was discussing ways to exploit various themes—including gay and lesbian issues.

"We're not going to go out taking that issue on," Dole said sharply. "We're not going to pick out a group and discriminate against them for political gain."

Lacy had Dole's pollsters conduct a national poll of likely Republican voters. Dole was favored by 44 percent, a number consistent with other national polls. But there was trouble. The support was soft. When asked, "Are you *definitely* going to vote for Bob Dole or just *probably* going to vote for Bob Dole?" 15 percent said definitely and 29 percent said probably. Lacy knew from extensive polling work that normally half of the support for a candidate should be hard. In Dole's case, it should have been 20 to 22 percent. Soft support was a front-running campaign's darkest fear. Part of the support was just name recognition or people choosing Dole over a list of relative unknowns. In practical terms the 15 percent solid support meant Dole didn't have a whole lot more than Phil Gramm, whose numbers were approaching 15 percent. And Gramm's support was almost all hard and committed.

The campaign needed a press secretary. Will suggested a longtime protégé of hers, Nelson Warfield, who had worked in communications with her during the last six months of the Reagan administration, and then had been press secretary to Estée Lauder heir Ron Lauder in his 1989 campaign to be mayor of New York, doing daily combat with the

New York City tabloids. Warfield, 35, was 6 foot 5, an articulate man who wore glasses, in many respects resembling a larger version of Mari Will's husband, George Will.

"Dole doesn't like staff being quoted a lot," Will said. It was a paradox, because for Dole that included his press secretary. "What are you running for?" Dole occasionally asked staffers who were quoted by name in the newspapers. Lacy said that it was important that the press secretary be someone who was not afraid of Dole.

Reed finally called and offered Warfield the job on a temporary basis —a press secretary on approval, meaning they or Dole could send him back. Warfield didn't like that. Reed proposed making Warfield the deputy press secretary, just in case it turned out he did not get along with Dole. At all costs, Reed said, they wanted to avoid stories about staff shake-ups or people not working out, because in 1988 Dole had shuffled his campaign staff several times in embarrassing public bouts of infighting. They just couldn't afford to have a press secretary coming and then going. Warfield proposed they hire him as press secretary just for the announcement tour the next month, and if it didn't work out they could note he was a temporary consultant. Reed agreed.

Warfield's meeting with Dole lasted seven minutes. Dole asked several New York political questions and wished Warfield good luck twice. Here perhaps the next President of the United States was hiring his campaign spokesman, one of the most personal and important decisions, and Dole blew it off. Warfield felt somewhat slighted.

Will told him not to worry. "He is not a yeller, not a screamer," Will added. If Dole didn't like someone, he would just freeze them out or bypass them. "Tell him what you think," she advised. "That's what you get paid for."

Warfield went to many old Dole friends or staffers to ask a simple question, "Tell me how I survive Bob Dole?"

Mike Glassner, Dole's loyal, attentive 31-year-old traveling aide, said that the first rule was to speak when spoken to. Since Warfield would be going on Dole's plane for the weekend campaign trips around the country, Glassner explained that Dole had little or no private time, and it was important for Dole's peace of mind to let him stare out the window if he wanted. It did not mean he was bored. And when Dole sits down for a media interview, especially for television, he gets settled and focused. Don't go up to him with suggestions or tips. "Recognize that this is not a man given to praise," Glassner also advised.

Warfield's first campaign trip with Dole was March 13 for New York

Governor George Pataki's endorsement. One reporter shouted a question at Dole about the pledge to seek only one term and Dole gave an ambiguous answer. Afterwards, Warfield was sitting next to Dole when another reporter phoned for clarification. As Warfield tried to explain and downplay Dole's comment, Dole offered advice and monitored everything Warfield said. Warfield vowed never again to try to manage a reporter or a story with Dole hovering over him.

Later, on the plane, the subject of an anti-tax pledge came up again.

"I don't know whether it's a good idea," Dole said privately. "Won't Gramm just take a tougher pledge?"

Three days later, Dole held a press conference while in Ohio for some endorsements. Asked about his reason for running, Dole said, "What we are talking about is, how do we make the government smaller. . . . We think it is time for some conservative, common-sense changes in the country."

Warfield took a transcript of Dole's remarks and answers, and did a content analysis, marking the various portions. Some 82 percent had dealt with process and politics. Only 17.8 percent had been message. It was passed to Dole, hoping he would see he needed to spend more time talking about his message and what he wanted to do if elected president.

Scott Reed had a long history with the National Rifle Association (NRA), one of the most potent lobbying groups in the country. Over the years he had learned how they played games. During February, his first month on the job, he had noticed that a meeting with the top NRA people just appeared on Dole's schedule. Tom Korologos, one of Dole's oldest friends, was the NRA's top lobbyist and virtually had instant access to Dole. Korologos had been the Nixon White House lobbyist with the Senate, and he was a big fund-raiser for the Dole Foundation, the charitable foundation Dole had set up to help disabled people.

Reed had the meeting postponed for several weeks, hoping this would be one of the issues the Majority Leader's Office and the campaign would have a chance to coordinate. Reed knew that the NRA believed there was no such thing as a bad gun. The group had featured Phil Gramm on the cover of their magazine, and Gingrich too was engaged in an active outreach program to the gun people. Gingrich had appointed a task force on firearms issues consisting of six junior congressmen who supported a repeal of the assault weapons ban. In the same period, the Dole campaign was having a big finance meeting with some 80 business CEOs, many of whom were rabid gun guys.

So, earlier in March, Dole had finally met with the NRA people and Korologos in his office. Reed was there, as were Dole's gun experts from his staff. The NRA representatives argued that they had been instrumental in helping the Republicans take over the Congress, including the 11 new freshmen Republican senators, more than the margin of Dole's new majority in the Senate. They wanted Dole to pay attention to their agenda. It was a cordial meeting, no screaming or yelling. Everyone was respectful when they got around Dole in person. Dole's Senate staff discussed sending a letter to the NRA thanking them and so forth. Soon Reed received a draft copy of a letter from the Senate staff. He wasn't fully sure of Dole's position and faxed back a note saying it looked fine with him but asked if they were breaking any new ground. He never heard back.

On Saturday morning, March 18, Reed was driving in for the weekly campaign meeting and listening to the news on the radio. A report said that Dole had sent a letter to the National Rifle Association promising to seek a repeal of the "ill-conceived" ban on assault weapons passed the previous year in Clinton's crime bill. The letter said Dole hoped to have a bill on Clinton's desk this summer. What the hell? Reed thought. Why was Dole pledging to return assault weapons to the streets?

What happened? Reed inquired immediately. He never got a satisfactory answer. Some pro-gun staff member had drafted the letter and the final copy hadn't even been signed by Dole! Reed concluded that nobody in Dole's Senate office could be counted on. It was a classic product from the floating crap game over there with no clear lines of authority.

Korologos read the letter addressed to Tanya Metaksa, the executive director of the NRA, and someone Korologos privately considered "a nut." The letter was strong and went beyond the meeting, and now that the letter was out, the Democrats and some liberals, like Senator Dianne Feinstein of California, were hollering bloody murder. Korologos was delighted. It couldn't have been orchestrated better.

Dole, who had voted against the assault ban the previous year, nonetheless wished he could have the letter back. "I don't have any problem with the meeting," Dole said, "but I guess I'd have a problem with the letter again. If we'd just meet, and say okay we had a good meeting." Dole wasn't sure what to do. As a first principle, the campaign didn't want to flip-flop on any issue. And no Senate office wanted to acknowledge that many, many letters—even important ones—went out without the senator reading them carefully, if at all. Many other letters were signed by automatic signature pens or by longtime staffers adept at duplicating the senator's signature.

Dole started getting asked about the assault weapons in public and he received phone calls from some big-time supporters. "Why would any law abiding citizen want an assault weapon," Dole said at one point, "it's a good question." He even approached Feinstein on the Senate floor one day. "You know I don't want anybody to get shot with a gun," Dole said. He was looking for an alternative, requiring an instant check to make sure those who purchased a gun did not have a criminal record. Still he wasn't sure what to do. He wasn't ready to label it a mistake in public, and he wasn't sure if it would be an act of political courage to reverse himself.

9

As Clinton continued assessing his position and reaching out, one person on his wide panel of informal advisers was Senator Joseph I. Lieberman, the Connecticut Democrat who represented the decidedly centrist, New Democrat side of the party. Lieberman, a 52-year-old Orthodox Jew known for his independence and civility, was in bed when one call came after 11 P.M. in early 1995. He later joked to his wife that it was like being a fireman or worse. With a Clinton call, Lieberman had to be able to go from a deep sleep to the full alert of high-intensity intellectual conversation in a few seconds. As a Yale Law student 24 years earlier, Clinton had worked in Lieberman's successful campaign in New Haven for the Connecticut Senate, so the two shared an old bond. As a Democrat, Lieberman had been a particular curiosity in the Republican year of 1994. He had won reelection to the Senate with a smashing 67 percent of the vote.

Clinton had offered his congratulations. In subsequent calls Clinton sounded to Lieberman like he felt unappreciated. The president indicated he had not been treated fairly. All of the piling on about the Democratic setback had been intense and was directed at him. Lieberman was aware that like most politicians, Clinton was taking it personally. Some were telling him the problem was that he had tried to do too much, more than the public could absorb, digest and appreciate, Clinton said.

Lieberman said that a key problem had been Clinton's massive health care reform plan, which had gone down to a crushing defeat. It was too much. The reconnection that Clinton as a candidate had made to the middle class in his 1992 campaign had been severed in the health care debate. The middle class, the Reagan Democrats, the New Democrats interpreted his health care plan with its emphasis on universal coverage for some 40 million uninsured people as a step back. Clinton was going to take something from *them* and give it to those who didn't work and to the poor.

That was not a fair assessment, Clinton protested, because their health care plan was going largely to help people who were working.

It was a subtlety that had been lost in the debate, Lieberman agreed.

Yes, Clinton said, continuing to insist that the problem with the health care plan was not the substance. He had lost the communications and the political war. That was the screwed-up part.

Lieberman disagreed. He felt that Clinton had forsaken the Democratic center as exemplified by the Democratic Leadership Council (DLC), which Clinton had helped found in 1985. As a fellow member of the DLC, Lieberman had broken with Clinton on his health care plan. The DLC had kept telling Clinton, why don't you do welfare reform first? Welfare reform, getting non-workers off the government handout, was what would have galvanized the Reagan Democrats.

At the same time, Lieberman sympathized with Clinton's dilemma. Clinton sat atop a very diverse, tumultuous Democratic Party. The political reality was that many Democrats were liberals. Clinton also had a genuine concern about poverty, inequality, and the plight of the poor. While intellectually Clinton might feel most comfortable with DLC centrists such as Lieberman, the political reality and his personal feelings tugged at each other.

In ongoing conversations with the president, Lieberman reminded him the president had a different role than the Democrats in Congress. There had to be times when Clinton would do things he wanted for the country, for what he determined was best, and for his own political standing that wouldn't please all the Democrats. The country was frustrated with both parties. He had been elected in 1992 as an agent of hopeful change. He had redeemed many of his promises on the economy and deficit reduction.

"You know," Lieberman said in the wise, optimistic tone of a rabbi, "people haven't given up on you. Some people love you, some people hate you. And there's this group in the middle, which is probably still the majority, that is open to hearing you out. This thing can flip back as dramatically by 1996 as it did in 1994."

Vice President Gore realized that the 1994 loss of Congress was very much like 1980, when Clinton had lost his first reelection bid as Arkansas governor. In Arkansas, Clinton had been ousted and had to stage his 1982 comeback from exile without his office. In 1994, Clinton had effectively been beaten—his party had lost—but he didn't have to leave office. He could stage a comeback from the highest office in the land. That gave Clinton considerable advantages, and time to find his bearings.

Gore continued to have some apprehension about Dick Morris. His doubts were at times mild, and at other times serious. Gore considered himself an advocate for the political center, and he thought Morris was a new force in Clinton's life and was helping Clinton sort out where he wanted to go.

Clinton asked Gore to help him use Morris and his advice, to see if they could find some way to test-drive some of Morris's ideas and see if Morris could mesh with the White House staff. Clinton wanted to be careful and tentative.

Gore could see that Clinton and Morris were like a straight line and a curve in geometry that get closer and closer together but no matter how far they are extended never actually touch: an asymptote. Clinton and Gore had discussed throwing the long ball, taking strategic risks. They now needed a full, real reelection campaign effort. Campaign money wouldn't do it alone.

Morris was pushing for a new role.

"Mr. President," Morris said, "I advise that we set up a team."

"I can't do it alone," Clinton said. He agreed that Morris could assemble a new team, including a new pollster and media consultant for some specific tasks.

Morris was delighted; he considered it a mandate. Gore saw Clinton's decision as more tentative. They would start by building a media campaign for the Democratic Party and getting on television.

Morris approached an old-time friend and adversary, Robert Squier, a veteran Democratic media consultant. At one time in 1990 Squier could have claimed accurately that he had helped elect 20 percent of the Senate. Squier, smooth and almost boyish, often sported a Florida tan. He was known for his boisterous and frequently stinging humor. Though he looked 40, he was 60. His joke-a-minute style concealed a highly literate and talented filmmaker. Squier had made much praised documentaries on William Faulkner and Herman Melville, and he had spent years working on a Hemingway film. He was also a master of the negative political ad. If accurate, they were an often effective technique because such ads could inflict immediate damage, and the subsequent attempts to present the other side rarely got the same attention as the attacks.

In 1982, Morris had hired Squier to assist in an election eve telethon for Clinton's comeback as governor. For years, Squier had been media consultant to Vice President Gore and was one of Gore's best political friends and advisers. In 1986, Morris and Squier had handled media for the opposite sides in the bitterly fought Florida Senate race—Morris for Paula Hawkins, and Squier for Bob Graham. Just before the election, Morris had publicly announced that he had a poll showing the race tightening to within 2 points. Squier responded saying he didn't believe the poll and charged that Morris was "the Julia Child of cooked polls."

Then, in 1992, Squier had quietly prepared close to 40 percent of the media advertising for the Clinton-Gore campaign behind the scenes. Morris felt Squier was the best Democratic media consultant and invited him to join the new effort. No one had a clearer record of making memorable, often searing ads. Over months Squier's ads would subtly connect to each other, building a thematic message.

Six months earlier, Clinton had brought a former investment banker into the White House as a deputy chief of staff. He was Erskine Bowles, who had headed the Small Business Administration during the first part of the Clinton administration. Bowles, a calm, 49-year-old North Carolinian, had done a large study of how Clinton was using his time, and he had been asked to try to bring more order to Clinton's decision making. "When there is no front door to the way of doing things," Bowles said, "everybody uses the back door." He wanted to eliminate the back doors to Clinton. The Morris channel threatened to derail Bowles's efforts.

Beginning in March, Clinton began calling evening strategy sessions, generally on Wednesday or Thursday nights, in the Treaty Room of the White House which he used as his study. Joining him were Gore, White House chief of staff Leon Panetta, Harold Ickes and the new campaign team of Morris, Squier and two pollsters, Doug Schoen and Mark Penn. Ickes, the standard garden-variety liberal, was going to be the chief mechanic for the campaign. But Morris and his team were going to be in charge of message. At these initial meetings, Ickes was comparatively passive, asking only an occasional question, often on technical issues about polling samples.

The tension between Ickes and Morris was obvious. So Clinton put Bowles, not Ickes, in charge of trying to coordinate the work of the new campaign team with the White House staff. Bowles wanted everyone coming through the front door to Clinton. But Clinton, by temperament and habit, loved back doors.

Hillary Clinton did not attend the evening campaign meetings. She and her husband had decided that her participation would feed suspicions about her role as the hidden hand of the administration. Any direct role could obviously hurt his reelection chances. Her thoughts and advice, which were plentiful, would be given to him alone in their private time together.

The third year of her husband's presidency was a difficult time for Hillary. She was continually battered in the various Whitewater investigations. And the outright rejection of her health care reform plan was more than an incidental setback. It hit directly at the core of the definition of herself as a competent, if not visionary, policy maker. Her failure on health care also undercut the notion of the partnership she had hoped to have with her husband, and the expected sharing of his presidency. She seemed jerked around by the muddled role of First Lady, as she swung between New Age feminist and national housewife. Her place and her role were not clear. Her high sense of purpose and doing good had been thwarted.

She was reaching out and searching hard.

Jean Houston and Mary Catherine Bateson had followed up their weekend at Camp David with a series of letters to Hillary, proposals and ideas on defining her role as First Lady and rising above the criticism and attacks. Houston had strongly encouraged Hillary to write a book, and Hillary had begun one on children. Hillary invited Houston and Bateson to the White House in the spring. Houston noticed a big picture of Eleanor Roosevelt in Hillary's office. As a teenager, Houston had met Eleanor Roosevelt about six times, and she recounted those encounters to Hillary. Houston and Hillary talked more about Eleanor and her lifetime of struggle on behalf of the poor and against racism and sexism.

"God," Houston thought, "this is really a serious Eleanor Roosevelt aficionado." Clearly Eleanor was Hillary's archetypal, spiritual partner, much as the Greek goddess Athena was for Houston. In the first month of the Clinton presidency, Hillary had said publicly that she had imaginary discussions with Eleanor. "I thought about all the conversations I've had in my head with Mrs. Roosevelt this year, one of the saving graces that I have hung on to for dear life," Hillary had said February 21, 1993, at a New York dinner to raise money for an Eleanor Roosevelt statue. Hillary had said then that the questions she put in her head to Eleanor included "How did you put up with this?" and "How did you go on day to day, with all the attacks and criticisms that would be hurled your way?"

On a visit to the White House in early April 1995, Houston proposed that Hillary search further and dig deeper for her connections to Mrs. Roosevelt. Houston and her work were controversial because she believed in spirits and other worlds, put people into trances and used hypnosis, and because in the 1960s she had conducted experiments with LSD. But she tried to be careful with Hillary and the president, intentionally avoiding any of those techniques.

Houston and Bateson went up with Hillary to the solarium, a sun parlor with three sides of glass windows perched atop the White House. It was afternoon and they all sat around a circular table, joined by several members of the First Lady's staff. One was making a tape recording of the session. The room, which Hillary had redecorated and which was her favorite place for important meetings, offered a spectacular view to the south of the Washington Monument. Fresh fruit, popcorn and pretzels had been set out.

Houston asked Hillary to imagine she was having a conversation with Eleanor. In her strong and self-confident voice, Houston asked Hillary to shut her eyes in order to eliminate the room and her surroundings, and to bring in as many vivid internal sensory images as possible from her vast knowledge about Eleanor to focus her reflection.

We admire you, said Houston, who thought Hillary was a great woman. She was trying to create an atmosphere of mutual admiration.

Hillary settled back in her seat and shut her eyes. She had just returned from a ten-day trip with her daughter, Chelsea, through South Asia, India and Nepal—a trip Houston, an old Asia hand herself, had encouraged her to make.

You're walking down a hall, Houston said, and there's Mrs. Roosevelt. Now let's describe her.

Hillary did. She had a wonderful description of Eleanor smiling, outgoing, slightly frumpy, always engaged, always fighting.

Go there to Mrs. Roosevelt and talk about the possible future of the children, Houston said.

Hillary gave a long answer. Children were her subject, 25 years of legal and policy advocacy on their behalf.

Houston asked the First Lady to open herself up to Mrs. Roosevelt as a way of looking at her own capacities and place in history. Houston regarded it as a classic technique, practiced by Machiavelli, who used to talk to ancient men. What might Eleanor say? What is your message to her? she asked Hillary.

Hillary addressed Eleanor, focusing on her predecessor's fierceness and determination, her advocacy on behalf of people in need. Hillary continued to address Eleanor, discussing the obstacles, the criticism, the loneliness the former First Lady felt. Her identification with Mrs. Roosevelt was intense and personal. They were members of an exclusive club of women who could comprehend the complexity, the ambiguity of their position. It's hard, Hillary said. Why was there such a need in people to put other people down?

Houston encouraged Hillary to play the other part, to respond as Mrs. Roosevelt. The discourse with a person not there, particularly an historical figure in an equivalent position, opened up a whole constellation of ideas, Houston felt.

I was misunderstood, Hillary replied, her eyes still shut, speaking as Mrs. Roosevelt. You have to do what you think is right, she continued. It was crucial to set a course and hold to it.

Houston thought that in many great people's lives a period of isolation and betrayal was followed by their most productive years. Attacks made their mission clearer. She had studied 55 creative people and found that most felt they had an archetype, a kind of spiritual partner. But Hillary was facing much greater toxicity and negativity from others than Eleanor had.

Houston explained that the rise of women to a level of partnership with men was not yet accepted. But women became more resourceful through adversity and backlash.

Hillary reviewed various attitudes and setbacks she had encountered. Each time Houston asked her, How would you explain this to Mrs. Roosevelt? And what would she respond?

The White House had been a shock, Hillary said. She had not been prepared for the kinds of attention she had received for every statement or move she made in the first two years. Unintentionally, her allies often isolated her as much as her opponents, giving rise to impossible expectations, placing the spotlight on every aspect of her words, actions and past.

Houston said that Hillary needed to see and understand that Mrs. Roosevelt was not just an historic figure but was someone who also was hurt by all that happened to her. And yet Mrs. Roosevelt could go on doing her work. Hillary needed to unleash the same potential in herself. In adversity she needed to find the seeds of growth and transformation. It then would become possible to inherit from these mythical or historic figures, and to achieve self-healing.

Bateson, who was watching more than participating in the session, considered the activity a kind of meditation, reflection or even prayer.

Next, Houston asked Hillary to carry on a conversation with Mahatma Gandhi, the Hindu leader, a powerful symbol of stoic self-denial. Talk to him, Houston said. What would you say and what would you ask?

Hillary expressed reverence and respect for Gandhi's life and works, almost drawing his and her own lives together with her words, opening herself up wide, acknowledging the level of his exertion, empathizing with his persecution. She said he too was profoundly misunderstood, when all he wanted to do was to help others and make peace. It was a strong personal outpouring—virtual therapy, and unusual in front of a large group.

Talk with Jesus Christ, Houston proposed next. Jesus was the epitome of the wounded, betrayed and isolated, and Houston liked to quote his words in the Gospel of Thomas, "What you have within you that you express will save you, and what you have within you that you do not express will destroy you."

That would be too personal, Hillary finally said, declining to address Jesus.

After about an hour, the session was over. Chelsea had called her mother earlier and had complained of an upset stomach. Hillary wanted to go see her daughter.

Houston and Bateson said they would be available to meet with Hillary at any time in the future. Of course, they would not charge the government or Hillary for their services, but they wondered if it was possible for Houston to get a reduced government airfare from her home in New York State. It turned out not to be possible.

Most people in the White House did not know about Hillary's sessions with Houston and Bateson. To some of the few who did, the meetings could trigger politically damaging comparisons to Nancy Reagan's use of astrology, which had heavily influenced if not determined the schedule of her husband, President Reagan. Astrology only changed timing, and it was a kind of pseudo-science that could be fun or worth a laugh. Yet the Reagans had been ridiculed. Hillary's sessions with Houston reflected a serious inner turmoil that she had not resolved.

Later, Houston and Bateson gave a kind of seminar for Hillary and her staff at an evening summer barbecue at the home of one of Hillary's staffers.

Houston told the group that if they were going to have so much work and so much stress, they ought to set up what she called "a creative teaching-learning community." She proposed various physical and mind exercises to help them nurture one another. One was for individuals to get up and voice their appreciation for one another, the work they did and the support they gave one another. Many got up and spoke, including Hillary, who seemed to love the bonding.

Hillary continued her meetings and in-depth discussions with Houston and Bateson about the parallels between her life and Eleanor Roosevelt's. Houston was writing her 15th book, a kind of autobiography called *A Mythic Life*. She sent one chapter to Hillary that was called "The Road of Trials." Hillary said it really struck home for her. The chapter was built on Sophocles' notion of "wisdom through suffering." The sufferings, or "woundings," as Houston called them, were necessary for growth and could be converted into opportunity. Houston claimed that by going into a trance for five to seven hours at a time over a period of four days she had dissolved a lump the size of an orange in her own right breast—all to the total astonishment of her doctor.

Hillary told Houston that she was moved by the chapter. The First Lady also said that both she and the president had read Houston's book *Manual for the Peacemaker: An Iroquois Legend to Heal Self and Society.*

Houston felt that she, Hillary, Bateson and some of Hillary's staff formed a kind of "old girls' club." Within the club they often communicated with a single word, a laugh, a joke or a lifted eyebrow. So Houston did not have to ask Hillary directly one of the key questions from the "Road of Trials" chapter, "Where and by whom were you wounded?" It was obvious that some of Hillary's woundings had come from the media, her former Whitewater business partners Jim and Susan McDougal, the relentless Whitewater investigations and her husband's past infidelity. But Houston did not raise these issues, nor did Hillary.

Houston had at least one other deep, reflective meditation session, in which Hillary closed her eyes and carried on an imaginary discussion with Eleanor Roosevelt. Houston's purpose was to move forward so Hillary could put her "wounding" in the middle of her story, ending with the birth of a new grace.

Houston regarded this as intensely difficult. Hillary was not there yet.

During the 1992 campaign, Hillary had been interviewed for the campaign film biography of her husband entitled *The Man from Hope*. In sections not used in the final film, Hillary talked about her personal relationship with him.

"Bill asked me to marry him a couple of times," Hillary said, "And, it was just a hard decision to make because I was very reluctant about, I mean, I was in love with him but I just couldn't envision what it would be like, leaving all of my friends and my family and moving to a place I'd never been."

What bound you together? the producer asked.

"I, you know, I don't know if I can describe it, I don't know if you could ever really describe why you love somebody or why you are committed to somebody, but, you know, I thought we complemented each other in lots of ways, but I also thought that, um, we cared deeply about a lot of the same things. I mean, it's real corny. It wasn't as corny 20 years ago as it is for some people now to say that, Bill and I really are bound together in part because we believe we have an obligation to give something back and to be part of making life better for other people."

In 1995, this articulate woman of great intelligence, talent, stamina and genuine caring seemed not to know what course she was on or where she was heading.

In public she kept up a good front, declaring that she felt no confusion or pain. She laughed, giggled and dismissed most suggestions or questions about her apparent setbacks and difficulties.

Hillary frequently began the mornings by exercising on a treadmill in the White House residence. She had a speakerphone nearby and called various staff members or friends during her workout. From under her heavy breathing, staffers could get the first hint of her frame of mind and what she wanted to accomplish that day. They referred to these as "the treadmill calls." The first calls from Hillary were in turn followed by a round of phone calls between her staff in the East Wing and her staff in the Old Executive Office Building, the main offices adjacent to the White House. The essential question each morning was, What's her mood?

On occasion she snapped at people, even blew up, providing a momentary glimpse of inner rage. She seemed angry, bottled up. Hillary was smart and determined, knew what she wanted to happen. When she was focused and directed, she often seemed not to recognize when she was hurting people. She frequently reduced her personal traveling aide to tears, once because the aide, who was responsible for carrying the First Lady's belongings, didn't have a piece of paper that Hillary needed. Unlike her husband, who tended to soften up after a rage, Hillary turned silent, often icy. Such incidents would not blow away, and all was not soon forgiven by Hillary as it was by her husband.

At the same time Hillary inspired intense loyalty among her top staff.

Hillary spent a lot of time thinking about Vince Foster, the deputy White House counsel who had committed suicide in 1993. Foster was from Hope, Arkansas, along with Clinton, and later had been Hillary's law partner. In the Arkansas years she would have ranked Foster as among the three most together people she knew. The fact that he, of all people, had killed himself was jolting. "From the outside it just looked like he was absolutely rooted, connected," Hillary told an associate. "Suicide is as old as time so there are some things you really can't avoid, but really when you think about it, it's the ultimate example of not being equipped. For whatever combination of reasons, you've got to be able to dig deep down and you've got to be able to hear your mother's voice, your father's voice, your brother's voice, you've got to be able to hear that and you've got to be receptive to that."

Voices were on Hillary's mind. Whether the voices of Eleanor Roosevelt or Gandhi in the sessions with Houston and Bateson, or voices from her immediate family or her own past, the First Lady seemed to be straining to hear them.

She continued to speak out to her associate, almost as if she were giving herself a pep talk. "Part of being equipped is to know yourself well enough because of the inputs you've gotten from other people, starting with your parents, to be able to make adjustments, to be able to say, wait a minute, this is not working, this is not right for me, *how do I get myself out of this?*"

Hillary remarked that she was sure that good habits were the key to survival. "I really believe you can change the way you feel and think if you discipline yourself. You know, there's that great phrase, I think it's in

Alcoholics Anonymous, that somebody once told me, 'Fake it till you make it.' Because there's a certain way in which making up your mind that you're going to be a 'fill in the blank'—a grateful person, a happy person."

"Life throws a lot of crap at you," Hillary added. "When the inevitable crap comes, which it will in anybody's life, and not just once but several times, that there is a cushion of capacity there, and there is a structure that gets you up in the morning."

"The more I see of the world, the more impressed I am that the vast majority of people do that every day. You know it's amazing to me that people actually stop at stop signs, that they do feed their children."

Hillary was searching for discipline, for order, for the rhythm and routines of life—"Fake it till you make it." She needed an adjustment mechanism.

This was what Bill Clinton faced at home as he was seeking reelection; to say nothing of the mounting frenzy of the Whitewater investigations, which increasingly seemed to focus on the financial practices, legal ethics and truth telling of his wife.

The Clintons had determined that as long as the Whitewater investigations continued, there was no way they could speak out and win politically. Their private lawyers had convinced them they had to pledge cooperation and hold their tongues—good legal defense strategy to avoid any contradictions that might come out later. In addition, it was impossible to win the public relations war with prosecutors, the lawyers argued. This was very hard for both Clintons—to be pilloried and to run up vast legal debts that could bankrupt them, all in utter silence.

In the first 100 days of the new Congress, Speaker Newt Gingrich and the new Republican majority in the House kept their promise to bring all ten items in the Contract With America to a vote. Every item passed the House except term limits. Gingrich, the Republicans and the Contract were taking virtually all of the oxygen from the political atmosphere, and Gingrich was going to celebrate with a nationally televised speech Friday night, April 7. Unprecedented for a Speaker of the House, he was claiming a role for himself equivalent to the president, delivering his own prime-time State of the Union address of sorts.

Clinton at first planned to answer Gingrich with an education message. Leon Panetta began mobilizing the entire federal government and cabinet for a Clinton speech and a series of proposals on education—an issue that had been central and successful for Clinton as Arkansas governor. Clinton knew that education, including support for everything from job training to school lunches and college loans, was the best possible investment in people and in their future increased earning power. But it was difficult to give the education issue political lift and immediacy. The payoffs in education programs and investments were generally years if not decades down the road. The speech drafts and proposals emerging seemed tedious, cumbersome and old.

Dick Morris believed that Clinton had not defined cleanly and crisply what he was doing in the era of the Republican Contract. Clinton needed to say, This is why I'm president. This is what I want to do. With Bill Curry in the White House as counselor, Morris had some leverage. One night at a meeting with Panetta, Stephanopoulos and several others, Curry made the argument that a Clinton speech on education was not sufficient. "Why not give a speech on ornithology?" he asked sarcastically.

A direct Clinton response to Newt's Contract, Stephanopoulos replied, would unnecessarily legitimize and elevate it.

"You can't just make general statements," Curry said. "You've got to figure out what to do."

After the meeting, Curry pressed Stephanopoulos some more on the argument that Clinton needed to engage Gingrich.

"This is like 1964," Curry said, "and the Beatles are opening in Shea Stadium, and we can't open in some little joint across the river."

Morris and Curry then began crafting an answer to Gingrich. Morris noted that some of the themes in the Contract With America had been part of Clinton's original 1992 presidential campaign. Morris reviewed the items normally associated with Republicans that Clinton had supported—deficit reduction, welfare reform, middle-class tax cuts, smaller government, tough anti-crime measures. At the same time, Clinton would veto Republican proposals such as one repealing the ban on assault weapons.

On the computer, Morris and Curry developed two categories: "Olive branch" and "Fuck you." Clinton had to say clearly whether he was going to extend the "olive branch" or say "fuck you" to the Republicans on each of the important or pending issues of the day. Using this formula, they crafted a long speech for Clinton to give setting his course.

On the morning of Tuesday, April 4, three days before Gingrich's speech, Clinton decided to bring the two strands of his administration together.

He had his chief White House speechwriter Don Baer, a former reporter, sit down with Morris to work out a speech for Clinton to give to a meeting of newspaper editors in Dallas the day of Gingrich's televised address. Baer, who had been Clinton's chief speechwriter for a year, read through the Morris draft and found much of it overwritten, flowery and full of clichés. Some of it was downright weird. But underneath the decoration were some strong fundamental ideas.

Baer began to rework some of Morris's ideas into plausibly presidential language. As they worked together, Baer realized that this was the secret world that Clinton had been drawing on for months in other speeches. The speechwriter now knew that he had collaborated with Morris before—but without knowing it—with the president as the intermediary. They came up with a new draft.

The White House chief of staff did not fully understand what was going on. Panetta had met with Clinton and Morris, and he knew there was a secret world, someone with powerful lines into the president, but Clinton had not made it clear that Morris was the source of all these new ideas. He had only vaguely referred to someone named "Charlie," a codeword for this secret input. Panetta also knew he didn't like the angle "Charlie" was providing.

A former congressman and the budget director for Clinton's first 18 months as president, Panetta had been brought in as chief of staff ten months earlier to address pervasive management problems. He was to help Clinton organize his presidency on everything from policy development and implementation to Clinton's daily routine. Panetta had tried to have all contacts with Clinton filter through him—especially contacts with outside political consultants. This had proved impossible because no one could keep up with Clinton, who would dial around all hours of the day or night or call people to the White House for dinner or late-night meetings. Even bringing Erskine Bowles in as the deputy to organize Clinton had not solved the problem.

The brutal reality, Panetta knew, was that both good ideas and good people had to be sacrificed for political survival. He now saw himself getting caught in the meat grinder. Panetta strongly identified with Clinton's desire to craft a program that could be sold with the moral intensity of a preacher. Clinton was looking for the Churchillian message to explain what the war was about, but his search had gone far astray in Panetta's eyes.

Less than 24 hours before Clinton was to give his speech to the newspaper editors, Panetta was presented with the new draft. This wasn't the preacher and it certainly wasn't Churchill. The new course bordered on a repudiation of the Democratic Party. He expressed his opposition.

Clinton countered that warmed-over ideas or federal programs or rhetorical pronouncements about education wouldn't hack it. The president was particularly attracted to the lines in the new draft that were the purest articulation of the Morris triangulation strategy: "We need a dynamic center that is not in the middle of what is left and right but is way beyond it."

The speech draft included the line, "The old labels of liberal and conservative, spender and cutter, *even Democrat and Republican,* are not what matter most anymore."

Ickes argued against the speech also.

Drafts flew around with revisions and ideas stacking up like airplanes waiting to land over an airport, circling in the air.

Gore liked the idea of a bold centrist direction. But he was concerned about some praise for Republicans that emerged in one early draft. He called the speechwriters.

"Did you get that shit out?" the vice president inquired.

They had.

On the day of the speech, Clinton was able to stitch it all together as he constantly revised and shifted parts, preventing a midair collision.

In Dallas that Friday, April 7, at the meeting of the nation's newspaper editors, Clinton delivered his blueprint. The speech was an hour long, and at its core was Morris's "dynamic center." Clinton even noted that the only two of the ten items in the Republican Contract that also had passed the Senate and been signed into law by him "were both about political reform, and they were also both part of my 1992 commitments to the American people." One held Congress to the same laws that are imposed on everyone else, and the second limited Congress from imposing requirements on states and local governments without providing the funding, what were often called "unfunded mandates."

The overall concept of the speech had been Morris's but the expansiveness was pure Clinton. His delivery was smooth but typical of Clinton as he threw in a vast laundry list of issues, including promised vetoes on matters he considered extreme such as lifting the ban on assault weapons. The additions muddied Clinton's central message: that he was trying to chart a new direction designed to preempt the Republicans on their issues. The speech was widely interpreted as a classic Clinton smorgasbord of New Democrat, Old Democrat, compromise and veto threats. House

Minority Leader Richard Gephardt had called the Republican Contract "unconscionable, reckless and fundamentally unfair." Clinton's speech had none of the accusatory rhetoric used by other Democrats.

Gore realized that the speech represented a pivotal moment for Clinton. That day the vice president had lunch with Chris Dodd, the new chairman of the Democratic Party. Dodd had been under considerable pressure from the Panetta-Ickes camp to weigh in against the speech before it was given, which he had declined to do. At lunch, Gore explained why he liked the speech and the approach. It was a bold step necessary for Clinton to regain the initiative. The speech was a declaration of centrism. Clinton was saying that Gingrich and his band of revolutionaries could go their merry way, but he would stop them when they were headed in the wrong direction, and embrace them when he agreed.

Afterwards, Dodd called Clinton to praise the speech.

The president, the vice president and the party chairman—all Democrats—agreed that the old political categories were, as Clinton had said in his speech, "defunct," and party was no longer what mattered most.

Gingrich gave his nationally televised speech that night, laying out a simple core theme. The federal budget had to be balanced in seven years. This was Gingrich's great moment, the completion of the first 100 days, though he had had to share top billing with the president.

The next day Clinton was elated. Good headlines. It had worked, he declared. "Why in the hell were we giving a speech on education?" he said to his senior staff. How could they have thought an education speech was the appropriate match-up with Gingrich's 100 days agenda? "I've got to get into this debate," he said, and the speech had begun to lay out a course.

Panetta was losing control of the White House operation, and he went into a depression. He was supposed to coordinate the ideas and formulate a political and communications strategy, and Clinton instead had vested authority elsewhere. His initial reaction was to resist, and he turned out his staff dogs and underlings to criticize Morris.

"I'm not going to take this shit," Panetta told one of his assistants. "I'm an adult human being and I've been around a long time, and I'm not going to take this squirt running around, gumming up the works."

How can I do my job? Panetta asked. He realized he had a choice. He could quit. He could continue to snipe and resist. Or he could find a way to accommodate and include Morris.

Panetta had several very blunt conversations with the president.

"I've got to have a strategist!" Clinton said. "I've got to have someone who's thinking where we need to be in November." And that strategist needed to be able to work backwards from November 1996 and provide the steps to get to a winning position.

As Hillary often reminded him, the whole apparatus of the White House was structured to deal with each individual day or week. There was little long-term planning. Morris would serve that role.

"You have to filter out half of what Dick says," Clinton told Panetta. "He can get wacky." The president said he could separate the good Morris ideas from the bad Morris ideas. "He's going to think strategically. He thinks like I do in terms of where we need to be and what we need to do."

Panetta could see that the reelection campaign was beginning to inhabit the body of the president more and more.

"I want him in," Clinton said.

"Well, if he's in," Panetta insisted, "he's got to be part of the process that I run." He proposed that Morris be included formally in the White House process so the senior staff could hear him directly, deal with him, so they could get his ideas, vet them in advance, incorporate them. That way new ideas and speech drafts would not come racing down the pipeline with only 12 minutes to go. More important, Panetta argued, George Bush had lost the presidency to Clinton in 1992 in part because of the dysfunctional, debilitating relationship between the Bush White House and the Bush campaign. The two were never coordinated properly. Panetta said he did not want to oversee a similar big fat trainwreck in 1996.

Clinton agreed and put out the word that he wanted everyone to work together and to work with Morris. Morris would come to Washington for three or four days a week and be integrated into the White House operations.

George Stephanopoulos was going through hell with the elevation of Morris. Stephanopoulos, a former aide from the Democratic Congress, had been like a younger brother to Clinton and was often thought to be the chief presidential soulmate. But Democratic orthodoxy was now less useful to Clinton, casting Stephanopoulos into a state of semi-exile. Stephanopoulos felt he was on a journey through the Valley of the Shadow of Death. He was being pushed more and more to the fringes of important policy decisions and meetings. Still, in the White House he often had a chance to weigh in late on speeches and tactics and was forced to engage that spring in a rearguard action. Clinton obviously trusted Morris's instincts on how to position himself more to the Republican center. Previously, instincts had been part of the Stephanopoulos portfolio.

Stephanopoulos was surprised by the April 7 speech. Up until that point Clinton had been against drawing those lines against the Democrats. Obviously Morris had immense influence with Clinton. But to have the speech virtually just appear on the day it was given? The White House and administration couldn't live like that. Something like that couldn't just be dropped on the whole executive branch as if from the sky without planning, without a strategy for explaining it or communicating Clinton's intent.

But as Stephanopoulos examined the speech, the reaction and the press coverage, he concluded there was no way to know what the speech meant on an operational level. There was enough on both sides. Was Clinton going to stop the Republicans? Or was he going to be for them? It was ambiguous enough, he figured, that both sides—the new Morris faction and the old Panetta-Ickes-Stephanopoulos faction—would live to fight another day.

Clinton, aware of the fissure, told other senior staff members that he wanted them to continue to deal with Morris, and if there were any questions about what Morris was proposing or what Morris wanted done, they should come directly to him, the president. Of course, as a practical matter that was neither likely nor possible. Who was in charge? What were the lines of authority?

The Clinton White House teetered on the edge of management chaos.

Morris didn't let up. He was seeking more forums for Clinton. He proposed that the president speak at a service to be held in Warm Springs, Georgia, on the 50th anniversary of Franklin D. Roosevelt's death there. FDR was a huge national symbol and his Little White House at Warm Springs was almost sacred ground.

"Fuck it," Panetta said. He didn't think it was a good idea.

Morris appealed to Clinton, who agreed to speak.

On April 12, Clinton addressed the commemorative service. He enlisted the architect of the modern welfare and social services state in his own cause.

"My fellow Americans," Clinton said, "there is a great debate going on today about the role of Government, and well there ought to be. F.D.R. would have loved this debate," Clinton declared.

"He wouldn't be here defending everything he did 50 years ago," Clinton insisted. "He wouldn't be here denying the existence of the information age. Should we reexamine the role of Government? Of course, we should. Do we need big, centralized bureaucracies in the computer age? Often we don't."

In many ways it was a preposterous speech—trying to speculate on Roosevelt's attitude toward current government, the information age and the computer. Mercifully, it received little attention. To Panetta, it proved that it would be difficult to separate good Morris ideas from bad Morris ideas, and that his influence could career dangerously out of control.

Stephanopoulos watched Morris dip into critical issue after critical issue as both conceiver and author, dashing off radio addresses and speeches with incredible speed. Morris once wrote and proposed a full Saturday radio address for Clinton in about 12 to 15 minutes. Stephanopoulos concluded that Morris had no filter between the back of his brain and what came out of his typewriter. The ideas or speeches would often be brilliant, or they would be totally crazy. For instance, on race, Morris argued that Democrats were hurt because they were perceived as too close to minorities—an embodiment of mushy-headed liberal thinking. But Stephanopoulos felt that Morris didn't understand Democratic voters very well and the importance of the race issue to them and to Clinton. Stephanopoulos was heading a review of affirmative action programs for Clinton, and he could see that Morris was working to undermine both the programs and him. Others in the White House told Stephanopoulos that Morris was constantly attacking him behind his back. But Morris had the cards, the confidence of Clinton. Stephanopoulos wasn't sure what to do from his weak position.

Erskine Bowles knew. He argued that it was not unusual for a business to bring in a consultant or facilitator to cause the executives to think. Often such people cause great discomfort, but it forced the chief executive officer to plan where he wanted to go. Morris was filling a void, and forcing some needed thinking and planning. The president had to listen to a wider group than the one Bowles referred to as "the little cabal at the White House." But several times Morris had taken the president's silence on an issue as a yes, and the wires were getting crossed.

So Clinton agreed to institute follow-up meetings in the Oval Office the day after the evening campaign meetings with Morris and the other consultants. Attending the follow-up meetings would be Clinton, Gore, Panetta, Ickes and Bowles—not Morris. That way they could discuss what the previous evening's Morris monologue had really meant and what Clinton had accepted and what he had rejected.

Bowles wanted the rest of them to amplify what Clinton had decided, not what Morris wanted Clinton to have decided. As the implementer, Bowles made sure they went over all the issues, then he made sure they all understood the president's decision, and then it would be over, no more debate.

On April 14, Clinton formally took the first steps to set up his reelection committee. He filed with the Federal Election Commission so they could legally raise money. Terry McAuliffe set up a campaign office in downtown Washington that was almost exclusively a fund-raising operation. The first mailing, intended for 1 million of the most loyal Democrats, was written, reviewed by Clinton and sent to the printer.

"Terry," Clinton said in a phone call, "I'm rethinking this letter. There's a sentence I cannot live with." He wanted a line about his efforts to grow the middle class and shrink the underclass.

"Yes sir, Mr. President, we'll change it."

McAuliffe immediately called the printer, who said the run had begun.

Stop, McAuliffe said. The change cost about $10,000.

"In a few days, I will formally announce my decision to seek reelection as President of the United States," Clinton said in the final version of the letter. As if it was a secret, he added, "Before meeting with the press, I wanted to contact you personally to give you the news." He invited each person to join his "National Steering Committee," an honorary position that required no meetings or formal duties. The pitch for funds still remained soft, only mentioned in the postscript and the response card. In the letter to Democrats dated April 19 Clinton was not triangulating. He labeled the Republican agenda "radical and dangerous."

Money from the direct-mail appeal soon began pouring in, $2 million eventually. Since most of that would be matched with federal funds, the real value was $4 million. After the $400,000 printing and mailing costs, McAuliffe calculated a net gain of about $3.6 million, an unusually high return.

• • •

At the end of April, Ickes arranged a long dinner for himself, Morris and Stephanopoulos at Kinkead's, a fashionable late-night restaurant just three blocks up Pennsylvania Avenue from the White House.

Ickes left after about an hour and a half so Morris and Stephanopoulos could talk and get to know each other.

"I want to work together," Morris told Stephanopoulos. "The president needs us to work together."

Stephanopoulos said he wanted to work with Morris.

They discussed Clinton, comparing him to FDR. Clinton obviously now wanted the same kind of creative staff tension that existed in the Roosevelt administration with everyone competing and everyone a little off balance, they agreed.

But Clinton liked one big happy family, Stephanopoulos said, and had limited tolerance for family warfare given the violence and alcoholism in his own upbringing. Clinton resisted open discord. "He hates being presented with it," Stephanopoulos said. "He hates seeing it. And it gets him agitated and very angry."

Morris saw the point. He too was under tremendous pressure from Clinton to fit in. Morris talked and talked, outlining his theories, the triangulation, getting the Republican issues off the table, trying to figure out a way they could work together.

Stephanopoulos had rarely seen anyone with such incredible ability not to tire of explaining himself.

"I got it," Morris finally said. "I got it, I got it! I'm the strategist, you're the tactician." Morris would be long term, George would be short term. Morris would be outside the White House, George inside.

Okay, Stephanopoulos said.

After five hours, the dinner was over. Stephanopoulos concluded that Morris was a cynical guy and that Morris was trying to own him.

Morris later settled on a basketball analogy. He would be the playmaker; Stephanopoulos would be under the basket.

10

On Monday, March 20, 1995, Patrick J. Buchanan, the columnist and television commentator, appeared in New Hampshire before 200 supporters to declare he would run for president.

Buchanan, 56, was the roaring wind in the Republican Party. He had challenged President Bush in the 1992 Republican primaries, reminding everyone that Bush had broken his "Read My Lips" pledge and raised taxes. Buchanan had won 37 percent of the New Hampshire primary vote, though Bush beat him with 53 percent in New Hampshire and eventually captured the Republican nomination. Buchanan's intense rhetoric and pointed critique had weakened Bush and undoubtedly contributed to Bush's defeat in the 1992 general election.

"We may have lost that nomination, my friends," Buchanan said, referring to 1992, "but you and I won the battle for the heart and soul of the Republican Party."

As he laid out his message, he made it crystal clear he was pointing his rhetorical missiles at both Democrats and Republicans. He would make "America first" again, he said, criticizing a weakened defense system and trade deals which he called the "sellout of the American workers." The enemies were Wall Street and the bankers, the politically correct liberals who favored permissiveness in schools and the rewriting of history to "defile America's past."

Many journalists and political figures treated Buchanan as a fringe candidate, a protest vote in the making. I had known him going back more than 20 years to the Watergate scandal when he had been a top aide and speechwriter to President Nixon. I had always found Buchanan a strange mixture. He could crank out the hottest, most extreme rhetoric. He could also be a pragmatist. Buchanan was often just plain fun, and he genuinely enjoyed the give-and-take of politics. At times he also made truly stupid, inflammatory remarks with racist and anti-Semitic undertones.

In dealing with him, you always had to try to figure out which of the four Buchanans you were getting—the extreme, the pragmatic, the playful or the stupid. Or what mixture. Assessing his seriousness was always difficult.

For example, back in 1973, when it was revealed that Nixon had secretly tape-recorded his conversations, Buchanan had made a suggestion to his besieged boss. Destroy the tapes, Buchanan recommended in a memo, take them all out on the White House lawn and burn them—an idea which came to be known as the "bonfire" approach. All four Buchanans were reflected in this recommendation. The suggestion was indeed extreme, and it was practical. In hindsight, if Nixon had destroyed all his tapes and with them the devastating evidence they contained, he almost certainly would not have been forced to resign. The suggestion was also made part in jest so it was playful, but it appeared stupid to Nixon's lawyers, who thought destroying the tapes might be illegal, an obstruction of justice.

Then when the famous smoking-gun tape surfaced that showed Nixon had led the illegal cover-up, Buchanan, who had been one of his most vehement supporters, showed his pragmatism. In Nixon's final week at the White House, Buchanan made the case for the president's resignation to Nixon's daughter, Julie Nixon Eisenhower, and the rest of Nixon's family. "Hell, I understand why he wants to stay on. But he'd be blackened, Julie. It's a straight road downhill—for him, for the conservative cause and for the country. There comes a time when you have to say, 'It's finished, it's over.' "

"The problem is not Watergate or the cover-up," Buchanan continued. "It's that he hasn't been telling the truth to the American people."

Five days later Nixon resigned.

Because of this strange mixture of personality traits, I was always perplexed by Buchanan as I watched and listened to him over the years. Often his words were outrageous, and strongly peppered with deep undertones that suggested racism, bigotry and sexism. He had to know the power of his words; he'd spent his life crafting them. Yet he also was a fighter, seemingly provocative at times just for the sake of a battle. Was he serious, or was he throwing mud in the eyes of the political and intellectual establishment, looking for a reaction? How would his words translate into action if he was ever elected?

"Rail as they will against 'discrimination,' women are simply not endowed by nature with the same measures of single-minded ambition and the will to succeed in the fiercely competitive world of Western capitalism," he wrote in a newspaper column after the defeat of the Equal Rights Amendment, suggesting that women were not psychologically equipped to compete with men in the workplace.

Homosexuals "have declared war upon nature," Buchanan often said. "Homosexuality, like other vices, is an assault upon the nature of the individual as God made him."

Of Adolf Hitler, Buchanan wrote in 1977, "Though Hitler was indeed racist and antisemitic to the core, a man who without compunction could commit murder and genocide, he was also an individual of great courage, a soldier's soldier in the Great War, a political organizer of the first rank, a leader steeped in the history of Europe, who possessed oratorical powers that could awe even those who despised him."

Holocaust survivors, on the other hand, had been shown in medical papers to have imagined their experiences, Buchanan claimed in 1990. "This so-called 'Holocaust Survivor Syndrome' involves 'group fantasies of martyrdom and heroics,' " he said.

In discussing immigration, Buchanan had rattled a lot of nerves when he asked rhetorically, "If we had to take a million immigrants in, say Zulus next year or Englishmen, and put them in Virginia, what group would be easier to assimilate and would cause less problems for the people of Virginia?"

Even some of Buchanan's ideological allies were alarmed by his rhetoric. William F. Buckley, the conservative commentator who was one of his role models, wrote emphatically in the *National Review* in 1991, "I find it impossible to defend Pat Buchanan against the charge that what he did and said during the period under examination amounted to anti-Semitism."

Buchanan maintained he was not a racist. I wanted to give him the benefit of the doubt. But I wondered, why had he time and again selected language that he knew would appeal to the worst in people instead of the best? Why Zulus?

Part of the answer was in his 1988 memoir, *Right from the Beginning*, about his Washington, D.C., childhood in the 1940s and 1950s in a

Catholic family of nine children and an authoritarian father. In it, Buchanan voices his undying respect for and devotion to the late Joseph McCarthy, the senator from Wisconsin who gave his name to an era by making ruinous and unsubstantiated charges that government officials were Communists.

Buchanan noted that McCarthy was still highly popular with the public in the 1950s, even after most of his charges were disproved and he was censured by the Senate. People "supported him, I believe, not because of precisely what he said, but because of what they *understood* him to be saying. To the Americans who sustained Joe McCarthy for four years, he was saying that the governing American Establishment, our political elite, was no longer fit to determine the destiny of the United States."

Buchanan's goal was to set himself up as the little guy determined to overthrow the reigning establishment—with the backing of people who supported him not because of precisely what he said, but because of what they understood him to be saying.

"There is a simplicity that exists on the far side of complexity," he had written in his memoir, "and there is a communication of sentiment and attitude not to be discovered by careful exegesis of a text."

Five months before he announced that he would run, I drove out to see Buchanan at his sprawling white brick home in McLean, Virginia. The date was Monday, November 7, 1994. The next day the Republicans would win both the Senate and the House.

He had just returned from hosting his radio show when I arrived. A tall man with wayward brown hair, he had grown plumper since his Nixon days, but he still had that same impish face that could change from the stern and scolding father to the cunning and mischievous little boy. When Buchanan smiled, his brown eyes narrowed and almost closed, a gigantic grin overpowering his face often accompanied by loud, pumping laughter. We went into his book-lined den with his ten-year-old cat Gipper, named after Ronald Reagan. After Nixon, Buchanan had worked for both Presidents Ford and Reagan.

Buchanan said he did not know if he was going to run again.

"You're a realist," I said to him. "When you look at this situation, it would be real hard for you to win the nomination."

He disagreed. "Winning the nomination," he said, "it seems to me— and maybe I'm a roaring optimist—would be less difficult than winning the general because in the party I've got a constituency." He noted he had received 3 million votes in 1992 and was well known. Like many political figures he at times referred to himself with the wrong pronoun, as if he were talking about someone else. "Let's say you get into Iowa. Dole wins, let's say. If I came in second in Iowa, I would have won Iowa.

"Then you go to New Hampshire," he continued, "if you come out of there strong, if you win New Hampshire or come out there very strong, and you're one of the last two or three standing, and you go South, I don't know why I shouldn't have as good a chance as anybody else. It depends on doing well. If I don't do well in Iowa and New Hampshire, I think it's all over.

"I mean, it's a long shot but it's a shot. Let me say this, I wouldn't go into it unless I believed there was a shot, and if I conclude there isn't any, I wouldn't go."

"But," I said, "if the Republican elders sit down, wouldn't they kind of say to themselves, look, we've got a real chance here to beat Clinton. We need to nominate somebody who's conservative but not of the red-meat right because that's where we're going to get the votes—in the center."

Buchanan waved me off hard. "The Republican elders can't deliver a thing," Buchanan said. *"Nobody pays any attention to them."* He had been out talking, listening. "I don't think they amount to a hill of beans in a place like New Hampshire and Iowa. No, I don't. If they did, I mean, I wouldn't even bother getting into it because I don't think they're in my camp."

What about the critics who charge that you had helped defeat Bush?

"They say, you know, 'Buchanan divided the Republican Party,' " he said. "I didn't divide it, I just exposed the division that was there, and there's no way I could have gotten 5 percent of the vote against Ronald Reagan."

He noted that Texas billionaire Ross Perot had gone on the Larry King show and launched his own candidacy two days after Buchanan's strong showing in the New Hampshire primary.

"You've got to have either JFK personality or McGovern/Goldwater issues I think are the only things that can beat clear front-runners like Dole," he said.

Buchanan was high on Phil Gramm. "Gramm is smart, he is tough, he understands our movement." He noted with a chuckle that both Gramm and he each were running about 3 percent in the latest polls. "I still believe that Gramm is the most underrated of the candidates."

He said that Gingrich's Contract With America was bloated with too many specifics. "It should be clean house, anti-Clinton, anti-tax. It's strategically such a mistake."

Buchanan turned to the future of the Republican Party, which he was trying to work out in his own mind. "You can't go back to Ronald Reagan. Reagan was a great man, a wonderful man and a great president in my view. But the Cold War is over and his issues are. That era is over. It's just like Democrats going back to FDR and Truman. It's over."

Buchanan naturally turned to the subject of fighting and fighting back, and he brought up Clinton's performance in the New Hampshire primary in 1992.

"I thought he was finished in New Hampshire," Buchanan said. "I said, that guy ain't coming back. I've never seen a beating like that, like he took on the draft evasion and on the women thing. I just said the guy's gone.

"I tell you I admire him. I admire him. He came back up there, he smiled through that beating, and all the crowds surround him and he came back."

Buchanan said that every candidate was going to get a beating. "If you do well and you come out, come back to people, they're going to say, wait a minute, let's take a look at this guy. And you'll have free media, you'll have television, you'll have radio, you'll be able to stand up there and talk directly to the country and redefine yourself. You can do it. But, look, there's no way I'm going to stop people from dumping stuff on me and calling me names.

"All the demonology, you know, you can overcome it in this day and age, and television is the reason, and so is talk radio and so are these direct shows where you get on, Larry King."

Buchanan said he ceased being a believer in free trade, a traditional Republican position, after he looked at the loss of manufacturing jobs in the last 25 years—nearly 50 percent in Michigan and New York, for example. "Why do you think there's such rage and anger out there?" he asked, his hands cutting the air in tiny chops. "The median income of the average American worker has gone down 20 percent while people who write books," Buchanan said, nodding toward me, "and people who do talk shows and people who give speeches," he added, pointing to himself, "our income has gone up." The American worker was being forced to compete with $1-an-hour Mexican labor and 25-cent-an-hour Chinese labor. "I've got nothing against those countries or people."

Buchanan said that if something was not done, people would be thrown out of work more and more, be forced into lower-wage jobs. "You're risking social stability just so some of these corporations' profits can be dramatically increased, they can move factories anywhere.

"I think I can make that case out there," he said.

"Let me tell you," he declared, "economic nationalism's coming in Europe. It's going to come to the United States. It is the future of this country just like the tough line on illegal immigration is the future, just like an anti-interventionist foreign policy. People aren't going to run around the world, send American troops to Pat's Crusade for Democracy. All these ideas are coming. They're winners, every single one of them. I think they're winning ideas in '96."

Though he said he had not made up his mind, it was apparent he was going to run.

I suggested that if he was right about the jobs and the economic decline and the potential social unrest, it might not be apparent for another five or ten years, elections in 2000 or 2004.

"So I get clobbered," he said. "So I get beat."

It doesn't bother you?

"It never did," he said, laughing hard and deep, his eyes squinting. "I've never won one. I've got 33 straight losses." He lost all the 1992 primaries. "You may be right, maybe it'll be by 2000 or 2004, but I'm going to go out and say this is what I'm going to campaign on, this is what I'm going to say, this is what I believe, and if I go through and I get clobbered, I get clobbered. I've had a good life. I've got no complaints."

Buchanan, a man of camaraderie, always loved the feeling of being on a team, driving against the establishment. I suggested that running again would enhance his public profile, implicitly raising the question of whether there might be another reason for making the run.

"I don't need any more money, but this is what I believe, and if I can do it, why not do it? Why not this time? Because you're going to get beat? Because you're going to get pounded? So what, you know, when it's over, you say, we got pounded the last time. I'm glad I did it. No apologies. No apologies, no regrets."

Did he think he could get a fair shake from the media? I asked. Was it settled in his soul that the media had a leftist tilt?

"I think the national media is probably the greatest single bulwark that liberalism and the Democratic Party has left," Buchanan said. "I think that the national press, the Washington press is viscerally hostile to my position. There's no doubt about it. And if you ran against, if you happen to have a general election against Clinton, that would be our biggest problem."

Buchanan said that the one thing that might keep him out would be if Ross Perot entered the race as a Republican, which Buchanan said he had once half expected. "If he got in as a Republican, I mean that would be a real reason for me to rethink it, because I mean it takes too much of your votes that you're trying to put together. But it doesn't look like he's going to get in now on the Republican side, so he'll get in third party. If he gets in third party, I think it hurts us badly because he'll take off a huge chunk of the anti-Clinton vote and I think that hurts us very badly. The way for Clinton to win is to get a real bloodbath in the Republican Party that has not healed and Perot running third party.

"Dole I guess is leader of the party, but there's no leader of the movement which is the heart of the party.

"I don't look on Dole negatively at all," Buchanan continued. "I like Bob Dole. If Dole is nominated, I'd support him all the way." Buchanan said he would support almost any Republican who won the nomination and was trying to remove Clinton. "Look," Buchanan said, "as long as they say, you know, that I'll support Buchanan if he's nominated, I'll support them if they're nominated."

On March 23, 1995, California Governor Pete Wilson announced that he would set up an exploratory committee to run for president. It was the culmination of a two-month behind-the-scenes struggle by some of Wilson's closest political advisers to talk him out of running.

Bob White, Wilson's alter ego and chief of staff for 26 years, was adamantly opposed. Wilson had pledged repeatedly not to seek the presidency when he was running in a tough reelection battle for governor as recently as six months earlier. He had given his word, White argued, and he had to stick to it. Trying to fudge it wouldn't work. Wilson should serve out his term as Ronald Reagan had done as California governor. The year 2000 would be Wilson's chance.

Wilson disagreed. He had to seize the chance. If a Republican won in 1996 and it wasn't him, the person would probably be reelected in 2000 and the office wouldn't likely be open until 2004, when Wilson would be 69. That might be too late, he might be too old. Wilson and White had a real screaming match over it.

White said that it was a choice between a speculative quixotic adventure versus the opportunity to be a great governor, the best in this century.

His national role would fall into place naturally if he did the other job and kept his word. The intensity of White's opposition only seemed to make Wilson more determined to set his own course.

White reluctantly agreed to help him, but Wilson failed to convince some of his key longtime advisers to join his presidential campaign. Larry Thomas, his first press secretary when he was the mayor of San Diego 24 years earlier, and a longtime member of Wilson's inner circle, declined. Thomas, a small man with patient eyes and a radio announcer's voice who had been in and out of politics, cited personal and family reasons.

But Thomas had deeper concerns. Breaking his pledge had raised the question of whether Wilson would keep his word, whether he was a truth teller. Thomas could see it would hurt Wilson's reputation. It was becoming a character issue.

"It's a fucking disaster," Thomas began saying privately.

Within ten days after announcing, Wilson recruited a chairman for his campaign—Craig Fuller, 44, who had been Vice President Bush's chief of staff from 1985 to 1988. Fuller was the vice president of public relations for the Philip Morris Company, making about $1 million a year. Wilson and White had taken Fuller on a Sunday night to the upstairs dining room of Frank Fats, a celebrated political hangout in Sacramento, and offered him the job of chairman and day-to-day manager of the campaign. Fuller, who had known Wilson for 20 years but had never been that close to him, was shocked. It had never crossed his mind that he would be offered the top spot. He almost needed oxygen. After Bush had been elected president in 1988, Fuller had lost out in the competition to be the White House chief of staff for Bush, and he had left politics. This was the call back from the political cemetery.

Bob White later told Fuller he was burnt out and he would not want to be White House chief of staff if Wilson was elected president, clearly dangling the prospect in front of Fuller. Fuller stopped him before any explicit deal was offered because he didn't think the two jobs should be linked. Soon Fuller accepted the position.

In the meantime, Wilson underwent elective throat surgery to remove a small growth or cyst on his vocal cords. He had strained his voice speaking, and the growth caused his voice to break in a high pitch at times. The operation was supposed to be simple, with rapid recovery.

Fuller would, more or less, be supplanting George K. Gorton, Wilson's campaign manager in four successful statewide races: two for senator and two for governor. A bearded 47-year-old student of Eastern religions and meditation, Gorton was often called "Mr. Zen" by those in the Wilson circle. He was an emotional man, who believed the essence of campaigning was television advertising. As manager of Wilson's come-from-behind 1994 reelection victory, Gorton had immense standing in the California political community. Wilson had already had Gorton prepare a budget and feasibility study for a presidential race, and it was widely assumed that Gorton would be the boss.

Wilson told Gorton that not only was Fuller coming in as campaign chairman but that Gorton would have to report to Fuller. He would be the campaign strategist. Gorton went ballistic. It was a slap in the face. "I'm getting fucked here," he said. "I'm a 25-year friend. I can't believe this." He left town and didn't say where he was going or how long he would be away. He told some that he had "resigned" and was leaving permanently.

Finally, two days later, Don Sipple reached Gorton by phone.

Gorton was hurt and felt underappreciated. He let his ego splatter all over, recounting his achievements and his sacrifices for Wilson.

The presidential campaign strategist gets the credit in these things, not the chairman, Sipple said. "In '88, Atwater got all the medals, not Baker. In '92, Carville got the medals, not Kantor!" If Wilson won in '96, Gorton likewise would get the credit, not Fuller.

Gorton was not buying it.

Sipple reached Wilson, whose voice was still terrible from the surgery.

"Don," Wilson said in a hoarse whisper that was more croak than human voice, "have you talked to George?"

Yes.

"What the fuck is the problem?" the governor inquired.

Sipple wanted Wilson to reach out to his longtime campaign manager. "Look, Pete, it's as simple as this. I think this came out of the blue. The message to George is there's been a precipitous decline in his authority and a precipitous decline in your confidence in him."

"Oh, it's an ego thing," Wilson whispered.

Wilson met with Gorton for two hours. Then Fuller and Gorton had a long lunch.

The result was a campaign with divided authority. Gorton would handle strategy and message. Fuller, as chairman, would launch Wilson onto the national scene, and develop a communications plan. But Wilson's voice got worse not better, and soon Fuller or Gayle Wilson, the governor's wife, were out giving Wilson's speeches.

Wilson was astounded by the level of media scrutiny of his past and his entire public career. Wilson proposed that Fuller handle the reporters who wanted to do the most comprehensive work, keeping them away from him. Fuller realized that Wilson always resisted penetrating coverage. George Bush likewise had complained that reporters wanted to put him on the couch for what amounted to psychiatric inquiry. It had been a large nuisance for Bush, who wanted to say what he believed and what he wanted to do and then leave it at that.

"Welcome to the world of presidential politics," Fuller told Wilson. "If you offer yourself up to the country as somebody who deserves to be their president, the country is going to learn a lot about you."

11

Bob Dole had spent the first several weeks of that spring preparing for a ten-state tour to announce formally he was running—a ritual declaration of candidacy that provided a trial run for the campaign organization, enormous free media, and a chance to deliver a message.

The afternoon of Wednesday, March 29, pollster Neil Newhouse presented Dole with information showing that people were concerned about his age. But the concern they voiced, Newhouse said, really reflected a concern about his health—that people his age often begin to have health problems. So taking it easy and relaxing the schedule were critical. Not only would it be better for his health, but everyone knew Dole looked ten years younger when he was rested. "You're your own worst enemy on this," Newhouse said.

Dole didn't like that comment one bit. "Aaggh! I need some help," he said. "You guys got to lighten up on my load." That night Dole gave three speeches.

Bill Lacy enjoyed the jokes and sly asides about a future Dole White House that made the rounds among the inner circle. Do you want to be on the day staff in the Dole White House or the night staff? The day White House chief of staff or the night chief of staff? The shift that begins at 4 A.M. or the one that ends at midnight?

Lacy didn't want to have anything to do with it. Scott Reed began voicing similar sentiments. He was convinced that Dole would be a good president. "I'm also convinced I'm going to have nothing to do with it," Reed said.

Lacy wanted to have polling and survey research on everything that Dole might say in his announcement tour speeches. From a mechanical point of view they were going to do what Stan Greenberg, Clinton's controversial pollster, had done for his candidate: when words came out of the candidate's mouth, it would not be the first time they had been heard. Public reaction would have been tested.

Mari Will had been drafting the announcement speech for several weeks. It included the three Rs—rein in the government, reconnect the government to people's values and reassert American influence abroad. The second day of the announcement tour in Ohio was going to focus on values.

They had done the small focus groups and some national surveying. But Lacy wanted the process refined. One of the best methods, he felt, was the so-called dial group. Here a controlled group of voters sat before a video screen, each person with an electronic dial in hand. As they watched clips of the candidate speaking or being interviewed, they turned their individual dials, indicating a level of approval from 0 to 100. Groups sat for hours listening and turning their dials, which were connected together to give an overall average reading of the candidate's approval at any given moment. Such a group provided an instantaneous and very precise read. In practical terms, anything scoring over 80 was considered very good.

Dole was videotaped giving segments of his speeches for use in such a dial group. He was not happy to be there but he stood still long enough to videotape several 15-minute chunks of the speeches. They also taped him making other pronouncements or statements that might be used in the speech.

On Thursday, March 30, Reed, Lacy and Will flew to Atlanta so they could watch the dial groups as 30 people responded to a draft of the Dole announcement speech and potential message. Dole hit the political jackpot—a 93—on welfare reform, with a line that Washington had failed and the federal government had to get out of the way and let the individual states run welfare programs. He hit 90 on lines about government demanding more and more authority over our lives, on his renewed pledge to eventually pass a balanced budget amendment, on the claim

President Bill Clinton and First Lady Hillary Rodham Clinton at a meeting of the Democratic National Committee, January 21, 1995.

Senate Majority Leader Bob Dole and his wife Elizabeth Dole at a Republican gathering in Washington, D.C., on February 9, 1995.

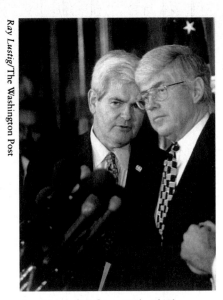

ABOVE LEFT: On January 3, 1995, former Secretary of Defense Richard Cheney became the first major prospective contender to announce that he would not run for the Republican nomination.

ABOVE RIGHT: House Speaker Newt Gingrich and former New York Congressman Jack Kemp at a news conference. On January 30, 1995, Kemp said he would not run for the Republican nomination. Gingrich announced on November 27, 1995, that he too would not run.

BELOW LEFT: Former Vice President Dan Quayle declared on February 9, 1995, that he would not be a candidate for president in 1996.

BELOW RIGHT: Massachusetts Governor William Weld said on February 27, 1995, that he would not seek the Republican nomination.

Robert A. Reeder/The Washington Post

Robert A. Reeder/The Washington Post

ABOVE LEFT: Texas Senator Phil Gramm was the first to announce formally for the Republican presidential nomination, on February 24, 1995.

ABOVE RIGHT: Former Tennessee Governor Lamar Alexander began planning a presidential campaign in 1992, before President Clinton took office. He formally announced on February 28, 1995, four days after Gramm.

BELOW LEFT: Patrick Buchanan announced on March 20, 1995. He won the New Hampshire primary and vowed to stay in the race even after Dole had the needed delegates to be nominated.

BELOW RIGHT: Publisher Steve Forbes entered the Republican race late, gained attention for his flat tax proposal, but dropped out March 14, 1996.

© *Lisa Berg* 1996

Robert A. Reeder/The Washington Post

Jim Bourg/Reuters

*Craig Herndon/*The Washington Post

*Ray Lustig/*The Washington Post

TOP: Republican presidential candidates pose before a television debate in Manchester, New Hampshire, a week before the first-in-the-nation primary. From left are: Alan Keyes, Morry Taylor, Steve Forbes, Robert Dornan, Bob Dole, Richard Lugar, Lamar Alexander and Patrick Buchanan.

LOWER LEFT: California Governor Pete Wilson declared his candidacy in March of 1995 and withdrew six months later.

LOWER RIGHT: Pennsylvania Senator Arlen Specter entered the race on March 30, 1995, and ended his bid for the presidency eight months later.

Dudley Brooks/The Washington Post

ABOVE: After months of speculation, former Chairman of the Joint Chiefs of Staff General Colin Powell declared on November 8, 1995, that he lacked the fire in the belly to run for president. With his wife Alma at his side, he also publicly stated for the first time that he was a Republican.

Vice President Al Gore and President Bill Clinton on November 28, 1995.

OPPOSITE:

TOP: Clinton's chief political consultant, Dick Morris, appears on a video monitor in Richmond, Virginia.

CENTER: Clinton media consultant Bob Squier, who designed the early, aggressive ad campaign.

BOTTOM: George Stephanopoulos, the senior adviser to the president for policy and strategy, had much of his role supplanted by Morris but was involved in the quick responses to Dole from the White House.

© *Ken Bennett, courtesy WWBT-12*

Ellsworth J. Davis/The Washington Post

Ray Lustig/The Washington Post

White House chief of staff Leon Panetta.

Mike McCurry, the White House press secretary, on January 5, 1995.

*Ray Lustig/*The Washington Post

*James M. Thresher/*The Washington Post

National security adviser Anthony Lake, who devised the Bosnian Endgame Strategy in 1995, and Clinton walk back to the White House after a meeting.

Scott Reed was hired as Dole's campaign manager in early 1995, but did not gain control of the entire operation until midway through the Republican primary campaigns.

Dole campaign press secretary Nelson Warfield, Bob Dole and Dole's chief campaign strategist, Bill Lacy, talk with reporters on a flight during Dole's announcement tour in April 1995.

© Brad Markel

Ray Lustig/The Washington Post

Photo by Tracey Attlee

TOP: Sheila Burke, Dole's chief of staff in the Senate Majority Leader's Office.

BOTTOM: Dole speechwriter and campaign communications director Mari Will.

Dole, with back to camera, meets with his campaign advisers: from left, pollster Tony Fabrizio, chief campaign strategist Don Sipple, chief of staff Sheila Burke, campaign manager Scott Reed, political director Jill Hanson.

© *P. F. Bentley*/Time *magazine*

President Clinton and Senate Majority Leader Bob Dole shake hands in the White House on December 19, 1995. Vice President Al Gore and chief of staff Leon Panetta are in the background.

White House and congressional leaders meet on January 9, 1996, in the Oval Office for their last attempt to reach a seven-year budget deal, ending more than 50 hours of meetings. From left are House Majority Leader Dick Armey, House Minority Leader Richard Gephardt, Senate Majority Leader Bob Dole, Vice President Al Gore, President Bill Clinton, House Speaker Newt Gingrich and Senate Minority Leader Tom Daschle (with back to camera).

White House Photo

that government had become the enemy of religion, and on proposals for tough drug law enforcement and a call for a simplified tax system.

Lacy was very pleased. "We are not going to budge from this," he told the others. "You're going to have to kill me, and if you want to kill me, if you want me to leave the campaign, fine." They had the right issues and had to stick with them.

For Reed, it was a question of maximizing what he called "meat" in the speech—popular, concrete conservative proposals.

Will continued to work on the draft, and seemed to have control of it.

But the next day, a mole in Dole's Senate Majority Leader's Office informed the campaign that there was a competing draft of the announcement speech in the works. It had been written by Richard Norton Smith, a staffer and the ghostwriter of Bob and Elizabeth's 1988 book *Unlimited Partners,* a biography of the couple which had been designed to boost the 1988 campaign.

Reed and Lacy braced themselves. Could the competing drafts mean the old Dole had reemerged?

The next morning, Saturday, April 1, Dole came to the campaign headquarters to practice the speech with a TelePrompTer and video-recording equipment. He also told the others about the Rick Smith draft. It had lots of Reaganesque rhetoric. "We got to have the meat," Reed said. They were ten days away from the announcement date, which was written in stone, and dueling drafts were still flying around.

Over the weekend, Dole took both drafts home, saying he would combine them. He liked multiple drafts. He wasn't going to have anyone in any position say, "Here's your speech, now if you want to change it, you change it." Dole wanted lots of eyes on it, lots of hands and lots of ideas. He didn't want one person sitting down and having the power. He wanted the power himself.

Early the next week, Clarkson Hine, Dole's Senate press secretary, called to tell Reed and Lacy that he had been tasked to put the two speeches together. "You've got to understand," Hine explained apologetically, "I'm not messing with the speech. I'm not getting in anybody's way. Dole told me to do it." Hine said he was just cutting and pasting portions of the two speeches, all at Dole's direction.

Lacy soon received the amalgamation of the two speech drafts. It was the opening and closing from the Rick Smith draft with most of the issues and meat from Will's in the middle. The speech, however, was not ready for prime time.

Will called and said she was ill. She was being treated for breast cancer, and would not be able to work further on the speech or even accompany Dole on the week-long announcement tour. So Lacy took personal control of the speech. Lacy took a line from Dole's 1988 campaign film and dropped it in, "I've been tested, tested in many ways."

Burke was opposed to the anti-tax pledge scheduled for New Hampshire. "I don't think it is good policy," she said. She understood it was good politics, but said that such a sweeping promise could later haunt Dole, as it had come to haunt and perhaps defeat George Bush.

Reed told Dole that they had to face the fact that any privately drafted Dole anti-tax pledge would be suspect. It would become the issue and might be torn to shreds. Frankly, Dole didn't have a lot of credibility on the tax issue. Dole had to go with a tried and trusted anti-tax pledge. Grover Norquist, head of Americans For Tax Reform, had a "Taxpayer Protection Pledge" that had been used for years by candidates, the one that Dole had refused to sign in 1988. The pledge merely promised to oppose any increase in the income tax rates and any reduction or elimination of tax deductions or credits unless matched dollar for dollar with cuts in income tax rates.

"Who is this Grover Norquist guy?" Dole asked. "I know him, but I don't know all his background."

The bottom line, Reed said, was that Norquist was the most credible anti-tax authority around. Dole was giving ground, slowly but not entirely.

"Okay, I'd like to get Grover over here on Friday," Reed told Dole midweek. Dole would sign the pledge quietly but keep it under wraps until the announcement in New Hampshire. Norquist himself would witness Dole's signature, giving it a seal of approval. Reed wanted a total surprise. "I'm going to sneak him up to New Hampshire Monday"—the day of the announcement. They would unveil the pledge, have Norquist there to explain and verify, have everybody popping—media, Gramm.

Dole liked that. Meanwhile, he was blowing off the video practice sessions for the speech, which anyhow wasn't finished.

On Thursday, April 6, Dole showed up for an evening practice session. Good God! Reed thought, Dole looked like he had been in a fight. He had cut his neck shaving, and the white in one of his eyes had gone partially but intensely red. Reed had a similar malady—from nerves and exhaustion. A day of relaxation and a good night's sleep would cure it. They all urged Dole to stick to a scheduled weekend in Florida.

"How would you like to have a TelePrompTer in Florida?" Reed inquired. They would have to make arrangements and hire someone to operate it.

That wouldn't be necessary, Dole said. He would be fine.

Dole talked with Elizabeth.

"I don't think with the hurly-burly," Elizabeth said, "Bob, there won't be time in Washington." If it was going to be off the cuff as usual, that was another thing, but if it was going to be the TelePrompTer, then he would have to practice.

Elizabeth called the campaign. Yes, she said, they should have a Tele-PrompTer in Florida.

Dole figured this was big time, the announcement tour, this was what it was all about. If everyone was making recommendations and he didn't follow them, he realized they would say—again—this guy doesn't listen to anybody. Here the campaign and Elizabeth were making the same recommendation. Elizabeth rehearsed everything. She would get to the point in a speech where she hardly looked at her notes, and people would marvel at it.

On Friday, Dole called Reed. "Let's have a TelePrompTer in Florida," he said. That was, if he went. He wasn't sure about the entire Florida trip. The weather looked bad. He was the sun worshipper, followed the sun. It relaxed him, and an hour in the sun took ten years off his appearance. But if there was going to be no sun, what was the point of going to Florida? "Won't go," he declared.

Reed and Lacy wondered if they ought to fake a favorable weather report just to get him down there. They finally called the cabana boy at the Sea View in Bal Harbour, where Dole and Elizabeth had their condo on the top floor, a three-room unit on the oceanfront.

Going to be beautiful, reported the cabana boy.

Dole agreed to go, and as usual before a trip they called ahead and had someone there put some milk, apples, bananas and cereal in the kitchen. Dole knew that everything just sort of slowed down when he walked in the Sea View door.

On Friday, they had one last rehearsal scheduled for noon in Dole's office in the Capitol, where Dole was meeting with California Congressman Sonny Bono, the singer of Sonny and Cher fame, now a freshman in Congress at age 60. Reed stashed Grover Norquist in a hideaway office to wait. Norquist had a private camera crew trailing him. A little media monster in his own right, Reed thought, it was ridiculous. But the staging was complete. Norquist walked into Dole's office and shook his hand with his camera crew capturing it all. Then Reed had Norquist looking over Dole's shoulder while Dole signed the Taxpayer Protection Pledge with his formal "Robert J. Dole." A couple of still photographers from the campaign snapped it all. Reed wanted photographs to release on Monday. He had run a three-week campaign with Dole for this moment.

Reed extracted a promise from Norquist to keep the secret. "I don't want to hear about this until Monday," Reed said. They agreed to meet in New Hampshire.

Lacy told Dole that he wanted to come down to Florida to be there at the speech practice. He also wanted to bring along Stuart Stevens, who Reed had just hired as their media consultant. Stevens, widely considered the most artsy of the Republican media gurus and probably the most politically moderate, had been very successful in 1994, winning 100 percent of his races, including that of Massachusetts Governor William Weld. A mod dresser, Stevens—who looks like a cross between a ski instructor and a movie actor—had written a novel about a political consultant called *Scorched Earth*.

In making his pitch for the Dole account, Stevens had argued that there were two truths in a presidential campaign. The first truth was that paid advertising was probably the least important in presidential races of any political contest because of the cacophony of messages that bombard the airwaves, especially about a front-runner like Dole. The second truth was that because of the cacophony, the paid advertising was the only thing that a campaign and the candidate could control. Therefore it was hugely important.

Saturday, April 8, Lacy and Stevens flew down to Fort Lauderdale, Florida, together and arrived at the Sea View around lunchtime. Dole and Elizabeth were already there. Dole was focusing on his own speech and had paid little attention to the speeches given by Clinton and Gingrich the day before. Even though Lacy had worked for Dole on and off for ten years, he had never really seen Dole in a totally social or personal setting. As proof that Dole was delegating, Stevens had been hired by Reed. He had never really met Dole before.

At the Sea View, Lacy and Stevens were directed to a huge patio area above the pool where drinks and lunch were being served. Dole was sitting there, wearing a tennis shirt, shorts, purple Nike shoes and Nike socks. Just one of the guys. Among the group were some of Dole's best friends who were also in their 70s: Dwayne Andreas, chairman of Archer Daniels Midland Company and one of the biggest political money givers to both parties of all time, and Robert Strauss, former head of the Democratic National Committee.

Lacy was surprised to see Dole relaxed, so at ease—so off the normal Dole tempo. They agreed to meet at 4 P.M. to begin a rehearsal. Lacy and Stevens then went to eat lunch, and soon Strauss was on to them. Strauss liked to play the bipartisan gadfly and get into everyone's business: In 1993, he had arranged a peacemaking lunch between President Clinton and Dole when they were at each other's throats. Strauss wanted to find out who Lacy and Stevens were. What was going on? When he learned that they were staff, he expressed total amazement. Never, never had he seen Bob Dole have staff down to the Sea View. To practice a speech? Unheard of, never, ever before. Strauss said that he thought Dole was the right man for the times, the right choice, and that he thought very highly of him. "But that son of a bitch is a Republican," Strauss finally said, getting to his punch line, "and I'll never vote for a Republican."

One other thing, Strauss added, the recent Dole letter to the National Rifle Association about promising to repeal the assault weapons ban was a mistake, wasn't going to fly, he couldn't believe Dole would think it was time to get more high-powered weapons back on the streets.

At about 3:15, Lacy and Stevens set up a podium in the Sea View's large meeting room. A young TelePrompTer operator from one of the local television stations had been hired to run the machine and she was late arriving.

About 4 P.M. Dole's personal aide Mike Glassner came in and said that Dole would be down any time. He wanted to read the speech once, Glassner said. Dole was worried about his voice. After one read-through, he was going to go upstairs and relax for an hour and then come back for one more read-through.

Oh great, Lacy thought. Not nearly enough. He wanted Dole to know the speech. Full immersion. About half an hour later, Dole appeared. He was wearing an old, blue seersucker summer suit and a tennis shirt—a sort of Don Johnson circa 1958 look. How do you like my announcement outfit? Dole joked. It was the very suit he had worn at the 1972 Republican Convention in Miami, Dole explained, chuckling. Nixon had a suit just like it, he added, in touch with the old master.

He went to the podium, and they began.

Stevens took the view that there was no way to try to coach Dole, who had a style ingrained over decades. Any attempt to modify it would look artificial and would surely backfire. As Dole went through the speech, Stevens and Lacy could see that he wanted to hurry, get it over with.

Dole was bored. But he had once heard Bob Hope say he was still using material that was 30 years old, so he persisted. Still, he wanted to hurry.

Stevens explained that in his opinion the only way the speech wouldn't be successful was if somehow it was rushed. Dole was obviously comfortable with the speech. He only had to show that comfort. The speech had been designed not to get in the way of the deliverer. It was written to be delivered, not read.

Dole did another run-through.

Wait, Stevens and Lacy occasionally interrupted, don't step on your applause line. Dole matter-of-factly read some of the material at the end about revisiting Northern Italy and the battle sites of World War II where he had served and been wounded. Don't fight the emotional points, Stevens suggested. Slow the cadence of honest recollection.

". . . memories of the heroism, the sacrifices and pain men and women suffered," Dole said, stiff in his seersucker suit at the podium.

If you feel a surge of emotion at any point, Lacy suggested, try not to bat it down, just let it come on out.

Dole marched through it again. A number of times he asked, "What does that mean?" Mari Will's prose soared but it wasn't simple or clear enough for him. They changed some words, broke some longer sentences into shorter sentences, which always helped.

It was 6:30 when Dole left. He had put in two and a half hours, and agreed to come down in an hour for one more read-through. At 8 P.M. Dole came to the room again for another half hour of work before they shut down.

That night Lacy phoned in the changes to the campaign to make sure they were reflected in the master text. There were variations to the speech for Tuesday emphasizing values and for Wednesday emphasizing foreign policy. Lacy wanted to go through those.

Sunday morning, Lacy and Stevens went jogging on the beach. Dole then came down and worked with them for another half hour on various parts of the speech. Lacy got 45 minutes to himself in the sun. He was almost in shock. Dole was so relaxed and willing to practice. He was even allowing himself to be handled around the margins. Lacy had three strategic goals for the announcement. First, to stake out the message ground of Dole as a conservative. Second, to show the party activists and the media that the Dole campaign knew what it was doing, that it could conduct itself professionally and on a large pre-presidential scale. Third, they wanted to advance the image of Dole as a possible president.

When Dole had balked on some conservative message material, Lacy had said, yes, some people are going to accuse you of pandering. But that's all right. They accused George Bush of doing the same thing, Lacy noted.

Dole had sat and nodded. He clearly liked the Bush reference.

There isn't anything that you're saying that you don't believe, Lacy said at one point, and there isn't anything that you are saying that arguably isn't supported by your record. You voted consistently for voluntary school prayer, for example. And you voted against the creation of the Corporation for Public Broadcasting, which in the speech he said he wanted to abolish. There's nothing here that's inconsistent. It's inconsistent with what the media wants you to be because they want to see you as a centrist, so yeah, there's going to be a little tension.

Dole had just nodded his way through this.

Lacy had a basic view of campaigns: *Never build your strategy on something you can't control.* And this speech could be, would be controlled.

That afternoon, Dole, Elizabeth, Lacy, Stevens and Glassner flew to Topeka, Kansas, where Dole would make his first official announcement of the tour the next morning.

The Dole campaign had invested heavily in the announcement tour, renting a large commercial jet that was normally used for the Yankees baseball team. It was temporarily christened "The Leader's Ship."

Reporters and staff flying from Washington to Topeka were greeted Sunday morning at National Airport's charter terminal with a spread of bagels, muffins, rolls, fresh fruit and coffee. Everything was there but the white-hatted chef making gourmet eggs to order. Several former senior campaign and government media experts had been brought in to make sure all the reporters were happy, hotel rooms were in order and everything ran smoothly. An 18-page schedule was released for the tour that would take Dole to ten states in four days—Kansas, New Hampshire, New York, Ohio, Iowa, Colorado, Texas, Florida, South Carolina, North Carolina and then ending back in Russell, Kansas. Nonetheless, some of the veteran Dole watchers in the media were certain that Dole would explode, steer off message or reroute the plane. "Delicious fun," one reporter said, anticipating a good story about an inevitable derailment of one sort or another.

Sheila Burke was flying out to Kansas on the plane and then going to Arizona for a vacation. She was trying to find out who else was on the plane, and she noted with evident disdain that she had been unable to obtain a list from the campaign. The division—and tension—between the leader's office and his campaign was continuing, through mostly low-intensity skirmishes.

In Topeka that night, Lacy set up another brief practice session with a TelePrompTer. He took Synhorst aside. "Tom, you just aren't going to believe it." Dole was practicing, his delivery was great, no asides, little sarcasm. Dole ran through it again, and the speech was down to about 20 minutes. After the equivalent of seven full run-throughs over the weekend, Lacy believed that Dole had taken ownership of the speech, not just on what Lacy called the "macroscale" but sentence by sentence, even word by word. All portions, ideas and key words had been adapted to make Dole comfortable.

The announcement speech was planned for the steps of the Kansas State Capitol, but Wizard of Oz weather struck—rain and intense wind. Reed had consulted Reagan's old media manager Michael Deaver on the setup. They had pictures of the site and diagrams. For weeks, Reed had held countdown meetings every two days on the entire announcement tour with 30 to 40 people. That night with less than 12 hours until the speech, Reed called a meeting of the key people to consider whether to move the event into the giant convention hall, the Kansas Expocentre. Changing locations would entail massive logistics, and they would have to do it overnight. But that was something that could be controlled. It would be in their hands. The weather wasn't.

"I think we ought to move it inside, does anybody disagree?" Reed finally said.

Everyone assented. Reed went to inform, not consult, Dole.

That night, Reed had a 15-minute talk with Glassner, the body person.

"The number-one job in the world is to make sure the guy never falls on ice," Reed told him. It was freezing in Iowa and New Hampshire, ice everywhere. Glassner had to do everything in his power short of getting out the snow shovel or salt to ensure that Dole had an ice-free track everywhere he went. It really didn't need to be said. A fall or an injury would remind everyone of Dole's age. It could be a catastrophe.

Monday, April 10, the Expocentre had been transformed from a sports arena into the site of a small political convention, complete with signs and bunting and balloons. When Dole gave his speech, he seemed a bit tense and halting at times. But the rehearsals probably saved him. His delivery was slow and his voice and cadence very strong. There was no dramatic news. He emphasized his experience going back to World War II, and he used the word "values" nine times. He insisted that as president he would cut taxes and balance the budget at the same time. The anti-tax pledge was being saved for New Hampshire later in the day, and word had not leaked. The news from the morning was simply that Dole had formally announced.

Reed and Lacy were immediately out talking to the reporters, giving precisely the same spin to the speech: Dole was the only presidential candidate who could give that speech. Caught saying that exact same thing to one reporter, Lacy felt they would look like assholes. To the contrary, Reed felt they were just doing their job—one recognized by reporters perhaps more than others.

Dole's speech had elements from the messages of the other major Republican candidates: Lamar Alexander's power to the people, Gramm's balance the budget, even Pete Wilson's anti-crime themes, and Gingrich's talk of societal transformation. All wrapped in the steady, experienced hands and voice of Bob Dole.

Soon they were back on "The Leader's Ship" for the three-hour flight to New Hampshire. The state had been Dole's Waterloo in 1988, and the campaign staff always treated it with a kind of foreboding while at the same time trying to power through any problem. The TelePrompTer did not function at the announcement outside the Exeter Town Hall, and Dole had to read his speech. Lacy stood in the front off to the side, wagging his head purposefully and conspicuously in a slow, steamy no, no, no! Some of the speech was up on the TelePrompTer screens so Dole could read, but it was backwards or jumbled and very distracting. Dole seemed distant from his own words. His delivery was mechanical but sufficiently resolute.

But a murmur was coming from the crowd of reporters at the front. The campaign press office had just handed out photocopies of Norquist's Taxpayer Protection Pledge with Dole's signature. What's this? One reporter called Norquist's Washington office by cellular phone. But the campaign produced Norquist right there to explain and certify Dole's newfound anti-tax credentials.

The reporters went to a filing center where they had 30 minutes to send out their stories. The story was the anti-tax pledge, a big clear shift by Dole. While boarding the plane, with only a local pool television camera crew present, Dole raced up the steps. As he turned to wave halfway up, his feet slipped out from under him and he went down hard on his good arm. He recovered quickly; it was as if someone had thrown cold water on him and he was up in a split second.

I was on the plane at the time and didn't see the fall, but when I heard about it, I broke campaign-plane protocol, which relegated the press to the back of the plane unless invited up. I went up to Dole in the forward compartment and asked if he was okay. "Oh, yes, yes," he said. He showed me the bottom of one of his shoes. They were new, with shiny leather soles. With his red, bloodshot eye and the general nervousness and pressure in the campaign not to screw up anything, Dole seemed tense but fine.

A still photographer got a picture of Dole right after the fall while he was still on the steps, but he was smiling. Only the virulently anti-Dole conservative *Manchester Union-Leader* and a handful of other papers ran the picture.

The local station, WMUR, had video of the fall but it had been taken while they were going for an exclusive interview with Dole on the plane. Two of the networks were going nuts asking for the film of the fall, arguing that it was pool footage to be shared with everyone. Senator Judd Gregg, the New Hampshire Republican who had endorsed Dole and was present on the plane, confidentially called an executive at the station. As a personal favor, please don't feed the video to anyone, he asked. The tape never got out.

Elizabeth worried. If she had known they were new shoes, she would have scratched up the bottoms of the soles to give them traction.

Reed and Mike Glassner looked at each other.

"I remembered our talk," Glassner said, referring to the worry about ice. It had been more than 50 degrees that day in New Hampshire, and he had been scared to death when Dole fell.

It wasn't anybody's fault, Reed said.

Former Senator Rudman, who was aboard the plane, found someone to blame. No rubber treads on the steps up to the plane, and brand-new shoes, Jesus, Bob! "That's stupid," Rudman said.

Rudman had been offering additional advice to Dole. He understood the necessity to take the anti-tax pledge. But guns were different. The pledge to repeal the assault weapons ban made no sense. "I'm sorry, Bob, but people are tired of everybody being killed."

The next day, headlines about the announcement focused on Dole's anti-tax pledge and his experience, his longevity and age.

Reed and Lacy worked to keep Dole away from the reporters so he would not be quizzed on his anti-tax pledge. They wanted his signature to carry the message, not new spontaneous words that might qualify or clarify or even take back what he had promised.

A reporter asked Rudman why things seemed to be going so well on the announcement tour.

"Because Bob Dole is not the campaign manager," Rudman replied.

Dole overheard this and burst out laughing.

The Dole plane flew to New York City for a giant fund-raising dinner run by Senator D'Amato that raised $1 million. Reed wanted to make sure they ended on a big money event that would drive the headlines, which it did in part.

On the second day of the tour and the sixth city, Denver, everything was late and the discipline finally broke down. Dole turned his 20-minute announcement speech into a 45-minute ramble. It was 11 P.M. Mountain Time when he finished his 20-hour day.

Elizabeth explained to the staff that her husband rambled on when he was tired. His appearance changed, his voice changed. Yes, he had the energy of ten men, but they had to be careful.

Dole ended the week in his hometown. Russell is a very small, flat town near the dead center of Kansas, made even smaller and flatter by the enormous sky. It is the town where Dole was born and raised, where he returned after his war injury and his neighbors pitched in to pay for his operations, where he launched his political career as Town Attorney. Russell is where Dole's brother Kenny died in 1993, and where his two sisters, Gloria Nelson and Norma Jean Steele, still live. The commercial stretch on Main Street is three blocks long—beginning on one end with a used-car dealership and the sign, "Everybody Drives a Used Car," and ending by the railroad tracks at the light blue grain elevator Dole's father Doran used to operate. Painted on the towering elevator in white letters, sky-high, are the words: "RUSSELL, HOME OF BOB DOLE."

The small brick house Dole was raised in, at 1035 North Maple Street, had been kept by his sisters just the way it was when their mother,

Bina, died in 1983; her spices still arranged neatly in the kitchen window, opposite a shiny red stove. This house, his sisters said, is where Dole returns for strength. A tall flagpole and three limestone pillars—symbols of old prairie fenceposts—adorn the front lawn.

On Friday morning, Dole attended a pancake breakfast at the VFW Hall and then went to Good Friday church services at noon. After that he wanted to drive around town with Elizabeth. They stopped at the A & W drive-in stand for root beer and hot dogs where Stuart Stevens's crew filmed the impromptu lunch. Next they went to a nursing home. All politicians want to be filmed at nursing homes so Stevens was ready, but word came down, no filming at the nursing home. The reason was obvious.

Russell was opening a new plant, to extract gluten from the Kansas-grown wheat, that would employ 35 people. Dole realized that was a big-time number for Russell, and he wanted to attend the ceremony. Up on the platform the Kansas wind was blowing dust at nearly 45 miles an hour. As the wind came roaring, Dole reached for his hard hat which the wind was lifting. He jerked his good left arm back quickly, catching the hat but pulling some critical muscles in his shoulder.

The next morning he couldn't even comb his hair, and the doctor said it took baseball pitchers three or four months to heal similar injuries. Dole protested that he had to shake hands, wave and be ready to go. When it was suggested that he put his other hand under his arm to rest the bad shoulder, he protested that he only had one arm he could use and that was now also on the injured reserve list. A series of unpublicized icepack treatments began that would continue over months. For a long time, he couldn't even reach the neckties in his closet at home in Washington.

Before taping NBC Television's *Meet the Press* with Tim Russert the next day, Lacy and some others sat with Dole to review the possible questions and angles of attack he would face. They walked him through the issues—his high-visibility and more conservative stands on affirmative action, taxes, gun control.

On *Meet the Press,* broadcast live from Dole's childhood home, Russert said, "You want to be president."

"I've thought about it a lot, yes," Dole replied.

"Why?"

Dole said experience, leadership. "I'm a conservative candidate," he added, returning to leadership, then mentioned reining in the government, reconnecting government with the people, and back to leadership.

Lacy watched in some agony as Dole dribbled the most obvious question into the outfield. Lacy blamed himself for not once again walking Dole through the celebrated "why" question. It could have been a home run. Dole didn't treat the question with the kind of sitting-up-straight-in-his-chair, now-I'm-going-to-get-your-attention answer that Lacy wanted. Dole's answers on the other questions were okay, worked fine, but they were not sharp.

"I'm not extreme in any way," Dole said at one point, protesting again, "Bob Dole is not an extremist."

Lacy didn't think it was a particularly good or necessary line. No one was going to accuse Dole of extremism. He did not need to protest.

The ten-state announcement tour was followed by a good deal of press commentary and analysis. "Dole's Right Turn: Real or Opportune?" asked *The Washington Post*. *Time* magazine headlined a column "The Brand-New Bob Dole," noting that the Republican Party was "seething," but not Dole, who was adapting himself to "the changing center of gravity in his party."

The Doles, Lacy and a few staffers flew back to Washington in a small jet. Lacy proposed a toast to the senator who had pulled it off. Elizabeth gave a long toast to the staff. She was effusive, bubbly, warm. When it was Dole's turn, he said, Yeah, great tour, good group.

Reed was delighted. Though there was the inevitable sniping, there were no news stories asking, Where's Dole's organization? Or, Where's Dole's message? Reed wanted to take advantage of his new stature. Early on he had made a run at Sheila Burke, Dole's Senate chief of staff. Reed was not so much troubled by her moderate image. It was the chaos in the leader's office that Reed thought was her fault. People on Dole's Senate staff came to work in the morning and just played defense. There was rarely a plan or real strategy. "There's no nothing," Reed said. Now with his stock high with Dole, Reed was going to try to get her out. Reed had a candidate in mind, Kelly Johnston, an aide to conservative Senator Don Nickles of Oklahoma, to take over as Dole's chief of staff from Burke.

"What are we going to do about Sheila?" Reed asked Dole. "We got it now, we're really rolling, we're in the high campaign."

"She doesn't want to leave," Dole replied, indicating that they had talked.

"Okay, fine," Reed said.

So Reed asked Burke, "What's up with you and Dole?"

"He hasn't talked to me yet," she said.

At first Reed didn't know what to believe. Dole obviously loved her in the job. She was a great buffer. When there was a problem with the conservative senators he could say or act like, oh, that's Sheila, you know. She had been there 18 years.

When Dole and Burke finally talked, "What is it you want me to do?" she asked. Maybe he needed a conservative chief of staff. The conservatives hated her, thought she was the devil.

Dole said he wanted to leave it up to her.

Becoming the permanent Secretary of the Senate was the alternative, an appealing option. Burke was already serving temporarily in that post in addition to the chief of staff position. The Senate Secretary received some $35,000 more in pay, had shorter hours, and a staff of some 220 versus the mere 20 on Dole's majority office staff. Though the title sounded big, it was really a factotum position, chief administrative officer of the Senate, away from the inside action. She finally chose to stay in the lower-paying position near the action. But she knew it was never really at the center.

Burke felt it was a big mistake that Dole didn't have an alter ego, someone who knew the whole picture and could fill in for him, speak for him in any instance. He was secure about himself and his own judgment. But the self-reliance meant he had built all these defenses, these walls. Burke understood it from her three years of work in a hospital, where many people just lived within themselves. "This means he is alone," Burke once said. The disorderliness of the staff, she felt, was a reflection of Dole's style. He was not a planner, he took each day as it came.

Dole felt Burke was an exceptional person. She had married his former administrative assistant David Chew, was raising three small children, had lost her mother and father within a year's time, had relatives all over the country. "She's intellectually honest, I think that's the key," Dole said.

Reed had failed to do away with Burke, so he decided to hold her close. If he could only help her focus and plan, and if he got into her loop on the Senate business, then it would be okay.

On Friday and Saturday, April 21–22, Dole campaigned in Iowa, including six town meetings. On the plane, Dole saw a report that Phil Gramm had earlier compared Dole to "1930s British appeasers" when Dole had endorsed a big-government compromise on health care the previous year. The British, Gramm noted, later stood up to the Nazis, and he pointedly added, "they didn't turn to somebody who yesterday was for appeasement." Dole was furious. Gramm was saying that Dole was Neville Chamberlain and that he, Gramm, was Winston Churchill. What an outrageous comparison.

"Don't let Gramm have the fight he wants," urged Nelson Warfield. Gramm had clearly sought the most inflammatory comparison that could be made to someone who had fought in World War II. Say nothing in response, brush it off, Warfield urged, adding what he knew would be a compelling analogy for Dole, "Treat Phil Gramm like George Bush treated you in 1988."

"Yeah," Dole growled.

At none of the six town meetings was the subject raised by anyone, including Dole.

In the evening, Dole was scheduled for a dinner speech before 1,000 people. Given the apparent success of the announcement speeches and the on-message media reviews, he spent three hours that Saturday afternoon practicing with a TelePrompTer.

Tom Synhorst attended the dinner and carefully watched the Tele-PrompTer speech. Dole was serious and presidential, but he lost his connection with the audience. Normally, he was funny, full of jokes, almost uncontrollable with the jokes, but there were none. He had stuck to the text. Synhorst was worried. It was important that Dole be loved in Iowa, like Senator Charles Grassley, who had won reelection in 1992 with 70 percent of the vote. Dole needed a reservoir of affection so that when the inevitable negative ads started to fly in the two months before the caucuses, voters would not give credence to whatever charges might be leveled.

Synhorst later reported to Lacy: on message, off audience.

Maybe they should just put the jokes in the text on the TelePrompTer, Lacy suggested half seriously. He knew it was Dole. After every good performance, he would come up with a bad one. There was no way to control or predict it.

Though Lacy and the others could not acknowledge it in public, the campaign was basically playing defense. But to avoid that appearance, to keep everyone busy and to advance the candidacy, Lacy believed that they had to carefully play offense. They had to select a few high-visibility things to do and to make sure they were done well. So Monday, April 24, Lacy wrote a one-page memo to the senator with some proposals.

"We need to amplify our arguments in the announcement and in Iowa over the weekend. A big opportunity, the California swing beginning the end of May. Los Angeles is the perfect place to do a 'thoughtful speech' on the entertainment industry's contribution to cultural decline and also a good chance to name names."

Dole returned the memo with the approve box checked, and the campaign went to work on the speech.

12

Dole picked up a Sunday front-page story in *The New York Times* May 14 headlined "Dole Isn't Being Dole, and Aides Call It Strategy."

"Senator Bob Dole, master legislator, has in recent days looked like anything but," Dole read from the lead paragraph. The story cited problems Dole was having passing a legal reform bill and handling President Clinton's very controversial nomination of Tennessee obstetrician Dr. Henry W. Foster, Jr., to be Surgeon General. Foster had performed abortions, and Republicans were out to stop his nomination. Lacy was quoted saying that much of the Senate business was "inside baseball" and the important matter was maintaining Dole's conservative credentials. Overall, the story suggested that Dole was wandering around bumping into himself in his dual roles as both the Senate majority leader and presidential candidate.

The next morning Dole called the campaign and said he wanted to have a meeting late in the day with Reed, Lacy and Jill Hanson, the political director. It was the first time he had summoned them so directly.

Lacy polled Reed and Hanson. What did they think the meeting would be about? Reed said he thought it was just to get a firsthand update on what was going on. No, Hanson said, she suspected it was to give them fatmouth about the *New York Times* article. Lacy agreed it was the article. He even went back and reread his own quotes to see if he had said something that was inappropriate or impolitic. He concluded he had not.

Dole had a very traditional 1960s or 1970s view about aides talking to the media. He didn't see why it was necessary. An aide quoted by name still often got a sly look from Dole or even a cutting remark. Since Lacy had been around Dole for ten years, he and Reed had decided it was better for Lacy to answer the reporters' questions and take the hit from Dole if he was irate.

At the meeting Dole asked some general questions, but clearly he was upset. Something was on his mind. He was not good at concealing. And then there was this article, he finally said. Had they seen it? It belittled Senate business, and showed him not fully managing or conquering his dual roles.

You know, Reed said, we have to present our case, our side of the story. We can't take a negative story without responding.

Dole almost immediately backed off, and he soon began running through the usual rhetoric: What's going on? Where's this guy? What's happening here?

The meeting degenerated into something like a tennis match with the ball going Dole-Hanson, Dole-Hanson, Dole-Hanson, with a state-by-state update.

By the end of the meeting, Dole seemed to have calmed himself down.

Later, Reed revisited the subject with Dole on the phone.

"My reputation is not as a hot dog," Reed said, "and I'm sure not going to start being a hot dog now." He said he was taking the campaign manager's job with utmost seriousness. "You've got to understand that there are times we have to be in the story, and we're going to have to and you just have to. If you're mad, tell me, don't go telling all the little Munchkins on the Hill who then go around and yap."

"You're right," Dole said. He was cool, agreeing that it wasn't a big deal.

Reed hoped the story would get the attention of Sheila Burke and the rest of the Senate staff. They needed to see that what they did had enormous political splatter on Dole's presidential campaign.

On Friday, May 19, Lacy read conservative Paul A. Gigot's weekly column in *The Wall Street Journal*. The column was an important pipeline into what movement conservatives were thinking. The headline read: "For 1996, Dole Leads, But Newt Looms." Lacy plunged into the column, which said that Dole's approach was "mechanical and uninspiring." Dole had not hit on the self-confident emotional appeal of House Speaker Gingrich. Dole sounded defensive and talked legislation. All the talk and interest about House Speaker Gingrich running for president was because of Dole's failure to step forward to represent the Republican Party's traditional economic growth and optimism, the columnist declared. "If there weren't a vacuum, no one would be asking if Mr. Gingrich might fill it."

The column resonated with Lacy, in effect saying that Dole had not conquered the philosophy question. It drove at the core of Lacy's strategy. He dashed off a memo to Dole.

"Subject: Message.

"*We will win if we stay on message,*" Lacy began, underlining the sentence. "Every speech or interview should reinforce or illustrate one of our key themes."

"Mari, Nelson, Stuart Stevens and I should begin regular sessions with you, Q & A and look at videotape of past performances."

Lacy knew that Dole was very independent and did not want to be handled, but he was exasperated.

Dole ignored the suggestion that the staff regularly review his performances.

As part of the campaign routine, Dole had set up a regular 8:30 A.M. Tuesday meeting, called the steering committee, of Republican senators who supported his presidential bid. The group consisted of about a dozen senators, including D'Amato and Bill Cohen.

Dole didn't attend the meetings himself even though they were held in his office. Instead, Reed ran the meeting. He and Lacy were there to listen, take notes on any and all suggestions. They bobbed their heads up and down in unison as one senator after another offered advice. Dole avoided the meetings like plague, once literally having his driver circle the block and calling into the office on the car phone, "Are they gone?" After the meetings ended at about 9:45 A.M., Reed often saw Dole in the hallway coming in. Reed realized the meetings made the group of senators feel part of the campaign, gave them a feeling of ownership in the process. So when it came time for them to tow the line on something critical to Dole's stature as Senate leader, they were more willing to go along.

Lacy found the meetings a pain. It was such rambling chaos—sort of like the Senate itself. He listened carefully, and the group of senators would get focused on something like a floor statement that Dole was planning. As good as they might be as politicians, Lacy was surprised how they would get so inside themselves and think and act like the world revolved around the Senate.

Dole had scheduled a Senate recess for the Memorial Day week, and he was going to be on the campaign trail, ending in California. The plan, as Lacy had proposed in April, was to attack Hollywood directly on the grounds of sex and violence in movies and popular music. Mari Will, who was back at work, had spent some time drafting the anti-Hollywood speech. In her conversations with Dole, she returned repeatedly to the theme of values. "The country really aches to hear about values," she said. And they needed to hear directly from him, not in cryptic partial sentences or Arrggghhh. For Dole, words were often a way of dancing around, avoiding confrontations or ducking a direct criticism of someone. She could interpret his likely meaning. But that wouldn't work with the public. He needed to step up in a forceful and direct way if he were going to get and retain attention, particularly with conservative voters, she said. So Will had interjected some high-voltage rhetoric into the speech. Hollywood was guilty of the "mainstreaming of deviancy," with loveless sex and mindless violence. Too many of the movies and songs were "nightmares of depravity." She cited Time Warner by name for some of the foul lyrics on its music labels.

Will finished the draft of the speech on Friday, May 26, sent it over, and then spoke with Dole on Saturday. He had read it and said he liked the speech. He seemed in a good mood about the speech, even its directness.

John A. Moran, a California oilman who had been the Republican National Committee finance chairman for two previous years when some $115 million was raised, headed Dole's presidential finance committee, as Terry McAuliffe did for Clinton. But big $1 million fund-raisers were unusual and Dole had to slowly eke out the money event by event. Since it was a heavy fund-raising week, Moran was traveling with Dole.

Moran had read the speech draft and said he was very concerned. Though most well-known Hollywood figures were Democrats, there were plenty of Republican big givers in the entertainment industry who would be attending the speech. He opposed a confrontation with the money

people. The speech was too harsh, too direct, Moran said. The donors
didn't like to be fingered.

Moran was one of Reed's best friends, but Reed thought Moran
had little political savvy. Reed had laid the groundwork with the local
California fund-raiser who was managing the event.

"This is going to be tough, but trust me," Reed said. Yes, it was risky,
fairly risky. "This is the right thing for us to do politically."

Nelson Warfield could never erase his first image of Moran from
several months earlier at their initial meeting. "Here comes the Monopoly
Man," one of his aides had said.

"What are you talking about?" Warfield asked.

"You are about to meet John Moran," the aide replied.

Moran had walked in, and sure enough he looked like the guy from
the Monopoly board game—the billionaire in the pinstripe suit with a
sack of cash on his shoulder, striding out with a big smile beneath his
mustache.

On Tuesday, May 30, Dole was in his suite in a Chicago hotel. A
TelePrompTer was set up so he could practice the Hollywood speech—his
only chance because they were flying to California the next day, first to
San Francisco for a fund-raiser and then to Los Angeles to deliver the
speech. Dole ran through it once, went off for some other meetings and
then came back later that night to the suite to practice. Warfield and
Glassner were there, and Dole invited Moran up.

Moran said that the phrase "sold your soul" was way too strong.

"Well, can we use the word 'rent'?" Dole proposed, laughing.

Moran and Nelson Warfield faced off about the speech.

Dole realized it was a very heavy speech. He went back and had them
get exactly what he had said on the topic earlier. He also read some of
what various other critics had been saying about the entertainment industry, including Democrats like Senator Bill Bradley of New Jersey. Dole
thought if he took a shot in the dark, whhhsssttt, he would get chopped
off as had happened before, criticized for taking a cheap shot. So he
started taking some stuff out of the speech, putting in some of his own
material. Changes were sent back to campaign headquarters where the
master draft was being finalized so it could be released to the media in
advance. Dropping an evening speech in California when it was 10 P.M.
on the East Coast was the media equivalent of doing nothing if it was

not released ahead of time. The speech draft went back and forth that night.

Moran had an alternative draft, a speech that would accomplish virtually the same goal without using what he called "inflammatory language."

"Senator," Warfield argued to Dole, "we can have the sort of punch if we have a strong speech like this. Trying to split the difference of this is going to result in a yawn. It could even be worse." Warfield wanted to see if they could make national news with the speech.

"You know, inviting these people in," Dole said, "I'm accepting their contributions. I'm going to blast what they may actually do for a living."

Warfield reminded Dole that he would be talking to a much larger audience. "You're talking to America. You're a presidential candidate, you're the front-runner. When you speak in that room you're speaking through the cameras to America, to every voter out there, to the world."

"It'll offend them," Moran said, appealing to Dole's sense of manners.

During a break, Warfield had a chance to phone Mari Will to report the latest threat to the speech. Moran was urging a major pushback, Warfield said, and it was particularly poisonous because Dole would likely try to build consensus among his advisers.

Will laid out the arguments for Warfield to give back to Dole. "These people are going to be flattered to have the speech given to them even if it doesn't directly affect a lot of them because they're going to be at work the next day and this is going to be in the papers, and they're going to say, 'I was there,' and it's a compliment," she said. Will argued that audiences of activists and donors wanted to be taken seriously.

She urged Warfield to remind Dole that this was a presidential campaign, not a race for the Senate. "It is insulting to go before audiences in this role and not take them seriously and not take the office seriously. . . . It's an insult to go to them and just say bland nothings, to just sort of wander through something without a point." The speech would give the audience credit for having a moral conscience, she argued.

Warfield went back with the full force of the argument.

"Well," Dole said, "I don't think people want to be treated like props." At this point Dole kind of glanced at Moran as if he was giving Moran part of the argument.

Moran took the cue and continued to cut away at the specific language. At one point, Moran suggested that such an in-your-face speech could cause fund-raising problems down the road.

"I would rather have the issue than the money," Dole declared. He looked at Warfield, as if he knew Warfield had scored a point. Dole had a habit of shooting looks at Warfield when he had used one of Warfield's lines or points in a speech or interview—almost as if Dole had given him something.

The back and forth continued. Dole never banged down the gavel and said the jury was dismissed, but rather just let the conversation wander on. In the end, he wouldn't authorize the Washington headquarters to hand out copies in advance.

Warfield called Reed to report, "This is not a sure thing."

On Wednesday morning, May 31, the campaign had the latest speech draft all neatly typed out in three and a half pages on "Bob Dole for President" letterhead, ready to give out to the press. But without Dole's authorization, Reed was initially unsure what to do.

Reed suggested strongly that Lacy fly out to Los Angeles that morning. Dole was going to use a TelePrompTer, and some time had been allocated for practice.

Lacy hated to travel and be away from his wife.

Message and an opportunity for a dramatic offense were on the line, Reed noted.

"I don't look forward to this," Lacy said, "but if you want me to, I'll just get on a plane and get out there."

"Yeah," Reed replied, "I think you should."

Lacy headed to the airport. His mission: Protect the speech draft.

That morning Dole left Chicago for San Francisco. Reed reached Warfield by phone on Dole's plane.

Lacy was on the way to hook up with them, Reed said, seeking the latest status report. "Is he going to give it?"

"Well, I think he's going to give it," Warfield said. "I *think* it looks good."

Reed noted that to generate a turnout they would have to show a little leg, and he wanted to get on the phone to reporters to alert them, pump up interest, major speech coming. Perhaps even release the text in Washington that morning. "Is it okay to do it?" Reed asked.

"We ought to do it." Warfield said, stopping short of making a full recommendation. Lacy on the scene would be a plus. "My *prediction* is he's going to give it," Warfield said, again stopping short of giving a full assurance. He figured he already had enough gray hairs from the campaign.

Reed decided to gamble and release the text on his own authority. He later reached Warfield. "Well, it's out, we're out. We've got tremendous interest so you're going to get a good turnout tonight."

Dole arrived in Los Angeles that afternoon. A visit with former President Reagan had been arranged.

Warfield was happy because it looked like the campaign was going to get a photo showing Dole with the former president—a trophy certain to make news. A Reagan-Dole meeting could suggest a modest if indirect endorsement. Later Warfield learned that Dole was only going to get a private meeting with Nancy Reagan at the Reagans' home. The former president was in such bad shape that he was not going to attend the meeting. He was 84 years old and suffering from Alzheimer's disease, the incurable neurological disorder that steadily destroys memory. Riding up in the car ahead of Dole's limousine, Warfield was wildly pissed, cussing and carrying on at some length about the lost opportunity for the magical Reagan-Dole summit photo.

For Dole, the stop was more personal than political. The former First Lady told him that her husband was getting up and going to work each morning and was playing some golf.

"It's really tough, really tough dealing with it," she said. That's all she would say, but it was clear to Dole she was very sad about her husband's condition.

Mrs. Reagan gave him a copy of the book *The Wit and Wisdom of Ronald Reagan*. She tried to be upbeat and noted that the former president had autographed it to Dole but had made a mistake and had to scratch out and correct a word. "That will make it more valuable," she added.

And she had lots of questions. What's happening? How's Newt doing? How are you doing?

As Dole answered, it was apparent to him that Mrs. Reagan was keeping pretty close tabs on the Congress and had a pretty good fix on where things were heading. Two matters didn't come up in the conversation: the 1996 presidential race, and Dole's forthcoming blast at Hollywood. Dole wasn't sure how she might receive his criticism. After all, acting was also her former profession. She would hear about his speech the next day.

. . .

Dole was trying to learn to talk about values. He remembered that back as far as 1988, Mari Will used to fuss at him. "You've got to get up and let people know who you are," Will had said. "It's not just that you get up and make a speech." He had to go further and answer questions, she said. "Who is Bob Dole? What's he all about? Is he complicated? Where does he come from?"

He was very uncomfortable with these questions, then and now, but Dole knew that the Hollywood speech was an opportunity to provide some of the answers. He saw it as a little test. Could he talk about the things that he hadn't really talked about before?

Dole connected values with religion. "My parents weren't religious in a sense," Dole told me a month later during a Saturday afternoon interview in his Senate office. "They wanted us to go to Sunday School but they didn't attend church often and there wasn't any driving force there at all. Probably believed in hard work, and we all worked Saturday, Sundays, evenings, whatever. We could find jobs, and you know I remember getting my mouth washed out with soap a few times for using language." Four-letter words that he had picked up in Russell, Kansas— words that he had thought could be used to emphasize a point. "We had a strict household." Dole claimed he had learned that points could be made without foul language.

My questions about values triggered a discussion of housework.

"My mother was a nut for cleanliness," he volunteered. "We didn't have a lot of clothes. She'd take 'em off at night, and we'd wear 'em again in the morning, but they would be spotless, you know, she'd see to that."

Those were the things he remembered when the talk turned to values —religion, hard work, cleanliness, not talking dirty.

Maybe it was generational, Dole figured, but he was very uncomfortable with the Hollywood values speech. Maybe the opportunity and the little test just weren't worth it. He considered not giving it.

Lacy arrived at the Century City J. W. Marriott in Los Angeles on the day of the speech and had a few hours to spare and make some telephone calls. He read the speech carefully—the draft that Reed had handed out. He wanted to identify the words that Dole might not like, so they could spend the time redoing portions or simply replacing words. He wanted to focus the debate on words, phrases, not on themes or the entire speech. It was a diversionary tactic so that Dole wouldn't toss out the whole speech.

About 5:30 P.M. Dole arrived at the Marriott with Moran and War-field. They went to a second-floor room equipped with a TelePrompTer so Dole could practice. Dole said he was still not sure what he was going to do.

Lacy coaxed Dole to stand up at the TelePrompTer. Dole took his place.

Lacy asked him if the text was at the right height?

To check, Dole had to read some of the speech.

Lacy wanted to hear how it sounded. Soon Dole was going through it.

As Dole read, Moran interrupted with his same objections.

It's going to be fine, Lacy said. He understood the speech might offend some of their finance people, but it would play well politically. It's going to play well, Lacy repeated.

The line about "selling" or "renting" their souls came up. Dole said he wanted it dropped entirely.

"I think it's okay, we can take that out," Lacy said. "We don't neces-sarily need that in there."

Warfield didn't argue.

A few minor changes were made to remove the "I" lines which Dole hated. For example, the line in the draft, "I have risked my life" to defend freedom, was changed to read, "Many, as I have, have risked our lives to defend it."

Dole read it through several times and then everyone left but Lacy, who wondered if this was by design since he was the designated baby-sitter.

As they sat down together, Dole again expressed his concern. There was not much time.

Lacy had one case to make. What they were doing wasn't something that two kids had concocted and brought in from the backyard. It had been very carefully thought through. It was a dramatic and sophisticated critique with a strong populist punch. The speech as a whole was coher-ent. Parts could not be thrown out at random and others substituted. There was a line of logic that had to be followed and retained.

Of all the thousands of speeches that Dole had given in his career, he had often felt good before giving them. Other times he felt good after he had delivered them. And some he wondered why he had given them at all. On this speech he had many trepidations. Soon, however, he was standing before the audience glancing around and wondering if some would be so offended that they would get up and leave. There had to be some Hollywood people from the entertainment industry out there, he knew. This was not only in their business, it was in their face. People had paid money to hear him, and he was going to cut their legs off.

Momentum was often the final decision maker for Dole, and he was capable of giving a full extemporaneous speech. Neither Dole nor Lacy knew for sure what he would do.

After Dole was introduced, a honking, forcefully cheerful song that sounded like the background to a video game played as he took the stage and stood between the flags of the United States and the state of California at a podium emblazoned "DOLE for President."

"I accept the nomination," he joked, drawing mild chuckles from the audience. "Why not?" he added. Dole's nervousness was palpable, and he began to ad-lib.

"I know in California there may be other candidates or at least one that I read about, but I would say right up front all these candidates are friends of mine."

Lacy could hear him stalling.

"I've been in California many, many times," Dole continued, off message, off text. "Over the years, campaigning in good times and bad." Pausing, his eyes darted quickly back and forth, gauging the audience. "I've met a lot of people here, made a lot of friends over the years and I come out here and I speak a lot and I talk about the party and I talk about what's happening."

Jesus.

There was nothing but the words, on TelePrompTer screens to either side of his face. Dole exhaled deeply.

"But I want to talk about a specific matter tonight," he said, licking his lips, taking one more quick look around the room and then, mercifully, going to the text. "I may not win an Oscar, but I'll talk about it anyway."

"It's good to be back in California," he inserted, drifting, veering sharply. Oh, no. "And John, I do thank you for that introduction," Dole repeated, referring to Moran whom he had already thanked. "And I do thank everyone for being here tonight." Slipping, slipping.

But there on the TelePrompTer were the words, and finally Dole plunged in. "I want to talk to you tonight about the future of America—about issues of moral importance, matters of social consequence." That was the point of no return. He probably couldn't just make it up now. He was onto "moral importance" and "social consequence." Dole looked worried, nervous but in control. Like the experienced doctor who has bad news for the patient but knows it must be told.

The entertainment industry was becoming "coarse," he said, sticking to the text. Then the punch in the face.

"A line has been crossed—not just of taste, but of human dignity and decency. . . . About a culture business that makes money from 'music' extolling the pleasures of raping, torturing and mutilating women; from 'songs' about killing policemen and rejecting law. The mainstreaming of deviancy must come to an end.

"We will name their names and shame them as they deserve to be shamed.

"And let me be specific," Dole said, pointing his left finger to the ceiling in front of his face for emphasis. "One of the companies on the leading edge of coarseness and violence is Time Warner," he said, naming and describing some of their products. "And I would ask the executives of Time Warner a question: Is this what you intended to accomplish with your careers? Must you debase our nation and threaten our children for the sake of corporate profits?"

The line hit right at the self-image of a generation of well-educated people determined and insistent that their lives make a difference. Dole had told them their work was rotten and they were rotten, that they were money-grubbing and willing to sell out the children. His voice grew steady and stronger. But still, his head jerked between the TelePrompTers to his side. He glanced around to see if anyone was departing. No one was. He named some of the bigger money-making movies to recently hit the screen—*Natural Born Killers* and *True Romance*—and music groups Cannibal Corpse, Geto Boys and 2 Live Crew. Incorrectly, he implied that Arnold Schwarzenegger's *True Lies* was a family-friendly film.

When Dole finished, many in the audience flocked to him. Boy, that was right, someone said. I've got a son at home, said another. Someone else said they had a little girl. Bo Derek, the actress who had appeared nude in the movie *10*, and TV actress Tracy Scoggins praised Dole on television.

Afterwards Dole attended a private high-dollar fund-raiser in the hotel restaurant. He was pumped up and actually repeated some of the lines from the speech. Later, crammed in a small plane to fly down to Orange County for the next day, Dole was animated, cracking jokes. Warfield had only seen him like that once before, after he had done a pace lap in a race car.

The advance team plopped the morning papers in front of Dole's door the next morning. Yeah, front page in the Orange County paper.

The New York Times played the story of Dole's speech above the fold on the front page. The headline read:

DOLE ATTACKS HOLLYWOOD WARES
AS UNDERMINING SOCIAL VALUES,
Senator Moves to Front of Conservative Critics.

The *Times* ran pictures of five of the movies he had mentioned, dividing them into two categories: "Friendly to Families" and "Nightmares of Depravity." His speech was called "a withering attack."

It was giant news. The impact was way beyond anything in Dole's entire political history. This was entirely new territory. Columns, debates, giant affection from Republicans and the right wing, and even outspoken praise from many Democrats and liberals.

The *Jerry Springer Show* wanted Dole to appear across from Bushwick Bill, the foul-mouthed one-eyed midget rapper from the group Geto Boys who had burned a Dole campaign poster in protest. That was real connection and impact.

Dan Rather wanted Dole on the *CBS Evening News* that night. Dole, in Las Vegas for a fund-raiser, had to appear from what looked like a closet.

"Ah, went pretty well, didn't it," Dole said to Reed the next day.

"Yes. It's working out well. You ought to see it from back here. We got the front pages," Reed said, referring to the East Coast papers.

"Ahh, uhh, aarrgghh," Dole replied. When he saw a video of the speech, he felt that he hadn't done as well as he could have, and concluded he should have practiced more with the TelePrompTer.

On the same day, Pete Wilson signed his first executive order cutting back on affirmative action, but the Dole speech virtually drowned out Wilson's efforts to gain attention.

The Washington Post had largely missed the Dole Hollywood story and came back the second day with two front-page stories.

As the impact and discussion continued, Scott Reed realized the campaign had made two mistakes with the speech. First, Dole was receiving some legitimate criticism because he had to acknowledge that he had not seen the movies. Reed should have made Dole watch the movies so he could speak with authority. But Reed figured they had barely convinced him to give the speech, and long sessions watching movies would have likely increased his resistance. Lacy knew that Dole had sat through a portion of *Murder Was the Case,* a 13-minute short film starring rapper Snoop Doggy Dogg, but Lacy wasn't around when the inquiries came in from the media.

Second, the mention of Arnold Schwarzenegger's movie *True Lies* in a list of the top-grossing movies that "were most friendly to the family" made it appear as if Dole were endorsing it. The movie was one of the most violent in several years. Since Arnold Schwarzenegger was one of the few outspoken Republicans from the acting community, it appeared that Dole was pandering.

Lacy believed the speech and the intense reaction to it helped Dole see the difference between the politics of his own generation and Lacy's generation. The speech graphically demonstrated the importance of ideas and mass communications. Dole, Lacy increasingly realized, came from the Huck Boyd school of politics—McDill "Huck" Boyd, the newspaperman and Kansas Republican kingmaker who had discovered Dole in the spring of 1960, was a classic 1950s and 1960s pol, a relic of the days when campaigns were won by going around, shaking hands, seeing and being seen. It was ground organization, person-to-person. Dole didn't fully appreciate how power today flowed from mass communications, and its inevitable role in a national campaign.

Lacy realized that when Dole spoke publicly, he was trying to connect with every individual in the room. Before Dole spoke, he liked to circulate in the crowd like the father of the bride. He would try to greet everyone if the group was small. Elizabeth even picked up the habit of going to the crowd before talking. Dole didn't realize fully that he was speaking to the TV camera and the millions who might see a 10- or 20- or 30-second sound bite.

Reed recognized that Dole was not fully comfortable with the speech, even though other senators, Dole friends, and the intense campaign watchers in the media and in Washington seemed to get it. There had been no downside—an almost unheard of situation for a high-profile campaign move.

Dole told Mari Will that he was struck by the power an idea could have and how it could tap into great feelings. Will emphasized that talking to those people about what they were actually doing with their lives highlighted the moral concept of individual responsibility. It gave them credit for having a moral conscience.

What was next? Dole wondered. Should they do more Hollywood? A lot of people were advising him to ride the wave, and hit hard again.

No, Will said, now's not the time. Let it play out. The topic and idea were so hot. She believed that sometimes things got so hot they could explode in the hand that held them. They could come back to Hollywood when the issue was cooler. Not until the fall, Will suggested. She had an idea for Hollywood II. It would be about sex on television.

Will said they should switch to another hot issue. The liberal academic elites have been pulling down pillars of the society—teaching in foreign languages and presenting American history by concentrating on the worst moments such as McCarthyism and the rise of the Ku Klux Klan. The English language has been the great unifier of diverse races and religions in America, and it was under attack.

Hhhhmmmm, Dole said. Hhhhmmmmm.

13

With things going well, Reed and Lacy turned momentarily to the fatigue question. Reed had canceled one of Dole's scheduled marathon sojourns into New Hampshire—a non-stop eight events, nearly as many towns, three hours in the car.

Dole admitted that a reduced schedule was better, and started asking, "Do I need to do this every moment?" He was wondering if running for president had to be so all-consuming.

Reed worried that Dole was eating crap, garbage on the campaign trail. Airplane food, a snack on the run, a full meal while standing up. Elizabeth was focusing on his diet, getting him to eat fruit and vegetables more. Even with cutbacks on the schedule, Reed didn't know how Dole did it.

When Reed encountered anyone really close to Dole, he urged them to reinforce two things with Dole: slow down, and stop doing the Sunday morning and other weekend television talk shows. Reed calculated he had enlisted about 30 people. When one of the senators at the Tuesday morning steering committee meeting raised the fatigue question, it was just a question of whether Reed or Lacy would be the first to say, "You go tell him that." They hoped Dole would listen.

Dole didn't think people were raising the fatigue question very often. He could recall more of them wondering aloud to him why he had so much energy. Most of the senators had to go lie down for a nap or rest during a long day of Senate business, Dole knew, while he stayed out there on the floor driving his race car, the U.S. Senate.

Nonetheless, Reed and Lacy persuaded Dole to ratchet back the campaign schedule for the summer up until Labor Day. They would cut it in half. Lots of weekends off, Sundays off, some trips to his condo in Florida. It looked like Dole agreed to take off most of the July 4th weekend, and he and Elizabeth were talking about going to New Hampshire for a week or ten days in August. This would include some campaigning but it was supposed to be mostly vacation.

One of the legacies the campaign had inherited was the Better America Foundation, a supposedly independent group that Dole had set up the previous year as a miniature think tank to provide some intellectual weight to his political persona. "Hire some geniuses over there and crank out ideas and papers," Dole said. He was aware of the considerable influence of the established conservative think tanks in Washington, which seemed at times to dominate or even frame the political debate. Dole wanted one of his own. Gingrich had all these groups and political action committees, lectures and courses he taught. Got Newt in lots of trouble, but also Dole could see their power.

Under Dole's direction, the Better America Foundation went on a fund-raising blitz, pulling in some $4 million.

It was tricky. The aim of the Watergate reforms on presidential campaign financing had been to build a shield of sorts around presidential campaigns, ensuring that what was inside was open to scrutiny. These laws had three purposes: prohibit corporations from contributing in any form; limit individual contributions to $1,000 per person; require full disclosure of the identities of those contributors.

Dole's Better America Foundation could skirt all these limitations since it was ostensibly a foundation with no direct connection to a presidential campaign. The $4 million had come in from donors who were promised their identities would be kept secret. Many corporate givers donated up to $250,000. Some of them had offered to give up to $1 million, but Dole had declined. The secret list read like a Who's Who of American business: $100,000 donations for example from the chairmen of AT&T, Ernest & Julio Gallo Winery, RJR Nabisco and Philip Morris Co.

These were precisely the type of out-of-channels high-finance donations that the Watergate reforms were supposed to prevent. But the appeal of "geniuses" who might bolster Dole, especially well-financed "geniuses," was too great. Dole knew the foundation could not do political ads for his campaign, but he felt they could do general advertising, what he called "generic ads." He said the goal was "Sort of lofty ideas for TV around election time."

It was a figment of his imagination. Dole knew political interests are rarely, if ever, generic.

In the summer of 1994 Dole had personally picked his Senate deputy chief of staff James Whittinghill to head the foundation. "Have you ever thought of running the foundation?" Dole had asked one day to Whittinghill's total surprise.

No, Whittinghill said.

"Well, you ought to," he said. And then Dole just walked away leaving Whittinghill to stew.

Dole told Tom Synhorst on the plane in 1994, "I was thinking why not have him do it."

Synhorst felt that Whittinghill, a former aide to a Texas congressman, was not very bright.

But Whittinghill accepted the assignment. He set up offices on Pennsylvania Avenue in a red brick town house, and began telling people he was the braintrust of the Dole campaign. Whittinghill had a short television commercial made promoting the foundation. The first version featured only Dole, and the lawyers said it would have to include other political figures to blunt the accusation that the foundation was a front for the Dole presidential campaign. So the final ad showed Dole, Gingrich and an American flag with an 800 number to call to give money. In the fall of 1994 when Reed was still executive director of the Republican National Committee, Whittinghill brought the TV spot over for Reed to see. Reed found it laughable. Hmmmmm, Reed had thought to himself, there aren't that many smart people around Bob Dole.

The TV spots ran at an incredibly high cost of $1 million. Less than 2,000 responses came in—an awful return. From his first weeks at the Dole campaign, Reed began saying, "The Better America Foundation *better* do something!"

Dole visited the offices twice.

Whittinghill began telling people that he was lining up congressmen to support Dole's presidential bid—one of the clearest political acts and an obvious violation of the restrictions on the foundation. Dole was aware that Whittinghill had tried to get Representative Susan Molinari, a New York Republican, and other Republicans to support him.

Finally Whittinghill did something. He gave an interview to the Associated Press, published on May 26. "Yes, there might be some things we do that Dole talks about in the campaign," Whittinghill said. "At some point it's hard to separate." Dole's campaign could benefit indirectly, or not so indirectly, from the foundation's poll results, reports and advertising.

The campaign lawyers told Reed that this would guarantee an investigation from the Federal Election Commission, which oversees the campaign financing.

Reed wanted to seize the opportunity to close Better America down, but he and Lacy wavered. Free anything in a campaign is very attractive, and the remaining $4 million in the Better America coffers was very tempting. They tried to see it as a public relations problem, a perception problem, and not a legal problem.

Some of the younger people in Dole's campaign, including Warfield, were horrified. They were adamant in their recommendations: Disclose the donor list and close down the foundation. But that was the kind of self-denying action that hard-pressed campaigns resist.

Warfield had to field the press calls, and when he learned all the details, he made it his purpose in life to get the foundation closed. "We're starting out in a bad situation so let no one hereafter say I said I'd make a good story out of this because I can't. It's a bad story."

One of the other lawyers explained that the foundation had done everything properly. Why can't you just go out and explain that we've operated perfectly within the law? the lawyer asked.

"Because that would put me out there saying we're keeping a secret we don't have to, we're not embarrassed by it but we're going to keep it secret anyway because we can," Warfield argued.

Reed was reluctant to disclose the donors, and was buying the arguments of the lawyers.

"We have a substantial public relations problem," Warfield argued, "that can only be made significantly worse as we get closer to the election, as we attempt to stonewall and as we fail. You're not going to keep everybody quiet. We've already screwed up with Whittinghill. This guy's already shooting his mouth off and calling me after the fact to say he's talked to a reporter. Well, that's swell. I'm a press secretary, not a priest, and don't call me into the confessional and say, well, I just did this."

We can sustain this, the lawyer argued.

Jo-Anne Coe, the finance director, said that there were some big-name contributors, high-profile names, who expected confidentiality.

All the more reason the information was going to get out, Warfield said, insisting, "It's going to happen."

Coe said they couldn't just blithely puncture the promise to the donors.

Warfield acknowledged that this was a legitimate, heartfelt concern, but the donors had given for the betterment of Bob Dole and helping Dole now entailed disclosure.

Reed saw the big chunk of money and wondered if there were not some good that could be done with the $4 million. Why not give it to the Republican National Committee's educational foundation or something like that? Reed proposed.

The money was tainted, Warfield persisted. "You've got a situation where you've got a presumption of proceeds from some presumably ill-gotten process and now you're going to go seek more influence with it?"

No final decision.

So Warfield resorted to whispering in Dole's ear out on the campaign trail or on the plane. In answer to Dole's perpetual inquisition about what was going on and what Warfield might have heard, Warfield said in the most grim and foreboding way, "You know we've got a problem going here?" Dole was all ears as Warfield outlined the situation and repeated his arguments. Dole, as usual, uttered a few Arrggghhhs but provided no directive.

The situation remained unresolved. Warfield was astounded, complaining, "There's this feeling that, well, it's going to be a bad story so let's just ignore it, let's just close our eyes." He noted that Gingrich was being battered about his various fund-raising activities, from GOPAC to his college course. The process was inexorable and eventually going to force disclosure, he was sure.

"Stupidest fucking idea," Warfield declared. Why? What is the game here? What benefit was there or came Dole's way from that risk? Dole clearly had a blind spot on this because he was convinced that he was not for sale and would never be swayed by these donations or any campaign contributions.

The Better America Foundation had some of the ingredients of a major disaster. Watergate was an out-of-channels operation that had high-level approval and was well financed and allowed to be run by cowboys. The Iran-contra scandal in the Reagan administration was an off-the-books renegade operation that was also well funded, operated in secret, had high-level approval, and whose operations officer was another cowboy, then Marine Lieutenant Colonel Oliver North.

Finally, Reed recommended strongly to Dole that they do away with it and return the remaining millions.

Dole agreed. He concluded that neither he nor his campaign got any benefit. "Six people got jobs, I guess," he said, "and we're going to mail money back, which is probably unprecedented."

It was a serious brush with scandal. Money, secrecy, special deals and cowboys were more of a problem than Dole grasped.

Clinton continued throughout the spring to search for the political center. In one of the 1992 presidential campaign's more memorable lines, he had promised to "end welfare as we know it." But he had made little effort in more than two years as president. The welfare system as it existed created permanent dependence, and it had become a symbol for the country. Clinton didn't want it to become a symbol of the economic and racial divisions. Welfare dependency was a documented fact, with millions of women and millions of children caught in a lifelong trap of monthly checks and unemployment.

To many, the program symbolized what was wrong with government programs—their permanency, the unintentional discouragement of personal responsibility and the undermining of the work ethic, the role of the states that received federal matching funds in the program, and the vast federal bureaucracy in place to determine eligibility and administer the program. Clinton didn't want to kick the poor or beat up on them. But something had to change. Welfare took away dignity. It was bad for children because it perpetuated the cycle of dependence. His main goal was to get jobs for those on welfare who were capable of working. At the same time, he did not want to cut off the truly needy.

Clinton wanted the issue off the table, legislatively and politically. It was a broken program that needed fixing, and he realized it was a loser for Democrats. He decided to try to make a secret deal with Bob Dole.

After a rare meeting that spring with the congressional leadership in the Cabinet Room, Clinton pulled Dole aside. Dole felt he was being lured out of the way so they could speak in private.

"Is there any way we can work out welfare?" the president asked. "Nothing will ever be said beyond this room, me and you."

"I don't know," Dole replied, very surprised, "pretty big jump." A welfare bill had not yet reached the Senate floor, and there was a big fight brewing among Republicans on the issue. Gingrich and the House Republicans were working on legislation that would be very harsh in welfare cutbacks and restrictions.

Clinton said he understood Dole's delicate position in the primary fight with Phil Gramm, who wanted to make the welfare reform bill much harsher. Gramm was one of the conservatives who had launched an attack on the "teen moms," and he wanted to stop welfare benefits to unmarried teenagers and to ban women who were already on welfare from receiving additional payments if they had more children. The president and Dole were closer to each other than Dole was to Gramm. "Just between you and me, never be repeated," Clinton said again. He made it clear he understood Dole would be vulnerable to political attack if the deal ever became known—there goes Dole again, making a deal again, making a deal with Clinton, the devil.

"I don't know what's going to happen on our side," Dole said, referring to the Senate Republicans. "We don't even know yet if we get a bill." Dole realized that because of Clinton's 1992 pledge to change welfare, he might be willing to go as far as Dole wanted while retaining as much of the safety net for poor children as possible.

"I'm not going to go out here and next year say Bob Dole made a deal on welfare," Clinton promised. Even if Dole became the Republican nominee, he said, he would not use it. They would work together for higher purpose. "This was just something that we did because it was the right thing to do," the president said, underscoring why they could work together in secret. "And we didn't do it for any political gain." They would just get the issue off the table.

"I'm not sure that can be done," Dole said, "but, you know, I'll keep you clued in."

Dole left somewhat dumbfounded. He would remember the encounter distinctly. On one hand, there was the immense risk of trying to do a deal secretly with anyone, especially the president, especially the man who held the job that Dole wanted. On the other hand, Dole realized that his natural ally on the issue might be Clinton, who was not looking to blow up the program entirely. Dole too wanted modest reform. And welfare reform was one of those unique issues that brought together the major questions of the day, much more vividly than health care reform or even the debate about the entire federal budget.

Welfare was vastly misunderstood, going back to charges from Ronald Reagan about "welfare queens." Aid to Families with Dependent Children (AFDC), the basic federal welfare program, provides a cash grant matching the programs in each of the 50 states. Currently 16 million children and single mothers were on the program. Three quarters of the children supported by AFDC remained on it for more than five years. This was the essence of the permanent underclass. Reform would raise all the questions about the relationship of the federal government to the states. How much should be controlled by the federal government? Was basic uniformity desirable? How much should the states decide? The House Republicans wanted to convert the entire program to a block grant to the states and let them largely decide what to do with the money. Clinton had given 25 states waivers to experiment with new welfare programs, and he was chiefly concerned with reform that would move people from welfare to work.

Dole thought that he might have some leverage now. He realized that many Republicans thought it was better to come up with a welfare bill that Clinton vetoed. Then the Republicans would have the issue. But in Dole's view it was better to have welfare reform. He didn't mention Clinton's secret proposition to anyone on his staff or in the Senate, but went to work quietly to see if a Senate welfare bill already in the works might also be acceptable to Clinton.

Later that month, Sheila Burke, Dole's chief of staff, held a meeting with the leaders of key conservative groups to discuss welfare reform. Representatives from the Christian Coalition, the Heritage Foundation and the Traditional Values Coalition attended her meeting. Burke was opposed to summarily dropping mothers off welfare. She was trying to broker a compromise and move the groups more to the center, but the hostility toward her could be felt.

"Don't give me that look," Burke said to a representative of one group who had expressed skepticism. When discussion turned to the thorny question of welfare and illegitimacy, someone said that the group represented real people.

"What do you mean, real people?" Burke replied. "Do you think Senate staffers are not real people? I'm a nurse!"

The meeting escalated into a screaming and yelling match, and ended very bitterly.

Judy Haynes, who was the liaison between the Dole campaign and the various coalition groups, went to see Bill Lacy.

"My phones are ringing," she reported. "We have a problem." She described the many calls she was receiving about the Burke meeting. These were the conservative activist groups who were deeply suspicious of Dole—the very groups they were trying to court for the campaign.

"I can't imagine Sheila doing that," Lacy said matter-of-factly. "I just don't believe it." Burke was tough but not stupid, he felt.

Lacy called Burke to check. Burke said that a couple of the people had really been nasty and rude. They had provoked her and she had returned the favor.

Scott Reed received a report in Boston where he was on vacation.

"It's a fuckup," Reed replied, "because one of these 20 little right-wing nuts is going to run out." Someone would report on the meeting to conservative columnist Robert Novak or someone from *The Washington Times,* he was sure.

In a newspaper column, Novak branded Burke a "militant feminist," and other conservatives piled on charging darkly that she was manipulating Dole. "Men of his generation don't know how to handle aggressive women," declared Paul Weyrich, a leading conservative. As a test of Dole's conservatism, Weyrich was demanding that Dole get rid of Burke. Reed said, "Weyrich thought this was an opportunity to be a man in his weird manhood way." The stories and columns continued, some reporting that Reed himself wanted Burke out. *Wall Street Journal* columnist John Fund wrote that Burke controlled access to Dole.

"What a joke!" Bill Lacy said, after reading the column. "That's the biggest problem with Dole is that there is not control. There *is* no control."

Reed realized finally that conservatives were engaged in 18 years' worth of payback to Burke, who had functioned as the moderate check on Dole. Reed felt Burke had brought it on herself, sparking the reactions by having the meeting with the Christians and conservatives.

Burke's insecurity grew as the attacks escalated. She began to question Reed and the campaign, and soon she was spending as much time worrying about herself as she was about Dole—jeopardizing the synchronization that Reed wanted between the campaign and Dole's Majority Leader's Office.

One morning during the public controversy, Burke asked Reed, Lacy and Warfield to her office. Did they have a strategy for how to deal with the stories about her? she asked.

Yeah, the three from the campaign said in several variations, don't talk to reporters, keep your mouth shut.

So Reed defended Burke publicly, disputing published reports that the campaign was at odds with her. "The real unwritten story about this campaign is the value Sheila Burke has given to Dole," Reed told the Associated Press.

Having failed to oust her quietly himself months earlier, Reed had little choice but to embrace her.

Warren Rudman sent Burke flowers with a card saying, "Roses are red/Violets are blue/Novak's a nut/We still love you."

The flowers arrived while Burke was meeting with Dole and Gingrich. She read the card and then passed it to the other two. Dole and Gingrich broke into hysterics.

"Bob," Rudman told Dole in a phone call, "this is the first shot. At some point you've got to stand up and be counted."

Dole said he would defend his chief of staff.

"It's coming from probably some very conservative people who figure you're apt to be the president and they want to shape your administration a year before you're even nominated," Rudman said. "It's the ultimate in cowardice. They're attacking this wonderful young woman because they're afraid to attack you and trying to prove you're a liberal."

Dole defended Burke mildly. He was quoted in *The Washington Post* as saying he didn't know why "my friends" were "out there attacking Sheila." He added, "I suppose next they'll be after my dog."

Scott Reed's best friend was Joe Gaylord, Gingrich's chief political adviser. The two had been trying to get Dole and Gingrich together for a long dinner for about a month.

The dinner was arranged for the evening of Monday, June 26, in Dole's office. Just Dole, Gingrich, Gaylord and Reed.

Dole was delayed on the Senate floor haggling with the Democratic leader, and he arrived about 15 minutes late.

"How do you deal with these guys?" Gingrich asked after Dole sat down and explained his lateness. "I talk to the president, the vice president, the chief of staff, the Secretary of State and the national security adviser." Gingrich explained that he let his number two, House Majority Leader Dick Armey, handle the floor business. "I don't worry one minute about what's going on on the floor," Gingrich stated.

"Well, yeah," Dole said, "I'm the Dick Armey of the Senate, I'm the majority leader." Not the Speaker, who by tradition didn't normally even vote and could stay in his office.

Gingrich wagged his head hard. He knew it was so much tougher in the Senate. He advised, he even lectured Dole a bit, on how he ran the House differently. He was getting it down to a system—his system.

Dole and Gingrich then sort of patted each other on the back about how well they were doing, transforming America. Both discounted the various news stories and rumors about how they really didn't like each other. *We* get on very well, Dole said.

"Okay, you're the nominee," Gingrich said in his self-assured manner. "You're the next president. How are we going to govern?" The smile on his face was broad. He had said it. The words were clear, but it was like many things he said. Dole took it only to mean that Gingrich could handle it if Dole became president, no more. It was also an acknowledgment that Dole was currently in a strong position, and again, no more. It was not an endorsement.

Gingrich said that all his guys thought Dole would win. "Look," the Speaker added, "short of you ending up in a hospital or some unforeseen reason, I'm not running." It was less than an absolute declaration. What did "unforeseen" mean? Gingrich didn't say, and no one asked.

Dole had Reed give an update on the presidential campaign. Rolling out the big numbers—140,000 individual contributors, $13 million raised, all the trips and endorsements—Reed tried to paint as impressive a picture of an irresistible force as possible without going overboard. Everyone at the table knew what he was doing, deterring Newt, and he didn't want to be stupid.

They turned to the fall legislative strategy and the rest of the year. Dole had set up a working group with Ken Duberstein, the former White House chief of staff in the last year of the Reagan administration, and various senior people who had worked with Reagan's chiefs of staff.

The express purpose was to examine how the Democratic Congress in the 1980s had caused the most problems for the Republican president on the 13 various appropriations bills each year. With this knowledge and a plan, Dole and Gingrich wanted to cause the most pain to Clinton. A lot had to do with the order in which the bills were handled and how the Senate and House could coordinate.

They hoped to take dead aim at Clinton, cause him problems wherever possible and make him look bad.

Dole and Reed emphasized that they needed to be in the loop on all the issues, decisions and plans.

"Whatever you want," Gingrich said.

After Gingrich and Gaylord left, Dole and Reed sat around, later joined by Sheila Burke.

Dole thought Gingrich was not a bad person. He was just undisciplined.

Reed felt that the meeting had been a good use of time. It was important among the conservative activists—Newt's base—that there be both a perception and the reality that Dole and Gingrich were working together.

14

Dick Morris continued trying to reshape Clinton's image. He was looking for occasions in which Clinton could show toughness in foreign affairs—another traditionally Republican strength. As Clinton was flying home from a Russian summit in early May, he had received a fax from Morris proposing a text for the president's Saturday radio address on May 13 on Japanese trade. Morris's draft stated bluntly that Japan would no longer get away with unfair trade practices and it threatened retaliation. Anthony Lake, the national security adviser, was shocked at Morris's inflammatory language. The tone was slightly chilling, almost suggesting that the United States had won the war 50 years ago and now would finish the job with trade. It would be wonderful, raw-meat rhetoric for auto worker voters in Michigan, but showed no understanding of U.S. relations with Japan, trade issues, the U.S. automobile industry or the subtleties of diplomacy. If Clinton were to give the speech, he would launch a full-scale trade war.

Clinton rejected the draft. This was one of Morris's bad ideas. In the radio address, Clinton said only that the United States was "hitting a brick wall" after 20 months of talks with the Japanese. The annual trade deficit with Japan was a record $66 billion, largely because of the closed auto market in Japan. "I am determined to open Japan's auto market," Clinton said in the bland address. "We don't want a trade conflict with Japan, but we won't hesitate to fight for a fair shake for American products."

But Morris didn't give up.

Before the Memorial Day weekend, Morris met with two of Clinton's speechwriters—Donald Baer, the chief White House speechwriter, and Bob Boorstin, the speechwriter on the National Security Council staff who had been with Clinton since the 1992 campaign.

Morris said that he wanted to use the president's Memorial Day speech at Arlington National Cemetery for a significant foreign policy statement. He began dictating to Boorstin an attack on state-sponsored terrorism, perpetuated by what he called the "rogue states" such as Iran, Iraq and Libya. In the post–Cold War era, the containment doctrine for holding off communism had to be turned on these terrorist states, Morris continued.

Boorstin dutifully started taking notes because Morris had indicated he wanted someone to take dictation.

Morris, speaking as the president, fired up the rhetoric, declaring that the terrorism of these states and their clandestine sponsorship of terrorism would no longer be tolerated. "We face no Hitler, no Stalin, but we do have enemies, enemies who share their contempt for human life and human dignity, and the rule of law.

"Our generation's enemies are the terrorists," Morris said. Terrorists kill children, the innocent and the peacemakers. "The threat to our security is not in an enemy silo but in the briefcase or the car bomb of a terrorist."

Morris had dictated almost non-stop for five to ten minutes in one of his legendary creative jags.

"I'm sorry," Boorstin said. "I can't do this." He had been around Clinton and his circle for four years. Management and policy making were often incredibly loose, but this was out of the question.

Morris looked at Boorstin with some dismay. "This is the kind of thing we have to do," Morris said. "Show we are strong."

Boorstin said the presidential speech on Memorial Day was traditionally a poem and a tribute to the war dead. The theme was sacrifice. "This is the wrong forum," Boorstin argued. It was a cemetery and the audience was almost exclusively military, always a difficult group for Clinton, who had not served in the military. Best to get in and out, make no waves.

This was precisely what was wrong with the communications operation in the White House, Morris said. Opportunities needed to be seized. No presidential speech should be routine. Going through the old, stale motions was no longer an effective communications strategy.

"I have no permission or instructions," Boorstin said. Tony Lake, the national security adviser, had said nothing about this. A new policy, if that was what it was, could not just be drafted by speechwriters.

Morris persisted.

In any event, Boorstin said, a saber-rattling speech that was so threatening could put Clinton in the position of not being able to follow up. It could turn out to be a problem in the 1996 campaign if there was a terrorist incident and Clinton's deeds were not able later to match these words. "I'm not going to do this," Boorstin said.

Morris consulted with Baer and Bill Curry, the presidential counselor who was Morris's representative in the White House. They agreed to stick to a Memorial Day poem. On Monday, May 29, Memorial Day, Clinton did not mention terrorism or rogue states. He instead referred to Normandy, Iwo Jima, Korea and Vietnam. "At this sacred moment," Clinton said, "we put aside all that might otherwise divide us to recall the honor that these men and women brought to their families and their communities and the glory they bestowed upon our beloved Nation."

The next morning at Panetta's 7:30 senior staff meeting, Lake, who was always turf-conscious, vehemently protested Morris's effort to turn Clinton into some menacing war dog. He noted the absurdity and the hazards of allowing political consultants to back-channel on sensitive foreign policy issues. Leon had to get control, please, Lake said. This was truly dangerous.

Panetta was still fighting Morris, who continued to be a shadowy master at circumvention. He increasingly found Morris abrasive and arrogant. Panetta again put out an APB—All Points Bulletin—directing that anyone on the White House staff should immediately report to him their sightings or dealings with Morris.

The next month Clinton was in San Francisco for an address at the 50th anniversary of the United Nations Charter. Morris sent the president a one-and-a-half-page fax with his previously rejected ideas on terrorism. At the last minute Clinton went over the fax with Lake, and inserted a couple of paragraphs in the speech.

"Today," Clinton said midway through the United Nations speech, "to be sure, we face no Hitler, no Stalin. . . . Our generation's enemies are the terrorists and their outlaw nation sponsors . . . the briefcase or the car bomb." He went no further, proposed no action, pledged no retaliation, and the remarks went largely unnoticed.

But for Morris, the back door still worked.

Clinton thought of himself as a deficit hawk, and could make a strong case for that belief. He had been elected in 1992 to fix the economy, and the very core of his economic plan—passed in his first year as president —had been a $500 billion reduction in the federal deficit over five years. Morris hounded Clinton on the subject of deficit politics, a central issue from both Ross Perot's and Clinton's campaigns in 1992, crucial to the Republican takeover of Congress in 1994 and now in the fore with Gingrich's latest goal of eliminating the annual federal deficit in seven years. Morris had polls showing its significance to voters. The deficit was basic to the overriding political questions of the day—the role of government and the well-being of future generations. The deficit had become an issue of values, even morals. Clinton had to have his own plan, Morris argued.

Clinton argued back that he didn't like the deficit. But he had not received sufficient credit for what he had already done on the deficit and the economy. Laminated cards had been printed up to highlight his achievements. "The Clinton Economic Record," a five- by seven-inch card, provided a side-by-side comparison of 15 key areas for measuring the state of the economy. The card compared the "Before" condition of what Clinton had inherited with "After 2½ Years." The annual deficit already had been cut nearly in half. Job growth, auto production, business investment and home sales were up, while the critical yardsticks that were supposed to be down were down: unemployment, federal employment, inflation and mortgage interest rates.

Christ, he had reduced the federal deficit three years in a row—the first time in more than 40 years! The back of the laminated card, "The Clinton Economic Record: The Best since. . . .

"*Deficit*: Coming down for 3 years in a row—first time since Truman was president.

"*Job Growth*: 7.1 million in just 30 months—better than any Republican Administration since Harding was president."

Another dozen figures were listed, including the so-called Misery Index, the combination of unemployment (5.7 percent) and inflation (2.7 percent), which was the "lowest since 1968."

Clinton was obsessed with the card, his press secretary Mike McCurry thought. Everybody in the White House and cabinet had to have one. McCurry had memorized it. The card was like a catechism to Clinton, the Apostles' Creed.

Clinton wanted to run on what he had done. "The things we set in motion in 1993," the president told his aides. "What I came here to Washington to do and started to get done here without a lot of help, without a lot of experience, without a lot of knowledge about how Washington works. What we started in motion in '93 was the right thing to do."

McCurry could see that as much as looking for a message for the 1996 election, Clinton was seeking validation of the direction and course he had set. He wanted self-validation. Had he got it right? Was he doing the right thing for the American people? Watching and listening to this, McCurry was reminded that the greatest politicians have all been fraught with a certain amount of insecurity.

But as he talked more and more about the past and his first-term record, Clinton saw that no amount of jawboning would get people to recite his laundry list of achievements or see it as an argument for his reelection. That's not what the presidency was about. "The presidency is about making an argument about where we go next," Clinton finally said.

Precisely, everyone from Morris to McCurry agreed. Morris focused on the budget, and urged that Clinton present his own balanced budget plan with a promise to eliminate the federal deficit at a date certain in the future to compete with the Republican seven-year plan. He needed one in order to compete for voter attention on the basic questions of government and the future.

Panetta was opposed. He said that Clinton could not move too quickly to balance the budget or he would upset the delicate balance among Democrats in Congress. Though Panetta was a deficit hawk, a balanced budget by a date certain would require cuts "too painful for our people," the chief of staff said. Make the Republicans pay and define what they would cut. It would be hard for them. Keep them out there. If Clinton proposed his own plan balancing the budget in ten or 12 years, the Republicans might just take him up on it. Get too close to the Republicans and they might embrace him and declare victory, Panetta said, throwing his arms out in a big bear hug, suggesting that Clinton might be swooped up.

Gore disagreed. He told Clinton that the administration would likely face a government shutdown in the fall because of the intensity of the philosophical disagreements with the Republicans and the likelihood of a massive miscalculation by Gingrich. "This is what is coming," Gore said, "and we have to prepare for it now. And when the crunch comes, we have to have a position that will be seen as reasonable. And we must, and our position must be, respectful of the opposition." The administration could not be in the position of opposing a balanced budget. "We can't go out and say to the American people, it's not important to balance the budget," Gore continued. That bridge had been crossed with the 1992 election when Clinton had promised to cut the deficit in half in four years. Their 1993 economic plan was basically a deficit reduction plan to do that. Perot was saying it. The Republicans were saying it. One broad theme was that the country had lost its capacity for self-discipline. Failure to balance the budget fell under that heading. Opposing would be untenable, put the administration on the wrong side. With a date-certain plan Clinton could then stand fast on principles that divided him from the Republicans.

Clinton was listening, nodding his head.

"We have to get right on the issue of balancing the budget," Gore said. They would get killed if the Republicans were able to present their program, saying, "We're just trying to balance the budget."

Clinton nodded again, indicating that he would think about it, but he did not say he agreed.

A very contentious debate followed among all of Clinton's major advisers.

Erskine Bowles felt strongly that a specific date-certain plan would show that Clinton was serious, fiscally responsible and prudent.

Earlier in the year, Clinton had submitted a budget calling for annual deficits in the range of $200 billion a year. That spring, Dole had decided to bring the Clinton plan to the Senate floor for a vote. It had been defeated 99 to 0. Even all the Democrats had voted against it, showing that such a plan had zero support even in the president's own party. Dole chortled that there could not be a more convincing demonstration that Clinton was way out of touch with the country, Republicans and Democrats.

The powerful repudiation stung Clinton. He told a radio interviewer in New Hampshire that he could balance the budget. "I think it can clearly be done in less than ten years. I think we can get there by a date certain."

Panetta, Stephanopoulos and Ickes went crazy. They knew that Gore and Morris had been pushing for this for weeks. Such a plan would cause too many cuts in Medicare for the elderly, Medicaid for the poor and education.

Four days later at a press conference, Clinton backtracked. "I believe that all Americans should be committed to bringing our budget into balance within a reasonable amount of time." Seven years would not be good policy, he said. "That would either require massive tax increases or massive budget cuts."

"What are you going to do?" asked a reporter. "What are you going to do, sir?"

"I'm going—well, for one thing, the Republicans have to resolve the differences between themselves," Clinton replied, and then ducked completely.

It was Morris's turn to be beside himself. The previous month Clinton had publicly declared, "The president is relevant." But now he was proving he was irrelevant. To be a player, a leader, Clinton needed his own plan, Morris insisted. He could not sit out on the sidelines.

Morris expanded his arguments to Clinton. First, balancing the budget was the right thing to do, government would be living within its means.

Clinton found this appealing. He had balanced his budget as Arkansas governor. He reviewed the 1992 campaign and his 1993 economic plan.

Second, Morris reminded the president that balancing the budget would be good for the economy and would reduce interest rates. Balancing the budget would be the single most reassuring thing he could do, Morris said. The action would ensure a robust economy all the way through 1996—key to reelection. Third, he said, it would preempt the most damaging attack on Clinton and congressional Democrats. For a decade the party had been labeled "tax and spend." Well, how in the hell could you be a tax and spend liberal if you balanced the budget?

Morris also presented the issue as having a Zen quality to it: There was no way to fight the particulars of a balanced budget, even someone else's, unless you embraced it.

Morris persisted. He just wouldn't give up until Clinton declared himself for a balanced budget at a time specific.

The Democratic leaders in Congress, Senate Minority Leader Tom Daschle and House Minority Leader Richard Gephardt, visited Clinton in the Oval Office and urged that he not proceed with his own balanced budget plan. Attacks on the Republicans for their plans to cut taxes for the rich in exchange for Medicare cuts for the elderly were just starting to take hold. Gore could see they were apoplectic.

• • •

On June 7 at 11:55 P.M., Clinton woke Senator Joe Lieberman out of a dead sleep. "Didn't wake you, did I?" Clinton asked.

No.

Clinton said he was considering a pledge to balance the budget at a date certain. What did Lieberman think?

Lieberman thought about the old Hebrew saying, Don't ask the rabbi a question unless you know the answer. Clinton seemed to be looking for fortification. Lieberman played his assigned role. He agreed strongly that it was very important, that it would take guts. Yes, Clinton should engage the Republicans on principle and national goals, with a balanced budget by a certain date. "The sooner the better," Lieberman said. "You don't have to present a full plan." It would make Clinton almost "sublime" while the Republicans were still out there arguing with each other about the details.

Lieberman considered Dick Morris's influence the best occurrence of the year in the Clinton White House. Morris was almost a New Democrat mole among the traditional liberals, and Lieberman thought his arrival an "act of God" to save the party.

Clinton decided he had to get on the playing field, and a speech was drafted. "We can't be the party of the deficit," he said. Gore personally called the four television networks requesting live coverage for five minutes at 9 P.M. on Tuesday, June 13.

"Tonight I present to the American people a plan for a balanced Federal budget," Clinton said. In a dozen long paragraphs, he said his plan was designed to help working people, avoid cuts in education, strengthen Medicare, save Medicaid, cut taxes for the middle class, cut welfare and protect the environment. "Balance the budget in ten years," he proposed. "Now mind you, we could do it in seven years, as congressional leaders propose. But the pain we'd inflict on our elderly, our students, and our economy just isn't worth it.

"But this debate must go beyond partisanship."

Clinton faced a virtual insurrection among Democrats. Many felt blindsided. Representative David Obey, the 26-year veteran Wisconsin Democrat, said, "I think most of us learned some time ago that if you don't like the president's position on a particular issue, you simply need to wait a few weeks."

The New York Post headlined the next day: "Bill Flips Again & Pushes For Balanced Budget."

• • •

Morris was exultant. He had broken the system. He had broken Panetta, and Ickes and Stephanopoulos. He figured now he could get control of the White House staff, place his people in key positions. Message and political strategy were not enough. He would now move on personnel.

Clinton would win in 1996, Morris said. The victory party would be publicized to the American people through paid advertising on television, he only half joked.

Stephanopoulos was beginning to think that if Morris didn't want to convert Clinton to a Republican, he at least intended to make him not a Democrat.

Mike McCurry was deeply worried about the Morris strategy. Taking all the Republican issues off the table sounded well and good, but if it worked the Republicans would be issueless. In that event they would surely fight with what remained. "They can only win by doing the single most dangerous thing for Clinton," McCurry said, "which is to totally destroy him as a human being." With the Whitewater investigation the Republicans were trying to destroy the First Lady, and next they would turn to the president. "They will do everything they can to turn him into a liar or turn him into a cheat or turn him into a philanderer. That basically is the danger here if you don't have a substantive grounds for debate. I despair of that more than anything."

On June 15, the Clintons went to Canada for the G-7 economic summit meeting. Hillary received an honorary degree from a women's university. It cited her work and leadership on health care reform. The Canadian citizens and doctors she met praised her, going on and on. They claimed to have read the 1,300-page health care reform bill and they said what she was trying to do was absolutely right. It was so discouraging for her to see that the Canadians understood she had been right, while it seemed nobody in the United States thought so.

The previous month Hillary had been in the Ukraine touring a hospital, and the minister of health had taken out a copy of her Health Security Act and asked her to autograph it. The plan was brilliant, the minister said. It diagnosed health care problems on an international level and he hoped she knew how useful it was in guiding the Ukrainians as they attempted to figure out how to rebuild their health care system.

Hillary burst out laughing, but the bitterness was evident. "You know," she remarked, "this is getting really embarrassing. I travel around the world, and this has happened to me dozens of times now, somebody from another country tells me that they've read it and analyzed it. More people have read it in the Ukraine probably than read it in the United States."

All this reminded her of a point her husband had made in his inaugural address, that nearly every problem had already been solved someplace but we didn't learn from each other.

Morris was determined to expand Clinton's communications strategy as much as possible. That meant not just focusing and redirecting his statements and actions as president. It meant political advertising on television. Too many other people—opponents, the media—were defining Clinton and his ideas. Clinton had to get out front and define himself in the most controlled and directed environment: the political ad. Going on television with ads would move poll numbers up, which in turn would allow Clinton to generate more money for his campaign. Morris wanted to attack the crime issue—another traditional Republican issue. Political advertising by a sitting president was a dicey undertaking, especially more than a year before the election and especially since he didn't have a primary challenger. Being too proactive so early could look like desperation. The advertising couldn't be half-assed in quality or scope. The project would require millions of dollars. Would the money be available?

On June 19, Terry McAuliffe invited his national finance board to Washington for a meeting at the Mayflower Hotel and a reception at the White House. More than one third of the 200 members had already shipped in or were about to deliver on their midyear quotas of $25,000, which was half of their $50,000 overall yearly goal. That added up to nearly $2 million. McAuliffe had already made almost a dozen trips to New Jersey, where in three days the first Clinton-Gore fund-raiser would amass well in excess of $1 million. Same for the next fund-raisers in Little Rock and Chicago—$1 million each. McAuliffe was traveling around the country to major fund-raising cities to meet with the top Democrats and local fund-raisers. "Folks," he said first, "we are coming to your city once. Now you're used to primaries where we come five, six, seven times. We're coming in once. It's the only event we're doing." He wanted the checkbooks open.

On Thursday, June 22, Clinton flew to New Jersey for the fund-raising dinner at the Garden State Convention Center. The place was jammed and about 300 people who had paid $1,000 a plate didn't initially have seats. Clinton was beaming, seeming joyous as he moved around to the VIP receptions for those who had sold a large number of tables. It was a security nightmare as the president moved around.

"Isn't this great!" Clinton said buoyantly. There was no draw like the president.

"I can't believe it," Ickes declared, surveying the turnout. It was a huge boost, and Clinton was even more pumped as he was introduced and took the podium just before 9 P.M.

He thanked McAuliffe and the fund-raising crew for their efforts, "So I can devote my energies to being President and to running in a responsible way."

He did not lay out the election as a contest between Democrats and Republicans. Instead, he said there were extremists in Congress. "There are people today in Washington who believe that the federal government is absolutely worthless except for national security." Presumably they were Republicans, but Clinton kept referring to them as "people today in Washington" who didn't want the government to protect the environment or who thought the answer to crime was to lock more people up for a longer time. At one point he said it was a battle between right and wrong. "You can have a decent humane budget and still balance it if you do it in *the right way,* not *the wrong way.* That's the difference between us!"

"Bring this country together," Clinton said. It had been one of Richard Nixon's campaign slogans in 1968.

The total take was $1.2 million.

Erskine Bowles was pleased by the big fund-raising push. It made business sense. "The best time to go fishing is when you can," he said. "The only better time is when they're biting."

The next day Clinton raised more than $1 million in Little Rock, Arkansas. McAuliffe would have more than $9 million raised by the end of June, a terrific first three-month fund-raising sprint. Now Morris had money to spend for television advertising. He had Bob Squier make a series of 30-second spots on Clinton's successful efforts to ban deadly assault weapons.

In one of the TV spots, an Ohio police officer who was wounded by an assault weapon comes on screen and says, "President Clinton is right. It's not about politics. It's about a ban on deadly assault weapons." Another ad began with a black and white film of police and citizens who were killed by assault weapons, shifts to color close-ups of assault weapons being loaded with ammunition. The announcer intones: "An officer.

Killed in the line of duty. A father. Gunned down at work. A student. Shot at school. A mother. Murdered in cold blood. Victims killed with deadly assault weapons. Bill Clinton did something no president has ever been able to accomplish. He passed and signed a tough law to ban deadly assault weapons."

Clinton himself appeared in another spot, saying, "Deadly assault weapons off our street. 100,000 more police on the streets. Expand the death penalty. That's how we'll protect America."

Morris checked on how much cash the new Clinton-Gore campaign had to spend. He pitched Clinton a proposal to spend $2.4 million to run the ads in 20-some major television markets in key electoral states for several weeks.

Bowles was opposed. Looking at the matter as a businessman he said that advertising was not effective so far ahead of the decision point, which in this case was nearly 18 months away. Such advertising would be too early and ultimately have no impact. Clinton would be able to utilize those resources better later on, he said.

Ickes put it more directly. "The biggest fucking waste of money," he said. Why? Who would remember? What could possibly be achieved? The ads would undermine the plan to keep Clinton looking presidential. "Money doesn't grow on trees." These were precious funds.

Clinton approved the expenditure.

The White House publicly and privately offered a number of explanations for the unprecedented advertising blitz. McCurry said the ads were not campaign spots but were to demonstrate how vital it was to preserve the assault weapons ban, which Bob Dole had promised to try to repeal. Though no legislation was pending, it was a kind of preemptive strike.

Dole thought the ads were directed at his promise to seek a repeal of the ban. "Oh, right at me," Dole said in his office. "No doubt about it," he added, laughing somewhat uneasily. "I picked up on it."

But the ads were central to the Morris triangulation strategy of repositioning Clinton. After the ads ran, he was claiming progress. "Moved him 10 points!" Morris said, referring to some in-market surveys where the ads had run. He compared these surveys with areas where the ads were not running, the so-called outmarket.

"What are you guys, nutty?" McAuliffe asked. He didn't believe they had spent so much money.

Neither did Ickes. He believed in it even less, and went nuts himself.

Stephanopoulos decided not to fight. "Total horseshit," he said. A temporary bump in the polls was possible with two weeks of solid ads in one state or region. Did it mean a damn thing? No. Affect Clinton's national ratings? No.

This was an education for them, Morris replied. Going on the air was generating better numbers, which would make it possible to generate more money, which in turn would pay for more ads. They would see.

On Friday night, June 30, Dole and Elizabeth went out to dinner and then had a rare evening at home in their Watergate apartment. They tuned in to the C-SPAN public affairs cable television coverage rerunning some early Senate floor debate. Dole had made six speeches on the floor on subjects ranging from the Fourth of July and somebody's retirement to Japanese trade talks and welfare reform. Then he argued on the floor with two of the most liberal Democrats, Senators Paul Wellstone and Carol Moseley-Braun.

"How can you do all these things?" Elizabeth asked. His life was so intense. He had to juggle so much.

"Well," Dole replied, "so far, so good. I think the first six months were the hardest."

The next afternoon, Saturday, July 1, I interviewed Dole in his Hart office for two and a half hours. Wearing casual khaki pants, a blue dress shirt with cufflinks, and purple Nike tennis shoes, he was very relaxed. I was again the last appointment of the weekend for him. After an hour and a half, he seemed to grow slightly tired. At the two-hour mark, I turned off the tape recorder for the last half hour and we just "visited," as he called it, off the record.

"We're trying to pace ourselves," he said during the taped interview, his voice and demeanor suggesting some ambivalence about the reduced schedule. "It's like today I'm not traveling, which is hard to believe. Tomorrow we go to Iowa, get back at 1 A.M. We're off all day Monday." That was July 4th. "Then we go to New Hampshire," he said with relief in his voice and apparently in pleasant anticipation.

On the early theme of his campaign, Dole said, "I didn't want to be in a contest with Phil Gramm on who was the, quote, 'most conservative.' I'm mainstream." Dole said he didn't think he had to shout the loudest, and expressed disdain for Gramm's "take no prisoners" style.

Yes, he was still working on his message, even after all these efforts to win the Republican nomination, the 35 years in Congress. The speeches that Mari Will prepared had to make sense to him, he said. "You just can't read something that somebody's written and say, 'Oh, boy, this is dynamite.' You've got to have a feel for it and you've got to think, Jimminy, this might work. And this is the message. And I think we're still testing it, and I think you can't say that if I said this on day one, it's going to be written in stone forever."

I said that I didn't think his message was clearly defined yet. "There's something people are waiting for somebody to say that no one has said yet."

"Right," Dole answered. "I think you're right." He volunteered no new possibilities.

His strategy, he said, was to keep running the campaign the way it was. "As long as we're on target, on message, and got money in the bank, and people are signing up, we're mostly doing the right thing," he said, adding wistfully, "But I also have been around long enough to know that somebody can make a mistake and it'll be all over, too."

Dole made one key point about the divided roles of managing the Senate and running for president. He realized he couldn't be a presidential candidate first and the majority leader second. The 54 Republican egos in the Senate would not hear of it. He first had to be majority leader, trying to direct legislative business and his Republican colleagues. Only then could he be the presidential candidate. The Senate was hard, he acknowledged. "Somebody has to manage it. And it may not be manageable. It isn't, you know, it's a frustrating place sometimes but generally it works out."

Though Dole seemed a little tired, he seemed to be in no hurry. I was not out of questions but I too was growing tired, and it seemed time to stand up and thank him.

At the end, Dole handed me a copy of "Ten Laws for Winning Presidential Elections" by Gerald F. Lameiro. He said someone had just given it to him. Dole was pretty excited about it and had a staffer making photocopies this Saturday afternoon of the Fourth of July weekend. The laws tried to reduce winning to a formula, noting the importance of optimism, economic prosperity, consistency, and a campaign built around an offense. Law number seven was the "Law of the Dominant Issue. There is usually one dominant issue in each election campaign."

As I read it over later, I realized that neither Dole nor anyone in his campaign yet knew what that dominant issue might be. I certainly didn't. What was going to drive the campaign?

• • •

The morning of Thursday, July 6, Clinton called Dick Morris from the car as he was on his way over to Georgetown University.

"Watch this speech," Clinton said. He wanted to make sure that both Morris and Stephanopoulos tuned in to a speech he was giving called "Responsible Citizenship and the American Community." Nearly everyone on the White House staff, including Morris, had not wanted Clinton to give the speech, but Clinton had insisted.

So the two aides went over to Bill Curry's office in the Old Executive Office Building to watch the address.

"Today I want to have more of a conversation than deliver a formal speech," Clinton said, but then lectured for nearly an hour on the need for "common ground," a favorite theme that he had used before.

"I've got it!" Morris yelled, almost jumping out of his chair midway through the speech. "What's happening here is the president has to go give a speech to the whole country to get us to listen to him."

Stephanopoulos was astounded by Morris's comment. It was so self-centered, almost megalomaniac.

Don't you get it? Morris asked. Clinton was talking to them the only way he could. He did not want a sampling of a little from the left, a little from the right, a little Republican or a little Democrat. He was talking about a true dialectic—taking the thesis and the antithesis and achieving a genuine synthesis. Something new and above. He wanted them to agree, work it out. "Common ground."

Stephanopoulos knew that Clinton's efforts to get on course were always painful exercises to watch. And Morris was the latest instrument of his course correction, the most painful one Stephanopoulos could imagine. Morris often talked gibberish. Morris was small, Stephanopoulos concluded, no big-league strategist.

Morris and Curry for their part felt that the White House staff, embodied by Stephanopoulos and Panetta, and by Harold Ickes most of all, had perfected the art of passive resistance to new ideas, even Clinton's. They just talked, debated and raised questions. They didn't need to provide answers or a strategic direction. They just played to Clinton's penchant for the fullest consideration of all alternatives, and won delay.

Later, when negative stories about Morris began appearing more and more in the media, Morris and Curry began to refer privately to Ickes's operation as a "thugocracy," because they felt he was trying to intimidate them both politically and personally.

. . .

On Friday, July 14, at 2 P.M., Bill Lacy and pollster Neil Newhouse went to Dole's Majority Leader's Office to report on the latest survey.

Dole was favored by 52 percent of the Republicans, the new poll showed, the first time he had been above 50 percent. More important, 22 percent of the Republicans said they were definitely for him. By comparison, Lacy said, George Bush did not reach 22 percent definite support until January 1988, a month before the Iowa caucuses that year. So in this sense, Dole's position was six months ahead of Bush's. The best news was that Dole's support among Republicans who identified themselves as conservatives had risen above 40 percent. Phil Gramm had dropped into the abyss. Dole's anti-tax pledge and the Hollywood attack had paid off, Lacy said.

Looks pretty good, Dole said. He latched onto the big bump among conservatives. Hollywood sure was an attention getter. What do we do next? he inquired.

Number one, Lacy said, most important of all we keep staying on our message. Number two, we come back and tap this entertainment industry theme from time to time without overdwelling on it. Number three, prepare for a big economic speech in September, which Dole had just agreed to do. They needed to come up with something for working people, to show the middle class how a Dole administration would make their lives better and allow them to keep more of their paychecks.

Most immediately, Lacy had been arguing that it was time for Dole to take Clinton head-on, and Mari Will had prepared such an approach for Dole's upcoming speech at the Republican National Committee meeting in Philadelphia the next day.

But Dole was resisting, telling Will that he didn't want to give any scripted speech to the Republican Committee. "I know these people," Dole said. "I've been working with them." Over the decades he said he had accumulated knowledge about their lives, their families, where they worked. He had been Republican Party chairman 25 years earlier when Nixon was president, and there were two or three good old souls still on the committee from those days. "I've always felt sort of a family relationship," Dole said. That was his crowd. "Those ought to be Bob Dole supporters." He wanted to set himself apart from the rest of the pack of presidential candidates. "It will be insulting to them for me to read just a political speech."

Will understood what he was striving for—a personal connection, the campaign trail of small-town Kansas. She thought Dole wanted to be like Reagan, get up and say, just let me talk to you, push the scripted speech aside. Dole wanted to sound more sincere than a political speech.

Will had gone on vacation and some of her assistants had written the draft attacking Clinton. Often Dole felt that when he indicated he wanted things taken out of a speech, they would send back to him the same stuff thinking he would forget about it in the next draft. So he watched closely, reading each draft very carefully, noting when his deletions had been restored.

"Not much new and exciting in it," he scribbled on the draft.

Next, Lacy and the speechwriters made three little changes and sent it back saying they had dealt with his input.

This time they had made his cuts but it was still dull, Dole felt. "This is the same," he wrote back.

A few more changes were made in the next draft. Lacy argued that it was worth playing tug-of-war with Dole on this. Let's stick to our guns and not make lots of changes.

"This is the same speech you sent me before with minor changes," Dole wrote back.

Of course, that was the point, Lacy felt. That was the speech they wanted him to give.

Dole finally signed off on the speech. Scott Reed decided to go up to Philadelphia with him July 15. On the plane Dole clearly still wasn't happy with the speech.

"It's too boring," Dole said. "It's boring." Reed said he thought it was an important red-meat speech that reporters would like because a good, sharp attack on the sitting president by the opposition front-runner would get lots of play on television and in the newspapers.

Nelson Warfield was one of the assigned blockers for the occasion, supposed to keep people, especially old Dole friends and advisers, away from the candidate as he moved about before his speech. But as Dole walked through a public hallway, a senior Dole campaign deputy from 1988 approached him. There was no way to keep this old friend away. He reported that Phil Gramm had just really gone after Dole in his remarks to the meeting, saying that tough welfare reform should not "perish on the ramparts of compromise and status quo and deal-cutting in Washington." Gramm's words were directed squarely at Dole. Respond, the former deputy said, invoke Reagan and Dole's own service to Reagan.

This threw Dole off. He went out and did another one of his off-the-cuff Jay Leno routines, neglecting the prepared speech. At one point he referred to the Republican gains the previous year, saying, "It all started in 1944." He corrected himself, saying, "1994," but the slip underscored that he was World War II vintage.

Reed was appalled. Dole was stepping all over himself.

Dole told the party leaders that he understood the yearning for another Ronald Reagan. "Well, I am willing to be another Ronald Reagan. If that's what you want, I'll be another Ronald Reagan," he said. The remark came out sounding like he would pander to the majority no matter what. Party leaders and delegates ridiculed him. Grover Norquist, author of the anti-tax pledge that Dole had signed, really stuck it in, saying publicly that Dole would dress up in a clown suit if that pleased the most people.

Warfield realized he had failed as a blocker. He also saw that Dole didn't deal with abstract suggestions very well such as the one about invoking Reagan. He needed more direct suggestions or there was no telling what would come out.

On the plane back, it was mostly happy talk. Reed and Warfield didn't realize the magnitude of the Reagan line until they saw it in the newspapers the next day. Reed had spent most of his time walking around with Dole instead of trying to guide reporters.

The New York Times ran a front-page story about Gramm and Dole fighting over welfare reform, with Gramm pushing the more conservative ideas such as cutting off payments to unwed teenage mothers.

Charlie Black, Gramm's chief strategist, called Reed on Monday morning laughing.

"You took our bait!" Black chided.

Never again, Reed vowed to himself.

That line, "If that's what you want, I'll be another Ronald Reagan," haunted Dole as much as any.

No matter how Warfield and the others in the Dole campaign tried to spin what Dole had said, their sale sounded a little ridiculous and not many reporters bought it. Warfield figured the political reporters for *The New York Times* had Dole's line programmed into their computers and with the stroke of a single key the quote would be inserted into their stories on Dole. "It pops up all the goddamn time," Warfield complained.

In an interview later, Dole said, "Well, I felt a little later on I could have gone back and cleaned it up, and I didn't. I sort of left it hanging out there. What I wanted to tell those people who are all great Reagan fans was that I'd worked with Reagan, we'd cut taxes together, and he had made a [positive] statement about my leadership, that he sort of started the revolution. Probably should have said it that way."

But Dole had another problem with making an unbridled attack on Clinton such as the one in the speech Will had prepared. Some very important matters that went beyond the value of one political speech were yet to be worked out with the administration—welfare reform, the budget and Bosnia.

15

The Dole campaign had decided to release all of Dole's medical records and a summary history of his health going back to World War II. Dole wasn't wild about the idea and resisted. But Lacy, Reed, and Nelson Warfield argued that it had to be done. Dole had to get out in front of the age question by showing he was in excellent health. They decided to release all the records the day before July 22, when Dole would turn 72. The birthday stories or references were inevitable. This way they would be combined with the excellent health stories.

"Where's the draft of the health records?" Reed asked just days before the scheduled release. "I want to read 'em, I want to read 'em, I want to read 'em." When he read them, Reed realized it was doctors' work, and the headline would be in effect, "Dole's Health Problems." The World War II injuries, previous elevated cholesterol levels, the 1991 prostate cancer, mild hearing loss, color blindness and the latest shoulder injury all added up.

Nelson Warfield went to see Dr. John Eisold, the Attending Physician of Congress, who had compiled Dole's records. As Dole's personal physician, Eisold wanted just to issue a one-sentence statement about Dole's excellent health.

Warfield said that the plan was to release all the details, leave nothing undisclosed. As they went over the records, Warfield had to fight to include each previous treatment and medication. What phone number do you want us to give out to the media so you can take questions? Warfield finally asked.

Well, I can't take questions, Eisold replied. Why can't the records speak for themselves?

The plan, Warfield said, was not only to be comprehensive but authoritative, and there were words and medical terms that no reporter could understand.

Eisold asked, Why couldn't he brief Warfield so he could answer the questions?

Even the credibility of a paid doctor would be questioned, Warfield said, but the candidate's press secretary would have close to no credibility on such matters.

Eisold called in his assistant. "You have to understand that Dr. Eisold is bound by the Hippocratic Oath that ensures confidentiality," the assistant said.

Warfield promised a signed, notarized statement from Dole waiving confidentiality within ten minutes, but Eisold would not give in. Finally Dr. Charles Peck of Walter Reed, who had treated Dole for ten years, agreed to be available to answer media questions.

Warfield took the records. Nothing was left out or changed, but a new emphasis was made. The press release declared: "Doctors Find GOP Frontrunner in 'Excellent Health.' " The details were put in chronological order so someone would have to wade through Bob Dole World War II survivor before getting to Bob Dole prostate cancer survivor.

In fact by all measurable tests, Dole was in remarkable health. There was no sign of the cancer returning and his heart was good. The average male Dole's age could be expected to live another 11 years. All this was summed up in nine pages of records.

Warfield suggested that since Dole got on the treadmill at his home to exercise regularly, they ought to accompany the story of his good health by letting some photographer in exclusively to photograph Dole exercising.

"Whatever you do," Mari Will told Warfield, "get him out of that outfit he was wearing on *60 Minutes*." A 1993 profile on *60 Minutes* of Dole had led off with video of Dole strutting out on his treadmill wearing a long-sleeve dress shirt and shorts that resembled boxer underwear. He had looked out of touch and grandfatherly.

Warfield and Mike Glassner went to Hecht's, a downtown Washington department store, and found the perfect running jacket and shorts for Dole to wear.

Reed and Warfield had opted to give the exclusive photo and the records to *USA Today,* which had guaranteed front-page coverage. Reed knew the popular paper with the shortest stories had the shallowest writers—just right for the positive visual they sought. A *USA Today* photographer was scheduled to meet Dole for the treadmill picture at his Watergate apartment.

"Senator," Warfield said, "we're going to have some clothes there for you for the photo shoot we're doing tomorrow. And Mari really recommends that you wear 'em."

"Might have something that works on my own," Dole replied.

Oh, shit, Warfield thought.

When Warfield arrived, Dole was dressed in a long blue dress shirt. With cufflinks! And his Tommy Hilfiger shorts. Purple Nikes and white socks. Initially, Warfield wimped out, said nothing, and walked out to let the photographer get the picture. Then Warfield felt no, he couldn't, he owed it to the man at least to say something. So he went back in.

"Senator, this is embarrassing for me to tell you this but I've got to tell you that if you pose on the treadmill in this outfit, some people are going to think that you're standing there in your underwear."

"Whaaaat!" Dole grunted, snapping and effectively flicking Warfield away. "This'll be fine."

Warfield went to the campaign photographer who was also there and asked a big favor. "When you go in there, tell me if he looks like he's in his underwear when he's on the treadmill. If he does, I'm going to do something to cancel the photo shoot."

"Naw, he looks fine," the campaign photographer reported.

The picture was taken.

Warfield told Lacy about the photo.

"Oh, shit," Lacy said, "this is going to be awful. Awful."

Warfield later realized that Dole resisted in part because he couldn't zip up the running jacket, and he wore a pad under his white T-shirt to give equal thickness, size and balance to his withered right shoulder.

Dole continued to question the decision to release his medical records right up until the end.

"You're 72," Reed said forcefully, "we got to do something about this."

The records were released Friday, July 21.

Dr. Peck came in to answer reporters' questions all day.

Time magazine—the flagship publication of Time Warner, which Dole criticized by name in his Hollywood speech—wanted to do a major story about Dole, his age and his health. Dole gave them an interview. On his Saturday birthday, Reed called. "Looks like you're going to be on the cover," he told Dole. Reed realized that *Time* was going to stick it to them.

On Sunday night, Dole received an early edition of the magazine. He was on the *Time* cover. Thank God, Reed thought, it was just a headshot with Dole in a suit and tie, not the underwear shot which ran inside. In the cover photo, Dole looked a little pasty.

"Is Dole Too Old For the Job?" the headline read. "The G.O.P. presidential front runner says he's 72 years young, but the age issue won't fade away." To the poll question of whether Dole was too old to run for president in 1996, only 14 percent said yes, and 75 percent said no.

The campaign had let it all hang out and there were no secrets to uncover and no real unanswered questions. Within 24 hours, Dole was joking, "I went after Time Warner and they put me on the cover."

"I'm now a full-disclosure kind of guy on everything," Reed said.

There were some jokes about the treadmill picture, but it wasn't a problem. How else would anyone expect Dole to appear? He was being himself. The dress shirt, cufflinks and shorts were in character.

Some of the senators on Dole's steering committee were still on Dole about letting himself get run-down, attending all these receptions around town, bouncing around all evening from event to event. Some, including D'Amato, complained to Reed. But then D'Amato said once, "By the way, Scott, can you get him to stop by . . . ?"

Reed finally decided that attempting to micromanage Dole's day was not the best use of his own time. It wouldn't work anyway. So Reed tried to focus on the period from about 2 P.M. on Friday when the Senate adjourned until about noon on Monday when it reconvened. He could make the weekend campaign trips smooth and avoid the rest.

At the end of July, both Dole and Clinton were to speak at a Governors' meeting. Dole wanted to give a welfare speech. That was the issue that mattered to the governors, he thought. He was on their turf, and should speak to their issue. Clinton was also speaking the same day on welfare. It would show Dole if a deal with Clinton was possible.

How can we do Dole versus Clinton when basically we are in agreement with Clinton on welfare reform? Mari Will asked. She worried that Clinton might just agree with Dole. The feud on welfare was within the Republican Party; Gramm had the more conservative position, and from what she was reading, Gramm was winning the battle. The whole campaign strategy was not to allow Gramm room on the right, or they would be handing Gramm a win, Will felt.

After both had given their speeches, the news coverage highlighted the points of agreement between Clinton and Dole. ABC Television's Brit Hume noted, "What separates the president and the senator on this issue is not so much the issue, they both want to give the states more control, but they both want to be seen as the leader on it—and they both want the same job."

Clinton had made no more overtures to Dole about a deal on welfare reform, and so Dole let it rest for the moment, but the ingredients of an agreement seemed to be there.

In late July, Dole had introduced his own anti-affirmative action legislation to end any "preferential treatment" on federal contracts or employment for minorities and women. He said that such programs, designed as temporary remedies, had become permanent and amounted to a "ridiculous pretense of quota tokenism."

At the next Tuesday morning steering committee meeting for the pro-Dole senators, Scott Reed said he thought the unveiling of the affirmative action proposal had worked out well. It wasn't a front-page story in the newspapers, and they didn't want it to be. But Dole had put a marker down, and no one, including Pete Wilson who was aggressively pushing to end affirmative action in California, was going to get to the right of Dole on the subject, Reed explained to the senators.

"That's fucking bullshit!" D'Amato erupted. "It's outrageous." Raising his voice and turning red, he lectured Reed and Lacy that opposing affirmative action would hurt Dole politically. "You're going to lose this election! You may have cost Bob Dole this election. I cannot believe you guys are giving him this advice and getting him to do this."

"Are you letting your speechwriter, that Mari Will woman, drive the issues and the intellectual side of this campaign?" D'Amato shouted. Mari and her husband, conservative columnist George Will, strongly opposed affirmative action. They were running the campaign, D'Amato charged. "If you're doing that, you're crazy!"

"That's just not true," Reed replied, exercising maximum discipline, biting his tongue. "Mari didn't write that speech, Mari didn't have anything to do with it." The matter had been handled out of the leader's office.

D'Amato would not let it go and continued his tirade, a ballistic harangue. He was nearly out of control. More than half a dozen other Republican senators sat in silence—some apparently appalled, some amused, most amazed.

"I think we disagree on this," Reed finally said when the D'Amato storm abated. "Why don't we talk about this later." Half of Reed wanted to fight the condescending lecture, but the other half knew having an outright fight with D'Amato would amount to an automatic loss. More than 200 years of protocol made a direct confrontation by a staff man impossible and foolish.

Right after the meeting when the senators had left, Dole wandered in, making his usual late appearance. Lacy and Kieran Mahoney, a D'Amato aide, explained to Dole that they had just witnessed one of D'Amato's crazy episodes.

Dole registered little reaction.

Bill Lacy was furious. D'Amato had not erupted because of a philosophical difference. Lacy had never seen D'Amato talk philosophy. It was about politics—that the position might hurt Dole. Lacy turned to Mahoney. "I had the courage to take him on because I'm not scared, but I didn't do it because I was afraid he would have considered that a direct frontal challenge to him, and it would have made things worse. Did I make the wrong decision?"

No, Mahoney said. "Alfonse is a rational person most of the time, but when he is irrational, you do not go head to head with him."

D'Amato called Reed that afternoon. Reed waited until the next day to call back, and D'Amato apologized.

"I respect you," Reed replied, "you're a senator, but you can't talk to me like that again in front of all these people." His anger getting the better of him, Reed had his own eruption. "If you ever do, I'm going to tell you to fuck off right in front of everybody else."

"Oh, Scotty . . . ," D'Amato said. He liked personal nicknames, even calling Dole "Dolie" at times.

"You've been hanging around with Claudia at the Hamptons too long," Reed continued. Claudia Cohen was D'Amato's new girlfriend, the millionaire ex-wife of Revlon heir Ronald Perlman, and the Hamptons were the posh summer resort communities where she summered on Long Island in D'Amato's state of New York. Reed really let loose. D'Amato had logged too much time with the chablis crowd, lost touch with reality.

"We've been talking about affirmative action for three months," Reed reminded the senator. "You were in on the early talks with Dennis Shea [a senior Dole aide] who's from New York, who wrote the whole plan. We've been talking about it at every one of these breakfasts. Every one of 'em. You don't listen."

"Uh, ah, Scotty. . . ." D'Amato wanted to make up.

They agreed to be friends.

Clinton's 1992 campaign theme, "It's the economy, stupid," had been critical to his victory. The economic stewardship role of a president was central, and Scott Reed suggested to Dole that he ought to speak out and develop his own economic plan. Dole agreed that Reed should set up working groups to examine the alternatives.

Dole and Gingrich had months earlier appointed a tax commission headed by Jack Kemp. Technically, the commission was going to make an independent recommendation that would amount to a tax and economic plan. But Reed wanted to tell them how to do it based on his own work, steer it to politically acceptable ground.

Reed, like Kemp, favored some form of a flat income tax rate of about 20 percent. Some deductions, like the popular home mortgage deduction, would have to stay. But Reed was determined to make Dole king of the flat tax. It would be politically very potent, Reed believed.

"I think it's the whole campaign," Reed had said on Capitol Hill as he was making the rounds. "If we pull that off as well as we can, I think we're pretty much securely on the offense."

In early August, Dole met with Reed, Lacy and Mari Will. At the meeting Reed and Will went over the arguments for the flat tax. It would be fair, everyone paying the same rate, everyone treated the same. They had a chart showing the impact on people of various income levels.

"How can you call it fair," Dole snapped and suddenly spun around in his chair, "when these rich people, these fat cats get the big tax break?"

Reagan and lots of other conservatives had looked at the flat tax and rejected it. People making $400,000, $500,000 or $600,000 a year would get a giant tax cut, paying the same low rate as the working person, Dole said. One of his wealthy contributors had sent him an article showing the tax rates and said in a little note, "Bob, this tax would be great for me but it would kill the Republican Party."

That was enough for Will. She realized immediately that Dole would not be proposing a flat tax.

As the meeting proceeded, Dole complained about a lot of other things. It was almost as if he had a list of what was bothering him.

"Iowa doesn't feel right," Dole said. His instincts told him something was wrong.

"Senator, wait a minute," Will interrupted. Back in 1988 they used to call Iowa their Magic Kingdom, flying in there in the little planes, all the other states turning sour, but Iowa had felt great, was great. "Iowa doesn't feel right?" she repeated incredulously.

"Yeah," Dole said, turning to her and saying with unusual intensity, "it doesn't feel right, and when I'm on the plane with Tom, he doesn't tell me anything. I have to pull things out of him, I have to ask him 20 questions. I don't hear anything from Tom."

Will was stunned. She knew that in 1988 Tom Synhorst had been into all the details, not just the time of day but how the watch was made, and knew all the organizers, even their family troubles. Tom was like the town gossip for an entire state, Tom was Iowa, Tom had made it the Magic Kingdom. But Will knew that Synhorst's reticence with Dole had more meaning. Not talking was the code among campaign people when they didn't have good news.

After the meeting, Will called Synhorst. A big straw poll among Republicans in Ames, Iowa, was just two weeks off. Anyone with a $25 ticket who showed up could vote, even from out of state.

"We're having trouble," Synhorst said. "That's right, it is a problem. We're having trouble getting people to say they're going to come. It's not the same."

Will knew there was always a tendency to run the last campaign, and eight years was a long time. Things had changed, but there was more to it.

Dole talked to Synhorst. All the other Republicans, particularly Gramm and Buchanan, were out in Iowa beating up on Dole all the time, every single day, "And we're not anywhere to be seen," Synhorst said. Do some call-in talk radio shows, he suggested, and other media interviews.

"I'm not going to do that," Dole said. "All I'm going to get is questions from Gramm people that, you know, the trash that they've been laying out there."

It had happened to other candidates, Synhorst reminded Dole. Like in 1980 when Reagan had been the target of all the attacks, and Reagan had lost the state.

"I'm just not going to do it," Dole said. "You find somebody else to do it." He suggested getting surrogates to come in and speak for him.

"I've just got to spend time in these other states," Dole said. "We should be able to win Iowa without me spending a lot of time there."

Synhorst said they would win.

Dole thought to himself, "Well, God, he did it in 1988, he's the best in the business."

The week of August 7, Warren Rudman called Dole. He had just appeared as a surrogate for Dole at a giant successful fund-raiser in New England.

"Look, Bob," Rudman said, "I'm traveling all over this country, and I'm talking to a lot of people who are your friends, people who want to be for you and generally are for you. But I've got to tell you, Bob, they're getting nervous." Rudman said that the rightward tilt in the campaign had gone too far.

"I've got to deal with Gramm," Dole replied.

"I know the strategy has been to make sure that Gramm gets too far to the right," Rudman said. Dole's tilt was designed not just to pick up conservative votes but to push Gramm to the fringe. "At some point if Phil wants to walk off the plank and fall off the plank to the right, I don't want you following him over."

Dole said he agreed, but the campaign staff had been very concerned about the Christian Coalition. "They're our constituencies," Dole said.

"Bob," Rudman said, "you've gone as far to the right as you have to go. This is Warren Rudman talking."

"You mean The Oracle," Dole teased, using his nickname for Rudman.

"I'll take that," Rudman replied. "That's better than most people get." He turned to the general election. "I don't care what you want to say about Bill Clinton, he is one of the smartest campaigners . . ."

"You're absolutely right," Dole interrupted. "He's terrific."

"I don't care if he only got 43 percent of the vote," Rudman continued. "I don't care if every expert in the world goes on CNN and says it's impossible for him to win the election. I want to tell you, Bob, it is possible. And the way he will win this election is for the Republican Party to scare the American people that they have got a rightward bent to them that is really far greater than the American people would accept." Rudman said he was now convinced that the 1994 election was the revolution that wasn't. People were not voting for each part of Newt's Contract With America. They were voting against Clinton. But basically the public was never comfortable with rapid change, and the Contract was too much, too fast.

Dole said he agreed about the 1994 election. "It was a referendum on Clinton," he said.

"Let's take affirmative action," Rudman continued in his quick, intense northeastern accent. "Bob, I don't disagree with some of the things you're saying." Some of the programs did need to be reviewed, but Dole's harsh language about "tokenism" was too much. It sounded like Dole was totally against affirmative action like some of the others, that Dole was saying minorities have made it in America and they don't need any more help. "You don't believe that, you don't believe that for a minute," Rudman said, knowing that part of Dole's core was with the disadvantaged. "Bob, you haven't vacated your basic civil rights beliefs, but people think that!"

"I've got to talk more clearly about it," Dole agreed.

Rudman said that Dole was getting off the charts, departing too much from his own record on equality and the notion of assisting the disadvantaged. "I want to tell you so you'll understand," Rudman added, "and nobody has to listen to my advice, but the nice thing about my advice is it's free, it doesn't cost you anything, and you're free to disregard it."

Rudman said he was telling Scott Reed and the Dole campaign staff to moderate a bit. "Nixon gave this great advice," Rudman said, "that for the primary you run to the right and then you run back to the center for the general. That would be fine if the primary were in Tahiti! But it's not."

Dole laughed hard.

Ross Perot was holding his United We Stand America (UWSA) Convention in Dallas where all the Republican candidates had agreed to speak. Perot's 19 percent of the vote in 1992 was a powerful enticement and no one wanted to offend him or his supporters. Politically, Dole had no choice but to attend. Lacy had concluded, based on his survey research, that if Perot ran he would make Clinton viable. Because of the electoral college with a solid Republican South, Clinton was not viable as long as Perot or a strong independent stayed out of the race. Clinton's chances of beating a Republican such as Dole head to head in the electoral college were the equivalent of drawing an inside straight in poker—less than a 10 percent chance, Lacy felt at this point.

Mari Will regarded the Perot event as something Dole had to get through. Dole was the bête noire of the Perot voters—everything they couldn't stand, the eternal, old Washington hand in the old Washington system of politics as usual.

Dole received the first draft of a proposed speech for the Perot event. It leaned heavily on old themes but included a new pledge to end taxpayer financing of the national political conventions held by both parties—a very popular idea in Dole's private polls. Surely that was something that would appeal to independents, Reed thought.

"It's a zero," Dole scribbled across the speech, "the kind of speech that will bomb with this audience." He also took the unusual step of directly calling the brainy young speechwriter who had drafted it but had never met Dole personally.

It's a lousy speech, Dole growled.

Mari Will undertook a rewrite. There was much back and forth. It was the last week of the Senate's legislative session, and Dole wouldn't give his approval to the speech.

Perot was calling Reed almost every day complaining that Dole was going to keep the Senate in session through Friday, August 11. That was the day his convention was supposed to start, and a number of other senators were supposed to speak. Reed considered Perot a total flake and untrustworthy. In 1994, when Reed had been executive director of the Republican National Committee, Reed felt that Perot had lied to him several times.

About 5 P.M. Thursday, Reed told Perot not to worry about the Senate. There were no votes scheduled for the next day and everybody would be able to get to Dallas. But later the Democrats tacked on amendments to a bill, and Dole decided the Senate had to stay for a Friday session.

"You're screwing me!" Perot yelled, reaching Reed at home 10:30 P.M. Thursday. "I can't believe you're doing this, you're deliberately sabotaging my weekend!"

Reed tried to explain the reason for Dole's decision. But Perot was out of control. It was like his off-the-wall allegations in 1992 that dirty tricksters were planning to sabotage his daughter's wedding. Perot was acting as if he thought everything that happened was directed at him. He was the center of the universe. It was frightening, Reed thought.

When *Newsweek* had quoted a Dole adviser calling Perot "a borderline lunatic" earlier in August, Reed figured he had better call Perot and assure him that none of the senior people had made the remark. When Perot called back, he flew into an absolute rage.

Reed and Lacy conferred, agreeing that neither had been responsible for the quote, though it perfectly reflected their opinion.

On Friday, Reed flew down to Dallas and late in the afternoon he called Dole, who had not yet left for Dallas, and had still not approved the speech. Dole wanted to make news every time he spoke.

"Please read the speech," Reed said in one last pitch. "Just give the speech." A favorable national poll was coming out. "All the press guys are talking about it," Reed said. "Let's get in and out."

On Saturday, Pat Buchanan gave a passionate, rousing America-first speech that was interrupted by standing ovations.

It was finally Dole's turn to speak to the thousands in the large arena.

"I've been watching on television," Dole began. "I think I watched a couple of hours last evening, and heard a number of good speeches. I took a little of each, put them together, and here I am."

Mild laughter. Mari Will thought it was precisely the wrong beginning—Dole as an amalgam, a vague sprinkling of all the others.

Dole departed from the text, dipping in and out of it at random. He mentioned how many Democrats were his friends, and he said the federal government did a lot of good things. He promised a vote on term limits, tried a joke about his age, and said no one cared about foreign policy but him. "You may not find perfection," he ad-libbed at the end. "You want somebody who has been tested and tested on the crucibles? Then take a look at Bob Dole." It was as if he were asking them to test-drive a used car.

Will watched him straining to connect with the audience. All his muscles were tight trying to reach them, and say, Hey, I'm a good guy, I'm not like that, I'm not what you think I am. She could see him glancing at the text once in a while. There was no way to diagram the speech, no beginning, middle or end. His sentences didn't really work. He was trying to take the force of his personality and project it, burning his eyeballs into them. She almost ached for him.

On Sunday, August 13, *The New York Times* ran a front-page story headlined "Dole Defending Middle Ground In G.O.P. Race." In an interview Dole had explained that he was not Gingrich or Phil Gramm. Dole, adopting Rudman's recommendation, said he was not an "in-your-face," uncompromising conservative.

"Hallelujah!" Rudman said after reading the article.

But Reed felt it was exactly the message they did not want to send.

Reed was beginning to look at the campaign as a long football game; they would move the ball forward but then they would get a penalty, move the ball down the field and then get another penalty. "That's the way it's been, and I think it's what it's going to be," he said. But he also realized that the seesaw quality of conservative message versus moderate assurances from Dole was becoming more and more a problem. Frankly, he felt they had a monumental communications problem.

Will had a quiet moment alone with Dole. Dole inquired about another long article a *Time* magazine reporter was researching on him. "How do you think that's going to go?"

"I think he's going to write that you're a moderate," Will replied.

"I don't understand why these people are writing this. Don't they look at my record?"

"Well," Will replied, "I think it's because you keep telling them you are, Senator."

That summer, Morris moved into an out-of-the-way suite of two offices at the Clinton-Gore headquarters on the seventh floor of 2100 M Street Northwest, in downtown Washington. He hired two assistants. His wife, Eileen McGann, helped him select dark-wood furniture from the Bombay Company for his office. The transition was not smooth. Morris blamed a delay in getting his phones and a paging system set up on a "malicious" effort by others in the campaign to undermine him. He was incensed that security guards required his wife to leave her driver's license to get a visitor's pass when she stopped in to see him. A negative newspaper story about him was posted on the campaign bulletin board!

In that hostile environment, Morris soon began doing most of his work from the White House and the Jefferson Hotel, where he stayed when he was in town. Most weeks he commuted from his home in Connecticut to Washington on Tuesday morning and stayed until Friday, giving him three or four work days and three work nights in the capital.

Morris wanted to ensure that Clinton was in position to maximize saturation television advertising in the coming primary season. Under federal election laws, any candidate would be limited to raising about $30 million for the primary season if he wanted to receive federal matching funds, which would normally mean another $15 million. The total of $45 million for the primaries was a lot, Morris realized, but given Clinton's fund-raising momentum and potential as a sitting president, was there a way to get more money?

The lawyers said that if Clinton rejected the federal matching funds, he would not have to abide by any fund-raising limits during the primary period. The possibilities would be limitless—potentially tens of millions of dollars more to spend on television advertising, perhaps even $50 to $60 million or more for an unparalleled media blitz. Morris decided that was the solution.

Panetta believed he finally had procedures in place with Bowles and Ickes at their follow-up meeting so none of Morris's ideas would get through to Clinton unfiltered. Morris pitched the idea of opting out of the matching-fund straitjacket. Ickes didn't like the smell one bit. He was 100 percent opposed, but Ickes had become an honest broker, promising to present ideas from Morris in the formal system. He outlined the idea in an August memo to Clinton but also noted that right away another $15 million would have to be raised just to offset the lost federal matching funds.

After a meeting, Clinton and Gore took Terry McAuliffe aside to ask what he thought.

"This seems far-fetched to me," Clinton said, but perhaps it was possible. If anyone could do it, McAuliffe could. What did Terry think?

"It's the dumbest idea I've ever heard," McAuliffe said. First, it would devastate the Democrats running for the Senate and House seats to have Clinton-Gore out there raising unlimited amounts of money. There was only so much money available and any excess money raised by Clinton-Gore would come out of the hides of other Democratic candidates. "We'll have a civil war on our hands," he added. Second, active Clinton-Gore fund-raising would also dry up the Democratic National Committee fund-raising next year, destroying what would be an important component for a coordinated campaign with Clinton-Gore. Third, McAuliffe added, it would make the president look like he was not playing by the rules and the spirit of the Watergate campaign reforms. "I just think it's too cute."

Panetta added that the president could not stab his own party in the back again, after caving on the balanced budget.

Morris argued to Clinton that he had to look out for himself, not other Democrats. And a civil war with Democrats would not necessarily be all bad. Clinton had to strike out on his own. Despite all the chatter and hubbub in Washington, Clinton's success in November 1996 would hinge on the amount of television advertising he could put on the air to pierce into the lives and attention of the voters, Morris said.

Clinton finally decided to go against Morris on this one. As candidate and president, Clinton had been on the side of political reform, trying to reduce the influence of money and special interests in politics. Operating outside of the existing federal election system, though technically legal, would open him to criticism which he felt would be valid and never-ending. And he was not sure he wanted to open this Pandora's box. Despite his momentary advantage raising money as a sitting president, Clinton wasn't sure he wanted to challenge Republicans in fund-raising, their traditional strength.

In August, Morris had new polling data on Medicare, the federal health insurance program for the elderly. The results showed that voters liked Medicare, trusted it and felt it was the one federal program that worked. Medicare was like Social Security—almost a third rail of politics that carried the highest voltage—the politicians did not dare touch it. And the Republicans were proposing cuts of $270 billion over seven years.

"You can shove it up their ass," Morris said.

Simultaneously, Mark Penn, Clinton's pollster, was working with some polling data showing renewed voter interest in values. They liked the notion of unity, working together and Clinton's notion of "common ground," for example.

Morris wanted more money from the Clinton-Gore campaign to run television advertising emphasizing Clinton's policy of protecting Medicare, not cutting it. The crime ads which had run earlier in the summer had been a giant smash hit, Morris was still arguing.

Clinton liked the idea and wondered aloud why they were not up on the air talking about his agenda.

Terry McAuliffe argued strenuously against spending more money on ads. "They'll be using our precision money," he said, since by law they could only raise about $30 million, which was going to be an absolute legal ceiling. The $1,000 limit on direct individual contributions to the presidential race made that money the hardest to get.

Harold Ickes said he agreed 100 percent with McAuliffe. The Clinton-Gore money was their insurance policy during the primary season. Even though it looked like there was no challenger to Clinton, one could emerge in a flash.

Bob Squier was an advocate of an early ad campaign. He believed an incumbent, even a president, was at a disadvantage because a challenger could define the incumbent and the issues. The incumbent had to strike early to define himself and set the framework of the debate.

Clinton wanted an ad campaign. Morris was pressing, Ickes and McAuliffe were resisting.

There was only one other place to get the money: the Democratic National Committee, which functioned as the unofficial arm of the Clinton campaign. And Clinton, as the head of the party, directed the committee's efforts. The committee could launch a new fund-raising effort as it had in 1994 when millions had been raised in a special effort to televise pro-Clinton health care reform ads. Though opponents of his health care reform plan had spent much, much more, the idea was sound. Clinton said he was not going to be drowned out this time, and directed a special fund-raising effort.

McAuliffe knew that if the president was behind a special fund-raising drive by the party, the money would be raised. Clinton did not make the fund-raising calls himself, but Vice President Gore made about 50 personal calls, and the party's chairman and entire fund-raising apparatus were turned loose. Because the money supposedly would be for the party, there were no limits on contributions—the so-called soft money loophole in the law allowing contributions for general operations. A number of large contributions in the $100,000 range were received.

Of course the distinction between Clinton-Gore money and Democratic Party money existed only in the minds of the bookkeepers and legal fine-print readers. It was all being raised and spent by the same people— Clinton, Gore, Morris and the campaign apparatus. In all, some $10 million was raised in the special fund-raising effort, and the Democratic Party went another $5 to $6 million in debt—drawing on its bank line of credit—to finance what eventually became a $15 million advertising blitz.

For several months, Morris and Bob Squier had been testing a half a dozen possible 30-second scripts and television ads a week for possible use. At weekly evening meetings in the White House, Clinton went through them, offered suggestions and even edited some of the scripts. He directed the process, trying out what he wanted to say, what might work, how he felt about it, and what it meant.

Morris jumped in most often, completing Clinton's sentences and finishing his thoughts.

Squier could see that the process was imposing a discipline on Clinton as he worked to formulate the precise message he wanted to convey. The concepts and the language they worked over in the scripts were showing up in Clinton's public statements.

The late summer was a difficult time for the Clintons. Senator D'Amato was holding hearings on the Whitewater scandal. The revelations of the hearings were minor, but D'Amato kept up a steady drumbeat as he called a parade of witnesses from the administration to testify in public. Joe Klein of *Newsweek* perhaps best captured the problem in an August 7 column, "The Body Count, The Real Whitewater scandal may be how the Clintons treat their friends." He recounted how Maggie Williams, Hillary's chief of staff, had to spend her own money on legal fees and had tearfully testified before the committee. "How could the First Lady allow her chief of staff to spend $140,000 on legal fees?" Klein asked. "Why hasn't she come forward and said, 'Stop torturing my staff. This isn't about them. I'll testify. I'll make all documents available. I'll sit here and answer your stupid, salacious questions until Inauguration Day, if need be.' "

Whitewater and the Clintons' response to it made them look sleazy. Their values were being increasingly called into question.

Bob Squier, whose experience went back to the 1968 Hubert Humphrey campaign, argued that presidential elections almost inevitably got down to clashing arguments over values. That was where the 1996 campaign was headed. Clinton needed to seize the high ground on a value-related issue. Protecting the elderly at the end of their lives was one of the most cherished American values. Clinton needed to build on that. Protecting the elderly was the popular Medicare program which the Democrats had created. It was their program, the party's child. Its grandfather was Social Security, also created by the Democrats. The Republicans had been stalking both Social Security and Medicare since their beginnings. Medicare was the Democrats' birthright, and the Republicans now wanted to cut it. Clinton's argument had to be to the voters: If you want something done about Medicare, you want Democrats to do it. Democrats would protect their child.

It was in this context that on August 10, Squier and Morris finally made the first 30-second television Medicare ad that would air. It was called "Protect."

The screen opened with a shot of a hospital heart monitor showing a healthy heartbeat—with a comfortable, reassuring ping, ping, ping.

Voice: "Medicare. Lifeline for our elderly. There is a way to protect Medicare benefits and balance the budget."

Flash to color footage of President Clinton standing by the American flag in the Oval Office reading some papers.

Voice: "President Clinton. Cut government waste. Reduce excess spending. Slow medical inflation."

Flash to black and white still photo of the Capitol with head shots of Dole and Gingrich on either side of the dome.

Voice: "The Republicans disagree. They want to cut Medicare $270 billion. Charging elderly $600 more a year for medical care, $1,700 more for home care. Protect Medicare benefits or cut them?"

Flash to the heart monitor going flatline and sounding an unnerving, loud, steady heart-stopped danger alarm.

Voice: "A decision that touches us all."

The next day, August 11, they followed with an ad that pulled out all the stops. It was appropriately called "Moral," and designed to intertwine the Medicare message with values.

The 30-second spot opened with a group of children raising an American flag.

A deep, soothing, authoritative male voice said: "As Americans, there are some things we do simply and solely because they're moral. Right. And good."

Flash to an elderly farmer working the fields, an American flag flying from the back of his tractor. Shift to elderly patients.

Voice: "We created Medicare not because it was cheap or easy. But because it was the right thing to do."

Flash to the head shot of the Capitol with picture of Dole and Gingrich.

Voice: "The Republicans are wrong to want to cut Medicare benefits."

Flash to Clinton again in the Oval Office by his American flag.

Voice: "And President Clinton is right to protect Medicare, right to defend our decision as a nation, to do what's moral, good and right by our elderly."

Closing to the fourth shot of the American flag which the children have finally raised to the top of the flag pole.

"We will defeat them in the air war!" Morris declared. He was delighted. The permanent campaign against the Republicans had begun.

"Their ground troops will be petrified by the bombing on Medicare," he said.

The first wave of Medicare ads was launched in states with moderate Republican senators—Vermont, Rhode Island, Maine, Colorado, New Mexico, Washington and Missouri. Morris was intent on smashing the Republican cohesion, breaking off the moderates. The spots were aired in major markets away from Washington and New York and Los Angeles where reporters might pick up on what was taking place. No one in the media really caught on.

Squier witnessed a big change in Clinton. Clinton, this very bright man, had been pulling on a rope to start the engine for the first two years of his presidency and too little had happened. All of a sudden it was working and Clinton seemed to be saying, This is how an engine is supposed to work.

Morris felt that politicians often failed because of their successes. Success could extinguish a political figure's agenda, forcing him to address issues that were not his and that would fall outside his electoral mandate so he would do poorly. "Limited success keeps you alive," he said. Clinton was alive.

As occasional news stories continued appearing about the growing influence of Morris, Clinton voiced surprise, downplaying his impact. Morris was just one part of the picture, a backboard for Clinton's own thinking. There was a creative tension between them, often a mind meld, but Clinton made it clear he was driving the strategy himself.

16

The upcoming straw poll of Iowa Republicans on August 19 was becoming a big deal. Conventional political wisdom had it that the Saturday night vote, six months before the Iowa caucuses that selected the delegates, would be a critical test of organizational strength. In fact, the straw poll was critical because it was basically the only test other than one in Florida coming in the fall. Under the bizarre rules, anyone who purchased or was given a $25 ticket to the event could vote—from in or out of state. Tom Synhorst had arranged for the campaign to buy about 3,000 tickets. He expected that about 90 percent, or 2,700 people, would actually show up and vote. He calculated this would put Dole comfortably in first place with something like 33 percent of the total vote—a win, but comfortably less than the 1988 caucus victory of 37 percent. A giant win with more than that would only build expectations for the real caucuses in February 1996.

Two months earlier, in June, Phil Gramm and his campaign strategist Charlie Black had realized they were stalled in the Republican race.

"The point is we've got to make news," Black told Gramm. He proposed targeting the Iowa straw poll. "We don't have to win, we've got to run a strong enough second." Everyone knew Iowa was Dole's state, so whoever finished second would be the news. "If we've got to spend a few extra bucks on mail," Black continued, "or telephones or barbecue or whatever, we could do it."

"Yeah," Gramm said, "I think we could do that."

"Let's really raise the importance of this event in the press' mind and in the political community's minds," Black said, "and then let's go see if we can't execute and pull a surprise."

In early July, John Weaver, the Gramm campaign's national field director and a 17-year veteran with Gramm, moved into the Courtyard Marriott on the outskirts of Des Moines, Iowa. He did not want anyone to notice he was living in Iowa. He set up his operation in a cubbyhole office at the Gramm headquarters. Weaver, 36, a tall, experienced organizer, had headed the successful George Bush for President organization in Texas for the 1988 race. Stealth and speed were important because if the Dole campaign learned what he was doing early enough, they could move to counter him. Weaver had 14 people working for him. Five mass mailings were sent out—one to Christian Coalition members, another to sportsmen (which meant gun owners). The elaborate flyers pictured Gramm with family, guns, dogs, Boy Scouts, actor Charlton Heston, policemen, the military and Ronald Reagan. Gramm personally approved all the copy. The cost was $200,000.

The Gramm phone banks completed some 40,000 phone calls at a cost of $23,000. Gramm personally approved the scripts. During the first ten days that Weaver was in Iowa, he spoke with Gramm twice a day.

About ten days before the straw poll, Synhorst and Reed started getting reports of trouble. Charlie Black was setting the bar as high as possible, proclaiming the event very, very important, with Gramm only shooting for a strong second-place finish. The Dole dream strategy was to win, have Pat Buchanan finish second, and Gramm third—positioning Buchanan as the leading conservative and perhaps extinguishing Gramm, or at least accelerating his decline.

Synhorst wrote a memo arguing that Dole, as the front-runner, was suffering from Reagan syndrome, meaning he was subject to attack from all the other candidates as Reagan had been as front-runner in 1980. The massing of criticism, Synhorst said, was beginning to hit home.

In the course of finding supporters, the Dole phone banks had identified 300 people in Iowa who said they supported Buchanan. So eager was the Dole campaign to promote Buchanan's candidacy that they sent the names over to Buchanan's operation.

After the fiasco of his speech at the Perot convention, Dole agreed to spend some time Saturday morning practicing his speech with the TelePrompTer. He and Elizabeth then flew out to Iowa.

"Something's wrong," Dole told Elizabeth, "it's not happening out here." Iowa was still not clicking.

Reed and Lacy flew in on a commercial flight to be on hand. In Ames, Iowa, more than 10,000 people were in the Coliseum. Reed and Lacy sauntered through like a couple of headquarters men at a kitchen appliance convention looking over the competition. Everything seemed fine. After a big Dole rally, they went to the holding room where the Doles were waiting before the speeches.

The five Republican candidates receiving the most support, money and attention were Bob Dole, Phil Gramm, Pat Buchanan, Pete Wilson and Lamar Alexander. The other five were Senator Richard Lugar of Indiana, a serious-minded and respected senior foreign policy expert; Senator Arlen Specter of Pennsylvania, a centrist, pro-choice on abortion and an advocate of tolerance in the party; Representative Robert Dornan of California; Morry Taylor, a wealthy wheel and tire executive; and Alan Keyes, a former State Department official who was probably the most powerful speaker in the group and a strong advocate of restoring traditional and family values to the country.

Tom Synhorst was very uneasy. Jesus, he said, he wasn't sure all their 3,000 people had actually made it. Before the formal speeches, each of the ten candidates one at a time was introduced on stage. It resembled the beginning of a professional basketball game, with flashing lights and a hyperkinetic announcer. Dole was introduced first and he received decent applause. At the Buchanan introduction, a huge roar rose from the crowd, particularly from one section where his supporters were sitting. Gramm also received a thunderous roar. Alan Keyes, too, received a big roar from one section. Reed was more than confused. The Dole people were spread out. Synhorst explained that someone in the Dole campaign had decided not to spend an extra $100 to reserve a section of 100 seats on the floor for the Dole people. Reed noted that was the basic campaign course 101, and they had badly botched the symbolism. Gramm had managed to get 600 of the 1,000 floor seats right in front of the podium by buying the seats the other campaigns had rejected.

As Dole was standing off stage before the speeches, he turned to Synhorst. "What do you think?"

"Sounds like a lot of Gramm people out there," Synhorst said.

"Sounds like a lot of Buchanan people out there," added Elizabeth.

"Are we going to lose this thing?" Reed asked Synhorst incredulously.

"I'm not sure," Synhorst said. "We may."

"Oh, shit!" Reed said.

Former Vice President Dan Quayle was the master of ceremonies, and he introduced Dole saying that Dole had been in public office all his life.

Will was watching on C-SPAN television. She thought the introduction was harmful. Quayle could have complimented Dole on his Hollywood speech, drawn some connection to what Dole was trying to do on values, rather than remind everyone of Dole's longevity. With the introductory music, Will's heart was in her throat. The music was all wrong, Will felt, terrible, old-fashioned, here-comes-my-grandfather music.

Dole went to the podium. "Minutes up the highway from here are farms and towns like the ones I knew as a boy," he said. He was looking out into the vast sea of people out front. He saw the Gramm section, the Buchanan section, even the sections of some of the other candidates. Dole noticed they all were sitting on their hands. Respectful but silent. "It's terrible," he thought. It was a little scary. He gave his speech and kept to the text, pumping his good arm and showing he was really into it. He was at a disadvantage without a vocal cheering section.

When Dole finally walked off the stage, he knew the results. He went to the holding room and found Reed.

"Where are all our people?" Dole asked sharply, darkly. "Why weren't they all in place?"

"I heard the crowd roar out there," Reed said, "and I just want you to know we may not win."

"What's going on?" Dole asked, restraining himself. His crack campaign team was coming to realize what was obvious.

"We're going to stay here," Reed said. "You go back to Des Moines and I'll call you when we know. We should know at ten o'clock."

Dole and Elizabeth went back to the Des Moines Marriott. Ten o'clock came and went. Dole was pacing. He had a campaign team with lots of paper and words. "Where's the beef?" he wondered.

Back in the hall, Synhorst was unnerved. It was so different to organize against people who prayed, the Christian right. They had an intensity, behaving and talking as if they were on a mission, as if they *had* to be here that night because it was a calling. Synhorst believed in Dole, but it was a political and secular belief which seemed weak in the face of the fervent support so many seemed to have for Buchanan and Gramm and Keyes.

Lacy immediately started giving out some pre-spin to several report-ers. "A competitive situation," Lacy said. "Could be a three-way race."

When they finally started calling the vote totals, Synhorst uttered to himself, "Oh fuck, fuck, fuck." But then it turned—incredible and implausible.

About 11:30 P.M. Reed called Dole with the final results:

Dole 2,582 votes or 24 percent.

Gramm 2,582 votes or 24 percent.

An exact tie.

Dole's immediate reaction was almost relief. He hadn't lost. Reed went on with the results: Buchanan 1,922 votes or 18 percent. Lamar Alexander 1,156 votes or 11 percent.

"I told you we had some weak people," Dole said, referring to the Iowa campaign team.

"You're right," Reed replied. "Let me get through tonight and I'm going to make some changes."

"All right," Dole said.

Dole did not sleep well that night. He was wondering why they hadn't been on top of this rather simple situation. The questions kept coming all night. What do I need to do better? Is it the candidate? Is it the message? Is it the organization? Did we spend enough money? Did we have the right people on the ground? Do we have the right leadership?

Back in Ames, Reed went to the press room and tried to beat back the wolves. They were out and it was tough. "We've said consistently that straw polls are meaningless," Reed told reporters. "We knew we had nothing to win. We treated it mainly as a way to test our organization. Other campaigns, especially Senator Gramm's, decided to really shoot their load here, with a lot of money."

In Gramm's holding room, the atmosphere was very upbeat, almost jovial before the vote totals were announced. When his staff had the totals, they raced to tell Gramm.

"Shit," Gramm exploded, realizing it could have been sweeter, "why couldn't I have gotten one more vote somewhere?"

"Phil," Charlie Black insisted, "you won." A tie was a clear Gramm victory. "We're going to get a huge ripple effect," Black continued in his soft southern drawl, which now had a conspicuous edge of excitement to it, "and it's going to bring people out of the woodwork. We'll do the same things and our money will be 50 percent better. And we'll have a lot of volunteers come out, they'll be a lot of people who were sort of for you but thought you couldn't win that'll now be willing to come on board.

You'll get a lot more coverage." Dole was not inevitable. The Dole band-wagon strategy was on ice.

Gramm went out to the cameras and had a field day, declaring, "If we can beat Bob Dole in Iowa, we can beat him anywhere in America."

Reed and Lacy canceled their 7 A.M. flight back home for the next morning.

Lacy had been so confident that Iowa would be a quick in-and-out that he had planned to wake up just in time, not even shave, and get on the plane. He had only brought hiking boots and shorts for the return trip.

Reed's first instinct was to blame Synhorst, the Iowa magician of 1988. Synhorst was spending much of his time in Washington and trying to manage the Iowa campaign by phone. He was in charge of Iowa but he wasn't there. It wasn't Reed's job to do bed checks every night to make sure those in charge were sleeping in their states. Clearly Synhorst had dropped the ball, playing senior member of the team on hand in Washington but not Iowa. Even Synhorst's own parents, devout Dole supporters, had not come to vote, apparently figuring that it was an assured victory.

"What the hell happened and why?" Reed asked Synhorst.

Synhorst said that he would make an assessment and tell him more in 48 hours, by Tuesday at noon. "If it will help the candidate's confidence," Synhorst said, "I'll move back there."

Reed wanted a detailed analysis, not just of what had happened in the straw vote but of what was going on in Iowa overall.

On Sunday morning after watching television and reading all the news accounts, Reed, Lacy and Synhorst went up to Dole's room. Lacy felt like a fool, the only one in shorts after Dole's presidential campaign had just taken its first dive.

Nelson Warfield was outside Dole's room waiting to go in. In his six months with the campaign, Warfield had never seen Dole really snarl and go wild, but this time he expected a blowup.

Mike Glassner let them all into the suite.

Dole was sitting at the end of a long glass-top table. Some 1970s reflective plastic furniture filled the room. A big accompanying 1970s-style flower arrangement was plopped down in the middle of the table.

"Here come the pall bearers," Dole joked. The humor cut some of the ice. Dole was tight, clearly not happy, clearly not cool. But he was not yet bouncing off the walls.

Elizabeth looked composed as always, but they all knew her exterior belied her inner intensity. The vote result seemed to have more of a personal impact on her, judging from her demeanor. She displayed none of her welcoming, upbeat Southern belle optimism.

They took their seats at the table, and Glassner removed the flower arrangment so everyone could see each other.

Reed didn't want to give Dole a chance to ask, so he started with three points. "This is not a reflection on you as a candidate," Reed said. "You gave a great speech. You're running a good campaign. The campaign let you down. Our people in Iowa failed and this is what our enemies are looking for." This was the setback that everyone was waiting for. "It's how we respond and how we react to this in the next 48 or 72 hours."

It was important, Reed continued, not to compound the problem. "You've got to go on national TV here this morning," Reed reminded them. Dole was due to appear on CBS's *Face the Nation*. Earlier in the week they had all argued that he shouldn't do a show that week, expose himself to questions the day after. But Dole had said yes to the show and now he had to go. "You've got to go out, put on a smile and we'll schlep this thing off."

Dole was listening, not saying much.

Lacy tried to reinforce the point. "It's not about the message or about you," Lacy said. "It's about organization, an organizational breakdown." He said they would reassess the organization and not let it happen again.

"I'll find out what happened," Reed interjected. "I'll have an announcement by the middle of the week." They would make changes in the Iowa organization. Reed looked at Synhorst. "Tom, we're going to make the changes as necessary."

Dole had a series of questions for Synhorst that showed he thought it should have been different. Why weren't the people organized on the floor? How many of his supporters had come from out of state? Where was it we fell short? He asked about a specific county.

"We've always been strong there, haven't we?" Elizabeth asked, underlining the seriousness.

Synhorst again promised to make his assessment.

"Well, it's over, we lost," Dole finally said. He had revised his personal assessment from the night before. A tie with Gramm was a defeat. "Spin it all you want," he said, "it was a good night for Phil Gramm. It was a bad night for us."

All Reed could do was move through this. He returned to the upcoming television appearance. Dole could not show any anger. "This is exactly what our opponents are looking for and everyone's going to be watching how we handle this." The way Dole accepted the result was far, far more important than the result itself, Reed said. The interpretation given to the press would be important. The future would be important.

Dole was thinking to himself, "I have to restrain myself!" He finally said to Reed, "You're right." Dole had his emotions tamped down. Okay. "Where we going next?"

It was over to the local CBS station. When Dole arrived, about 20 reporters were there. The station had let them into the studio itself—something never done. As Dole took his seat to look into the camera, all the reporters were milling about, watching for any sign of blood. Nelson Warfield went berserk complaining to the station management. Reed muttered about the stupid station and all the "cornseed heads."

On the air, Dole tried to joke. "I even saw a few people from Iowa there last night." Then somewhat reversing his position of a week earlier when he had been a moderate for *The New York Times,* he said, "I'm a good mainstream conservative, always have been probably as conservative as the others in the race."

What happened in the Iowa straw poll?

"There was some complacency," Dole said, adding that he was ahead in the polls. "I think you'll see in the next few weeks a number of very important endorsements coming our way which indicate that we're the preeminent favorite right now."

Dole told reporters later, "In my view, this is one pebble on the beach. There will be lots of beaches to cross."

Later Dole rode out to the airport with Synhorst. As he got out of the van, Dole turned to his young aide.

"Don't give up," Dole said. "We got a lot of work to do. I'm counting on you. You're the best there is, so let's not look back, let's look ahead."

From Dole that was almost a full hug and a kiss.

Dole went to the Iowa state fair, and then flew to Arizona for his next appearance. It was a quiet plane ride.

Flying back from Iowa, Scott Reed decided that he was personally going to take the blame. The most important thing was that he retain Dole's confidence, that he and Dole not have a split. Stepping up and pouring all the responsibility on his own head was the only way to keep the relationship with Dole. A defensive posture of blaming others would not work. More important than these external politics were the internal politics with Dole that would last for months, if not more than a year.

Gingrich didn't hold his tongue after Iowa. "I thought the Iowa results were the sign of a remarkably open race," the Speaker told reporters several days later. The lack of a clear winner would allow him to take his time deciding whether to run or not. "Iowa did nothing to discourage me from running."

"Fucking Newt!" Reed exploded, after hearing about the Speaker's remarks. "What a jerky thing to say. Totally undisciplined." Reed knew it would set him back with Dole, who expected Reed to have Gingrich under control through Reed's close friend Joe Gaylord, Gingrich's top political adviser.

When Reed talked to Dole next, Dole was furious about Gingrich's comment and, as expected, in part blamed Reed.

"Why does he talk like that?" Dole asked.

Reed tried to explain that Gingrich had no sense of discipline and just rolled out there and said whatever the hell popped into his head.

Reed began bad-mouthing Gingrich in private, spreading a little of his own poison. An article in *Vanity Fair* magazine by Gail Sheehy had just come out. Reed told his political friends that it was devastating to Gingrich, particularly the quote from Gingrich's wife, Marianne. "I don't want him to be president and I don't think he should be," she had said. The article disclosed some of Gingrich's past affairs and claimed he preferred oral sex with women so he could claim he had not slept with them. Reed even took to repeating the Jay Leno joke about Gingrich and his wife going to vacation in New Hampshire to stay at a "Desk and Breakfast"—a reference to the allegation that Gingrich had had sex on his desk.

In Synhorst's review of the Iowa straw poll, he found that about 750 of Dole's votes or 30 percent had come from out of state. That was good, what they had planned. The real snafu had occurred in the central Iowa counties where less than half those planning to come had attended. Even the faraway Iowa counties had bused in their share. Synhorst was pretty sure that the state organization was solid, better than in 1988.

But, he explained to Reed and Lacy, Gramm and Buchanan had developed clear, vivid messages with images that were taking hold with Iowans.

"Rein in the government, etc.," Synhorst said, referring to Dole's basic message, *"doesn't fucking do it*. You can delude yourself into thinking it's organization, but it's message."

"Does that mean that the message is wrong?" Lacy asked. "Or does that mean that we haven't been executing the message when we're in Iowa?"

For Synhorst it was both—the content and the execution. "I understand you've got to say it's organization to the outside world," Synhorst added.

Synhorst came up with four organizational recommendations that could be announced as the response to Iowa.

Reed had to cover the message problem with a visible organizational shake-up. He called Darrell Kearney, a longtime conservative activist he had worked with in the 1988 Kemp organization in Iowa. "There's got to be somebody in the morning giving all these kids direction," Reed said. Kearney finally agreed to take a leave from his own business and become the full-time, on-the-ground, hands-on manager in Iowa.

Reed reported the change to Dole.

"Been telling you we need to get an adult out there for a long time," Dole said.

Later in the month, John Moran, the Dole finance chief, called Scott Reed.

"We got a check for $1,000 from the Log Cabin Republicans," he reported. Log Cabin Republicans is a nationwide political action committee (PAC) that advocates gay rights.

"Don't deposit it," Reed said, "and I'll deal with it when I get back."

Within the hour, Moran was back on the phone. "Well, it was deposited back in June and it was on our last FEC report," Moran said. The Log Cabin group also had a letter showing that Moran had solicited the contribution to Dole.

"Great," Reed said. "Don't do anything."

Reed felt that the Log Cabin Republicans had set up the campaign. He chastised Moran for being so stupid to solicit the group. For four years Reed had watched the Log Cabin group position themselves to make news. He didn't want to just roll over and take it. In the wake of the Iowa straw poll, the contribution could not have come at a worse time. Gay rights were anathema to the Christian right, the key to Iowa.

Reed conferred with Lacy, who didn't agree that the Log Cabin group had set them up. They probably saw it as a chance to get some mainstream credibility, and after all, they were being courted and solicited by John Moran, Lacy said. "We can say that we disagree with these folks and we're going to give the money back," Lacy said, "or we can say, doesn't matter what these folks think, what matters is what Bob Dole thinks."

Of course, both knew that the question of "what Bob Dole thinks" was a big problem. In public and private discussions all his life, Dole had made it pretty clear he was against any discrimination. He had even waffled on gays in the military, saying earlier in the year that "I haven't made a judgment on that." He had later issued a tepid statement saying he opposed gays in the military.

Lacy said that keeping the $1,000 would present a problem down the road. "This is something that would make great Gramm fodder in the South and in the Christian community, not only is Dole for gays in the military, he's also taken gay PAC money." Lacy and Reed tried to project into the future. Right before and during the primary period the next year—February and March—Gramm could try to make it a big issue. They could picture the Gramm direct mail and radio and even television advertising allegedly outlining Dole's thoughts on gays. Gramm had done this shamelessly in his first Senate race in 1984 by attacking his opponent, Democrat Lloyd Doggett, for taking money raised by gays at a fund-raiser that Doggett did not even know about. Gramm had exploited the issue repeatedly, and many had attributed his victory to it.

Further, Lacy said that taking the $1,000 could make gay rights an issue and have the effect of inviting gay-bashing within the party and the primaries.

"I think we ought to give it back," Reed finally said.

Both agreed it would be best not to consult Dole in advance. The candidate should *not* be involved in such small decisions, Lacy was sure. If there was criticism, better they, the staff, take the hit. Asking Dole would put him in a difficult position. They had to protect him. And if they asked, he might want to do the wrong thing politically.

So Reed had the $1,000 returned.

The story was starting to leak out and it was becoming a press problem. Reed talked to Dole.

"Why did we do it?" Dole asked. He wanted to know why they had sent it back.

Reed explained. "We're going to take some lumps on it," Reed said, "but rather now than in February or January." A big blowup on the issue right before the Iowa caucuses or New Hampshire would be worse, and a blowup was going to happen at some point, he said. He used to read about letters the Log Cabin Republicans had sent him in the newspaper before he received them. "That's how these guys operate."

Dole couldn't believe he hadn't been consulted, but he did not protest immediately.

Reed had spent an hour with Richard L. Berke, the chief political reporter of *The New York Times,* hoping to get him going on a front-page story on Dole's upcoming speeches on the economy and values. But Berke was on to the returned $1,000 contribution.

Sunday's *New York Times* front-page story was headlined "Dole, in a New Bow to Right, Returns Gay Group's Money." The verbs in the story conveyed the situation—Dole was "scrambling" and "intensifying" his drive to court the conservatives, after a "humbling" tie with Gramm in Iowa, while he had to "cajole and compromise" to get legislation through the Republican Senate.

Not Reed, Lacy or anyone else in the campaign was able to come up with a public explanation for returning the $1,000 that washed. They couldn't claim that they were trying to protect gays from gay-bashing by others. And to announce that Dole didn't want to be open to distorted or outrageous charges during the primary season would make Dole look vulnerable and weak.

Nelson Warfield's mother had died, and he was at the funeral home taking phone calls and trying to come up with a rationale for returning the money. It was one of the most painful times of his life. His final answer was dubious and reflected the strain: "It's our policy that we won't accept contributions from groups that have a specific political agenda that's fundamentally at odds with Senator Dole's record and his views." Warfield acknowledged it was the first time the principle had been applied.

Richard Tafel, the head of the Log Cabin Republicans, hit the talk show circuit. "We've had lots of calls from pro-choice Republicans or moderate Republicans who've said, 'Hey, I was supporting Dole because I was afraid of Gramm. But if he *is* Gramm, what's the point of supporting him?' "

A *Boston Globe* editorial noted, "Dole has not returned campaign contributions to Time Warner even though he deplores the 'nightmares of depravity' in the entertainment industry." The *Atlanta Constitution* asked, "Will the real Dole please stand up?"

Dole was really unhappy now. In a meeting with Reed and Lacy several days later, he complained bitterly about the decision to return the $1,000.

"Who's making these decisions?" Dole asked again, knowing full well that it had been Reed.

"It was my decision," Reed replied.

"Why did we do that, I don't understand that," Dole asked.

Reed explained the political rationale again, adding, "I still think it was the right thing to do."

"Senator," Lacy piped in, "I fully concur. Scott and I discussed it thoroughly, and I still think it was the right thing to do."

"I don't like to defend this," Dole said. The clear implication was that it was a mistake, but he didn't suggest the campaign publicly change its position.

It's forgotten, forget about it, Reed and Lacy urged. Both felt confident they had avoided big trouble down the road. Lacy was sure that they would see attacks that would curl their hair, that would drive Dole and them absolutely crazy. At least one future problem area seemingly had been foreclosed, and Dole had been insulated.

Dole was concealing his fears. He decided that he would buy into his aides' plot with a straight face, though he didn't like it. He held his tongue. He had promised everyone he would not manage his own campaign. Yet he was the candidate. He was really hanging out there. Reed's and Lacy's names were not in the editorials.

Dole sought out Jo-Anne Coe, his longtime fund-raising manager who had been with him for 28 years.

"Jo-Anne," Dole asked, "why did we do this?"

"They just thought it was the best thing to do," she replied.

17

Anthony Lake, the 55-year-old national security adviser to President Clinton, had spent much of the last several months in his green-carpeted West Wing office agonizing over the three-year war in Bosnia, the thorniest foreign policy issue of the Clinton administration.

For years Lake, a former foreign service officer and professor who had worked in the Nixon and Carter administrations, had been a proponent of stronger action in Bosnia to halt the horror—the systematic ethnic cleansing, the random artillery shelling of cities, war on women and children, rape, pillage and destruction that had marked previous centuries. A pleasant man with gray hair and glasses, Lake had earned a reputation as a tough bureaucratic infighter. To him, it was often a question of just surviving. As coordinator of foreign policy for a president who wanted to be known for his domestic accomplishments, Lake was overseeing the part of the administration's portfolio that Clinton wanted kept on the back burner.

Earlier in the administration, Lake had written in a confidential communication to the president that the administration's weak, muddle-through strategy in Bosnia was becoming a cancer on Clinton's entire foreign policy—spreading and eating away at its credibility.

But the administration and Clinton had always found reasons not to act or else to employ half measures. It wasn't that Lake did not see the inevitability or the practicality in each decision. He did. But postpone-ment and avoidance eventually add up to failure.

U.S. policy in Bosnia was tied to the United Nations, which had an ineffective peacekeeping force on the ground. Thank God, Lake felt, that the UN force did not yet include U.S. forces. The United States had also agreed to operate within the NATO alliance and cooperate with its European allies. NATO airpower and bombing were being used selec-tively to try to minimize violence and reduce the heavy artillery shelling of the cities like Sarajevo, the Bosnian capital. These instruments of U.S. policy—the United Nations and NATO—had somewhat insulated the Clinton administration from full responsibility in Bosnia, but they were increasingly holding the administration prisoner.

The Defense Department didn't want to get involved. The dual ghosts of Vietnam and General Colin Powell walked the halls of the Pentagon. In the first year of the Clinton administration, when Powell was still chairman of the Joint Chiefs of Staff, he had argued that bombing in Bosnia wouldn't solve the problem and that 100,000 or more U.S. ground forces would be needed to guarantee a successful peace. Secretary of State Warren Christopher also was reluctant. He had been deeply embarrassed in 1993 when he had failed to persuade the European allies to adopt a more aggressive policy.

But by the spring of 1995, the Bosnian crisis had reached a new level. During May, hundreds of UN troops in blue helmets had been taken hostage by the Serbs, the aggressors in the war, and chained to telephone poles in yet one more humiliating international spectacle in the Balkan quagmire. The television networks, particularly CNN, had run haunting footage of young soldiers, who were supposed to be symbols of world peace, chained and tied and displayed as helpless. This had captured the president's attention, and Lake had watched Clinton erupt in several of his celebrated private blowups, his large body shaking and his voice bellowing. Clinton raged alternately at the aggressor Serbs, the United Nations' rules, the allies, and the situation. It was quite a show—power-ful, effective and a little chilling. When Clinton got livid, Lake knew that policy could then change.

Lake had been a senior official in the Carter administration when the Iranians had held fewer than 50 Americans from the U.S. Embassy hos-tage for more than a year—the event that as much as any had sunk the Carter presidency. The inability of President Carter to solve the Iranian hostage crisis for a year had become folklore in the study of failed presidencies, and Lake knew that Clinton was intimately familiar with the history.

It was in this context that Lake had gone down to the Oval Office for a meeting with Clinton on Wednesday, June 14, 1995. Clinton was having a formal session called a "pre-brief" with his senior foreign policy advisers prior to a meeting with President Jacques Chirac, the new leader of France, that would focus largely on Bosnian policy. After the routine briefing, sharing of views and discussion of other issues with France, Clinton turned back to Bosnia.

"We need to get the policy straight," Clinton said sharply, "or we're just going to be kicking the can down the road again. Right now we've got a situation, we've got no clear mission, no one's in control of events."

Nothing important in the Clinton White House was decided in a single day or week, Lake knew too well. But obviously Clinton was coming to a central understanding: he was not in control of his nation's destiny, certainly the first duty of all presidents.

Clinton spoke emotionally and with mounting frustration.

"I never would have put forces on the ground in such a situation," Clinton said. "The rules of engagement are crazy!" The members of the UN force, which was supposed to be keeping a peace that did not exist, were not permitted to shoot first to protect themselves, so hundreds had been taken hostage.

"It's the issue from hell," Vice President Gore added. "The Europeans are self-delusional." The NATO alliance was not acting aggressively to protect the UN force. NATO looked weak, and as the senior partner in NATO, the United States was looking weaker. "The need for us to protect and preserve the alliance is driving our policy," Gore said. For years, Gore had been a hawk, urging strong action to stop the war. He went on about the consequences of inaction. "It's driving us into a brick wall with Congress," Gore added. A confrontation with Senate Majority Leader Dole was right around the corner. Dole, too, for years had accused the administration of fecklessness and weakness in Bosnia. The Republican majority in both the House and Senate was behind Dole on this one, pushing legislation aimed right at the heart of the United Nations' and the Clinton administration's policy. Dole wanted the United States to break with the United Nations and unilaterally lift the arms embargo on the besieged Bosnian Muslims.

As a senator in 1992, Gore had favored lifting the arms embargo. The idea had a simple and powerful emotional appeal—help the victims in the war. Gore was now convinced it was a phony policy that would lead to more disaster. If the United States acted on its own, the Russians would in turn lift their arms embargo and help the Serbs, who would then overrun the Muslims. NATO might collapse, the British and the French would withdraw their troops from the UN peacekeeping force, and the United States would be left with full responsibility for the Balkans.

As Lake watched, he wondered if there were not some different course, some new route beyond the hideous cycle of crisis management. There had to be a way to break out from the past policies and the ingrained habits of meetings, planning, papers, talking, mounting frustration, presidential temper tantrums and then hesitation. How? Lake wondered. All U.S. foreign policy was at risk. The cancer image, which he and Clinton had discussed, was precisely the correct one—spreading and untreated. Lake could see that Clinton was being increasingly boxed in— by the United Nations, the NATO allies, his own State and Defense departments which didn't want to move, and now the Republicans and Senator Dole.

After the meeting in the Oval Office, Clinton welcomed President Chirac. Clinton and Chirac agreed that the UN forces in Bosnia needed a rapid reaction unit to protect their troops on the ground from incidents such as the humiliating hostage taking. But Senator Dole and House Speaker Newt Gingrich were refusing to support the United States' portion of the funding for the new force. They were determined to force the United States to lift the arms embargo. Clinton called Dole and Gingrich and asked if Chirac could come up and meet with them to make his arguments. Chirac visited them, and the result was a compromise agreement with Dole and Gingrich that postponed the funding issue. But once again Clinton's hands were tied, showing he was not fully in charge.

That evening the Clintons hosted a private dinner in the family quarters of the White House for Chirac and his wife Bernadette. After the dinner, Clinton and Hillary danced as the Marine Band played. Despite the day's events, Clinton seemed in a good mood. The French contingent finally left. Secretary of State Christopher, UN Ambassador Madeleine Albright, and Assistant Secretary of State Richard Holbrooke were standing in the North Portico seemingly enjoying the summer evening. The Clintons joined them, and the president brought up Bosnia.

"Mr. President," Holbrooke said, "I'm afraid that we may not have as much flexibility and options left." The secret NATO operations plan 40-104, already agreed to by the United States, called for the commitment of 20,000 U.S. troops to Bosnia if and when the UN force decided to leave or collapsed, as many, including the president, expected.

"What do you mean?" Clinton asked, answering his own question, "I'll decide that when the time comes."

"Mr. President," Holbrooke said bluntly, "it's been decided."

"Chris?" Clinton asked, turning to his Secretary of State.

"That's right," Christopher said. "This is serious stuff. We have to talk further about this."

Clinton said good night, took Hillary's hand and walked out.

In Christopher's view, a pullout or collapse of the UN protection force would be a disaster and had to be avoided at all costs because it would obligate the United States to live up to its commitment to supply the 20,000 troops to cover a retreat. Clinton could renege, but at the risk of destroying NATO. It would be unthinkable to abandon NATO, the most important alliance in the post–World War II period, the alliance that had been central to winning the Cold War.

Lake could see that Clinton was trying to work out a solution for himself.

"On this foreign policy thing, I know I can get it," Clinton said at one point, putting his fingers to his head as if he were driving something in, trying to sort it out. "I just need some time to think about this."

Lake figured he had better come up with something himself. In late June, he convened a Saturday meeting for three hours to brainstorm with his senior colleagues on the National Security Council staff. Most of their time was devoted to managing the latest crisis, the day's shelling or atrocity, never looking beyond. The president's image of "kicking the can down the road again" was precisely right. But who was kicking the can? The answer was everyone. And to what purpose? The truth was that everyone —the United Nations, the allies, State, Defense, the Congress—had a different purpose. Suppose, Lake proposed, they calculated where they wanted to be six months from now? Define that place and then work backwards? "Let's think from the end backwards," Lake said. "I don't want to hear about what next."

If they decided where they wanted to be at the end, they might be able to step the policy back and figure out where they wanted to be in five months, then four, and so forth. It sounded obvious, but they had been so mired in daily crisis management they had never taken the time to plan strategically. Lake called it the "Endgame Strategy." Of course, there was no endgame at all. For all they knew they were in the middle game of an endless and mounting crisis.

Several days later, Lake outlined the somewhat vague possibility of an Endgame Strategy to Clinton during a regular morning national security briefing in the Oval Office.

Clinton showed immediate interest. He was always calling for new ideas.

By defining where they wanted to be in half a year, they might devise a way to get there, an Endgame Strategy, Lake suggested. The obvious final goal would be some peace settlement or even full disengagement. The strategy would have to include both diplomatic and military initiatives. The existence of such a strategy might force everyone's hand, Lake said. "I want to try to think this through and come back to you with a coherent, comprehensive strategy," he said.

Clinton indicated he wanted to hear more.

"Mr. President," Lake added, "tell me if you don't want to do this, stop me now because the risks are very clear." Lake didn't want another false start. The risks, he said, were that it would fail and be an embarrassment like earlier U.S. efforts in the region that went nowhere. The second risk, ironically, Lake said, was that it would succeed.

Clinton fully appreciated the irony. Success would mean 20,000 U.S. troops on the ground in Bosnia in some form to oversee the UN withdrawal or to enforce a peace agreement. And a 20,000 troop deployment in the Balkans was more than risky. It had the smell of the beginning of Vietnam. Would the public support such a risk? Would the Congress?

Yes, Clinton said, go ahead and put some ideas down on paper. The current position was untenable. He wanted rethinking. They had to break out of the old mind-set. He hadn't heard anything new, Clinton said, and new was what he wanted.

Lake said that he would have to get State and Defense involved, and once he started down that road, a certain dynamic would evolve.

"Do it," Clinton said.

Lake then asked Christopher, Secretary of Defense William Perry, Chairman of the Joint Chiefs General John M. Shalikashvili, and UN Ambassador Madeleine Albright to write papers on Bosnia. Not option papers but a discussion of where the policy ought to be in six months. State and Defense offered a lot of resistance. This wasn't the time. Why stick our necks out? We could precipitate withdrawal of the UN force— a nightmare in itself. Why do we want to do this?

The president wanted some new ideas, Lake insisted.

Lake was supposed to be the honest broker among the others and present all the views neutrally. He could include his own, but State and Defense had to feel that the playing field was level. But Bosnia was too important, and Lake decided to violate his own rules for the first time. As the president had said, they needed to get the policy straight. Lake took his own paper to the president before Christopher or the others had seen it. The design was presented as the "Endgame Strategy."

Lake proposed that Clinton send him as a secret emissary to the allies so he could explain that Clinton had made firm and final decisions on the future course of U.S. policy in Bosnia. The foundation would be an assertion that the United States would implement this new long-term policy by itself, outside the umbrella of the United Nations and NATO, if necessary. Of course, the United States wanted to work with the United Nations and NATO, but the president had decided to go it alone if need be, and this was final and absolute. These preemptive decisions included what Lake called "carrots and sticks" for all sides to force a negotiation. It included massive bombing of the Serbs if they did not cooperate and agree to peace negotiations. It also put pressure on the Bosnian Muslims by saying the United States would lift the arms embargo as the Muslims wanted, but if the Muslims did not negotiate, the United States would leave the region, effectively abandoning them. This was called "Lift and Leave."

After Clinton read an initial draft, he sounded willing. He did not balk at the proposal to go it alone or to bomb heavily. But he was focused on getting the Serbs and the Bosnian Muslims into some negotiation to stop the war.

"I want to get the diplomatic process back on track," Clinton said, adding that he felt stuck because under the UN agreements the United States and the other allies were prohibited from talking to the Serbs, who were the aggressors. "We need to get them back to the table."

Two weeks later, Srebrenica, a former industrial city long under siege by the Serbs, had fallen. Clinton called Chirac on July 13.

Senior White House officials often listened in on these calls, which involved translators and diplomatic and military decisions that needed to be clearly understood.

"What do we do next?" Clinton asked Chirac.

Chirac was full of moral indignation. This was like World War II. The Serbs were separating the men and taking them off to camps. "We must do something."

"Yes," Clinton said, "we must act."

Chirac had a breathtaking suggestion. They ought to go in with French ground forces and American helicopters to recapture the city.

What would be done after that? Clinton asked, clearly stunned. Throw the Serbs out of the city, then would they liberate the rest of the country? Clinton made it clear that he didn't consider that practical and wouldn't go along.

After the call, Clinton said to his aides that the only time they had ever accomplished anything in Bosnia was when NATO had been tough and bombed the Serbs.

Clinton suddenly turned to the young Navy military aide who had set up the phone for the call.

"What do you think we should do on Bosnia?" Clinton asked.

"I don't know, Mr. President," the dumbfounded aide replied.

The next evening, Friday, July 14, about 7 P.M. Clinton was behind the White House chipping and putting golf balls onto his private green when Sandy Berger, his deputy national security adviser, and Nancy E. Soderberg, third in rank on the NSC staff, approached.

They had more details on the fall of Srebrenica. Some 15,000 people —mostly women, children and the elderly—had been rousted out of their homes and forced to leave, the largest wave of ethnic cleansing during Clinton's presidency. Berger described a horrifying trail of death and depravity.

"This can't continue," Clinton said, blowing up into one of his celebrated rages. "We have to seize control of this." Where were the new ideas?

Berger reminded him that Lake was trying to develop an Endgame Strategy.

"I'm getting creamed!" Clinton said, unleashing his frustration, spewing forth profanity. He was putting, and he did not look up at Berger or Soderberg as he stroked the balls one after the other to the hole. They kicked the balls back to him to putt again. Soderberg felt almost as if she had fallen into Clinton's mind, and they were witnessing the interior monologue of his anxiety. He was in an impossible position, he said. He needed to do something. The UN force was being treated like dirt, making the situation unsustainable. Why am I only getting bad and worse options? Why am I not in control of this?

Berger and Soderberg listened, occasionally mentioning why each apparent option had a strong downside.

Clinton said that Chirac was getting under his skin with his bold but unrealistic suggestions. Chirac was getting the attention with ideas that might make people feel good but would not solve the problem. He spoke as if he felt some competition with Chirac. "I'm getting increasingly squeezed."

The discussion was going nowhere, and after some 45 minutes Berger and Soderberg left. They reported to Lake that they had been the victims that night of a 45-minute Clinton diatribe.

"I know, that's why I'm doing this," Lake said, referring to his efforts to come up with a sustainable strategy.

Lake was able to use the Srebrenica horror to move forward. He immediately informed Clinton that he was having breakfast on Monday with the foreign policy team to go over the papers on long-term strategy in Bosnia, and he was going to plunk down his own paper then, recommending simultaneously a diplomatic initiative and intense bombing of the Serbs. He urged Clinton to drop by.

At the breakfast Monday, July 17, the foreign policy team met around the oblong table in Lake's bright corner West Wing office. Lake presented his Endgame Strategy to Christopher, Perry, Shalikashvili, Albright and Berger. The suggested approach was so completely out of character with most administration decision making, which generally focused on today's immediate problem, that Christopher and Perry kept returning to the immediate Srebrenica crisis.

Suddenly the president appeared, greeted everyone and took a seat.

"I don't like where we are now," Clinton said. "This policy is doing enormous damage to the United States and to our standing in the world. We look weak." He forecast more trouble. "And it can only get worse down the road. The only time we've ever made any progress is when we geared up NATO to pose a real threat to the Serbs." But he added, "I'm not sure what we should do."

Lake froze. Clinton had to be resolute.

"But we're in the worst possible situation," Clinton continued. "We are not in a position we can sustain. The Europeans could bring forces to bear but they prefer to whine at us." He reported on French President Chirac's bold idea. It had not been thought through, he said, but he welcomed the attitude. "We have a war by CNN. Our position is unsustainable, it's killing the U.S. position of strength in the world."

Clinton then left. He had been forceful but there was an out-of-body quality to it, as if he were not talking about his own policy, as if he had just come to realize what was happening.

Lake returned to his theme. "We need to make some policy decision that will affect where we are a month from now," he said.

"We have to look at this issue beyond Bosnia," said Albright. "I'm glad the president sees this in terms of American power in the world."

"Yes," Lake said, "this is larger than Bosnia. Bosnia has become and is the symbol of U.S. foreign policy."

All agreed to take home Lake's paper for study.

But they had all become accustomed to Clinton's method of making decisions. A clear direction or course was rarely set.

The fall of Srebrenica was a catastrophe, and the news was filled with stories of rape, mass genocide, and roads jammed with refugees.

The next day, Tuesday, July 18, Clinton gathered his team in the Oval Office.

Vice President Gore spoke at length. "The worst solution would be to acquiesce to genocide," he said, "and allow the rape of another city and more refugees. At the same time we can't be driven by images because there's plenty of other places that aren't being photographed where terrible things are going on." The top secret intelligence provided additional tales and pictures of horror not available to others. "But we can't ignore the images either," Gore said. He noted that the front page of *The Washington Post* over the weekend had described a young woman, just one of the 10,000 refugees from Srebrenica, who had committed suicide by tying a floral shawl and her belt together, making a noose to hang herself from a tree. A picture of the woman had run all over the world. Gore said she seemed to be the age of his own daughter.

"My 21-year-old daughter asked about that picture," Gore said. "What am I supposed to tell her? Why is this happening and we're not doing anything?"

It was a chilling moment. The vice president was directly confronting and criticizing the president. Gore believed he understood his role. He couldn't push the president too far, but they had built a good relationship and he felt he had to play his card when he felt strongly. He couldn't know precisely what going too far meant unless he occasionally did it.

"My daughter is surprised the world is allowing this to happen," Gore said carefully. "I am too."

Clinton said they were going to do something.

Gore forged on, noting that after the fall of Srebrenica they had to write off the city of Zepa, which was next in line. "But we now can't watch 65,000 people in Gorazde be helplessly subjected to the same treatment." In Srebrenica the Serbs had singled out the women related to the local commanders for gang rapes for the world to watch, Gore noted. "The cost of this is going to cascade over several decades. It goes to what kind of people we are. Acquiescence is the worst alternative."

Gore talked about Chirac, who was not involved in the mistakes of the last four years because he had just become president. "Chirac now wants to roll the dice and keep his own record clear." Chirac's rescue proposal was in the tradition of the grand French gesture, Gore noted. The United States needed a real alternative. "We have to come up with something practical to make military sense," Gore said. "Acquiescence is not an option."

"I've been thinking along similar lines," Clinton said. "So we all agree the status quo is untenable."

They returned to crisis management and whether there was anything that could be done immediately in the wake of Srebrenica.

"The situation underscores the need for robust airpower being authorized," Clinton finally said, adding, "The United States can't be a punching bag in the world anymore."

On Saturday, July 22, Clinton again met with his team in the Oval Office.

Christopher, who had just returned from London, reported that the allies had agreed on a more assertive use of NATO airpower and bombing to protect the Bosnian cities. "The closer the Europeans get to bombing, the more nervous they get," Christopher said, but added, "We still have to maintain allied solidarity."

Leon Panetta reported on the status of the Dole resolution in the Senate, which called for unilateral lifting of the arms embargo so the Bosnian Muslims could get weapons to defend themselves.

"There's a good chance it will pass," Panetta said.

Clinton felt the practical impact of a unilateral lift would be wholesale disaster because it would release the well-armed Serbs to go on the offensive before the Bosnian Muslims could be armed.

Lake said, "As long as it's still a unilateral lift we have to veto it, no matter what changes they make."

But Clinton then tried to draw people out on whether there were any circumstances not to veto the Dole resolution.

"If I were not to veto this," Clinton said, clearly looking for a way out, "we should say to our allies they have to do what was promised in London and make the Serbs believe that we're willing to kick the shit out of them. And this could increase the chances that we wouldn't need to bomb. And we would be able to be strong without ground forces." Clinton too seemed nervous about bombing.

After a discussion of the potential humiliation for the United Nations and NATO if the UN forces on the ground collapsed, Clinton said, "We need to think about whether there's anything more we can do diplomatically." Maybe there was a way to bomb the Serbs more effectively and avoid hostage taking. "But, by the same token," the president said, "we need to show the Serbs that there's some reward for half-decent behavior." Maybe the Serbs were like the North Koreans, who had made a deal on their nuclear program earlier with the United States, Clinton said. "They may prefer to make a deal with the United States than with others."

Clinton was going back and forth, trying to reach some conclusions.

"The stronger you are, the more you can afford to open channels of communication with the Serbs," the president summarized.

"Maybe there's some other proposals we could put on the table if we're dealing from a position of strength and we're not begging. We've got to change the rules of debate. We can only do it from a position of strength."

"We'd have to put some new things on the table and show both sides the benefits of peace. We can't only try to prevent something bad from happening."

For years Dole had wanted to help the besieged Bosnian Muslims, clearly the victims of the calamity in the Balkans. Dole was determined to pass a resolution unilaterally lifting the embargo. He had not only Republicans but many Democrats on his side, a veto-proof majority.

Behind the scenes, however, Dole made overtures to signal another possible solution. He privately told Secretary of State Christopher that though he strongly disagreed with Clinton, he was not trying to take over foreign policy. A strong Senate resolution to lift the embargo—the House had already passed one—would give Clinton leverage with the Europeans to claim that his hands were being tied by Congress. Clinton could then go to the British prime minister, "call John Major and say, here it is, I'm dead." Dole told this to Christopher and also passed word to the White

House National Security Council staff. "I'm just trying to give you guys some leverage. You don't have any leverage. I'm gonna give you some."

Tony Lake told every Republican senator he saw that if Dole succeeded, Dole and the Republicans would be taking responsibility for everything that happened in the future in Bosnia.

Clinton and Dole never talked privately about this.

On July 26, the Senate passed legislation 69 to 29 to lift the embargo in what was seen as stunning and direct repudiation of Clinton and his policy. Supported by 48 Republicans and 21 Democrats, the resolution was not one of the traditional, vague sense-of-the-Senate measures that did not have the force of law. It was binding legislation and an open challenge to Clinton's authority.

Clinton told Lake that now they had to pull out every stop on the Endgame Strategy. Lake would go secretly to the Europeans, present both the sticks and the carrots—bombing of the Serbs and peace talks. The window of opportunity was narrow. The allies would have to be told explicitly that Clinton would veto the Dole resolution but that he was not sure he could get the votes to sustain a veto.

"We're rolling the dice here," Lake said to the president. "It's imperative everybody be on board, and while you need to listen to all the views, you need to then lay out the marching orders. You have to make it clear, and this is dangerous, that you're going to act on this unflinchingly if the worse comes to worst."

Clinton normally kept Lake out of the discussion of the political or domestic ramifications of his foreign policy actions, but this time he didn't.

"I'm risking my presidency," Clinton said.

On August 7, Clinton gathered his foreign policy team in the Cabinet Room. Christopher was out of town and sent a deputy, Peter Tarnoff, the number three in the State Department.

Lake led off by presenting the various papers for the Endgame Strategy.

"We should bust our ass to get a settlement within the next few months," Clinton said. "We've got to exhaust every alternative, roll every die, take risks." He liked Lake's approach of going forcefully to the Europeans with the carrots and sticks. "But failing that," Clinton said grimly, "the only other option would be to get a cessation of hostilities while they haggle for over a year." So the options were few. "We should negotiate now from a position of real strength, or otherwise, if we let the moment slip away, the Serbs will start shelling Sarajevo again and we're history."

Lake said they could not be tied to past peace efforts and the old rules and agreements. The past needed to be leapfrogged, he said. "We need something bold."

"I agree we make a full court press to seek a diplomatic solution," Clinton finally said. He said Lake would go see the Europeans. "The question is, should this be a high-profile or a low-profile mission by Tony? If it's high-profile, we'll lose some operational flexibility."

"Don't leak it to the press," Clinton said. They would meet the next day to go over what Lake would say in Europe.

Lake didn't want any ambiguity and he drafted a series of precise points he intended to make on his secret mission. The key leadoff point was: "The decision the president has taken." Addressing the possible collapse or withdrawal of the UN force, Lake wrote, "We have decided what we will do in those circumstances." The president would veto the Dole resolution, but "We have at most until the second week in September before Congress considers an override vote." Unless there is progress, "We are not sure we can get the votes to sustain a veto. Therefore every day counts." Repeatedly he wrote, "The president has decided. . . . The president feels strongly."

At 6 P.M., August 8, Clinton met in the Cabinet Room with his team again. From a folder, he pulled out a copy of Lake's talking points outlined in a memo classified "Secret." It was almost unheard of for Clinton to work from paper at a meeting, and it signaled to the others that this was serious. Lake went through the points in detail to make sure everyone agreed. The essence was the series of concrete carrots and sticks to get all parties to the bargaining table. All would be presented as final presidential decisions. This included a strong bombing threat against the Serbs. But Lake was not going to give the Bosnian Muslims a free ride. He had to be tough with them also. "If the Bosnians are the bad guys, they don't get the strike or the arms," Lake said. "They get lift and leave." Everyone knew that would mean they would be overrun. If they agreed, they would get the lift of the arms embargo, training and strikes on the Serbs.

"Let's meet again at eight in the morning," Clinton said. "I want to see a new version of your talking points. I want to make sure that everybody else is comfortable with them. If everything is within reach, then Tony can leave at ten. If not, we'll delay his flight. We need to push this. Fortunately we're in a different situation than we were in 1993 and finally we're not asking for something that the Europeans won't like. This time we'll be pushing on an open door." The Europeans were getting frustrated themselves.

The meeting ended at 7:50 P.M.

The next morning, August 9, the meeting began 20 minutes early.

Lake wanted no ambiguity. Speaking to Clinton and the others to make sure, he said, "The line I'm going to take in the meeting with the allies is that this is the U.S. policy, this is what we're prepared to do if there is no settlement. This is what we intend to do. We hope you'll come with us. We won't be so inflexible to refuse changes to our approach but want to give them an accurate understanding that these are presidential decisions, this is a strategy we're wedded to and now's the time to move." At the same time, he said, he was going to tell the allies that the United States was willing to go it alone if necessary.

"The whole thing sounds pretty good," Clinton said.

"I'm fully supportive of this," Christopher said, but he added a cautionary note. "I agree it may work. It will be too difficult if we actually have to implement the worst-case option, fortifying the Bosnian state. Some of the allies will cringe at that if we're actually arming and training them." That would be difficult to sell, he said, and Congress might once again step in and try to force our hand.

"We now have the strength to carry out a diplomatic effort," Clinton said. "We may not have the ability to pull it off later." He added that the administration could manage congressional pressures if they had a credible diplomatic effort going.

"I'm going to lowball expectations in talking to the media," Lake said.

"Yes," Clinton said, "don't say we have a plan." Mention of a plan could build expectations. "I think this strategy's quite good," Clinton added, "and I think the presentation is quite good." He wondered if it wasn't best to present the carrots, the positive agenda, first, before the sticks—an approach that Lake later used.

Lake left on time for his mission, and in seven European countries he laid out the plan saying that President Clinton had already decided his course, urging them to join. The thrust was that they had better help get the diplomatic track going in earnest or all hell would break loose and the United States was going to do all these crazy things like bomb the Serbs. This was an old technique that Lake had learned 25 years earlier from his former boss Henry Kissinger, national security adviser to President Nixon. During the Vietnam peace negotiations, Kissinger frequently hinted that President Nixon was a "mad bomber" whom Kissinger had to control. In 1970, Lake had been Kissinger's executive assistant and had questioned the Vietnam bombing policies, and Kissinger had accused Lake of not being "manly enough." Lake had resigned in protest at the invasion of Cambodia.

Now, as Clinton's national security adviser, Lake was shuttling among European capitals as an advocate of bombing. The impending Dole resolution was a significant stick. In France, the power of the new Republican majority in Congress was so well understood that when Lake raised the Dole resolution, one senior French official asked, "How do we know that the president speaks for the United States?"

Lake was tired and got angry.

"When I get back I will send you a copy of the Constitution of the United States of America," Lake said sharply. "The president makes foreign policy!"

Lake's mission began to bring the Europeans on board. He was able to invest both a peace initiative and more aggressive bombing with the authority of the president. The Europeans loved the diplomatic effort with Clinton putting the reputation of the United States on the line, but they hated the idea of bombing. But Lake insisted that the two were bound together and that the president had already decided on U.S. policy.

Finally, in London, Lake met up with his old friend and rival, Assistant Secretary of State Richard Holbrooke, who was going to take over as the chief negotiator with the warring parties in Bosnia. Christopher had pushed hard for Holbrooke, arguing that he had the kind of aggressive style, ego and experience to deal with all the parties, including the Serbian war criminals. Lake and Clinton had finally concurred in the Holbrooke selection.

"This is what you and I dreamed about doing together 30 years ago," Lake said, referring to their efforts in the Vietnam peace negotiations.

All his life, Holbrooke had wanted to try the toughest negotiation in the world, and he realized he was about to get it.

"Dick," Lake said, "I'm literally going to be with you. If this fails, it's my ass on the line more than yours." Holbrooke agreed, but they both knew Clinton was the one with the most on the line.

Lake and Holbrooke went over the seven points. Holbrooke said that he would not negotiate viable military boundaries in a way that would abandon the town of Gorazde to the Serbs. That would create 65,000 more refugees. It would be unthinkable and immoral.

Lake agreed. The administration was giving Holbrooke unusual latitude to find peace. Holbrooke immediately began his mission to meet with the leaders of the three warring parties.

On August 19, while Holbrooke was in the Balkans, three senior members of his five-man negotiating team were killed in an accident when their armored personnel carrier slid off the road near Sarajevo. The dead were Robert C. Frasure of the State Department, Dr. Joseph J. Kruzel of Defense, and Air Force Colonel S. Nelson Drew of Lake's National Security Council staff. Holbrooke was shattered, and he reported directly to Clinton, who was on vacation in Jackson Hole, Wyoming.

"Mr. President," Holbrooke said, formally and in control, "we have the sad duty to report that three of our comrades have died."

"How does this affect the mission?" Clinton asked.

"I can't tell you, Mr. President," Holbrooke said.

"What do you want to do?"

"You sent us out as a team, Mr. President," Holbrooke said. "We will come back as a team, and then we will return."

Holbrooke brought the three bodies back to the United States, flying part of the way with his knees pushed up against one of the coffins.

Clinton flew back to Washington for the memorial service at Fort Myer chapel on August 23. He met with the families, widows and children. At the service, Clinton said, "Today we gather to honor three peacemakers." He spoke at length about each of the three dead men. "May God bless their memories and lift up their souls."

Death, Clinton later told his advisers, helped him put things in perspective.

Holbrooke gave Clinton an hour-long briefing on the preliminary discussions with the presidents of the three warring parties in Bosnia. Clinton was stunned. It was a negotiation that was going nowhere.

Bombing was the most important lever they had, Holbrooke believed. He privately began calling himself "a hawk for peace." It was the only way the Serbs would listen.

On August 28, the Serbs lobbed mortar shells into the Bosnian capital of Sarajevo, killing 37 people in a crowded marketplace. It was the deadliest attack in 18 months and in clear defiance of the Clinton-Lake-Holbrooke peace efforts.

"We've got to bomb," Holbrooke said from Europe in frantic phone calls to Lake and Christopher. They had lost three men, paid a fearsome price already, and the United States would have no credibility if there was no bombing.

Clinton, Gore, Christopher, Lake and the entire U.S. government pushed the hell out of the NATO allies. NATO finally acted, and a massive bombing campaign, the heaviest of the three-and-a-half-year war, was approved. More than 60 planes, including Navy bombers from the U.S. aircraft carrier *Theodore Roosevelt,* would strike to silence the Serb artillery. Upon getting the final news, Lake, the former Kissinger aide who resigned over the Cambodia invasion, phoned Clinton, the former Vietnam draft evader, who was back vacationing in Wyoming.

"Whooopppeee!" whispered the president.

18

Hillary was thinking about attending a United Nations world conference on women in China during early September. She wanted to condemn the abuses of human rights and of women, but pressure was mounting on her to stay out of delicate U.S. relations with China.

Jean Houston wrote Hillary a strong letter about her obligation and burden, on behalf of all women, to go and speak out. Houston enclosed letters from two friends also urging the First Lady to undertake the mission for all women.

Hillary said she cried when she read the letters. She told Houston that the appeals had made a difference and she had decided to go. Her speech at the conference in Beijing was front-page news.

Houston was struck by how emotional a woman Hillary was, crying easily, laughing easily, not repressed, expressing herself fully in private. She was a very rich emotional palette. She had not closed down, though in public she was still reserved and careful.

Hillary was being honed in the crucible, Houston believed. It was almost like a Greek tragedy. Houston had found Hillary to be as noble as anyone she had ever met, so much like Eleanor Roosevelt. But Hillary had been a golden girl in school, always the good and the best and the brightest, so the adversity of recent years had been more of a shock for her. Eleanor had endured years of suffering and rejection as a child and young adult, which prepared her for the trials she faced as First Lady.

Houston told Hillary that she was going through as much psychological abuse as anyone Houston had ever seen.

Hillary nodded.

She was creating a new type almost, the woman who could withstand it all.

Hillary nodded, clearly listening, not saying much.

They discussed the woundings from the news media. Houston recalled that early in the administration, Hillary had spoken of heroes and villains, and the need to have enemies who could symbolically be singled out to embody the opposition. That's the old male hero's journey, Houston said, and the female journey had to be different, better. "Do we have to have villains?" Houston asked.

Hillary implied that Houston did not understand at all. In politics, debate was always framed that way.

Houston found Hillary enormously warm and empathic, but realized that Hillary was not a soft woman. Her lawyer's training and her dislike for the news media had made her edgy, full of angles. Houston proposed a series of exercises to help Hillary think about the press differently, to think of them as human beings and respond heart to heart with them, to build up a field of empathy and humanity. She felt that Hillary broadcast her hostility through all kinds of subtle cues. She wanted Hillary out of the warrior mode.

Hillary said she would get savaged anyway. Some of the press had made an industry of demonizing her. She made it clear that she hated being muzzled, being forced to respond to the media projections and definitions of her. But if they won a second term she would have greater freedom to do and be the things she wanted.

Houston could anticipate Mozart getting his hands back again, Hillary her voice. She called Hillary a "world server," someone who would help all humanity.

Houston had encouraged Hillary to write a book about children, but the first draft had not satisfied Hillary. So in October and November, Houston virtually moved into the White House residence for several days at a time to help. One period was about five days, with an interlude, and then approximately another five days. During this period Houston got to see how intense, stressful and overwhelming life in the White House had become. Bateson came to help, too, at the end. They were spirit raisers, encouragers, idea people. Houston and Bateson did variations of chapters, which Hillary then took and rewrote. *It Takes a Village and Other*

Lessons Children Teach Us was published in early 1996 and became a number-one *New York Times* bestseller.

On and off during the year, Newt Gingrich had openly flirted with the possibility that he might run for the Republican presidential nomination. His public and private comments about those running, especially Dole, were critical, if not savage. He said no one running had come up with a strong message for the presidential campaign. He candidly acknowledged that keeping his options open was a good marketing strategy, generating more news coverage for his statements, the Contract agenda, and his best-selling book, *To Renew America.*

On September 7, Fred Steeper, Gingrich's pollster, sent the Speaker a private seven-page memo entitled "Your Public Perceptions." The news was bad.

Overall, 31 percent of the people polled had favorable impressions of Gingrich. But 52 percent had unfavorable impressions, and many of those used "a variety of abusive terms to describe your personal style—'coarse,' 'arrogant,' 'abrasive,' 'a loud mouth,' " Steeper said.

"Your expressed interest in the presidency is also being interpreted as inappropriate self-promotion," Steeper added. "The book tour and the presidential possibility only act to aggravate this 'out for himself' perception.

"I'm not sure of your reasons for not discouraging the presidential stories, but my conclusion is that they are hurting your image, rather than enhancing it. You should scuttle the stories, sooner rather than later."

Steeper said that Gingrich had an "excessive personality syndrome" that presented "a huge challenge." He added, "I had been thinking, without success, on how to 'fix your personality.' "

The memo did not persuade Gingrich to close off the option of running, and he continued to openly criticize the Republican contenders. If he won the seven-year balanced budget and the Contract was largely passed and signed into law, he could possibly run on a record of accomplishment. Gingrich and his spokesman, Tony Blankley, insisted that Clinton and the White House staff were seriously misreading Gingrich on the budget if they thought he would compromise. Gingrich was a revolutionary. Revolutionaries, intent on overthrowing the old order, didn't compromise. Period. Better to fail than to cave in, except Gingrich expected a big victory on the budget.

• • •

McAuliffe had spent the summer putting together a fund-raising extravaganza for September, with a series of presidential gala dinners intended to raise about $1 million each. In mid-September, he told Clinton that by the end of the month they were going to have a second quarter total that would exceed the first quarter, unprecedented. The first three months of fund-raising were always the best because the easy money from the devoted followers came in then. But with direct-mail appeals, solicitations by the steering committee and the gala dinners, they would bring in $10 million for the second quarter.

"Mr. President," McAuliffe said, "we will be able to finish all the fund-raising this year." They would reach the maximum of close to $30 million by then and with the federal matching funds would have about $45 million.

Gore was delighted. "Mr. President," he said, "you know we are now in the presence of the greatest fund-raiser in the history of the universe."

For most of the year, Steve Forbes, the 47-year-old head of the publishing empire that bears his name, had been brooding about Jack Kemp's refusal to run for president.

Kemp was the natural messenger for all the economic ideas that Forbes was certain could lift the country's economy and spirits. The core idea: that low tax rates would provide incentives for individuals and businesses to work harder, invest and stimulate economic growth, creating more jobs.

"You can't walk away from this," Forbes had told Kemp, arguing that history virtually required him to run. Kemp's personality and his message of optimism would be perfect for 1996. Was he going to let Bob Dole take over the party? How could he even think of that? Dole was the embodiment of the Eisenhower-Nixon approach. To Dole it was as if Reagan, who had lowered the top income tax rate from 70 to 28 percent, had never happened.

Kemp continued to say no.

Forbes was flabbergasted. He was an awkward-looking man with a puckish smile, a sprinkling of gray hair, and a cratered, uneven complexion. He often rocked his head and shoulders back and forth gleefully when he laughed. But underneath the jolly demeanor Forbes held serious and strongly felt ideas about the economy. He had helped Christine Todd

Whitman devise a tax cut platform in her successful run for the New Jersey governorship in 1993, demonstrating that not only could Democrats be beaten, but so too could the economic austerity crowd, made up of the old-line, traditionalist Republicans. When Clinton's health care plan had been devastated in 1994, Forbes believed the big-government, high-spending old order had just had their last spree.

The Republican takeover of Congress in late 1994 showed even deeper disaffection with the old order, Forbes thought. Republicans as well as Democrats had failed to understand the meaning of the end of the Cold War. In the Cold War, government had shaped everything, even domestic policy. There had been federal aid to everything. Government spending had saved the nation, winning wars, putting a man on the moon, even going to the forefront of the civil rights movement. But without the external enemy everything had changed, Forbes believed. The new economy and the information age, with the personal computer and the microchip, were the opposite of centralization.

The government should shrink dramatically as the economy shifted to global markets. America had to prepare for a century of peace. Some presidential candidate had to get on top of this, insist that the tax code protected the old political order and centralized, outdated business interests. The tax system needed to be dismantled and pulled out by its roots. Dole didn't and couldn't possibly understand this, Forbes believed. At best, Dole could only make a tactical accommodation to such ideas.

Kemp agreed with much of Forbes's analysis, but made it crystal clear he wasn't the man.

Forbes went to see Phil Gramm, the Texas senator and former economics professor who had been officially running since February. Maybe he was the hope. Forbes wanted a radical overhaul of the tax code, including some form of a flat tax rate of about 17 percent for everyone. It was the kind of dramatic cut that would encourage investment and trigger economic growth. Gramm's Texas colleague, Dick Armey, the House majority leader and number two to Speaker Gingrich, was pushing a similar flat tax.

"Dick Armey was an undergraduate when I was a full professor!" Gramm said dismissively. Gramm implied that professors like him had the answers, and thundered on about how he was going to cut the government.

Forbes said that was too static a view. In business, cutting costs alone was never enough. Investment, new opportunities, radical overhaul were necessary.

No, no, no, Gramm said. Eliminating the federal budget deficit was everything. He was staking everything on it.

Well, it wasn't everything, Forbes felt, and he left disenchanted. Gramm clearly had more intellectual candlepower than any of the other candidates, but he seemed to Forbes to think he was so smart that he couldn't learn very much from others. Gramm's supporters continued to pursue Forbes, insisting that Gramm wanted to expand his group and needed powerful businessmen like Forbes on the team. "Phil is ready to listen," one Gramm supporter told Forbes. Forbes went to another meeting with Gramm. After five minutes of preliminaries, Gramm pounded his desk and said, "Now, Steve, let me tell you why you've got to support me." For the next half hour Gramm lectured.

Forbes walked out convinced more than ever that Gramm was not the guy. And Forbes began to wonder, Why spend your time trying to educate? He felt he was locked in the mind-set of Henry Higgins trying to educate Eliza Doolittle in *My Fair Lady,* trying to create something that did not exist. All they're going to do is disappoint you, he thought, reviewing the possible field of candidates.

Forbes began to think about running himself, and confided in Bill Dal Col, the president of the Washington think tank Empower America of which Forbes was chairman.

"Are you serious?" Dal Col asked.

"Yeah."

"I think you're crazy," Dal Col said.

Forbes said he wanted to consider it.

"Do you know what you're going to get into?" Dal Col asked. "From my limited experience, I can tell you. It's going to be a cement mixer." Dal Col, 38, was nine years younger than Forbes. A willowy, pale man with a long face and a scrupulously attentive and efficient manner, Dal Col had run the 1984 Reagan-Bush reelection campaign in New York State, held Suffolk County board seats, worked on the 1988 Bush campaign in Washington and then had worked for Kemp. Forbes had worked closely with Dal Col for years.

"Anything you, your father, your brothers, your daughters, your cousins, your aunts or uncles have ever done is going to be on the front page," Dal Col explained.

"What's it going to cost?" Forbes asked.

"My guess is $20 to $25 million," Dal Col estimated.

Jude Wanniski, a former *Wall Street Journal* editorial writer and serious-minded gadfly economist who was one of the strongest advocates of supply-side tax cuts, had earlier sent Forbes a memo encouraging him to run. He said that the campaign law would permit Forbes to spend his own fortune on his campaign, but Wanniski recommended against it. "This can't be seen as a money grab by a Forbes rich kid on *Lifestyles of the Rich and Famous,*" Wanniski, a longtime Forbes friend, said. "Play within the rules."

Forbes called Jude and said he was very flattered by the memo, though he disagreed with the part about spending his own money. As George Washington said, if you were blessed with treasure as well as intellect and energy, you should share all three with your countrymen.

Forbes discussed the prospect with Sabina, his wife. A stocky, white-haired woman with a toothy smile, Sabina had a welcoming, maternal presence. They had been married for 24 years and had five daughters, ages 8 to 22.

What would it mean for the kids? Sabina asked in her deep, slow voice. What would it do to the family? Did he truly understand the magnitude of what he was considering? Up until now they had lived a small-town rural life in New Jersey—albeit privileged and private. Steve had been all business, shunning the high-profile, jet-set extravagance of his father, Malcolm Senior. This would put him and them square in the limelight that they had avoided.

Forbes said he wanted to weigh it carefully, but he just might want to go ahead. Sabina said she would support it, but he had to talk to the girls.

The oldest girls thought it was crazy. They never had envisioned their father as a candidate, and just didn't believe he would do it in the end.

Sabina had some heavy questions for him. Did he realize that he would be putting their daughters up on the public stage? And they could get hurt, couldn't they? If he won the nomination or the presidency, they would forever be public personalities. Is that what they wanted for their daughters? If he lost, what would life after the campaign be for them? Could they withstand it?

Forbes talked with his daughters some more. They were well aware of the publicity that had surrounded their grandfather, Malcolm Forbes, Sr., and his glamorous party-giving lifestyle and homosexual relationships during his latter years. They had read the stories and said they had no illusions that if their father ran, it would be just fun and games.

Forbes's father had run for New Jersey governor twice and lost. At the time Steve Forbes was a young boy, and he could vividly remember his father's deep disappointment. Later his father told him he had expected to go all the way in politics and become president. What struck the younger Forbes was how his father had put politics behind him, licked his wounds and gone on with his life in business. His father just buried it all, never hung around, never went back, never said, gee, should I run again? In the mid-1960s before Steve Forbes went to college at Princeton, he remembered his father saying, "I don't know how I ever did that. I could never do that again." He just closed out the whole chapter of his life and went on to the next thing. It was the way to do it, Forbes thought.

Forbes had a series of breakfast meetings with Wanniski, his old mentor and biggest promoter.

In urging Forbes to run, Wanniski argued that he would have to find a ground between boldness and the middle of the ballpark, tune his message so it was dramatic but plausible.

"You're going to make a lot of mistakes," Wanniski advised one day over lunch. "As long as you keep them in the ballpark, you'll be fine."

"Where's the ballpark?" Forbes asked.

"Well," Wanniski said, "when you get close to the walls, they'll scream."

Later in May, Forbes and Dal Col had met in the *Forbes* magazine boardroom and Forbes asked what it might mean to the family business.

"Shit," Dal Col said, "look around this boardroom. There's three generations standing on your shoulders. You screw this up, it gets *Forbes* magazine screwed up."

"Do you know what they're going to do to you?" Dal Col asked. "You could become the Pierre DuPont IV." DuPont, the former Delaware governor and a wealthy descendant of the chemical-manufacturing family, had run for president in 1988 and gone nowhere. Finishing fourth in the New Hampshire primary, 28 points behind George Bush, DuPont's campaign was over less than a week later. He was barely a mention in the 1988 campaign chronicles.

Forbes also had long talks with his younger brother Tim to review the pros and cons of running.

"How would I take it if I lost?" Forbes asked.

"If you fail," his brother said, "everyone would say rich boy tried to go in the big league and got his head handed to him." When would you get your reputation back?

Forbes wasn't sure. "How long would it take me to bounce back?" he asked.

"We're all salespeople in one respect or another," his father had told him at the youngest age. The old man had repeated it many times, and the old man had practiced it. "You're always selling." In some aspects, Steve Forbes's entire life from earliest childhood to the chairmanship of Forbes had been the successful, highbrow version of *Death of a Salesman,* in which Willy Loman's friend tells him, "The only thing you got in this world is what you can sell."

Forbes felt that political campaigning would just be another version of selling. He realized he couldn't outsell Clinton on personality. He had met Clinton briefly three times—twice at White House dinners. Unlike other presidents Forbes had seen at similar state dinners, Clinton had walked around after the meal casually talking to people. Forbes saw the skill, the remarkable charisma, the empathy, the warm, meaningful connection with people. But Forbes was convinced that Clinton hadn't defined the era. That was a president's big mission, and Clinton didn't realize it, hadn't defined a direction or set a clear course.

Still Forbes wasn't sure if he was going to run. He wanted to test himself.

On July 8, Forbes appeared on the CNN Saturday afternoon television interview show moderated by Rowland Evans and Robert Novak, the conservative newspaper columnists, to test-drive himself and his possible message should he run for president.

Forbes emphasized the void. "I don't know what Bob Dole would do as president. Do any of you?

"Where does he want to take the country? Where does he feel the country is right now? Where does he think it'll go? And unfortunately the whole crop of candidates—no point in singling out Bob Dole—give the impression that they do the political equivalent of painting by numbers. That isn't art. It isn't leadership."

Forbes compared himself to Jonas Salk, the developer of the polio vaccine, who had died the previous month. Salk's approach was not accepted by the medical establishment, Forbes noted, but it worked. "Millions of kids would have had polio if it had not been for somebody who was outside the mainstream," Forbes said. His vaccine was the overhaul of the tax code.

"Absolutely an atrocity," Forbes said of the tax system, "anti-growth, anti-honesty, anti-American—scrap it, start all over again." He wanted a flat tax, he said.

At the end of the show after Forbes had left, Evans and Novak discussed the performance on the air. "I give him high marks," Evans said. Novak said that Forbes could become the candidate of those who were saying, "Gee, are we going to give Bob Dole the nomination without any serious challenge?"

In August, Forbes met Dal Col for a two-and-a-half-hour discussion. What about the money? Dal Col asked.

"We'll take care of that," Forbes said.

"I don't buy the bullshit that you're going to raise any money," Dal Col said frankly. Without a political base or office, there was no fund-raising apparatus. Everyone would know the personal fortune was available. "They all say, you're going to raise this, you're going to raise that. What I think you're going to find is that everybody who says they'll write a check for you, when you go ask for it, they'll find a reason not to."

"I'm prepared for that," Forbes said. He would commit the tens of millions that would be necessary, he promised, but he didn't offer a final number or a ceiling, just said the necessary funds would be there.

What about your abortion position?

Forbes said that he did not like abortion, opposed late-term abortions, opposed abortion for sex selection, opposed government funding for abortions.

"I think it's going to be a problem," Dal Col said, noting that Forbes was not really pro-life. In fact, he sounded pro-choice, accepting of the standard first-trimester abortions.

"That's what it is," Forbes said.

"I ran three times on a right-to-life position," Dal Col said, referring to his local races in Long Island, "and that's not going to cut it. Just say those little words, 'I'm pro-life,' and it solves a huge problem."

"No, I'm not going to get pigeon-holed," Forbes said and shook his head defiantly.

They discussed Forbes's eyeglasses. Could he wear contacts?

No, Forbes said. He was almost blind in his right eye and the corrective lens was nearly as thick as the bottom of an old Coca-Cola bottle.

Some thought Forbes had a goofy smile. What should they do?

To Forbes, who had been looking in the mirror for more than four decades, the smile wasn't goofy. "I am what I am," he said.

Dal Col said that if Forbes got in, and they bloodied him bad real early and he dropped out in the first three weeks or something like that, it would be awful and more than embarrassing. Once you're in, you have to be willing to go the distance, he said.

Forbes agreed.

By the end of August, he told Dal Col, "I'm going to do it." He hired Dal Col to be his campaign manager at $210,000 a year. As Forbes worked on an announcement speech, he realized that he was declaring a two-front war—on the Republican Party establishment and on the media establishment, which would no doubt write him off.

On Friday, September 22, Forbes went before the press to announce his candidacy. At least they showed up, a giant crowd gathered at the National Press Club.

"There is an empty feeling in this campaign so far," he said. He laid out his flat tax plan of 17 percent. "I want to change the culture of Washington."

Forbes felt he had pulled it off. Inside, he thought he was going to go all the way simply because he felt he was seeing things in a way the others didn't—as a radical tax cutter, a genuine optimist, a well-funded total outsider with a sense of the future.

Forbes and Dal Col immediately began with millions of dollars in advertising in the early primary states—strong issues ads passionately advocating the flat tax and pointing up the weaknesses and inconsistencies in the other candidates, especially Dole. Forbes spent $1.5 million on television ads alone in the first month after the announcement, blanketing New Hampshire and Iowa.

Forbes said he didn't want the ads to be personal, nothing about Dole's age and so forth.

Dal Col agreed but wanted only one commitment from Forbes. If Dole or the other candidates started attack ads against Forbes, Dal Col wanted to go for their kneecaps and make them pay. "When they hit," Dal Col said, "we're going to hit back, but we're not going to play tap for tap. If they hit, we go for a real hit."

Forbes approved.

Don Sipple had been watching the Pete Wilson campaign falter for months. Over the summer he had gone along with Wilson on a weekend trip to New Hampshire. Afterwards Sipple wrote a three-page confidential June 26, 1995, memo to top campaign officials Craig Fuller, George Gorton, and chief of staff Bob White. "I believe we need to have a sense of urgency," Sipple wrote. After listening to Wilson, people "don't say 'Wow,' " he said. They needed a message and presentation that said "Wow." And within the campaign, he continued, "I have witnessed in-fighting and dissension . . . no one understands in whom or in what com-bination of people authority rests." He forecast "a self-inflicted disaster or series of disasters."

They came. The July and August fund-raising goal was $5 million. The Wilson campaign raised only $800,000. By September, the campaign hoped that a last-minute television advertising blitz in New Hampshire would boost Wilson into second place behind Dole in local polls, and that in turn would energize the fund-raising. It was a fantasy. The cam-paign was in debt.

On Wednesday, September 27, Wilson met with Fuller and White.

"I've written this out," Fuller said. "Just handwritten. Here's where I'm at." The piece of paper showed a campaign debt of $1.5 million.

"We've got to get out," Wilson said. He then picked up a briefing paper and began to prepare for his next event, a group of bankers in Orange County. Even though Wilson knew his campaign was over, he decided to continue with a fund-raiser in San Francisco the next day, and then announce his withdrawal the following day, Friday, September 29.

"I hope I haven't let you down," he told a group of supporters as he announced he was leaving the race. "I blame no one but myself."

Sipple realized that Wilson never had a good answer to the question of his pledge not to run for president. Never. He never even had a good fake answer, Sipple thought. When the pledge issue came up, Wilson's body language spoke volumes of discomfort. He turned a slighter, lighter shade of gray and just fumbled. It was a gateway to a whole series of issues that Wilson had changed his mind on—taxes, immigration, and affirmative action—and they were going to kill him eventually.

Wilson endorsed Dole, after the Dole campaign agreed that Dole would do some fund-raisers to retire the Wilson campaign debt.

On Sunday, October 1, Reed settled in to watch Dole on the CBS morn-ing show *Face the Nation*. No matter what he and the others said or did, Dole had a craving for these shows, which seemed to give order to his Sun-day. But the shows with freewheeling interchange from well-informed in-terrogators were high risk. The questioners were always looking for news.

On the current federal budget debate, Dole was asked about the target of $245 billion in tax cuts over the next seven years—a figure that seemed to have been agreed upon by both House and Senate Republicans. But even some of the most conservative senators had privately indicated to Dole that they were willing to compromise more and lower the amount of the overall tax cut. So Dole said, "Will it be $245 billion? I'm uncertain at this point."

"Shit," Reed exploded, "there goes my afternoon!"

For House Speaker Newt Gingrich, this was betrayal. The next night, Gingrich started calling some of the Republican governors—Steve Merrill of New Hampshire, John Engler of Michigan, and William Weld of Massachusetts. Did you see what Dole did? Can you believe it? We can't trust this guy, he declared. There he goes again. Tax cuts were sacred stuff. Gingrich said that as a result he was thinking even more seriously about running for president himself.

Merrill reported in to Reed that Newt was getting happy fingers dialing up the governors at night. Dole called a press conference, rejoining Gingrich. "As far as I'm concerned, $245 billion is the figure," Dole declared. Gingrich's chief adviser Joe Gaylord was out of the country and Reed believed the absence meant Gingrich had no one to talk to at 11 P.M. When Gaylord returned, they put things back on track. Soon Dole and Gingrich were meeting every morning so they would be in sync and speak with one voice. Everything—the Republican legislative agenda, the party's reputation and Dole's presidential candidacy—rested on some kind of coordination.

But the news of Gingrich's calls to the governors soon leaked, triggering new reports that Gingrich was thinking about running.

The controversy over returning the $1,000 contribution from the Log Cabin Republican gay organization continued to simmer. Earlier, one of Dole's supporters in the House, Representative Steve Gunderson, a 44-year-old Wisconsin Republican who is openly gay, had written Dole a stinging, anguished personal letter criticizing the decision to return the $1,000. "Are you rejecting support of anyone who happens to be gay? If this is so, do you intend to now reject my support and request those on your staff who happen to be gay to resign?" Gunderson asked.

"The Bob Dole I know would never sacrifice his personal integrity for political purposes. Please do not allow your historical commitment and integrity to be compromised by the politics of the moment." Gunderson asked for personal assurances, and released the letter publicly.

Dole called Gunderson at home that night after the letter was released to say that he regretted the decision to return the money, it was a "mistake," and he wished it had been handled differently. He assured Gunderson that gays were welcome in his campaign, and that he had not lessened his resolve to fight discrimination.

Scott Reed spoke with Gunderson, who was planning to go public with what Dole had told him. He urged Gunderson at least not to say publicly that Dole had labeled returning the money a "mistake." Gunderson agreed and told reporters just that he had received a reassuring call from Dole. The story of Dole's call appeared in the *Kansas City Star* and on the Fox television news in Washington, but it had not been picked up by many other news outlets.

Publicly, Dole continued to defend the return of the money. "What I didn't want was the perception that we were buying into some special rights for any group, whether it is . . . gays or anyone else."

Personally, Dole was still fretting. Were they going to have a litmus test for every contribution? Would they have to pass each contribution through radar saying, "Take, kill, take, kill"? he asked. Finally it occurred to Dole that he should adopt the policy Ronald Reagan had used in his campaigns, essentially, "You buy into my agenda, I don't buy into your agenda." That made a lot of sense to Dole, but he remained silent.

The inconsistency was left on the record for weeks until Tuesday, October 17, when Dole was interviewed by some Ohio reporters in his office. He said that his campaign aides had made a mistake and should not have returned the $1,000. "I think if they'd have consulted me, we wouldn't have done that, wouldn't have returned it." He also undercut his own rationale for returning money and the one repeatedly given out by his press secretary. "My view is because you accept money doesn't mean you agree with their agenda."

Reed learned about Dole's comments only after the story hit the news wires in Ohio. Furious, he and Warfield went into the bunker. They refused to release a transcript of Dole's remarks to other reporters and then issued a bland written statement: "The campaign returned this contribution to protect Senator Dole from distortions of his record." They declined to answer other questions or return phone calls from reporters.

Dole's direct criticism of his staff gave the story an added dimension, and the Log Cabin Republicans bombarded reporters with calls to note Dole's latest, newest inconsistent position. The story made the television news and the front pages of the newspapers, many with headlines about Dole saying his staff was wrong. Political reporters knew that Dole turning on his staff had been an early omen of the 1988 Dole campaign meltdown. Television, radio and the newspapers were filled with the story of Dole reversing himself. Gay rights groups and social conservatives voiced unusual agreement, both criticizing Dole.

Dole called Reed at the campaign three times the next day. Reed didn't take the call each time, claiming that he was too busy to speak to the candidate. Reed's anger was mounting. Friends and others in the campaign told him it was terrible what Dole had done to him, effectively rebuking him in public. But Reed wanted time to think. Getting angry and defensive wasn't the right reaction, he concluded. Given Dole's record and habits, Reed was no doubt going to be embarrassed many more times before it was over. He thought long and hard. What was the right reaction? The most effective for the campaign? For Dole? For himself? Reed had to get this one right.

The next morning, Thursday, Dole called and Reed took the call.

"How're we doing?" Dole inquired, using one of his trademark lines.

"We're not doing well, Senator," Reed replied. "This was a terrible, terrible mistake that you made yesterday that's hurting you. It's not hurting me. I'm a big boy. I don't really care what anybody thinks about me, but it's a blemish on your character the way you handled it, not only blaming the staff but by reversing something that you had very wisely gone out and defended for two months."

"Well," Dole replied, "I've been telling you I wasn't happy with it. I was sending signals about it."

"Senator," Reed responded, still boiling, "if you've got a problem you've got to tell *me,* you've got to bang on the desk, you've got to call me, but don't send signals through the press that you've got a problem *because you really don't.* If I made a mistake, and I've made many mistakes, it was I should have told you beforehand, but I thought since you agreed with me, it was okay. I can understand a little grumbling but you've got to have that relationship with me, you've got to trust me and tell me if something's fucked up, it's fucked up. It's also sending a signal that you have no confidence in me and your whole campaign team. And that's bad—not for me—*but we go back to the old Dole.*"

"Well," Dole said, "that's not true. I have total confidence in you and everything you guys are doing."

"That may be fine," Reed said, "but that's not what the people think now. So we've got to go back to kind of square one."

Dole was willing to take the heat from his campaign manager because he now felt better about himself. Yes, he was getting beat up, but the principle on gay rights applied elsewhere. At least he could face people and say, "I'm not going to discriminate against you, and that's not Bob Dole's style whether you're disabled, black or white."

Dole and Reed agreed they were going to have differences at times, and the disagreements had been minimal to that point. Soon Dole and Reed were talking about upcoming campaign matters, moving on.

Reed realized that few things could have been better designed to play right into the hands of Dole's detractors and enemies. Now there would be 45 cartoons. One of the saddest parts, Reed felt, was that just the previous weekend the Log Cabin incident had finally faded out of the news.

Two months later on a long plane ride back from Iowa, I quizzed Dole at length about what had happened, how he felt about it and what he had learned from the incident.

He acknowledged that the campaign staff had made the decision, which he said forced him initially to buy into their explanation and what he called their "plot."

"I didn't like to buy into the plot with a straight face," he said.

"Why," I asked, "when they told you, did you then go along with the plot?"

"Well," Dole said, "the old bugaboo: Bob Dole's trying to run the campaign." He was haunted by 1988, when he was roundly criticized for trying to be his own campaign manager. If he reversed Reed's decision, he said, everyone would start saying there Dole goes again. "We lost the straw poll and I'm not too happy about that, then this happened, then the next thing could have happened, Bob Dole's unhappy with the campaign, da-da-da, he's trying to run it," Dole said.

"I think what we learned from that mistake is that there are certain things that a candidate ought to clear," Dole said. "This gets into Bob Dole the person. It's not so much Bob Dole the candidate. It's the person. Is he tolerant? Does he tolerate different views? Tolerate somebody with a different lifestyle?" He added, "This is basic, this is what people ought to know about you. Are you going to just do this because it sounds good politically?"

He also said that he knew and was concerned that everyone was waiting for him to slip up like in 1988. The media and other political figures, he said, always talked about "When Bob Dole makes that mistake."

"Well, I haven't made it yet, maybe I'll make it tomorrow," he added.

"So my view is, I'll probably make some mistakes, but I wouldn't have made that one."

• • •

On October 17, the same day Dole declared to the Ohio reporters that it had been a mistake to return the $1,000, Clinton was speaking in Houston at a fund-raiser.

Referring to the 1993 economic plan of his first year in office that included a $250 billion tax increase, mostly on the wealthy, Clinton told an audience of high-rollers, "There's probably people in this room still mad at me about that budget because you think I raised your taxes too much. Well, it might surprise you to know that I think I raised them too much too." He said he wanted more cuts in government spending and implied that the Congress had made him raise the taxes.

Clinton's economic plan had passed without a single Republican vote in either the House or Senate, and Clinton had engaged in some extraordinary personal arm-twisting and dealmaking to win the Democratic votes. To get the last vote in the Senate, the president got in a shouting match with Senator Bob Kerrey, the Nebraska Democrat, and at one point grew so angry that he told Kerrey, "Fuck you."

Upon hearing of Clinton's reevaluation, Democrats in Congress, especially Kerrey, were furious. Kerrey wrote out a speech blasting Clinton that he planned to deliver the next morning on the Senate floor. He shared his plan with several other Democratic senators in the privacy of the Senate cloakroom.

About 6 P.M. Vice President Al Gore called Kerrey.

"I heard you're upset," Gore said.

Yes, Kerrey said.

"You have a right to be," Gore said.

Kerrey said it was unbelievably outrageous that Clinton would imply the Democrats in Congress had pressured him when he and others had pressed and pressed for more spending cuts in 1993, not tax increases.

Gore said that Clinton would soon be apologizing for the comment or clarifying it. Clinton had been tired at the Houston speech. It had been late and Clinton thought he was speaking to a meeting closed to the media.

Kerrey said he was still going to speak out.

"I hope you'll reflect on it," Gore said very politely, "before you give it."

Kerrey reconsidered. If he gave his prepared remarks and showed his heat, he thought his anger would be the story. He didn't want that, so he toned down his remarks substantially while still criticizing Clinton.

Clinton publicly offered a modified and qualified retraction. "If I said anything which implies that I think that we didn't do what we should have done given the choices we faced at the time, I shouldn't have said that. . . . What I meant to say is I think nobody enjoys raising taxes." Clinton even suggested that his mother had once warned him about late-night speechgiving.

Some news accounts attributed Clinton's initial remarks in Houston to the influence and strategy of Morris. How absurd, Clinton told several of his advisers. "Disneyland," he said. The people in the room in Houston knew what he meant. No one liked taxes, including him.

19

Much to Colin Powell's relief, his long-awaited memoir, *My American Journey,* was finally released in mid-September. He was a more emotional—even prickly—person than he conveyed in speeches or television appearances, and he had found book writing hard and frustrating. Powell had spent 35 years of his adult life in the highly structured and scheduled military environment, and he was unaccustomed to the loneliness and the long, intense task of writing.

"You're never fucking done!" Powell had said several months earlier in a moment of frustration. "I hate this fucking profession. I am an amateur, and I am leaving the profession. But we are as done as it's ever going to be. It's abandoned just about now. One more look and then the hell with it." He hoped the book conveyed that he had been a bit of a "shithead," as he put it, in his younger life but had pulled himself up. The book was so much about his march upward that Powell had once seriously entertained the idea of calling his memoir *Thank You, America.* The title was vetoed by Powell's advisers and publishers.

My American Journey was a giant hit, the biggest book of the year by far. Crowds jammed his five-week book tour to 25 cities, including London and Paris, which began September 16, 1995. It looked to many, especially the professional political reporting class, like the start-up of a run for the presidency. The intense hoopla, with the poised, well-dressed, articulate man behind the security and under the bright camera lights, looked and felt like a presidential campaign. At the first bookstore, 40 camera crews and a half-mile line of people seeking autographs showed up. Powell personally signed more than 60,000 books over five weeks— a monumental achievement. If he had signed ten books a minute, that would have been roughly 100 hours or four 24-hour days of non-stop book signing. Instead of getting tired, Powell drew energy from the attention.

"That was incredible!" he said, settling into the back of his car after one signing. He had never experienced anything like it, even during the parades after the Desert Storm Gulf War victory in 1991. The war victory had been about much else—General Norman H. Schwarzkopf, President Bush, the troops, erasing the stain of the Vietnam War defeat, national pride. This new wave of attention, however, was personal, exclusively about Powell. No Schwarzkopf, no Bush this time. The sheer power of directed public adoration seemed to boost Powell's already considerable self-confidence.

"Of course, people would turn out for Charles Manson too," Powell noted sarcastically in private. Yet he was treated with reverence and ogled over like a rock star. "There he is!" people from the crowds shouted, and those urging him to run for president—rich, poor, and in between— seemed genuine and sincere.

His personal and television appearances reinforced the impression of a man who knew himself and who was at the top of his game. Powell is a big, hefty man with a booming, directed voice. His expressions of approval can be infectious and his disapproval can be chilling. A powerful, natural speaker, Powell does not get tongue-tied and never gives up his advantage over an audience or questioner. Whether in a formal speech or a television interview, he seems on track and in control. He directs outward from the podium or the television, projecting an unusual sense of surefootedness.

Before his book was published, Powell had pretty much decided that if he ran for president it would not be as an independent. That would require money and an organization that he didn't have and could not possibly put together in the coming months. Besides, how would an independent be able to govern effectively with such a highly partisan Congress? No, Powell figured, if he ran, he would enter the Republican primaries. Though he was no conservative on domestic and social issues, he thought government had grown too big and unwieldy.

But he realized that at the end of the day a decision to run for president would get down to him, not others. What did he want? It was the right question, and one he could afford to ponder after all those years of taking orders. Asking precisely what he himself wanted was a somewhat novel and luxurious exercise. Even the chairman of the Joint Chiefs of Staff, the post he served from 1989 to 1993, took direct orders from the civilian leadership and had to ask the Secretary of Defense and the president, What do you want?

Powell was basking in his new independence. If he wanted to sleep a little later, read a book, gab on the phone with a few close friends, he did. He watched MTV, laughed hard at Dave Barry's humor columns, tinkered with one of the classic old Volvos in his garage, attended a professional wrestling match, or just went shopping.

He noted that he was carrying water for no one. "I'm in a wonderful position in life in that I don't have to appeal to, pander to, appease or try to champion anyone's position or any party's position," Powell said. He was the most popular potential leader in the country in the early fall. A *Time* magazine and CNN poll showed Powell, running as a Republican, beating Clinton 46 to 38 percent.

Powell's possible candidacy had already captured two cover stories in *Newsweek*—the first in October 1994 headlined "The Powell Scenario." It was a tease and offered no scenario other than the likely impact of his immense popularity. Two *Time* magazine cover stories had followed, one in July 1995 putting the question in the form of a dare: "If Colin Powell Has the Nerve, He Could Change America." The story was so fawning that Powell privately declared it "a major barf." *U.S News & World Report* restrained itself and ran only a single cover story, "The Man to Watch."

Powell nonetheless seemed, at times at least, to be keeping his feet on the ground. He knew about the half-life of fame. Close up, he had watched President Bush weather defeat in 1992. Even a president, a good man like Bush, could be forced out and fade away almost overnight. Powell was determined to explore as fully as possible the option of running. That was the key to understanding what was going on, which few did. Powell liked to weigh all reasonable options and not just as an intellectual game. He had trained his mind to approach big problems from all angles. His core work in the Army had been the analysis of options. His usefulness to Presidents Reagan and Bush had been his ability to lay out alternative courses of action sensibly and somewhat dispassionately.

• • •

Earlier in the year, Powell had watched some of the Conservative Political Action Conference Convention, a gathering of key conservative activists, on C-SPAN television.

"Can you imagine me standing up and talking to these people?" Powell asked his longtime friend and former aide Marybel Batjer.

"Yes," Batjer replied, well aware of his adaptability.

"Who needs it?" Powell replied.

During October, in the last week of his book tour, some of his Republican friends were urging him to temper his criticism of the Christian right, a powerful voice in the Republican Party. He had said previously and publicly that the religious right made him a little nervous for pushing their religious agenda into a political agenda. But Powell, after all, agreed with the Christian right's emphasis on family values. That could be a point of convergence.

As his book tour was ending, Powell appeared on CBS *This Morning* on Monday, October 16, and sounded this new, more conservative line. He said he favored tax cuts and much of the direction Newt Gingrich was trying to take the party. "And so I am generally in line with the Christian right," he declared at one point.

Richard Armitage, a 50-year-old former Assistant Secretary of Defense and Powell's closest personal friend, watched the morning TV show and was shocked. It had come out all wrong, making Powell sound like he was outright pandering to the conservative right.

"How'd it go?" Powell asked Armitage on the phone afterwards.

"Too wordy," Armitage said, suggesting they talk later. Armitage didn't want to reveal his shock while Powell was still on the road. Powell shouldn't lose any of his self-confidence, essential in the long march of book tour and possible candidacy. Armitage was continuing to advise Powell not to run. Even so, he could see the inexorable, almost hydraulic pressures building, and he wanted to assist and counsel his friend in every way if he chose in the end to run.

The next day, October 17, Powell, in Cleveland on his book tour, remarked that the decision might have to be made in his gut. "I need the passion that I had for the military, where every day I got up and said, 'C'mon, let's go!' Thirty-five years of that. Can I transfer that sort of passion over to being a campaigner as well as being an elected politician? That's probably the most difficult question."

How was Powell going to find this essential passion and the single-minded drive in the coming weeks? And how would he explain if he suddenly gained that passion effectively overnight? What event—internal or external—might cause such a shift? It was too much distance to travel in a short time.

Powell's formative experiences in senior roles had not been as a decision maker or even as a military commander in the traditional sense. Powell was an adviser. He had been national security *adviser* to President Reagan for a year in the late 1980s. It was the old Henry Kissinger job, but Powell was not a broad strategist. His job was to coordinate other opinions and present recommendations. Later, as chairman of the Joint Chiefs of Staff, Powell was by law the principal military *adviser* to the president, the Secretary of Defense and the National Security Council. By law he was the most senior military man in the nation, but he was not directly in the chain of command. His function was oversight and communications. He was the liaison between the military commanders in the field and the Secretary of Defense and the White House.

Powell was not accustomed to making hard, final decisions.

After his book tour ended on October 20, Powell imposed a deadline on himself. He would have to decide in the next month and planned to plunge, carefully and step by step, into the depths of the "run" option.

The most insistent of those urging that he run was a troika of self-appointed Powell promoters. All three were devotees of Dwight Eisenhower and the concept of a citizen president who would be above politics. First there was New York public relations veteran John Reagan "Tex" McCrary, who had helped persuade Eisenhower to run in 1952 by staging a series of public appeals. At 85, McCrary now saw Powell as the embodiment of Ike. He bombarded Powell with memorabilia, literature, mail and faxes about Ike, drawing historical parallels with the mushrooming support for Powell's candidacy. Five months earlier, on May 3, Powell had sent McCrary a handwritten note that was no doubt encouraging: "Dear Tex, Thanks for the bayonet, books, clips, advice, love. You're a piece of work! Colin."

Another avid and high-profile Powell promoter was Stephen Ambrose, the historian and Eisenhower biographer, who resigned as director of the Eisenhower Center at the University of New Orleans in the spring of 1995. Ambrose, 59, said he would devote himself full time to launching Powell's presidential bid and appointed himself a speechwriter for the general he had never met. He had concluded that it was Powell's duty to

run, and began declaring he knew for certain that Powell would run
because a man that capable would see his duty—at least as defined by
Ambrose. "I'm 99 percent sure he'll run," Ambrose said over the summer.

On his own initiative Ambrose crafted a first draft of an announcement speech for Powell but complained to Tex McCrary in a letter that
he didn't know Powell's views, cadence or language, making it difficult to
polish such a speech.

The third Powell promoter was Charles J. Kelly, Jr., a retired investment banker and the head of Citizens for Colin Powell. Kelly had headed
the campus Citizens for Eisenhower in 1952 when he was attending Yale
Law School. Beginning in late 1994, Kelly had virtually devoted a full
year of his life trying to persuade Powell to run for president. Kelly had
worked day and night out of his home in Georgetown to try to draft
Powell. A ten-page executive summary entitled "National Draft Movement" presented Powell as the "only person" to lead. He was unique and
inevitable, the summary stated.

Kelly had not spoken directly with Powell in the previous year but
had gleaned through conversations with George Weathersby, a classmate
of Powell's in the 1972–73 White House Fellows program, that Powell's
coyness stemmed from the legal requirements that no money be expended
on his behalf until a formal presidential exploratory committee was established. Kelly felt he was acting with Powell's tacit approval. After all,
Powell had the option of passing word that Kelly should stop, and he
never had.

Powell invited Kelly to his McLean home for Thursday, October 26.
Kelly and Weathersby arrived at Powell's house about 10 A.M. Powell's
old friend and key political adviser, Kenneth Duberstein, 51, the White
House chief of staff in the last year of the Reagan administration, also
was there. Powell and Armitage affectionately called Duberstein "Duber-
dog" or just "The Dog." Although he was now one of the most important
lobbyists in Washington, Duberstein had little experience in electoral
politics.

"You understand I have not made a final decision," Powell told Kelly
and Weathersby, but he wanted to hear where they were and what
they had.

Kelly delivered an extensive briefing book outlining the campaign
apparatus he had set up in major key primary states for the Republican
nomination. He had what he called "cadres" of seriously committed people in each. Since the most precious resource for a late-starting campaign
would be Powell's personal time, he would have to divide it between

fund-raising and voter contact, Kelly said. Powell should run on the future of the country, focusing on young people, he recommended. Major events should be scheduled at universities. He explained that either he or his cadres had talked with the governors or Republican state chairmen in key states.

"All agree on one thing," Kelly said, "that Dole cannot win the general election against Clinton."

"Yes," Powell said, "I understand that his support is very shallow. I hear that from others."

Kelly went through more of the campaign mechanics and outlined a possible budget of somewhere between $8.5 and $12 million for the period up to the end of the California primary at the end of March 1996.

They reviewed the poll numbers.

Kelly recommended an announcement at Powell's alma mater, City College of New York (CCNY), in about four weeks, the week of Thanksgiving.

After more than two hours, Kelly left, elated and absolutely certain that Powell would run. All of Powell's questions had been directed at "how," and he had never introduced the word "if." The morning had been all positive, and Kelly felt that Powell was very impressed with their work.

Powell realized at once that this was not an A-team of top professionals, not even close to what a presidential campaign would obviously require.

Over in Dole headquarters, Scott Reed was increasingly worried that Powell might jump in. Reed had a private, back-channel relationship with Ken Duberstein. The two talked once a week, trying to smoke out information, send signals and pick up intelligence from other campaigns.

"If he doesn't run," Duberstein had told Reed in one of their phone calls, "I'm with you guys."

Reed wondered what to do. Powell was getting unprecedented favorable news coverage beckoning him into the race. "All these blowjob interviews all the time from everybody," Reed said. At the same time, a reporter for the Public Broadcasting System had interviewed Dole and had asked Dole mostly about bad things—dyeing his hair and his divorce.

"This is one of the things there's nothing we can do anything about," Reed finally concluded. He developed a three-point plan if Powell got in the race. First, Dole would welcome Powell and not criticize him. Second, they would stick to their own game plan. Third, they would work to avoid any defections from their endorsers and supporters among the high-visibilty senators, governors and other local state officials.

Late in October, Nelson Warfield had come to see Reed. Ronald Lauder, the wealthy cosmetics heir, unsuccessful candidate for mayor of New York City, and Warfield's ex-boss, had said that Powell had called him the night before about 11 P.M. to see if Lauder would be available to raise money for a possible Powell campaign.

Reed believed that Lauder was a political joke and couldn't raise two nickels in a presidential campaign, but the direct contact by Powell was a dangerous sign. Reed decided to stir up a little trouble and had the word passed to two reporters about Powell's call to Lauder. The leak would possibly give Powell some second thoughts, Reed hoped, and show the general that if he ran he wouldn't be able to do much in private. It also would perhaps give Powell some doubts about Duberstein, who had urged the fund-raising calls.

After the inquiries about his calls to Lauder came into his office, Powell called Lauder. Why did you talk to anybody? Wasn't this supposed to be between us?

Lauder was somewhat dumbfounded and explained that he had just talked to some of his money guys to test their reaction.

The news stories of the Powell-Lauder call filled the vacuum of expectations about Powell's plans.

Reed was delighted with the stories. He considered Lauder a lightweight, and Powell's outreach made the general look like he was scrambling. On Friday, October 27, Reed talked with Duberstein.

"We had a better week than you did," Reed said.

"I don't know what he's going to do," Duberstein said, repeating his promise to support Dole if Powell said no.

Reed wanted to keep the heat on Powell in every possible way. Lacy had some new confidential polling data showing that in a twoway Republican race just between Dole and Powell, Dole would win, 42 to 29 percent. In addition, the polling showed that more than half the Republicans thought Dole was philosophically conservative while nearly half thought Powell was moderate or liberal. That meant, Lacy believed, that Dole would defeat Powell in a Republican nomination fight. Lacy went to see Warren Rudman, a longtime Powell friend.

"You've got credibility with Powell," Lacy said to Rudman. "Would you consider taking this data and sharing it with Powell so that he understands?" Maybe the data would discourage Powell. The Dole campaign didn't want to deliver the information in a threatening way or with an attitude of "we'll kick your butt," Lacy said. "Just as a friend say you're going to have trouble beating Dole in a primary situation."

Rudman called Ken Duberstein, who thanked him for offering to share the poll. They were looking at their own polling data, Duberstein said politely, and Rudman didn't need to send it over.

Armitage spoke with Powell regularly, sometimes two, three or more times a day. He could hear that his friend was seized with the weight of the decision. Powell was edgy. He was wrestling and admitted experiencing tremendous moodswings, even violent shifts in emotion. Quite a rollercoaster, he said. The expectations and the enthusiasm of others got to him. Some mornings, Powell said, he thought it might be yes. He would feel good for the first 15 minutes of the day, and then it would be downhill. On the mornings he started out thinking it would be no, he felt good all day. A sign perhaps. But then he thought about the word used by the organizers of the various draft movements—"duty." He believed he knew what the concept meant. But where was his obligation? Armitage noted that if Powell ran, he would have to feel morally superior to the opposition—Clinton or Dole or whomever. It would help to dislike the opposition. But Powell didn't declare enemies very easily. He was friend to the world, even liked and saw the strengths in Clinton and Dole, though he knew their weaknesses.

"These people, you know," Armitage said at one point of the potential opponents, "they're not Saddam Hussein."

On Wednesday, November 1, Powell asked Armitage and Duberstein to lunch to discuss his options.

Powell was in a very positive frame of mind, seemingly leaning toward running. Duberstein had researched the federal election laws outlining how a presidential exploratory committee could be set up.

Powell had some questions. What is an exploratory committee? How does it work? What do you have to do to set one up?

When it was explained, Powell said that he wanted Armitage and Duberstein to be co-chairmen.

Armitage asked if that would be the best use of his time. After all, he knew nothing about electoral politics. How about a role as foreign policy adviser—his specialty? Wouldn't people with well-known names and high political visibility be better?

This would only be for ten days, a bridge before he set up a full-fledged committee, Powell said. With the exploratory committee he could legally begin to raise money.

Turning to the question of where he might announce for president, Powell said that he was considering CCNY, his alma mater.

Next, they turned to the question of the campaign theme. They discussed economic development and racial healing, but the notions were general and vague. What would be driving the race? Could it be integrity? Coherence? Strength? The type of people now in government and the obvious case that Powell was different?

Armitage could see that Powell wasn't clear on why he might run or on exactly what he might want to do as president.

Powell asked if they thought he would win the New Hampshire primary. So much would hinge on the first state with actual ballot voting. No Republican had ever been nominated in modern times without winning New Hampshire. He didn't want to start with a second- or third-place finish, he noted. "How do you think I'll do?"

"I think you'll win New Hampshire," Armitage replied. Sure, Powell could do it. "You can go up there and slog around." But Armitage didn't want to think in terms of the pieces of a possible campaign, the details, when the most important question hadn't been answered. He turned a little emotional. *"I don't think you're ready for this,"* he said emphatically.

Powell didn't respond.

Duberstein said he also thought Powell would win New Hampshire.

Powell was moving through the parts. What about the money?

They noted he was way behind.

Powell was not so worried about the money. He sensed it would come in. He had hardly met a businessman or CEO who had not offered to help raise money beyond the $1,000 maximum individual contribution by soliciting others to give, the key multiplier in all successful fund-raising.

Armitage left shortly after 2 P.M. He was quite amazed. For the first time, he concluded that Powell was likely to run. Armitage liked to put percentage odds on decisions or outcomes. He thought Powell seemed to be 70 to 90 percent leaning toward it.

Duberstein arranged for Haley Barbour, the chairman of the Republican Party, to come to Powell's Virginia office. Most of the other candidates only scored a little breakfast with juice and muffins at Barbour's office so Barbour, a jolly Mississipian, could keep his stance of neutrality.

As he had with all candidates, Barbour said his job was to ensure the playing field was level, that the winner of the Republican nomination would have the chairman and the party's full support, and of course Powell was welcome to the party, welcome to run.

By Thursday, November 2, Powell's office in Alexandria was increasingly besieged. Fielding the phone calls, running the office, and attempting to manage the various tidal waves was a neat, compact, well-groomed man with thick, graying hair, a mustache and a cheerful smile.

"This is Bill Smullen," he said into the phone, carefully and politely identifying himself. Smullen, 54, was Powell's chief of staff, executive assistant and press spokesman. He had served 30 years as an Army officer, and he had retired as a full colonel in 1993 with Powell. For all four years of Powell's chairmanship of the JCS, Smullen had been his personal press spokesman. He was the only person Powell had hired from his staff when he retired.

Smullen had been there since the beginning of Powell's post-retirement life and had set up a small office in a seventh-floor suite of the Armed Forces Benefit Association in Alexandria, Virginia. Smullen had read, helped edit and fact-checked six drafts of *My American Journey.* He had been hard on the drafts and on Powell a number of times, pointing out parts he found too self-serving. In the acknowledgments, Powell called Smullen his "close friend" and "my confidant and protector." Smullen had spent months planning and orchestrating the book tour and had been at Powell's side during the entire five weeks on the road.

Low key but also a careful advocate, Smullen was one of the breed of military press officers schooled in the lessons of Vietnam. He had learned that the essence of sound media relations had to be persistent, aggressive realism. The message could barely get an inch ahead of the ground truth.

Smullen felt Powell's decision was almost getting down to a coin toss. The expectation level was so high as to be palpable in the office and seemingly about the country. Smullen could see these expectations bearing down on Powell, overpowering him. Since most requests to Powell funneled through Smullen, he saw that too many people were looking out for themselves, overlooking Powell's real interest and taking advantage of the man, who was nice to hundreds of friends and acquaintances.

That afternoon, Powell came into his Alexandria office and called Smullen in to solicit his views.

"You've left me alone on this and I appreciate it," Powell said. "You know me as well as anyone. I value your opinion. I want to hear what you think."

Smullen said that he had sat at the information crossroads—the book tour, fielding calls from reporters from all over the country and the world. He had picked up the phone from hundreds of average people calling in their encouragement, sifted through the bags of mail, seen the instant, near-electric surge of strangers when they heard of his association with Powell. "Sir, the support is real, genuine, heartfelt," Smullen said. And, he said, you have a chance to win—the Republican nomination and the presidency.

"I think I know you as well as anyone," Smullen said. "I know what is important *to* you, not *for* you. Family is the most important thing, and if it was not number one for you, you would not be the person I know." Smullen was aware that Alma strongly opposed a candidacy. Her unyielding opposition had to be given something more than serious consideration, Smullen said. He reminded Powell that he had said publicly that Alma's views would count 51 percent in the overall decision. With all Powell had said about the primacy of family, Smullen felt he did not have to add the implicit thought—if you are true to yourself, Alma's desires have to be given that 51 percent.

Alma suffered from depression and had undergone successful medical treatment for years. It was not a family secret. This had been known among Powell's friends and many in the media. When it had appeared recently in published news articles on Powell, the descriptions had been straightforward, not sensationalized. Neither Powell nor Alma had taken offense.

Smullen had been saving up his thoughts for months about whether Powell should run. "You've got to understand that Alma will have to be out there for 12 months," Smullen said. She would be expected to campaign. Elizabeth Dole had just taken a leave of absence as head of the American Red Cross so she could devote herself full time to stumping for her husband. Alma would be uncomfortable even in a dramatically scaled back version of personal campaigning. "Alma would not be a happy camper," Smullen said.

Powell laughed heartily and darkly. He understood the depth of the understatement. Stress could be the worst thing for a person with depression.

"Sir, you would surrender your privacy and the privacy of your family in a way that even *you* don't realize," Smullen said. They had seen it in the current frenzy of media coverage—unbelievable already. But that was not the real thing. That was just the warm-up act. Declare his candidacy and the media which had been widely criticized for puffing Powell would go to work with microscopes, shovels and every other instrument of scrutiny known to man. It could be like nothing anyone had ever seen before.

To illustrate, Smullen handed Powell a newspaper article published that day, by Martin Fletcher of *The Times* (London). The story referred to "uncorroborated rumors" about the lifestyle of someone associated with Powell. Of course, by their very nature rumors are uncorroborated. And in this case, apparently no effort had been made to check. There were no details in the story. Probably only a British or tabloid newspaper would print such a story. Smullen didn't even care about this particular article, didn't care about someone's personal lifestyle, thought it didn't matter, wasn't relevant. But if Powell ran, that would only be the start. The stories any publication chose to run could make their way into the mainstream media. Smullen was only raising it in the context of privacy.

Powell was grim. He didn't believe the rumor was true.

The point, Smullen said, was that the truth was often the least important and least relevant element in some news coverage.

Smullen wanted to finish. Maybe they were points only a fellow career military officer could make—the Army was like family, the brotherhood, both Powell and Smullen knew. Running for president was not something Powell had always wanted, Smullen noted, or something he had worked for all his life. It was only recently considered. "How do we get from here to there without a structure?" Smullen asked. In the military, there were always clearly defined functions—someone in charge of personnel, logistics, communications, intelligence, strategy, plans and policy, and operations. They only had Powell, Smullen and one other person in the office.

Powell's style, Smullen noted, had been to keep his views and intentions to himself, gather information from dozens and dozens of people personally. The result was that there was no central sharing point or organization or structure other than Powell's own mind.

A week earlier, Smullen had gone out with Powell's permission to look for possible office space for a campaign headquarters. He had found a whole floor that would be available in their current building. But then, Smullen said, he wondered who would fill it? The hoards of volunteers who seemed to be clamoring to go to work knew less about politics than they did. At best they would have a rocky start instead of a brisk start. Powell probably would not be able to have the immediate successes that everyone—supporters, the press—would anticipate. "Can we deliver the goods?" Smullen asked. "Frankly, I'm uncomfortable with our ability to do that."

Nodding and attentive, Powell encouraged his friend to continue.

Should Powell run, he might become the instant front-runner if the polls were to be believed, Smullen said. If not the front-runner, he would surely be watched the most and covered the most by the press. He could get as much media attention as all the other candidates taken together. Each step, each misstep, each non-step would be a story. Overall the immense expectations probably could not be met.

You need a political philosophy to run for president, Smullen said. You have to go beyond affirmative action and gun control and being pro-choice. What would you want to do as president? What program would you want to carry out? For example, one of the television stations recently had run a story about the peanut farmers being upset with the government. What was Powell's position on the peanut farmers? It seemed small and incidental, but the issue was very important in parts of Georgia, for instance. "Where's the enormous staff to work out your positions on this?" Smullen said. "It's nonexistent." No doubt there was a logical Colin Powell position on peanut farmers that was consistent with his other positions. But it would take time and people.

"You're right," Powell said. "I'm not steeped in these issues."

In addition, Smullen pointed out that if Powell chose to run he might win the nomination, be elected and then reelected. So he was potentially making a decision about the next nine years of his life—in essence the remaining portion of his working life up to age 67. Was this what he wanted to do?

There was that question again.

Smullen did not believe that ambiguous advice or carefully listed pros and cons would be of as much value as a bottom-line recommendation. He was willing to declare his opinion.

"If you're asking should you run or should you not," Smullen said, "I'm saying you shouldn't."

"Everything you say is true," Powell replied.

Smullen said that he thought there would be other ways to serve the country, and he personally hoped that Powell would be Secretary of State some day. Powell would know how to do that job and was probably the most thoroughly prepared person in the world for the post.

Powell soon gathered up his things and left the office for home.

It was their first meeting in over six years at which Smullen had talked more than Powell.

That day a dozen leaders of the anti-tax and anti-abortion right wing of the Republican Party held a press conference and tried to scare Powell out of the race. They said Powell was an insider Washington celebrity, a liberal and a member of the establishment who didn't belong in their revolutionary party. Leading conservative Paul Weyrich said that Powell was like a Gilbert and Sullivan opera character who had risen to "ruler of the Queen's Navy by polishing the handles on the big brass front door."

Powell did not have a chance to watch it on C-SPAN, and when he later received a report from Armitage, he said he was amused, astonished and a little peeved. But Powell was truly furious that some of those leveling the severest criticism of his military career had themselves never served.

In the evening, House Speaker Newt Gingrich went into his secret agent mode and didn't tell his staff where he was going. He arrived at Powell's house for a two-hour meeting. Providing a lecture on history, politics, Republicans and the future of modern civilization, Gingrich said Powell was more than welcome to run. But the Speaker had one central piece of advice: "You've got to think about it as a human being."

When Gingrich left, he had no idea what Powell might decide.

Friday morning, November 3, Alma wanted to talk to her husband. She had not received a clear answer from him. She wanted a clear answer. They had an extended quiet discussion at the kitchen table away from the phones and hubbub, advisers and politicians knocking at the door.

Alma repeated that she was opposed. She would not yield. It would be the wrong thing for him, for the family, for everyone. Perhaps it would turn into a disaster. She had meant it when she said publicly that she feared he would be shot.

They spoke seriously and intensely.

At the end, Powell knew that Alma would not budge. She had been consistent. His partner in life for 32 years was absolute in her opposition. As a practical matter, would running be possible? Would it be right in the face of this? His two daughters were also opposed. And though the temptation was there, Powell still had not found that essential burning passion and certainly not in the quantity to outweigh Alma's passionate feelings. The fiery enthusiasm was from others. It was not his. And at the end of the day, it had to be his. The decision to run had to come from the inside.

Powell stepped back from his own situation. The political atmosphere had become superheated, principally because there wasn't much else to grab attention. The celebrated O. J. Simpson trial was over. The race for the Republican nomination seemed stalled. The media fires were looking for pure oxygen. Reporters were looking for stories, and he had provided one for the last several months. If he had learned one thing from his military service, it was that you had to know what you were doing before battle and before the curtain went up.

After 8:30 A.M., Powell called Smullen, who was at the Alexandria office.

"How are things going?" Powell asked, always wanting the latest.

Fine, Smullen said.

"I'll be down this afternoon," Powell said. "I've come to a decision. I'm not going to proceed."

Smullen was relieved. But he quickly realized they would have to tell the world and they would have to find a way to say it exactly right. Sooner rather than later. "There is an engine running out there and we've got to shut it off," Smullen noted.

Pledging Smullen to secrecy, Powell added, "You're one of few people who know."

Powell spoke with Armitage and explained that the decision was heading way, way south. He said he was worried about what the reaction might be when he announced it was a no. There would be problems. He did not want to be seen as a quitter. He also didn't want to be seen as cynical about the country or politics. A lot of people might be angry.

"Your pants are falling down," said Armitage, noting that Powell had lost weight, close to eight pounds. "You're not sleeping." No one could allege that Powell had not given it the most serious consideration. After their talk, Armitage realized it was 98 to 99 percent over. What a swing from 48 hours ago when Powell seemed 70 to 90 percent leaning toward it!

Powell began trying to draft a statement. He decided to tell it the way it was. Family and an absence of passion prevented him from entering the race. He took the draft into his Alexandria office and met with Smullen. "These are the questions I think you're going to get," Smullen said, suggesting they go through some of them and review his answers when he made his announcement.

As they practiced the question and answer session, Smullen could see that the decision was still weighing on Powell very much. He was as tired and drawn as Smullen had ever seen him, even during the most tense moments in the Gulf War.

What about the vice-presidency? Smullen asked.

Powell said he didn't want to be vice president and wouldn't run for the office.

Later, Smullen returned to the vice-presidency question. What if the circumstances changed? They always did. What if the Republican presidential nominee came and pleaded?

"Hell no," Powell said adamantly.

The next day, Saturday, Powell checked in with Smullen.

"How do you feel?" Smullen asked. "No second thoughts?"

"Nope," Powell said.

Powell had to go to Florida to give a speech to Pontiac dealers, and on returning he learned that cameramen and reporters had staked out his house.

Armitage called that afternoon with the first report that Israeli Prime Minister Yitzhak Rabin had been shot. Rabin died shortly afterwards.

That day Alma offered a simple five-word statement to the family, "This ain't going to happen."

Yeah, Powell said, but inside he was still bouncing around.

The bouncing stemmed from his nature, his capacity to see all the sides, the trained option-study habits of a lifetime. There was a doubleness to Powell. He was a passionate person who could also be a cool analyst. He was sometimes profane but also the one to say, "Yes, sir, Mr. President." Powell was a black man up from Harlem and the South Bronx, and as such he retained a kind of vital outsider status. But also he was a Washington insider. He could be open, almost confessional, but also he was very public relations conscious and could close down. There was a core of compassion, even a genuine tenderness to him, but he could be hard. It was Powell who had stood before the map during the Gulf War in his full uniform and declared his strategy for defeating the Iraqi Army: "First we are going to cut it off, and then we are going to kill it."

Powell loved the system, but he could be deeply skeptical at moments about the system and its leaders, especially when it came to race. He loved to work with his mind, but also with his hands. He could be a tough realist, but also a dreamer. He would tell it like it was, but he also could tell it how the listener, especially a president, might want to hear it.

He had worked closely with Presidents Reagan, Bush and Clinton during the moments of some of their hardest decisions. In some respects,

Powell had been training for the job of president. He could do the job, he felt. But the politics and the process of getting there were foreign and largely unknown to him. He had seen how Clinton's instincts just hadn't worked in foreign and defense policy. They didn't apply very well, and his own might not apply to that strange, perhaps awful business of campaigning for the presidency.

On Sunday, November 5, Smullen arrived at the Alexandria office. It was quiet. He was jittery. Lots to do—too much. This could be handled badly. He checked in with Powell to see if there were any overwhelming second thoughts. Nope. Okay, Smullen said. They needed to move out smartly on an announcement of non-candidacy. Very smartly. Since the upcoming Tuesday was a local election day, and Friday was a holiday, Smullen had recommended Wednesday. Powell had initially said, "Let me get back to you on that," but had later agreed.

We need a place to make the announcement, Smullen said.

Yeah, check it out, Powell said.

Chuck Kelly, founder of Citizens for Colin Powell, had been expecting a phone call from Powell that Sunday to get the final go-ahead. Nothing. Duberstein and Armitage had been telling the press to expect a decision from Powell very soon, and media calls to Kelly were running about 200 a day. New Hampshire Governor Steve Merrill was supposedly expecting a signal from Powell too, and word was coming back to Kelly that Merrill and his staff were upset because the general had not sent one. Kelly ran into Duberstein at a party. They rolled their eyes at each other. Kelly was concerned. They should be working. The delay, silence and the assassination of the Israeli prime minister were very ominous.

That evening, Tex McCrary, the most unabashedly persistent of those pushing Powell, faxed Powell a letter at home, addressing Powell as "Mr. President" and Alma as "First Lady." He said, "Most relevant tonight, as I watch CNN's live coverage of the million mourners moving slowly past the soldier's coffin in which Prime Minister Rabin lies in state . . . a soldier/peacemaker *like you.*"

Tex continued, "I have never wondered or asked you, 'Will you run for president?' I have always known you would, because *you must.*

"You are the only leader left . . . and good buddy, you have passed your Point of No Return . . . D-Day . . . H-Hour . . . Moment of TRUTH!"

"Eisenhower was an idea whose time had come—so are you."

McCrary also suggested City College as the site for the announcement. "Bet Bill Smullen will fill the place with worldwide 'must' media."

The next morning, Monday, November 6, Smullen began searching for a place Powell could hold his press conference. In Alexandria, the Old Colony Inn near the office had a convention booked in its hall all week. The nearby Holiday Inn didn't have a parking lot big enough for television to bring in the trucks for live coverage.

Powell viewed his statement with increasing concern. He had already called Armitage and asked him to come by for a drink that night. Armitage was scheduled to play in a basketball game. It is really important, Powell said.

Armitage showed up with a few thoughts written out. Duberstein also came. Powell called Smullen about 7:30 P.M.

"We need one final meeting," Powell explained. But it would take Smullen 45 minutes to get there. "Well, this isn't going to be very long," Powell said. They got him on the speakerphone.

Powell went over his statement. First, it was crucial to express how honored he had felt by the outpouring of support, find the right language to express thanks and humility. Second, he needed to declare his optimism about the country and about politics. Third, he wanted to announce that he was joining the Republican Party. Fourth, he wanted to rule out the vice-presidency and say he would not seek any office in 1996.

Alma joined them for an hour of the two-hour meeting.

At one point, Duberstein asked, just to be sure, "Is it over?"

"It's over," Powell answered.

Tuesday morning Duberstein drove into the wide courtyard of the Armed Forces Benefit Association, a striking new red brick building, and determined that it would be fine for an outdoor announcement.

Smullen called Powell. The weather was going to be sunny but it would be in the 40s and windy. Everyone would freeze, and the wind would howl in the microphones. So Smullen arranged to rent the ballroom of the Ramada Inn the next afternoon at 3 P.M., pledged the manager to secrecy and negotiated the usual $1,000 rental fee down to $250. A couple of security professionals volunteered to help.

The next morning at 8 A.M., Smullen began making calls to the media saying that Powell would have a press conference at 3 P.M. at the Alexandria Ramada Inn.

Scott Reed was continuing to do everything to thwart Powell, who was dominating the campaign news. A recent poll in New Hampshire had Powell at an incredible 33 percent to Dole's 18 percent among likely Republican primary voters. After much courting, Reed had finally persuaded Governor Steve Merrill to endorse Dole. Merrill, incredibly popular in the first primary state, was thought to be the grand endorsement prize. Reed wanted to get the formal news out as soon as possible to lock it in and send another deterring signal to Duberstein and Powell.

Reed arranged for Merrill and Dole to announce the governor's endorsement on Wednesday, November 8, in New Hampshire.

On Wednesday morning, Dole was flying up to New Hampshire with some of his key backers from Congress, including Representative Bill Zeliff, the New Hampshire Republican who chaired the Dole campaign in the state. Dole and Zeliff were chatting in the back of the plane when Nelson Warfield came back to report that he had heard Powell was going to make some kind of announcement at a hotel in Alexandria, Virginia.

"What do you think that means?" Dole gruffly asked.

Warfield said he didn't think anyone would announce he was running for President of the United States from an Alexandria hotel, so it looked like a no.

Soon Warfield reported in again. Tim Russert of NBC was telling people he had it on good authority that Powell was going to say no.

Zeliff instantly clapped his hands over his head. "This is the greatest day of your campaign," Zeliff said.

Dole sat quietly with a thin smile on his face.

Earlier in the day, Powell got a haircut but he didn't have time to shampoo afterwards so his hair stood up more than usual and he joked that he looked a little like Don King, the boxing promoter whose hair stood straight up several inches.

He and Alma arrived ten minutes early at the Ramada. The only place to wait was the kitchen. Emotions were heavy.

"Maybe we can stay for dinner," Smullen joked to Alma, pointing to trays of salmon laid out in the kitchen and trying to lighten things up as much as possible.

She smiled.

"How do you feel?" Smullen asked.

"Wonderful."

"You happy?" Smullen inquired.

She smiled again. "I'm the happiest woman in the world."

At the press conference Powell, with Alma at his side, read an 11-paragraph statement with the key line right in the middle, at the end of paragraph six, "I will not be a candidate for president or for any other elective office in 1996." He said he based his decision on "the welfare of my family" and the absence of "a commitment and a passion to run the race."

He and Alma took questions for more than 20 minutes. It was widely seen and described as a gracious and masterful performance. But Powell was tired and spent.

At the end of the press conference, Powell looked out into the audience and noticed Chuck Kelly, the man who had spent a full year trying to draft him. There had been no time to call Kelly in advance. While leaving the podium Powell made his right hand into an imaginary phone with thumb at his ear and little finger at his mouth, signaling Kelly that he would phone him later.

That night at Powell's house, the relief and drop in tension were palpable. Powell made his calls, including the one to Chuck Kelly.

"I know you're disappointed," Powell said. He almost apologized, thanking Kelly for the confidence, but repeating the reasons he had stated —family and the lack of passion.

On November 8, after Powell's announcement, Clinton decided not to say anything publicly. He had heard all the analysis from his staff. Stephanopoulos had argued that it would be the best thing in the world for Powell to get into the race. Powell would probably lose and that would give Clinton a single talking point election: the Republicans killed Powell, they're too extreme.

McCurry, taking a different tack, had argued that it might be a good thing also because Clinton was always best when he faced a real challenge. And a Powell candidacy would make it difficult for the Republicans. Powell was black, his parents had been Jamaican immigrants, and as one of the heroes of the Gulf War he was a symbol of internationalism. McCurry argued that if Powell was in the Republican race it would be difficult for Republicans to run on race-baiting, racial quotas, immigration and isolationism.

"Who knows what it means anyhow?" Clinton said that day, shrugging his shoulders. He wanted to find some way to use Powell to improve race relations and wondered about setting up a commission or task force that would include Powell.

In the following days and weeks, as various people offered their postmortems, analysis and speculation, Powell realized he would not be totally free. He had entered into a political mythology of sorts, if only a minor chapter. And political myth has a staying power and a curiosity. His refusal seemed contrary to the great American drive. Was it plausible that someone would say no to such potential power for the stated reasons? "I just told it the way it was," Powell said afterwards. "People are rooting around trying to find some smoking gun. There isn't any. People will root around. No. You heard it.

"I've been as honest as I can on this. And people will always want to look for more, and they're welcome to do so, but you heard it."

Later, Powell filmed a public service announcement for the United Negro College Fund as part of his new private life and continued to give speeches around the country. Hundreds of letters were coming into the office each day. He and Smullen threw themselves at the mail as the new project. They doubled the size of the office. Powell was trying to answer the mail very carefully. Maybe it wasn't that important, but he felt some deep connection with these people. The mail was there, and it was something to do.

"It was never a yes," he said. "And everybody thinks that I was in a binary situation where I had to bawl my brains out or go into politics, and I never saw it that way."

Even before he decided, Powell had taken to introducing Alma only half-jokingly as "Mrs. Sherman," alluding to William Tecumseh Sherman, the Civil War hero who emphatically refused to run for president with the famous statement, "I will not accept if nominated and will not serve if elected."

Now, as a full private citizen, Powell was reading the letters of General Sherman and found them relevant. He was astonished that the professional encouragers and supporters had badgered Sherman for nearly 20 years after the Civil War. Did it never stop?

He read Sherman's May 28, 1884, letter to a friend carefully. "My career has been all my family and friends could ask," Sherman had written. "We are now in a good house of our own choice.

"Military men have an absolute right to rest and to demand that the men who have been schooled in the arts and practice of peace shall now do their work equally well.

"I have my personal affairs in a state of absolute safety and comfort. I owe no man a cent, have no expensive habits, envy no man his wealth or power." Sherman said he would "account myself a fool, a madman, an ass, to embark anew, at sixty-five years of age, in a career that may become at any moment tempest-tossed by perfidy, the defalcation, the dishonesty or neglect of any single one of a hundred thousand subordinates utterly unknown to the President of the United States.

"The civilians of the United States should and must buffet with this thankless office, and leave us old soldiers to enjoy the peace we fought for, and think we earned."

Powell was amazed. Sherman had covered every point. It was a perfect way to say what Powell had been feeling: Leave me alone. "My God," Powell thought, "I'm a reincarnation."

20

Near the end of October, Dole and Gingrich handed Clinton a political bonanza on Medicare, the federal health care insurance for the elderly which polls showed was the most popular government program in the country.

On Tuesday, October 24, Dole told a conservative group that he was among only a dozen House members who had opposed the creation of Medicare three decades earlier. "I was there, fighting the fight, voting against Medicare—one of 12—because we knew it wouldn't work, in 1965."

Dole later clarified his statement, insisting he had favored an alternative health bill that might have avoided Medicare's current state of near bankruptcy. But the quote standing alone made him sound like an opponent of Medicare.

The same day, Gingrich also spoke about Medicare, but directed his harshest comments at the Health Care Financing Administration, the agency that handles Medicare payments. "What do you think the Health Care Financing Administration is?" Gingrich asked. "It's a centralized command bureaucracy. It's everything we're telling Boris Yeltsin to get rid of. Now we don't get rid of it in round one because we don't think that that's politically smart, and we don't think that's the right way to go through a transition. But we believe it's going to wither on the vine because we think people are voluntarily going to leave it—voluntarily."

Gingrich later could argue quite persuasively that he was speaking about the financing administration, not about the Medicare program itself. But again the quote standing alone made him look as if he opposed Medicare.

Morris and Squier were thrilled. These were the kinds of comments —extreme, controversial and eminently quotable—political consultants are always hoping an opponent will provide for use in a commercial. On October 30 they made a 30-second television ad called "Wither."

"Finally," the announcer began, "we learn the truth about how the Republicans want to eliminate Medicare." Dole and Gingrich were quoted, then the announcer continued, "The Republicans in Congress. They never believed in Medicare. And now, they want it to wither on the vine."

These types of ads were tough but defensible, Morris and Squier felt. As long as the quoted words were literally accurate, the Republicans could argue all they wanted about context or intent. The ads were designed to bring the Republicans to the bargaining table on the budget or make them pay for staying away, while at the same time laying out Clinton-Gore campaign themes.

Morris and Squier saw the ads as a keel, a stabilizing, confidence-building force for Clinton. He was committing himself to a position through the advertising—not merely drawing a line in the sand, but in concrete. Once the president allowed something to be said in the ads, the line hardened and deepened.

Gore liked the ads, and he was also sticking to his points about the budget. If the administration's program was perceived as reasonable and if it treated the opposition with respect, they would win. He had told Clinton about the undergraduate thesis he had written at Harvard about confrontations between presidents and Congress. It showed that a president in a reasonable and respectful posture had tremendous institutional advantage over Congress, especially in a crisis. In the television era, the president could go on the air and speak to the nation as no one else. "We will absolutely prevail," Gore told Clinton.

By the fall, Clinton and the Republicans had not been able to reach agreement on the federal budget. Clinton told his senior advisers that he still believed that Gingrich wanted a budget deal. The last thing the first Republican Speaker in 40 years wanted was gridlock, the infamous buzzword from the 1992 presidential campaign. That would show that Gingrich couldn't do any better than the Democrats had done when they controlled Congress. The problem was tricky. Gingrich had to figure out how to keep his right wing in a cage, and at the same time continue to demonstrate that it was he who was the vanguard of the new Republican revolution. To do both, Clinton told his advisers, the Speaker might have to adopt a more confrontational posture, but in the end, Clinton believed, Gingrich wanted a deal.

How would a budget deal impact Clinton's reelection chances in 1996? Was it just a necessary hurdle? Would it be seen as a genuine accomplishment? Or an ugly compromise?

Clinton had his own set of political problems. Mike McCurry thought that Clinton had to define himself more clearly. He had both to explain and demonstrate that he was not just some old-time liberal. Clinton would be reelected president, McCurry felt, if he defined without any question or doubt what the phrase "New Democrat" meant. That definition could not come from Dick Morris. Triangulation was not enough to get someone reelected president, McCurry thought. Clinton needed to present himself and his philosophy as recognizable, a thoughtful contrast to the Gingrich revolution. The White House staff could not provide the definition. It ultimately had to come from the president.

Clinton's efforts had been mushy, McCurry felt. The previous month, on a trip back from California on Air Force One, Clinton had wandered back to the press. Wearing jeans and cowboy boots, he had held forth for an hour of free association. Sensing danger, McCurry had tried to call a halt. "Time out," he said at one point. "This is good food for thought, but these guys need real food too." It was dinnertime, about 7:30 P.M., nevertheless Clinton plunged on. "I'm also trying to get people to get out of their funk," he declared several minutes later. It was the height of mush, and it had led to a two-day feeding frenzy in the press. The word "funk" had obvious negative overtones, suggesting that Clinton was blaming the public, inviting comparison to Jimmy Carter's unfortunate suggestion that it was the country that was suffering from malaise. Three days later Clinton took his comment back, insisting he was optimistic and hopeful.

The incident was heartbreaking for McCurry because such wide-ranging exchanges could be useful to both the press and Clinton. But Clinton pulled back from the press again.

"I've got to figure out a way to get back in," Clinton said. He had to find a way to explain himself.

McCurry took the position that Clinton would just have to accept the culture of the media and of Washington.

"The thing is to outsmart this town, you know, not to kind of succumb," McCurry said.

Clinton was exasperated. "No matter how hard I work, how hard I try," he said to McCurry in private, "they're going to find a way to try to turn this around. So I have to figure out how to stay one step ahead of 'em. I can run faster than conventional wisdom. I can outrun them. I think I'm smart enough now to be able to figure this out." Clinton said he was convinced that the enemies of change, the entrenched were always out there ready to kill.

Clinton took to quoting a long passage from Machiavelli: "For the reformer has enemies in all those who profit by the old order, and only lukewarm defenders in all those who would profit by the new order. . . ."

McCurry concluded that it did not work for Clinton to be self-obsessed and reflect on the lost spirit of America. Bluntly put, people did not want a president to think in public. They wanted decisiveness, clear ideas and direction, inspiration.

Clinton was really agreeing. And McCurry was glad to hear him say one day, "Americans don't want me to help them understand. They just want me to do something about it." Clinton was looking for that extraordinary challenge that would rally people to his cause. McCurry was listening to Clinton very carefully, a large portion of each day, whether in public or private. But he had yet to hear the winning message for 1996.

During the early fall, Dole had become increasingly worried about the federal budget. The Republicans both in the House and Senate were moving on one track, on the verge of enacting a seven-year balanced budget. Though Clinton was on record supporting a balanced budget in ten years, the gulf between the Republicans and the White House was still wide. Dole wanted a meeting. On October 31, he had called Leon Panetta and suggested the Republican leaders and the president discuss the issue the following day after an already scheduled meeting with Clinton on Bosnia.

The session was set for the next afternoon in the Oval Office, but by then Gingrich was perturbed by some comments of McCurry's and was refusing to go. McCurry had charged that the Republicans wanted Medicare to "just die and go away," and had added a sarcastic aside, "That's probably what they'd like to see happen to seniors too." McCurry had retracted the comment, but then he had publicly described the upcoming meeting as an encouraging concession by the Republicans. Gingrich was still furious, but Dole persuaded him they had to sit down and talk with the president to try to work something out.

So on November 1, Gore, Dole, Gingrich, Senate Minority Leader

Tom Daschle and House Minority Leader Richard Gephardt met in the Oval Office.

As Gore shook hands with Gephardt, the vice president whispered, "We ought to sell tickets to this meeting!" Gore knew that Gingrich was roiling.

The discussion of Bosnia was straightforward. Clinton's emissary Richard Holbrooke had won agreement from the warring parties to meet at a peace conference in Dayton, Ohio, and everyone was hopeful.

When they moved on to the budget, Gingrich erupted almost immediately. "I can't tell you how angry I am!" he bellowed. Gore noticed that Gingrich was almost shaking.

"You have a chickenshit operation here, Mr. President!" Gingrich continued. He objected to the Medicare advertisements being run against them, and the innuendos and charges of extremism that were being leveled at the Republicans by the White House. Abruptly, Gingrich turned to Gore and whipped his finger in the vice president's direction. "You've been calling me extremist!" Gingrich roared, rising from his seat.

"At least we didn't accuse you of drowning those little children in South Carolina," Gore shot back.

Gingrich paused for a couple of beats at the reference to one of his recent and more outrageous comments. He had mused aloud that Susan Smith, a South Carolina woman who had drowned her children, reminded everyone how sick the society had become and how in need of change, and had said, "The only way you get change is to vote Republican."

"I didn't accuse you personally of drowning any children," Gingrich told Gore.

They turned to some of the differences in the budget. Clinton said he wanted to protect some of the programs slated for cuts—Medicare, Medicaid, education and the environment. He said he was deeply worried that the Republicans were out to destroy the federal government.

The discussion focused on reform of Medicaid, the federal-state program of health care for the poor. The Republican plan would essentially return the program to the states, and eliminate the federal law entitling the poor to automatic coverage.

Clinton said he didn't like what it was going to do to children, and he just wasn't going to go along.

Gingrich pressed hard, pointing out that the Republicans had the votes and that they reflected the new majority on cutting these government programs and balancing the budget.

"If you want somebody to sign your budget," Clinton said finally with flourish, pointing to the chair behind his desk on the other side of the Oval Office, "you're going to have to elect someone else to sit there because I'm not going to do it. You're going to have to get yourself another president."

Gingrich eventually returned to the exchange about the South Carolina woman drowning her children. "You make a good point," Gingrich said, waving his hand at Gore. "We all say some things in the heat of battle we shouldn't."

As they went through the issues item by item, Clinton said he just was not going to sign their budget. He promised a veto.

After the Republican and Democratic leaders had left, Clinton's blood was pumping. He and Gore felt they had clearly "won" the meeting. Gingrich seemed somewhat a changed person, they thought, and appeared to be on the verge of realizing he would have to modify the Contract With America.

They both noted that Dole's body language and near-total silence spoke volumes. Dole had rolled his eyes a couple of times, not just at them but at Gingrich. But neither Republican leader seemed to be setting up anything that would box Clinton in—nothing credible enough that he was going to have trouble if he rejected it.

For his part, Dole was not at all happy. It seemed as if everyone—Clinton, Gore, Gingrich and the other Democrats—was posturing. He wanted to get something worked out.

Around this time, Lacy received some alarming polling data from Iowa. Though more than 80 percent rated Dole favorably, the poll showed voters didn't know what Dole stood for, and couldn't identify him with any specific idea or action other than to say they had been contacted by his campaign to give money or had received a mailing. In one of their polls, Dole was running even with Gramm at 26 points each among Republican voters very likely to attend the Iowa caucuses in February. The poll also showed that in contrast to Dole, Gramm was identified as a strong conservative who wanted to balance the budget and cut taxes. Lacy's own doctrine on advertising was never to go on the air until the competition had, but the data demanded dramatic action. They needed to get some positive Dole ads on television.

Reed was opposed. Dole ads this early would be interpreted as signs of panic and desperation. Dole couldn't look defensive or reactive.

Lacy countered that they should take credit for the legislation that Dole had passed in the Senate, despite whatever might happen with a Clinton veto. If it was suggested that they were panicking, they would reply that they were taking advantage of this appropriate opportunity to highlight their candidate's accomplishments—that Dole was leading the Senate to balance the budget, cut taxes and reform welfare. This could be set up in an ad contrasting Dole to Clinton.

It was risky, Reed said. Maybe they should try radio ads. It would be seen as a big deal for the front-runner to go on television.

Lacy argued that the polling showed a fundamental problem with perceptions of Dole. Only television would provide the impact to change people's minds.

Reed finally conceded.

A 30-second ad was made that opened with Clinton taking the oath of office with Hillary standing next to him. The words "Liberal Agenda" flashed on the screen.

Announcer: "From Day One, Bill Clinton shocks America with his liberal agenda."

Next, the ad flashed to Dole with a group of young people waving flags. "Bob Dole leads the fight against the Clinton agenda. Dole rallies the nation and Congress passes historic conservative reforms."

For about $75,000, the Dole campaign purchased airtime of nearly 900 rating points in Iowa's three big media markets. That meant that about 90 percent of the voters would see the ad on an average of about nine times over a two-week period beginning in early November—an unusual saturation more than three months before the caucuses.

The key question was how to spin the advertising to the media in Iowa. Reed had the Iowa campaign manager Darrell Kearney explain the ad to the *Des Moines Register*, which then reported that the new advertising blitz was to "highlight the historic conservative change" that Dole was spearheading.

The New York Times ad-watch, a regular feature designed to test the truthfulness of campaign ads, also took the bait: "This is clearly a front-runner's commercial, made for a candidate so far ahead of his rivals for the Republican nomination."

Reed and Lacy were delighted; they got away with it.

At midnight, Monday, November 13, the federal government was going to close down unless Clinton and the Republicans reached an agreement on the budget. Ten months of partisan warfare and wrangling over the Contract With America were about to implode.

After the earlier unfortunate meeting in the Oval Office, Dole and Gingrich had repeatedly taken the public position that they wanted to sit down with the president but the White House had said no. The refusal to meet was the best and purest evidence that Clinton was dug in.

"Look," Leon Panetta said, "the government is going to shut down tomorrow morning. We can't be sitting here pretending that we don't want to invite them into our sandbox, they can't come play in our sandbox. We've got to look like we're at least making a good faith effort." Clinton agreed, and Panetta called Dole several hours before the shutdown and said the president wanted a meeting.

Dole was all in favor of a meeting. Shutting down the government made no sense to him, and he was trying to coax both Clinton and Gingrich into discussion.

"No," Gingrich told Dole, "I'm not going if they're going to bring the Democrats to the table." Gingrich felt that they, as the new Republican majority, held the cards. The only obstacle was Clinton, who alone had the veto power. Why negotiate with the Democratic leaders? It made no sense.

"The president called," Dole said. "We should go down. We said we were available at any time he called." The day before Dole had appeared on David Brinkley's show with a cellular phone, half-joking that he was waiting for a call from Clinton.

Nope, Gingrich was opposed.

"Now you're telling me because they're going to bring their people in we won't sit down?" Dole said. "Come on." He continued to coax.

Finally, Gingrich agreed. They would bring his number two, House Majority Leader Dick Armey.

Armey, 55, was the nuts-and-bolts organizer of the Gingrich revolution. A former economics professor in Texas, he viewed Gingrich with deep ambivalence. He was awed by Gingrich's self-confident rhetorical skills, but he was also privately resentful of the way Gingrich had jumped out in front to lead the new Republican parade and take personal credit. Armey believed that it was his own efforts, as much as Gingrich's, that were responsible for the Republican takeover of the House in 1994. But Gingrich had seized all the attention, and Armey lived in his shadow.

Armey had no such ambivalence about Clinton. He was sure that Clinton was weak. He was certain that Clinton would not put himself on the line. Armey had a bet with a close friend that Clinton would sign the Republican budget. He had also felt slighted by the president at congressional leadership meetings. Clinton seemed to have something for everyone in these discussions, except Armey. Over the last two years Armey had clashed publicly with Hillary Clinton on health care, and he had once said, "Her thoughts sound a lot like Karl Marx."

At about 10 P.M. Dole, Gingrich, Armey and their top staffers arrived at the White House West Wing entrance and were escorted to the Cabinet Room to meet Clinton, the top Democrats and their advisers. Panetta and Clinton's other key advisers were very concerned that Clinton might fold or show some willingness to compromise on the key issue. They had pressed him on the need to hold his ground this time—ground that had been carefully laid in the advertising by the Democratic National Committee and by Clinton himself in his public comments. Clinton was the protector of Medicare, Medicaid, education and the environment.

After everyone had gathered in the Cabinet Room, Clinton went on at some length about how he was not going to let the Republicans dismantle the government and hurt people. He had his principles, and he was going to protect the important programs for people. Wound up, he started waving his finger. Since Armey was sitting directly across the table, the president seemed to be directing his monologue at him. Armey figured this was a dress rehearsal for a speech that Clinton wanted to give to the American people. Armey wanted to make it clear it wasn't working on him. Clinton said he wanted to work together, but he continued to wave his finger a number of times.

"Call it my western upbringing if you like," Armey finally replied, trying to remain calm, "but I have to tell you it's very hard for me to relate to somebody who's lecturing me by pointing their finger in my face." He believed his words were carefully chosen to deflate Clinton. "But be that as it may, I have to tell you, Mr. President, I am totally unimpressed with everything you've just said."

"I didn't expect you to," Clinton replied.

"You can't call us ugly all year and expect us to go to the prom with you at the end of the year," Armey said. "You've run all these ads against us, and you've beat us up, and now you say come and sit down and let's be friends? You know these things don't work out that way." He complained about Clinton's Medicare scare ads. His wife's two aunts had refused to move his wife's grandmother into a new nursing home because they believed the ads, Armey said. "All that demagoguery may be all well and good for political purposes, but it gets played out in real people's lives and it's painful to watch an old lady lose her chance to move because two aunts believe these ads that you and I know are just plain bogus." His relatives, the people from his district in Texas thought they were not going to get Medicare. "They're scared to death. I think it's shameful."

"I don't need you to tell me about Medicare," Clinton replied testily.

"You don't understand how hard we worked," Armey said, referring to the months of back and forth just among the Republicans as they were working out their budget plan. People with heartfelt differences had sat down and wrestled out a hard-fought agreement. "These things hang by a thread. You don't throw away somebody else's work. You can't go back there, or people are going to have bitter disappointments. Look, these people stand for something."

"Look, I stand for something too," Clinton replied. "We worked very hard," he said, citing his 1993 economic and budget plan that he had to pass without a single Republican vote. The failure of a single Republican to join was a sore point with him. The president said they had worked hard on health care also. And Clinton finally brought up Armey's statement about Hillary, an obvious but unstated source of tension between them. "I never, ever have and never expect to criticize your wife!" the president said sharply.

The room was silent. There was lots of discomfort.

Armey had a line in his head to reply: "My wife has never tried to take over one seventh of the economy." No, Armey thought to himself, there was no need. He just stared back at Clinton and said nothing.

Dole and Gingrich stayed out of the Clinton-Armey fight, and after it died down, Dole tried to return to the subject at hand and move the discussion along.

One of the Democrats mentioned a budget plan that did not include tax cuts at all.

"Look," Dole interjected, "if you're going to talk about no tax cuts we might as well just end this meeting right now."

Panetta raised the prospect of an accommodation that might be worked out with enough Republicans and Democrats for a majority agreement.

"You don't understand," Gingrich finally said about 11:30 P.M., "I'm not doing a centrist coalition. It's got to be my majority." He said the Republicans had worked in good faith and honorably. "We've worked so hard. I can't go back to my members."

Stephanopoulos, sitting in one of the chairs that lined the room, thought that the Republicans ought to go talk about their hard work to their therapists. The argument had no resonance with him. He saw that the Republicans had become exclusively involved in their own group dynamic. They were the majority, so once they worked it out among themselves, they figured it was settled. Clinton, Hillary and the administration had made the same fatal error on health care, he remembered all too well. If Gingrich couldn't hold a majority of the Republicans—if the White House, Dole or something else, broke them—there was hope, Stephanopoulos thought.

The meeting continued for some time but there was no progress. Panetta summed up, "Look, you understand where we're at. You're just going to have to go ahead and pass your legislation, and we're going to veto it."

"What are we going to tell the press?" Dole asked, joking. "We're not going to tell them we went in to shout at each other."

Clinton asked them all to keep their comments positive.

Dole left thinking that the president was acting like he was in a strong position. Clinton's poll numbers were up a little, the Republicans' were down. Dole felt they were still all posturing, avoiding the crunch. The stakes were high. The presidency might be on the line, Dole thought. Dole knew there was only about 2 percent difference between the Republican and Clinton plans on projected Medicare spending. But he felt that Clinton was clearly looking out for number one—himself—and was willing to lie, painting the Republican plan as draconian. Clinton must have concluded that he had hit a big political nugget with Medicare, Dole felt. No way was Clinton going to approve the Republican budget.

"It really does boggle the mind," Dole said later in an interview, "that he can look right at that camera and make statements that just aren't accurate. You've got to have some confidence in the President of the United States whether it's election year or not." Dole recalled that his mother had been in that fix, having to rely on Social Security and Medicare. A president could frighten people. "You get a little worried if the President of the United States comes on and says you're going to lose, they're going to cut your benefits." Dole shared his thoughts with colleagues and friends, but didn't make his observation directly to Clinton. He wasn't confrontational like Gingrich or Armey. He'd seen how far it had gotten them.

Dole wanted a balanced budget and figured it would be a big plus for him, at least through the Republican nomination, if he could get it, so he was determined to press ahead. But he wasn't happy about the meeting. Finger-waving, loud talk, references to what someone had said about someone's wife was childish. In his view, both Clinton and Armey had gone too far. Both the boys needed a little spanking, Dole thought to himself.

At midnight the partial shutdown of the government began.

Two days later, at a breakfast meeting with reporters, Gingrich said he was being tougher in the budget negotiations in part because he felt he had been snubbed on Air Force One earlier in the month. On a 25-hour, round-trip flight to Israel for the funeral of Prime Minister Yitzhak Rabin, Gingrich said Clinton had refused to talk to him about the budget. Gingrich told the reporters he knew he shouldn't be so candid about his emotions. "It's petty," he said, "but I think it's human."

"You've been on the plane for 25 hours and nobody has talked to you, and they ask you to get off the plane by the back ramp," Gingrich said. "You just wonder where is their sense of manners? Where is their sense of courtesy?"

At the White House, McCurry at first refused to believe Gingrich's remarks. When convinced of their accuracy, McCurry later said publicly, "Maybe we can send him some of those little M&Ms with the presidential seal on it."

Afterwards Clinton met with his press secretary.

"Mike," Clinton yelled in private at McCurry, "why did you do it?"

McCurry thought Clinton's reaction was in jest and at first tried to get the president laughing, but as Clinton pressed on, McCurry saw he was outraged.

"Don't kick him too hard when he's down," Clinton instructed. "We can't." Ultimately Clinton wanted a budget deal, but on the administration's terms. That would require Gingrich, who had said in private that if he couldn't hold the House Republicans together, Clinton would be negotiating with the number-three Republican House leader, Tom DeLay, who was much more conservative and inflexible. "We have to be very conscious of Gingrich's standing," Clinton explained. "He's the only one that can pull it together. If we get something, and we put it together, he's got to be able to sell it." Clinton and Panetta were worried that the government shutdown could turn into a disaster for the White House. As president, Clinton could be held responsible for the closing of much of the executive branch. The political price would be high. It was critical that Gingrich remain viable, Clinton said.

In public, Clinton was soothing to Gingrich. "If it would get the government open," Clinton said gently, "I'd be glad to tell him I'm sorry." But the government remained closed, making everyone nervous.

The Gingrich flap about the plane ride was a giant story. *The New York Daily News* headline blared "Cry Baby," with a drawing of Gingrich in diapers, bawling.

McCurry felt that some things are just so wickedly perfect that he could let them go all by themselves, no embellishment or comment was necessary. But the White House had a picture of Clinton talking with Gingrich and Dole on the Air Force One trip. McCurry had copies of the picture mass-produced and released to the press, further undermining Gingrich's claim.

That night, Panetta went up to the Congress to chase down his successor as chairman of the House Budget Committee, John Kasich, who was Gingrich's point man on the budget. Kasich, 43, was a pivotal figure, hard-line but reasonable and one of Gingrich's most trusted lieutenants. As Kasich emerged from the House gym, he saw Panetta racing down the hall with hair flying. Panetta was clearly a desperate man, thought Kasich.

We've got to settle this, Panetta urged. He had a piece of paper in which Clinton would agree to the goal of a seven-year balanced budget but based on the White House budget office's own liberal projections. He handed it to Kasich. Should Panetta wait for Kasich to read it?

"You don't understand," Kasich said. "We are not going to cave in." The Republicans were insisting that their own Congressional Budget Office numbers be used.

"What is it with you guys!" Panetta screamed. "You're crazy. This president isn't going to blink."

Kasich again said no, wondering to himself why Panetta felt such pressure. Why was the White House so desperate to get the goverment open? Was it a bad poll? Were they worried that the conservative Democrats might join the Republicans?

At 9 P.M. Panetta wanted another meeting.

Kasich talked to Gingrich and they agreed to hold firm.

"What you've got here doesn't work," Kasich told Panetta.

Ross Perot called Dole's office on November 17 to weigh in on the government shutdown, and he spoke with the majority leader's press secretary, Clarkson Hine. Perot said he had an idea about how to help with the federal workers who were not getting paid. But more important, Perot said he was concerned about Dole doing both the job of majority leader and presidential candidate. Maybe Dole ought to give up the majority leader's job, Perot suggested, adding that he didn't like to see Dole being blamed for everything that wasn't getting done.

When informed of the Perot call, Dole was surprised and amazed that Perot seemed to be looking out for him. What did it mean? But he didn't seize the opportunity to respond to what might have been an olive branch. He brooded about it and didn't call Perot back.

Scott Reed took the attitude that there was no reason to talk to Perot ever again. Nothing they said to him was going to matter. Perot did whatever he wanted.

At the end of the week Florida Republicans were holding a straw poll, grandly named Presidency III. Only some 3,000 people were expected to cast ballots, but the event had grown in importance because Gramm had tied Dole in the Iowa straw poll three months earlier. Larry King was hosting a debate on his CNN television show that all the Republican candidates were expected to participate in the night before the vote.

Dole told Reed that he couldn't go to the debate because he was scheduling the Senate's final passage of the seven-year balanced budget, and he had to be there because a trainwreck was still likely.

But at the last minute Dole changed his mind in typical fashion and decided to debate.

Reed and Lacy were opposed. Dole had not prepared; he had not done a single debate prep session; and he didn't know the local Florida issues that might come up. He clearly was not ready.

No, Dole said he was going to do it.

Reed called Lacy who was in Florida.

"Put on your seat belt, hang on," Reed said.

Reed tried to salvage the situation. Sheila Burke arranged that the Senate would vote final passage of the seven-year balanced budget just as the live Larry King debate began in Florida. Then Dole could leave the Senate, arrive about ten minutes later at CNN's Washington studio for a satellite television hook-up to Florida. He would sweep in and announce passage of a full balanced budget.

That morning, Reed called Dave Carney, a giant, heavyset man, who was liaison between the leader's office and the campaign, and asked him to guard the door to Dole's office and keep people out so Dole could study his debate briefing books.

Dole did take several 30-minute study periods.

That night Reed watched Dole on C-SPAN on the Senate floor during the final passage. Then Reed shifted to CNN to watch the debate. He reached Dole in his car so Dole wouldn't enter into the debate blind. The first big question was whether the candidates would consider Powell as a possible running mate or for a cabinet position, Reed said. "It's dominating the first 30 minutes of this thing." It was the craziest debate, with three of the candidates in Florida and the rest at CNN's Washington studio.

Dole arrived at the studio and made his victorious entrance. He was comfortable, relaxed, and mentioned several Florida issues. He even sounded presidential reporting on the Senate vote. Lacy was astounded Dole did so well.

The next day, Dole flew to Orlando, Florida, for the convention holding the straw vote. Reed told Dole they had counted a solid 1,100 votes among those attending the convention. With an anticipated share of the hundreds of undecideds, he expected a big win with about 40 percent.

After speaking, Dole flew back to Washington.

The results came in. Dole received 1,104 votes, or 33 percent; Gramm 26 percent, and Alexander 23 percent.

Reed phoned Dole with the numbers.

"What happened?" Dole asked.

"It doesn't look like any of the undecideds broke our way," Reed said. They had picked up maybe only four votes.

Dole was clearly unhappy.

Elizabeth passed the word, "He wants to be told what went wrong."

Reed promised to look into it. The answer was as simple as the one he had provided the night of the vote. None of the undecideds went for Dole. Reed and Lacy began telling themselves that the convention was the ultimate retail situation and Dole had not been down there enough, accounting for the failure to capture the undecideds. Alan Keyes also had given a powerful speech, Lacy noted, and had won an unexpected 8 percent of the vote. Soon Dole was getting calls congratulating him, and everyone in the campaign decided they had psyched themselves up too much about expecting 40 percent and they should be pleased with the 33 percent. It was a win, and, after all, they only had to win. Soon they circled the wagons and declared victory.

For Reed, the lesson was clear. He would in the future be a little more conservative about delivering favorable expectations to Dole.

On Sunday, Dole stopped by his office to check on how the efforts to reopen the government were proceeding. Not very well, he learned, with paper proposals flying back and forth with the White House.

"Gotta get an offer on the table," Dole told the assembled Republican leaders in his office, S 230. Gingrich and the other key House Republicans were gathered in the large, ornate room around the fireplace. "I don't know about you, but that's enough of this foolishness," Dole said, laying down the law as much as he ever had with Gingrich and the House Republicans. Shutting down the government was a big mistake. They were not winning the battle. They had no way out, and they would pay for it, he said.

Clinton had already agreed to the seven-year balanced budget, the key, but the White House wanted a collateral agreement. The White House would agree to seven years as long as Medicare, Medicaid, education and the environment were protected. Dole and the Republicans added protection for agriculture, national defense and veterans.

"Let's put ethanol in there," Dole joked about the corn-based fuel that was the product of a company run by one of Dole's biggest supporters.

Gingrich was convinced it seemed a total win because the seven-year provision was the guts of what he and the Republicans wanted.

Clinton had been out jogging and returned to the residence to shower and change so he could make a statement that nothing had been worked out. But suddenly a fax came in from the Republicans.

"God," Panetta said, "this is something to work with."

Clinton thought that Dole's trip to Florida had helped because no doubt Dole had heard people complaining about what the hell was going on in Washington. It was always productive to get out of town, Clinton noted.

The temporary spending legislation would open the government the next day after a six-day shutdown, the longest in history, but would expire in a month. The agreement was more a recognition by both sides that something had to be done than a sign they had moved closer. It was the most expedient way to declare a cease-fire.

At 7:30 P.M., Clinton spoke from the White House briefing room. "This agreement reflects my principles. And for the first time, the Republican leaders in Congress have acknowledged the importance of those principles."

He was vague about his explicit agreement to balance the budget in seven years.

"The key is that nothing will be agreed to unless all elements are agreed to," Clinton said.

Dole and Gingrich held a press conference, also claiming victory. Next, they watched Panetta on television say, "If we can achieve it in seven years, fine. If it's eight years, fine." The next morning Panetta on the *Today* show said, "I don't think the American people ought to read a lot into what was agreed to last night." Privately, he still didn't like the seven-year budget commitment, which would require too many painful cuts.

Gingrich was sure the White House was acting in bad faith. Seven years meant seven years, and it infuriated him that the White House was already reneging on the agreement.

Clinton tried to bury the hatchet with Gingrich. "You know," he said in a phone call to the Speaker, "if I had it to do over again, I would have had you come up and have a drink in the front of the plane."

Dole was just delighted to have the government back in business.

On Tuesday, November 21, the presidents of the three warring parties in Bosnia initialed a peace settlement at talks in Dayton, Ohio. It was an enormous personal triumph for Richard Holbrooke, the U.S. negotiator. Lake's Endgame Strategy had worked.

The next day, Clinton and Gore met with the foreign policy team, Lake and Holbrooke. They all packed into the Situation Room of the White House.

Clinton had some questions but he said that they were going to make the peace accord work. "Any ambivalence that anyone in this room may have had is now over," Clinton said.

He later told his top advisers in private that Bosnia was no longer just a threat to his foreign policy. It was once again a threat to his presidency. "This risks reelection, but we have no choice," he said.

On November 26, the Sunday after Thanksgiving, Dole summoned his campaign team to their headquarters for a meeting in the third-floor conference room. It was a typical Dole meeting, with discussion wandering until Dole, almost out of the blue, brought up what was on his mind. The Bosnia accord signed in Dayton meant that Clinton was going to have to deliver on his pledge to send 20,000 American troops to keep the peace. Dole said that he had no choice but to support the president's troop deployment. It had occurred to him very early in here, he said, pointing to his stomach. He was an American. He was going to support the president. America's credibility was on the line, he believed. The president had signed an agreement, and the others had signed based on U.S. participation.

"Senator," Lacy interrupted with a shudder, "have you seen the polls? They're running at best 60 to 30 against this."

"Yeah, I've seen 'em," Dole replied, "but I don't have any choice. I feel obligated." He said he disagreed with the way Clinton had handled nearly every step in Bosnia, but he also believed it was the prerogative of the president to deploy the military forces.

"You realize what a difficult position that's going to be?" Mari Will said.

Dole didn't reply.

Reed and Lacy realized there was no way to argue him out of it. They met later with Sheila Burke to develop a strategy.

Several days later, Lacy went to see Dole. He tried not to hang around Dole just to be there, to have the precious face time so many in Washington seemed to covet. That way, Lacy figured, when he did seek his time, Dole would listen to him seriously and Lacy could be direct. Too often they didn't discuss the crucial matters. Bosnia was too important.

"Senator," Lacy said when they sat down, "I know you're going to do this. I'm not going to try to argue you out of it because I know it would be a political argument. But if you're going to do this, come out and say it, do it forcefully, explain why, build the rationale." In other words, handle it differently than most matters. Dole couldn't flounder around on this. "Let's put it behind us. Let's get it over with. Don't delay it any longer."

Dole listened but didn't react.

"Let's not screw around with this," Lacy continued, "let's not let it look political. If you're going to take some political gas on this for being a statesman, then go out and get it done and be a statesman. Don't look like you're fiddling around with it for two weeks and then you're coming out on the wrong side."

Lacy enlisted Burke, who told Dole she agreed. But she knew that Dole would be constantly evolving. He was thinking. It was coming internally. There was never a bright line drawn.

Dole finally started preparing a speech to deliver on the Senate floor supporting Clinton.

"You know, Senator," Burke said, "Gramm's going to snap at your heels regardless." Gramm would oppose Clinton and make a big deal of it.

Gramm, who had not served in the military, didn't have a chance given all of his draft deferrals, Dole said. "I will eat him alive on the floor."

Al D'Amato protested to Dole.

"Why are you doing this!" D'Amato yelled, steamy and hyperbolic. "You're making a big mistake!"

"Sometimes, Al," Dole said, "we're not going to be able to agree. I've got to do this. You're still my friend."

Clinton had been very solicitous of Dole, calling him for advice on Bosnia. The president had even wanted to know if it was all right if he came up to the Hill to get support.

"Listen, Mr. President," Dole had said, "you ought to go everywhere you can to get support." Clinton should come see the Republicans. Any president would do this.

"I won't bother you," Clinton asked, "won't bother you?"

Not in the slightest, Dole said.

On November 27, Gingrich finally pulled the plug on his own possible candidacy. "We decided we would explicitly, definitely close the door so there's no more speculation," the Speaker said at a news conference in his home district in Georgia. "I will not run next year for president." He acknowledged he would have had a hard time, and said he wanted to focus on decisions about the domestic agenda, which he said were the most important in the last 60 years.

In a televised speech to the nation that night, Clinton explained his decision to deploy the troops to Bosnia to enforce the peace accord. It carefully met Colin Powell's requirements for such a deployment: the mission would be precisely defined, with realistic goals that could be achieved in a specific time; the risks to the troops would be minimized; and support would be sought from Congress.

Later that night Clinton called Powell, who told him privately that he could support him.

Shortly afterwards the White House told Dole that Clinton was going to veto the giant one-year defense appropriations bill of $243 billion because it contained $7 billion more in defense spending than Clinton wanted. The Republicans and the White House had agreed to fund defense for a year. This dispute was over how much, and it was not part of the overall negotiations on the seven-year balanced budget. Dole was so astonished at the report of the impending veto that he called the president, who was about to leave on a trip to England and Ireland.

Dole argued that from the president's standpoint, he should please reconsider. Just as Clinton was going to try to sell the public on deploying troops to Bosnia, he was going to veto a defense bill? That wouldn't make a lot of sense to a lot of people, Dole said. There was some $600 million for Bosnia in that bill, he said. If Clinton vetoed it, he would have to come back to the Congress for Bosnia money. That would trigger a big Bosnia fight. "You don't need that," Dole said. "You're going to have people want to cut off funding. Over on the Senate side you could have a filibuster." The whole debate would be to question Clinton's policy.

Clinton said he appreciated the call, but there were some things in the bill he didn't like, particularly money for extra B-2 Stealth bombers the Pentagon did not need.

Dole reminded Clinton that he could take money from the large defense expenditures and reprogram the money for other defense needs up to a certain point. A president had latitude to redirect money in defense as long as the major congressional committees approved.

Clinton said he hadn't made up his mind.

Signing the bill, Dole said, would avoid another blowup, avoid a big fistfight in the House and the Senate.

He was going to Europe first, Clinton said, and he would take the bill with him.

"Let it sit," Dole said. "Think about it."

"I'll wait," Clinton replied.

Dole said he still had reservations about the decision to send troops to Bosnia, but he was going to come out and support Clinton and try to get a formal resolution of support through Congress.

Thank you, Clinton said.

Clinton had received a hero's welcome in Ireland, and in Belfast he was staying in one of the most bombed hotels in Europe. He rarely drank but someone had given him a great bottle of Irish whiskey, and he had made an exception that night. Clinton called Panetta.

The last ten days had been sobering as Clinton dealt with the deployment of the U.S. troops to Bosnia, making much of the budget debate seem puny. Clinton had had to look the military commanders in the eye. Though every precaution was going to be taken, the mission was far from risk-free, and it would no doubt result in U.S. casualties. In comparison, the budget discussions seemed nickel and dime: talk of continuing resolutions, seven years versus five years with these assumptions versus those assumptions. Clinton said they were going to have to stop the theatrics on the budget and get on with it. On the possible veto of the defense bill, Clinton knew he was giving up leverage in the budget negotiations, but he was in a very tough position on Bosnia.

"We need to deal with fundamentals," Clinton said.

He had decided against a veto.

"Yeah, you know," Clinton said, "we really don't have much of a choice here given what we've got to do."

On Thursday, November 30, Dole spoke on the Senate floor in support of Clinton on Bosnia. "Some would say, 'Well, if you do this you are supporting the President of the United States.' I say that is all right with me. We have one President at a time. He is the Commander in Chief. He has made this decision. I do not agree with it. I think it is a mistake. We had a better option, many better options. But as I said, he repeatedly rejected those options. Now it is up to high noon. The troops are on the way. They are looking to us for support."

On Sunday, December 3, Dole went to the CBS studio in Washington to appear on *Face the Nation*. Knowing he would be asked about his decision to endorse the president's Bosnia plan, he wanted reinforcement from Colin Powell. He had already paved the way with Powell's political adviser, Ken Duberstein. In the studio's "green room" hospitality suite before the show that morning, Dole phoned Powell.

"See, if you were a candidate for president you could be here," Dole said, half-joking.

Powell said he had gone to church and preferred that.

What was the position Powell was taking on Bosnia?

Powell said he supported the deployment if the United States did not go in aggressively.

Dole asked if he could mention that on the show?

Yes, Powell said.

Before the show Dole told Bob Schieffer, the moderator, about his conversation with Powell, so Schieffer asked about it on the air.

Dole answered, "I asked him about Bosnia, whether or not he supported the effort. He said, yes, he would not have supported it in a sort of belligerency status, but if they do have a peace agreement, support the peace agreement, supporting our troops there, certainly he does."

Dole had made Powell's private support public, but also given himself important cover.

In the White House, Lake still felt Dole's idea of a unilateral lift of the arms embargo had been a bad and absurd idea. But the pressure from Dole and Congress had helped build pressure on the administration to act. Also, Clinton had used the threat of a lifting of the embargo to sway the Europeans to support the administration's plan.

Dole never received credit for giving Clinton some leverage.

"Not publicly," Dole said in an interview later, laughing lightly. "I don't think privately, either. But that's all right. I mean, that happens. You know, hopefully, when I'm president there will be some kind senator up there to look out for me." He laughed again gently. "But I think we got him out of a crack."

Mari Will had a long session with Dole about message and his speeches. Although Clinton's Bosnia policy seemed to be going well, she said Dole's campaign was in real trouble. The retail campaigning was going to intensify, and he didn't have his stump speech down. While everyone was focusing on the Congress, the budget or Bosnia, he was supposed to be rehearsing on weekends. He had missed practice, and hadn't honed a basic speech for his campaign trips. She had presented him with text focusing on his conservative economic and values issues. "Why aren't you giving it?" she finally asked him.

Dole dodged and ducked, not answering directly, going round and round, half sentence after half sentence.

"You're really not going to give this?" Will asked.

"No," he said.

Will decided to propose a focused and structured communications plan. She sent him a five-page memo entitled "Iowa and New Hampshire Message Strategy."

Dole was not delivering his core beliefs and philosophy adequately, she said. Routine rallies, endorsement press conferences, headquarters openings and town meetings had dominated the last months. "It has put us behind the curve in our ability to drive home messages likely to energize our supporters," Will wrote, "let alone win new recruits among the culture/moral/religious voters I believe are the key in states like Iowa."

"It is no wonder our research reveals supporters scratching their heads," she wrote sarcastically, "as to what your message is, and reporting that the only contacts from the campaign they recall are requests to join or give."

Will proposed a careful schedule of what she called "vision themes" in which Dole would deliver short "three-minute newsmaking sound-bites" in different proportions in Iowa and New Hampshire. In Iowa, it would be three on the cultural issues for every one on economic and one on agriculture. "Theme formula: $3 \times$ culture $+ 1 \times$ economic $+ 1 \times$ agriculture," she wrote. She proposed what she called "Issue Clusters." Under the economic issues were taxes, budget, federal regulations, eliminating the four federal departments, small business and jobs. Under culture were Hollywood and television. She considered schools, crime and welfare cultural issues.

In New Hampshire where the economic issues were dominant, she proposed a theme formula of three economic speeches for each cultural and each defense or foreign policy presentation. So for New Hampshire, she wrote: "Theme formula: $3 \times$ Economic $+ 1 \times$ Culture $+ 1 \times$ Defense/Foreign Policy."

"I remain convinced that our supporters are generally in the 'low motivation' category," Will added, "which makes it hard to predict how we will do against the 'high motivation' supporters of Gramm in Iowa and Buchanan in New Hampshire, for example."

"As you know, I believe it will be the 'culture conservatives' who will be bounding out the door that snowy night of the caucuses, and it is they who are motivated by what they see as the real, personally menacing threat of a decaying community, which requires, in their view, redress by the political system."

She sent copies to Reed and Lacy, who greeted the precise thematic formulas with a good deal of hilarity. They couldn't really direct or focus the content of what Dole said. It was pure fantasy to think the proportions could be managed.

21

The Republicans in the Senate and House had finally reached agreement on all the details of a new seven-year balanced budget package, voted it through and sent it to Clinton, who was certain to veto it. It was a moment to relax. On Tuesday, December 5, Congressman John Kasich, the House Budget chairman, was over talking with Dole. Discussion turned to whether they would be able to get any of the blue dogs to join them to override the veto.

"Who are the blue dogs?" Dole asked.

"They're the conservative Democrats," Kasich replied.

"We don't have any blue dogs over here," Dole said, chuckling, "we have hot dogs."

Kasich laughed and smiled, his smirky boyish laugh.

"What about Snoop Doggy Dogg?" Dole said, knowing he had an appreciative audience. Dole remembered the name of the rap star from his speech attacking Hollywood.

Panetta's strategy on the budget was for them to hang tough, continue to pound the Republicans but also make it clear Clinton wanted to negotiate. This was always dicey and they had to work the problem day to day. The long-range goal was to get Gingrich to abandon his crazies. And in the process there was no telling when the Republicans would get smart and see they were suffering badly with the public. Panetta was also tired of the budget, convinced nothing would happen until the next deadline. One of his sons had just had the first grandchild in the Panetta family, and Panetta was planning a family holiday. At the moment he was more interested in his grandchild than the budget strategy. He didn't want to be sitting in the White House on Christmas Eve.

Morris continued to be a thorn for the chief of staff. Unbelievably, one of Morris's key Republican clients was Senator Trent Lott of Mississippi, the majority whip and Dole's deputy in the Senate. Lott was closer to Gingrich than to Dole. Morris made big claims in White House meetings about Lott's power in the Senate. "All roads lead to and emanate from Trent," Morris said. He said Lott was the key to both Gingrich and his House, and to the Senate. Clinton had authorized Morris to listen to Lott but not to undertake a separate track for negotiations on the budget. Panetta knew there was no way to know what was really happening in the Morris-Lott relationship, but Morris seemed to bring back some good intelligence that was handy. And the whole bizarre, intertwined series of relationships perhaps made Clinton seem a little more unpredictable to the Republicans.

The weekly evening meetings on the campaign were also getting to Panetta. Clinton and Morris would go on and on, willing to talk all night. Panetta often wondered, when is this going to be over? Sessions that should take only 20 minutes to decide on what ads, where to run them and how often they should be on the air lasted four hours or more. One meeting lasted until 1:30 A.M.

"I've got the whole goddamn White House to run," Panetta told one of his assistants, "and I've got to be here at 7:30 the next morning." He had to handle all the minutiae that could cause the White House or the federal government to unravel.

Morris was driving obsessively for a budget deal because getting those issues off the table and out of the 1996 political debate was one of his grand designs. A deal would almost ensure Clinton's reelection, he said. At one White House meeting, Morris said, "We're going to have an agreement even if it's December 31, at 11:59 P.M. and 59 seconds."

McCurry didn't go to the campaign meetings because he felt he was already perceived as way too political for a White House spokesman. But he received detailed reports after each meeting, "mind dumps," he called them. McCurry understood why the meetings were so long. Beyond Clinton's tendency to talk anything to death, formulating the campaign message was the candidate's toughest work. No one could do it for him if it was going to be genuine. Clinton's message had to be worked out personally.

The next afternoon, Wednesday, December 6, Clinton summoned the cameras and reporters to the Oval Office.

"Throughout our history," he said, "American presidents have used the power of the veto to protect our values as a country." He picked up a pen which had been sent from Texas. "Three decades ago, this pen you see here was used to honor our values when President Johnson used it to sign Medicare into law. Today, I am vetoing the biggest Medicare and Medicaid cuts in history, deep cuts in education, a rollback in environmental protection."

Clinton then tried to write his signature to veto the bill.

"Can you bring me some more ink, boys?" the president asked. His staff secretary Todd Stern had some on hand, and Clinton signed his veto.

George Stephanopoulos said publicly, "The Republican budget is dead, the Contract With America is dead. Now let's go to work."

White House polling showed that the president's message on Medicare, education and the environment was working magnificently.

More advertising, Morris insisted. Clinton personally approved the script for another ad that Bob Squier produced that day attacking the Republicans.

"Belle is doing fine. But Medicare could be cut. Nicholas is going to college—but his scholarship could be gone. The stakes in the budget debate. Joshua's doing well—but help for his disability could be cut. President Clinton. Standing firm to protect people. Matthew bought a house—but will the water be safe to drink? Mike has a job—but new taxes in the Republican budget could set him back. President Clinton says balance the budget—but protect our families."

It was simple.

Conservative radio and television host Rush Limbaugh, who understood a hard sell, complained on his radio show that the Republicans were not doing enough television advertising. "This budget battle is more important than the 1996 election," he declared, and the Senate, House and Republican National Committee needed to get to work.

That night Gingrich answered the phone to receive news that he had been cleared of all ethics charges involving his personal and campaign finances except one that would be investigated by a special counsel. Tears began streaming down his face. His wife Marianne also cried, and Gingrich broke down, weeping uncontrollably. His advisers and he later tried to insist the tears were mostly of joy and relief. But the revolution had been dealt a big setback. Clinton had not caved. The budget had not yet been balanced. Taxes had not been lowered. The social and health programs had not been cut or changed. Clinton stood firmly in the way.

There were no tears from Dole. When I went to interview him several days later in New Hampshire where he was campaigning, I found ambivalence. "Some in our party see it as a total failure if we got up to the five-yard line and couldn't score," he said. "My view is we did it, he vetoed it. Game's over. Start a new game." Dole added, "It just makes the case we've got to have a Republican president." The 1996 election could be about the difference between the Republican approach and the Clinton approach. "I'm not going to be too upset if we take it to the people," he said.

On the other hand—there was generally another hand with Dole—he said he wanted a budget deal with Clinton. "I think in the short term, particularly through the nominating process, it's a big plus for Bob Dole. If we don't get it done, I don't know how it plays." He said he was still worried about Phil Gramm's charges that the Congress did nothing, that the majority leader had made the Senate "a black hole" in which the Contract With America had been dropped.

At the same time Dole acknowledged that a full budget agreement with Clinton would boost both the economy and Clinton's reelection chances. "I think we put him on first base at least," Dole said, perhaps even "halfway to second."

Suppose Dole won the Republican nomination and lost to Clinton because of a booming economy? I asked. How would he feel?

"I won't feel too good," he replied. But people would get jobs and interest rates would drop, he said.

We talked at length about the political impact of a budget agreement and Dole's tendency to accommodate Clinton on foreign policy.

"I try to separate my own ambition when I can," Dole said. "After all, we're all in this together. And he is the president. Particularly when it's foreign policy, I don't think we ought to be playing games. Some people play games all the time."

·   ·   ·

On Thursday, December 14, Bob Squier produced a television ad called "Children" that savaged the Republicans for pushing more children into poverty, and making cuts in education, the environment and Medicare. Over $1 million of television time was purchased to begin the following day in key battleground states where polling showed the most undecided or persuadable votes.

With images of a child on the screen, an announcer's voice said, "America's children. Seven million. Pushed toward poverty by higher taxes on working families. Four million children get substandard health care. Education—cut $30 billion; environmental protection gutted." The images switched to Gingrich and Dole as the voice continued, "That's the sad truth behind the Republican budget plan. The President's seven year balanced budget protects Medicare, education, and gives working families with children a tax break. It's our duty to America's children—and the President's plan will meet it."

Late Friday, December 15, Clinton said publicly that the Republicans had broken off negotiations, and he wasn't going to give in, so the next day the federal government would shut down partially for a second time.

Dole wanted to open the government temporarily, but it stayed closed over the weekend.

On Monday, December 18, Clinton and his advisers realized the administration was playing a dangerous game. The Republicans might be getting all the heat on keeping the government closed, but Clinton had to show he was willing to talk.

He called Dole and proposed a temporary reopening and then serious talks between himself and Dole and Gingrich.

Dole was eager to talk, but he had second thoughts when 30 minutes later he saw the Clinton ads on television kicking the Republicans on Medicare, education and children.

Dole later told Scott Reed that he believed Clinton would say and do anything to get reelected. "This is what we're dealing with," he said. He wasn't angry or even particularly hot. Clinton was just a problem. "We have to understand—this is the type of person we're dealing with."

Dole figured the political season was on. In the budget negotiations he felt he couldn't be the first to speak because of widespread suspicions among Republican conservatives that he would make a deal with Clinton. At this stage just before the Republican primaries, he couldn't be seen as a moderate compromiser sharing some of Clinton's policies. So he let Gingrich or Armey present their proposals first.

Throughout 1995, Dole had felt he had to bite his lip about the Contract. "On the Senate side we were the bad boys, and we didn't get it done in 100 days." They didn't get it done in 200 days or in 300 days. The Senate was the black hole for Gingrich's Contract. But Dole felt the House Republicans had miscalculated. "There's a way to use power when you get it," he said, "and my view was that maybe they've just been a little too much in a hurry. You don't undo 40 years or 20 years or 30 years in 100 days or four years." He added, "President Clinton nailed us to the mast on the government shutdown."

Gingrich and Armey had been insisting that any Medicare reform include the so-called medical savings accounts, allowing those who put money aside to pay for health care to take a tax deduction. The greatest proponent of the idea was Golden Rule Insurance Company, which sold a version of such accounts, and its former chairman J. Patrick Rooney, who had given more than $1 million to the Republican Party and to various Gingrich spin-off organizations. Clinton and Gore opposed the tax deduction, believing it would favor the healthy and the wealthy who could most afford to set up the medical savings accounts.

In a phone conversation with the president, Gingrich complained about the $1.5 million in anti-Republican advertising that had just been launched, and he accused the president of bad faith.

"Well," Clinton replied furiously, "if you want to know about your Medicare program, it's a complete rip-off of the American taxpayer with Rooney and Golden Rule! It's an obscene political payoff. But, of course, I'd never publicly accuse you of that."

Clinton and Gore felt that the retort had been effective. Gingrich seemed to back off, and the Speaker much later said he wouldn't insist on the accounts.

Another White House meeting among Clinton, Dole and Gingrich was scheduled for Tuesday, December 19. That morning Reed called Gaylord, Gingrich's adviser.

"Look," Reed said, "we've got to make sure today is not fucked up." Dole had been sniping about Gingrich to Reed, accusing Gingrich of recklessly keeping the government closed, believing it would force Clinton to cave in. But Reed said he and Dole were determined to keep the relationship with Gingrich intact. Dole would not split with the Speaker despite Gingrich's unfavorable rating, which was climbing to nearly 60 percent. Reed said that after the White House meeting, Newt had to keep quiet. "Just stand there and let Dole carry it, and then they both turn around and walk away. Instead of Newt popping off and making the evening news and we're set back another day. That's what we need."

Gaylord said he would try, but Gingrich had just been named *Time* magazine's Man of the Year and was riding a little high.

Clinton, Gore, Dole and Gingrich met for two hours, seeming to reach agreement on a short-term reopening of the government with serious follow-up talks about the full budget. Dole and Gingrich left feeling they were making progress. But afterwards Gingrich did not stay quiet, outlining in detail to the media what he thought was the agreement. A White House plan would not be considered because it still used the wrong numbers, he indicated.

Vice President Gore watched Gingrich on television. An obvious distortion, he declared. He immediately marched over to the White House briefing room to explain that the White House plan would be part of the negotiations, despite what Gingrich had said. Gore felt a natural rivalry with Gingrich.

Later Gingrich could not persuade the House Republicans to pass a short-term spending bill to reopen the government. His top leaders voted 12 to 0 against it and him. They wanted to keep the government shut down and use it as leverage to force Clinton to sign a version of their seven-year balanced budget. The moment of truth was coming for Gingrich. He was caught. On one hand, Clinton and Dole were pushing for a deal of some sort and Gingrich, as a full participant in their discussions, had tacitly signed on. On the other hand, Gingrich's own team of House Republicans was willing to have an Alamo finish.

Dole was very unhappy, but he did not explode. He had decided he would have to keep cool, keep the pressure on both Clinton and Gingrich.

Clinton saw the opportunity. He called Dole to explain that he was going to denounce the House Republicans in public. Dole did not resist.

"My new best friend, Bob Dole," Clinton declared to his aides afterwards.

Clinton went public. He, Dole and Gingrich were on the side of opening the government. "Today, the most extreme Members of the House of Representatives rejected that agreement," Clinton said.

Clinton and his advisers believed they were close to breaking the

Republicans. Gingrich would either have to put his speakership on the line and force the House to reopen the government or Gingrich would have to break with Dole.

Everyone agreed to a four-day Christmas break in the negotiations.

On Tuesday, December 26, Clinton phoned his new best friend, but Dole was out. Dole called back about 3 P.M.

"What can we do to get the government running again?" Clinton asked.

"I'm not an advocate of shutting down the government," Dole repeated. "I'm not an advocate of paying people for not working, frankly. That's a point lost on some House Republicans."

Clinton agreed with that.

Dole said that Leon Panetta had given him a two-page proposal that might get them out of the impasse.

Clinton went into a long discussion of the technical issues of spending restraints and about whether it would be possible to have more money available in the sixth year and so forth.

"When are we going to finish?" Dole finally asked. He was very anxious and losing his patience. He liked to be straightforward and frank. "I've got to get to Iowa. My election is in February, yours is in November."

"Yeah, I know," Clinton said, sounding sympathetic.

"If we don't get this done, New Year's is coming up next weekend," Dole complained. "Do you think we can get a framework of an agreement by Saturday night if we work all day Friday and all day Saturday?" Dole wanted something.

"I don't know," Clinton said. "I hope so."

Dole said he needed to go to New Hampshire afterwards.

The president said he wanted to go to South Carolina for the famous Renaissance Weekend gathering of seminars, discussion and networking.

"I'd sneak down to North Carolina," Dole said, "and spend a day with my 94-year-old mother-in-law."

Clinton delicately turned to the subject of the other key member of their negotiating triangle. He said he hadn't spoken with Newt. Some earlier private phone conversations with Gingrich had been rough. Gingrich had accused Clinton of bad faith and complained about the negative television advertising attack on the Republican budget.

"Well, are you going to call Newt?" Dole asked. Clinton and Dole had taken to having private discussions about mood management of the Speaker.

Clinton wasn't delighted with the prospect.

"I can call Newt, and take his temperature," Dole said, taking Clinton off the hook.

Clinton said fine, and they ended the call.

Dole learned that Gingrich was taking some time off, and he didn't call the Speaker.

The next day, Dole picked up a column by Robert Samuelson in *The Washington Post* called "Budget Charade."

He read, "On policy matters, congressional Republicans have utterly dominated. They have set the agenda, and President Clinton has been a bit player. By contrast, the president has completely dominated the public relations struggle. He has constantly made the Republicans look mean, petty and silly." Samuelson argued that Clinton was really responsible for the two government shutdowns. Clinton, Samuelson noted, had generally adopted the Republican policies of budget balancing and tax cutting, and then engaged in a "Houdini-like feat of deception."

Dole agreed. They were being clobbered on the public relations front as the Democrats poured millions into ads. Where was Haley Barbour, the chairman of the Republican National Committee? Dole felt Barbour was spending too much time with the hard-line House Republicans, siding with them rather than him.

Dole took the Samuelson column and told an aide, "Fax a copy of that over to Haley, and put, 'Read carefully,' on it."

The Republicans had come up with a series of changes in Medicare that would restructure the program, and in Dole's view that was the only way to save it. If Medicare was allowed to run unchanged on automatic pilot, it would eventually bankrupt the federal government. The policy changes were the important steps, but they seemed technical. Elderly millionaires and those with no income were having the federal government pay the same share of their Medicare health insurance bills. It made no sense to Dole. But most of the debate was about how many billions would be cut, and that had scared people.

Just recently in one of their telephone calls, Clinton had told Dole, "Maybe I talk too much, maybe you should be talking more in these meetings."

Dole didn't say anything in response. "What do you say to the President of the United States?" Dole wondered.

"This is between the two of us," Clinton said, as he always did, "I'm not going to use this in the campaign."

Dole pushed for some real policy reform on Medicare.

"Oh, I'm willing to talk," Clinton said, "and I hear you."

They didn't talk any more about the campaign. The closest Dole came in his White House contacts was when Gore and he talked about raising campaign money.

"How much have you got in the bank?" Dole asked.

Gore said about $26 million was pledged but it hadn't all been collected. "I know you got about $24 million," Gore said.

So they were keeping track, Dole thought.

Indeed they were. By using the Democratic National Committee money for advertising, Clinton's managers were able to continue to save much of the Clinton-Gore campaign money. And the Morris-Squier advertising blitz was in full force. In the fall, the ads attacking the Republican budget had covered some 30 percent of all media markets in the nation. The December 30-second commercials followed the pattern showing Clinton as champion crime fighter and as the leader seeking tax cuts, welfare reform and a balanced budget that would protect vital health programs, education and the environment.

By Christmas, the pro-Clinton ads had been on the air in an incredible 42 percent of the national media markets. The advertising pattern was designed to project one theme as spot after spot showed Clinton as a figure of national reconciliation, a healer bringing the various sides together, who rounded the sharp edges of the Republicans. Clinton was shown as a man comfortable and above the fray, the president-in-office, not a candidate and certainly not identified as a Democrat.

The Democrats' meticulous and nuanced polling showed gains, often 10–15 points in favorability for Clinton, in the crucial markets in primary states such as Pennsylvania, Michigan, Florida, Illinois and Ohio, though not Iowa and New Hampshire, the first primary states, where the Republican candidates were on the air fighting it out among themselves. The Clinton advertising was more potent because there was no candidate on the other side and little or no advertising directed against Clinton. "Unopposed storytelling," Squier called it.

By the end of the year, $18 million had been spent on this extraordinary media campaign. Morris, Squier and the pollsters attributed a significant portion of Clinton's rise in the national polls to this effort. Ickes and Stephanopoulos disagreed strongly. Clinton and Gore, however, thought the advertising was a big plus.

The media didn't catch on immediately. Of course, when the Federal Election Commission report was filed the next year, the large expenditures would be disclosed. But that would likely be a one-day story. It was uncertain if anyone would figure it out. And next year it would be history. People would likely remember Clinton's stunning rise in the polls, not one of the contributing reasons for it.

Clinton continued to spend time most weeks reviewing the spots, honing down what he wanted said in 30 seconds. The focused advertising spots continued to impose more and more discipline on the president. Ideas, language and attitudes had converged with the protracted budget negotiations. So in the course of his working day as president, he generally stuck to the same lines and themes. The result was more consistency. Instead of projecting his ambivalence as he often had in the past, Clinton was staying on message.

Two days after Christmas, December 27, I flew to Iowa, where Dole was campaigning. As I flew back with him to Washington, we had a two-hour, uninterrupted interview. One of the subjects was the vice-presidency.

We began with 1976, when Dole as a 53-year-old senator had been selected as President Ford's running mate. Was it a surprise?

"When the phone rang that morning," Dole recalled, "I was stunned, surprised, shocked, but not completely."

Why?

Dole acknowledged that he had urged that he be considered for the vice-presidency in a discussion with former Secretary of Defense Melvin Laird, a close Ford friend. "I lobbied Mel Laird. I said, 'Mel, you're out here advocating, you named all these guys that ought to be vice president. You know you've got trouble in the farm belt, you got to mention somebody from the farm belt like Bob Dole.'" Dole recalled that Laird responded favorably, "Okay, I'll put your name in the slot."

So if in 1996 Dole became the Republican nominee and learned someone was lobbying to become his running mate, what would be his reaction?

"Well, I guess it depends on how they do it," Dole responded, citing a bunch of people who also had lobbied for him.

But you were lobbying for yourself?

"Only to the extent that I remember being there," he said, providing a classic Dole non-answer and dodging the question.

When you look back on 1976, were you ready to run for vice president?

"Probably not quite," he said.

Did you realize that at the time?

"I don't think so," Dole said. "I feel differently about it now." He probably should have had more experience and he could have handled running better. "On a scale of 1 to 10, I wasn't a 10."

What were you?

"I don't know, maybe a 7. But I was important from the standpoint of agriculture and veterans."

Ford wanted you to be the attack dog on Jimmy Carter?

Dole quoted Ford as telling him, "I'll stay in the Rose Garden and you go out in the briar patch."

Would you pick a vice president to be the attack dog?

"I think it would depend," Dole replied, saying that the polls and the various weaknesses of people he might select would play a part. Another factor, he said, would be "whether your running mate had credibility" to criticize the opposition. For example, he said, "I've never talked about Clinton and Vietnam." He added that he had never used Whitewater to attack the president personally.

What would be your criteria for picking a vice president?

"I'd want somebody I know pretty well," Dole said. "I wouldn't want to pick, you know, go back to the Nixon days and pick somebody that you didn't really know. Agnew," he said, referring to Spiro Agnew, who had been the Maryland governor when he was picked by Nixon in 1968. "Turned out to be a winning combination," Dole added, noting that Nixon-Agnew had won the election. He didn't mention that both later resigned. "But I want somebody I can work with. Somebody I can totally trust, and they trust me, and they know me, and there are a lot of people I think fit that description. We've got a crop of great governors out there."

Would you want somebody who's more than a 7 on a scale of 10?

"Sure," Dole said. "I'd want a 10." He volunteered that in 1988, George Bush probably didn't want a 10 because he picked Dan Quayle. "I might have been a 10 in 1988," Dole said, recalling that Bush did not pick him as his running mate though Dole probably by then had the experience. "But I think you always shoot for a 10," Dole added. With the exception of Nixon's selection of Agnew, Dole said, he admired Nixon because "he wasn't afraid of somebody smarter than him, and it doesn't bother me any."

What would be the process of selecting a vice president and who would work on this decision?

"Mostly me," he said. "I think I'll have some people around to check things out, but it seems to me that it's got to be the nominee's decision and not some board of directors out there sitting down [considering] geographically and electorally and da-da da-da da-da. There may be something to that but it's got to be—a partnership."

He added, "Very frankly, I think Vice President Gore was pretty well picked. In fact, I'm surprised at how the vice president interrupts, takes over, even in the budget discussions . . . which I think wouldn't bother me. I'm used to staff people interrupting me."

What did he think of Powell's decision not to run?

"I felt like here is a guy who really believes in his family," Dole answered, "really consulted his family. Who had a lot going for him. Wouldn't have been easy. He might even have not been the nominee, but he would certainly have been a challenger. And who knows where he'd be today? He might be out of it. He might be on top of the heap."

What about Powell's explanation that he didn't have the fire in the belly?

"Well, I thought that was probably legit," Dole said. "I mean, you're up there, you're on stage all day long. You're not supposed to make a mistake."

Though Powell said he wasn't going to seek the vice-presidency, Dole didn't think that Powell was ruling that out totally. "Sounds like he's not rejecting it out of hand," Dole had said to Sheila Burke, his Senate chief of staff, as he watched Powell on television announcing he wouldn't run.

"I don't think he'd be anybody's vice president," Dole said of Powell. But in the right situation, with the right nominee, Dole believed that a strong case could be made to Powell. Vice presidents were more active in recent years and could take a big load off the president. Dole didn't know if he would even try or be able to persuade Powell to take the vice-presidency. But the proper Republican nominee would have a pretty powerful argument to make to Powell, Dole said, adding, "Wouldn't be a bad Secretary of State either."

Over the years, Dole said he had watched Powell operate. Powell had been able to get along with nearly everyone in the Republican Party, from Senator Jesse Helms to Senator Bill Cohen.

Dole would love to see a black like Powell on the Republican ticket, have a "big tent" as they called it, the party open to minorities and everyone.

Neither Nixon, nor Ford, nor Bush had gone for the 10s in picking their running mates. Having witnessed all that history, Dole said he was set on picking a 10 if he became the nominee. No Agnew, no Quayle, not even a 1976 Dole.

22

After New Year's, Dole was totally fed up with the budget negotiations. His message of balancing the budget had turned into shutting down the government for more than two weeks. It was crazy. For over a month he had been saying his side had no plan for an endgame, and now polls showed the public supported Clinton's approach on the budget almost 2 to 1.

"I know a lot of people probably are out there muttering, what are these clowns doing back there?" he said later in an interview. "Why can't these clowns get together? I know how people sit around the pool hall or at home. What the hell's going on back there?"

On Tuesday, January 2, 1996, Dole went to the Senate floor. "Enough is enough!" he said, and pushed through a resolution to reopen the government. It took Gingrich several days to rally the House behind the resolution and he had to put his speakership on the line to get the votes, but the government was reopened. No permanent budget agreement, however, had been reached, though talks continued.

After sitting through the dozens of initial hours with Clinton in the Oval Office, Dick Armey had reached some conclusions. There were two Clintons—the outside-the-room political Clinton and the inside-the-room charmer who reached out to everyone. Armey felt Clinton was too insecure to continue to be in a room with a man that he hadn't properly courted and seduced. "I think I bugged him because he couldn't get me to love him," Armey said. He knew that Clinton didn't love him, but found that the president continued his personal outreach program.

At one point, Clinton came around the table and poured a cup of coffee for Armey. But Armey was not impressed. Another time, late at night, all the others were talking around the Oval Office coffee table, and Armey was standing apart from the group, thinking, let's get the hell out of here. Clinton left the group and came to Armey. He moved in real close and chummy.

"You know, Dick," Clinton said, "I have really enjoyed getting to know you in these meetings, and I've discovered you're not nearly as bad a guy as I thought you were." He praised more, then added, "If you'll accept it, I would like to apologize to you for that event we had, that blowup we had."

"Mr. President," Armey replied, "there's no need to apologize to me for that. It really wasn't a big deal. But of course I'll accept." Armey felt he was getting dangerously close to slipping into Clinton's orbit, but he was able to resist.

Bill Lacy had been monitoring Steve Forbes and his massive advertising efforts for months, much to the amusement of some others on the staff.

"Gramm's the competition here," Mari Will said, almost laughing in Lacy's face. "And we're going to get distracted by a straw man and we're going to take our eye off the ball, and we're going to lose the nomination."

On Friday, January 5, Lacy received their latest poll numbers. Forbes was ahead 7 points in Arizona and had moved into second place in Iowa! He was alarmed, realizing they had deceived themselves rather dramatically, and he blamed himself for not trusting his instincts. As always the heavy advertising was paying off, and Forbes had spent millions. There was only one comfort for Lacy. In the fall, there had been no way to win an advertising war of attrition with Forbes, who could spend millions more of his own money. Now, a month from the Iowa caucuses, the Dole campaign had a chance.

In New Jersey, Bill Dal Col had just received similar polling information. Forbes was so far ahead in Arizona that someone would have to wake up. Dal Col laughed, certain that Dole would erupt at Scott Reed. "My God," Dal Col said, "he's going back there, he's going to tell Scott, 'I want that rich little bastard and I want him now.' "

In Washington, Lacy went to work. He asked Stuart Stevens, Dole's media consultant, to come up with some initial scripts for negative ads attacking Forbes. The first scripts made fun of Forbes, treated him as a joke, a man who inherited a publishing empire, had never held elective office and now wanted to buy the presidency. Way too cute, Lacy thought. They had to take Forbes and his ideas seriously—and attack them.

Dole himself was pretty hot over Forbes's attacks.

"Yeagggrh!" Dole said. "The first negative ads said Bob Dole voted for this big subway and Bob Dole voted for a ski resort in Idaho. This guy running for president or Congress?" Dole sarcastically noted that Forbes's proposed flat tax would give Forbes a substantial tax cut.

Lacy argued that the polling showed Republicans didn't care that much about Forbes's money, what they cared about was their own money. Lacy and Stevens made an ad saying that Forbes would bring "untested leadership, risky ideas." The 30-second spot said Forbes's flat tax would increase the federal deficit. For good measure it also said Forbes opposed mandatory life sentences for three-time felons—the so-called "three strikes and you're out" legislation.

By Monday, January 8, before they had made a decision to air Dole's new ad, Lacy's internal polling showed that Forbes had closed within 6 points of Dole in Iowa, 30 to 24. Just as important, under the barrage of Forbes's negative Dole ads, Dole's unfavorable rating in Iowa had gone from just 13 percent in the fall to 30 percent now.

"We've got to take this guy out," Lacy said.

Scott Reed thought it was a very dicey call: front-runner goes negative. Would it look like panic?

Lacy said they had no choice, and he urged that they put the negative Forbes ad on the air in Iowa before an upcoming candidate debate sponsored by the *Des Moines Register* on January 13. Others worried that the ad would ignite Dole's temper and he might lash out at Forbes.

No, Lacy said, they needed to get the ad on the air immediately as a safety valve for Dole. If Dole knew the ad was taking on Forbes, he would not feel he had to attack Forbes personally.

Reed agreed, and talked with Dole.

"We've been the Boy Scouts in this field long enough," Reed said. Time to get Forbes's attention. With four weeks to go before the Iowa vote, they had the money to saturate television. If they moved quickly and bought up large chunks of airtime, even Forbes's millions wouldn't be able to outbuy them by that much. Only so much television time existed.

It was phenomenal, Dole said, that all the negative advertising could drive up his unfavorables so much. All that money Forbes used to attack, attack, attack! "Money speaks, money talks," Dole said. Fighting back was okay with him. He likened it to lifting the arms embargo in Bosnia. Yeah, all right, he said. "Lift and strike!"

Morris had continued to press Clinton on welfare reform, literally begging Clinton to sign a Senate welfare reform bill in the works. The pressure had seemed to be paying off earlier, when on September 16 he persuaded Clinton to give a Saturday radio address praising the bill and all but promising to sign it. Three days later, the bill passed the Senate 87 to 12, enough votes to override a presidential veto. Nearly all the Republicans and a majority of the Democrats voted for the bill called the Personal Responsibility and Work Opportunity Act of 1995. The bill imposed a time limit. A person could only collect welfare for five years. Getting the welfare issue off the table was one of Morris's foremost strategic goals.

But the Health and Human Services Department presented Clinton with a study showing that about 1.5 million children would be thrown into poverty by the bill because 75 percent of the children whose families were on welfare were on it for more than five years.

Though he initially seemed supportive, intense publicity about the study put Clinton in a crunch. Marian Wright Edelman, head of the Children's Defense Fund and an old friend and decades-long children's activist with Hillary, laid down a strong marker. She appealed publicly to Clinton's "moral conscience" not to go along with the Republican measure. The bill changed somewhat in negotiations with the House, and became harsher. The Senate on December 22 passed a final version 52 to 47. The publicity and the House's impact had won back all but one of the Senate's 46 Democrats. So 45 Democrats and two Republicans voted against it.

Dole no longer had the votes to override Clinton's veto. He spoke with Clinton after Christmas.

"I don't think the Senate bill we passed is that bad," Dole said.

Clinton cited the study about throwing 1.5 million children into poverty.

Dole said he had seen so many studies over the years he didn't know what to believe. The bill was a significant first step and was largely consistent with the principles that Clinton had outlined. "It's only a five-year bill and if we find out in a year that some of those things are true, we can change it," Dole said. "It's not that we don't meet every year." Dole's advice was to sign it. "We're going to be around. We're not cold-hearted up here. We've got a pulse."

Clinton said he thought the bill had changed too much and the cuts would be too hard on children, including some big structural changes in foster care, food stamps and the school lunch program.

"If you're going to veto it, Mr. President," Dole said, "you ought to set down why you're vetoing it, otherwise you're going to be hard-pressed."

"I'll do that," Clinton replied.

But Clinton shifted ground again. On January 6, 1996, Clinton offered to accept the five-year welfare limit as part of his overall balanced budget proposal.

Three days later, at 8 P.M., he shifted again. While Washington was still snowed in, Clinton vetoed a separate welfare bill based largely on the Senate version.

Dole took to the Senate floor the next day. "The president may have tried to hide this 'stealth veto' by doing it late at night, but he cannot hide the message he is sending to the American people," Dole said. "He will stand in the way of fundamental change and, instead, will fight for the status quo."

Clinton sensed that as they settled into 1996, Dole was more reluctant for a budget or any other deal. He seemed to be saying, forget it in the campaign year.

Dole still maintained he wanted a budget deal, but that he couldn't take any more meetings. "I've got to get out of here," he had said repeatedly to whomever was sitting next to him, including House Democratic Leader Dick Gephardt. He had met for some 50 hours with Clinton and the others. His eyes would glaze over. "Numbers, numbers, numbers!" he said. "It got to be an endurance contest." He felt like a potted plant or a prop. The winter snowstorms came. "Meet! Meet! Meet!" he said, wagging his head. "Snowstorm! Meet! Blizzard! Meet! Meet!"

Clinton remained heavily involved in the day-to-day presentation of his campaign through television advertising. The pre-Christmas ad called "Children" had accused the Republicans of wanting to cut tax credits for the poor, health care and education for children. A new ad was proposed saying the Republicans were willing to balance the budget on the backs of children.

Dick Morris and Bob Squier came up with the new ad, not very subtly called "SLASH," with the same theme about Republican cuts in health care, education and the environment versus Clinton's efforts to protect those programs. Pulling no punch, the ad put the choice in terms of "duty" to children.

Clinton said that he didn't want the standard visual of Dole and Gingrich flashed in the ad.

Squier disagreed strongly. It was a small point, but one that he and his ad specialists thought would make a difference. Right when the ad said, "Drastic Republican budget cuts," they wanted to put up the picture of two of the horsemen of the apocalypse—Gingrich and Dole. Other Republican leaders, like House Budget Chairman Kasich, were out there publicly calling the Clinton plan—and by inference Clinton himself—a turkey.

"Yeah," Clinton said, "but it's not Gingrich and Dole." The spirit of the budget negotiations was not to personalize their differences. They were trying to avoid personal attacks.

But they were the symbols of the Republican Party, Squier argued, and lashing Dole to Gingrich was a key part of the strategy to contrast Republican extremism with Clinton's reasonableness.

"Those are the guys in the room," Clinton said, referring to the budget discussions in the Oval Office, "and that's the way it is."

Squier pressed very hard. He thought Clinton was dead goddamn wrong.

No pictures, Clinton said. "That's the way it's going to be," the president directed, "and you do what I tell you to do."

"SLASH" ran without pictures or references to Dole or Gingrich. It was paid for by the Democratic National Committee (DNC) and was supposed to have nothing to do with the Clinton-Gore reelection effort.

Clinton personally had been controlling tens of millions of dollars worth of DNC advertising. This enabled him to exceed the legal spending limits and effectively rendered the DNC an adjunct to his own reelection effort. He was circumventing the rigorous post-Watergate reforms that were designed to limit and control the raising and spending of money for presidential campaigns. His direct, hands-on involvement was risky, certainly in violation of the spirit of the law and possibly illegal.

For practical purposes, Clinton's control of the party advertising—and his aggressive use of it going back to the first Medicare ads the previous August—gave him at least $25 million more for the primary period. That was in addition to the $37 million the Clinton-Gore campaign was authorized to spend under the law. And Clinton did not have a primary challenger. In contrast Dole, who had to fight his way through the expensive primaries and had no similar control over the Republican National Committee until the primaries were over, was limited to the $37 million. The playing field was not level.

I called Lawrence M. Noble, the general counsel of the Federal Election Commission, one of the premier non-partisan experts on money in politics. Noble had been with the commission for 19 years, and its top lawyer for ten years. I outlined the hypothetical situation of a presidential candidate deeply involved in his party's advertising, but without saying it involved any candidate in particular. Noble had one comment. "We have forgotten the lessons of Watergate."

The Federal Election Commission consists of six commissioners, three Democrats and three Republicans. Scott E. Thomas, one of the three Democrats and a commissioner for the last ten years, said the law had been seriously undermined, and new reform was needed. "The limits and prohibitions are basically out the window," he said.

Meanwhile, Dole still was fighting Steve Forbes. His first attack ad on Forbes aired Friday, January 12.

Almost immediately, Nelson Warfield received a call from a newspaper reporter who had checked the facts in the ad. Indeed, Forbes had said he opposed the "three strikes and you're out" legislation, but in the same sentence, in the interview the Dole campaign was using, he had said, "I believe in one strike and you're out."

"What the fuck!" Warfield screamed. He checked the backup material, and the reporter was absolutely right. Lacy and Stevens had rushed making the ad. Warfield, who was campaigning with Dole, pointed this out. The new big negative ad had a significant distortion in it, Warfield said.

Maybe we should pull the ad, Dole told Reed.

Reed was furious at the mistake, but said it would be unthinkable to pull the ad. That would be an admission of wrongdoing and it would become a huge news story: Front-runner pulls first negative ad because of unfair distortions. Too devastating. No way. They would find some way to brush it off.

Dole said okay.

Forbes saw the ad. My God, he thought, this is going to get nasty. They're going to knock me down.

Bill Dal Col had been waiting for some attention. "Why won't the media pay any attention to us?" Dal Col had been asking for weeks. Finally. He was delighted at the attention from the front-runner. The distortion was an added opportunity. "Boy, are we going to shove this up his nose." Forbes made a counter ad saying Dole was "desperate" and "deceiving voters."

Warfield finally put out a convoluted press release, arguing that the second part of the Forbes quote, "I believe in one strike and you're out," was clearly referring to another tough-on-crime issue, truth in sentencing. So it was fair to say that Forbes opposed three strikes and you're out, he asserted.

But privately Warfield was distraught. These ads were supposed to be researched within an inch of their life. They had to be bulletproof, not Swiss cheese. The more Warfield went over the simple ad, the more he realized it also was not very good, mixing too many issues, from the deficit to crime. And the central theme, charging Forbes with "Untested leadership, risky ideas," was not powerful enough. Two of those four words, "leadership" and "ideas," were positive, and "risky" was not so negative. A lot of people wanted to take risks, Warfield thought. Why were their ads so bad? he wondered.

On Saturday, January 13, at 1 P.M. all the Republican candidates gathered at the Iowa Public TV Studio on Corporate Drive in Johnston, Iowa, for the debate.

Lamar Alexander led off. "The Forbes tax plan is a truly nutty idea in the Jerry Brown tradition," Alexander said, referring to the former Democratic California governor who had previously run for president.

In a private holding room, Bill Dal Col and John McLaughlin, Forbes's pollster, were hysterical, jumping up and down with joy.

"Jackass," Dal Col said, "he just bought himself some trouble." Alexander was clearly the most frustrated of the candidates, seeing Forbes move into the limelight as he was still struggling to break out of the pack. They would have to hit Alexander next with a negative ad, Dal Col thought.

"And, Steve," Alexander continued in the debate, "the only thing you've ever run is a magazine you inherited and you raised the price of your magazine."

All right! Dal Col thought.

Next, Dole took a swing, suggesting that the money needed to run the government could be borrowed from Forbes. Gramm took a punch at Forbes about opposing a balanced federal budget.

In the Dole holding room, Reed and Lacy were pleased that Alexander and Gramm were also hitting Forbes.

Dal Col was still elated at the attention and the suggestion that Forbes's ideas were framing the debate. Dole was an automatic. He was going to attack. But Gramm too, great! Where was Buchanan? Dal Col wondered as the debate continued.

A few minutes later Buchanan said, "Since everybody's been piling on Steve Forbes, I want to be fair and I want to jump into piling on a bit, Steve."

The audience laughed. Dal Col was jumping.

Buchanan said that the rich could retire and under the Forbes plan pay no taxes on their investment earnings or profits—a plan "worked up by the boys at the yacht basin."

Where was Morry Taylor, the wealthy tire and wheel manufacturer who was also a candidate? Dal Col thought.

Soon Taylor took a crack at the Forbes tax plan. "It would have me paying no tax on $15 million of capital gains," Taylor said, "and my employees paying 17 percent. That's wrong."

Up on the stage, Forbes initially felt annoyed because the debate format did not allow him to respond to each of his opponents. But as the criticism of him continued to mount, he thought to himself: Do these people realize what they're doing? They are making me the alternative. Why doesn't one of these professional politicians realize the dynamics they've created and take a different tack? Are they so inflexible that once they're on a course, they can't change?

Afterwards, Dal Col went to Forbes.

"You did great!" Dal Col said, barely containing his glee. "They creamed you! You're going to be in the news!"

"This is it," Forbes said. "This is the new dimension. This is the real race."

Forbes realized that the central challenge of his campaign was at hand. He had established himself as a serious candidate, and the serious criticism would no doubt begin. His opponents and the media would draw some blood—a good deal of it. Forbes well knew that he was no Colin Powell or Dwight Eisenhower. He was starting fresh, with no national reputation to fall back on. What would happen to his support once the real piling on began? Once it became cumulative? It was one thing for him to hold his own on *Nightline* or *Meet the Press,* but what if the whole political establishment came down on him? What kind of toll would a continuous hammering take? What if the positive side of him and his message were not reinforced somewhere? What if everything else was negative? He wasn't going to win the endorsement contest with Dole, but he needed someone to stand up, some respected figure in the party, to rise up and say, Forbes is okay.

On Wednesday, January 17, Lacy went to Arizona to watch two focus groups on Forbes. By that point, Forbes had run close to $2 million of advertising in Arizona—an extraordinary amount, especially when no other candidate was running TV ads. The first focus group of ten men and women had been drawn from people who said they supported Forbes.

For two hours, Lacy watched in horror. One of the voters called Forbes an American hero. They all loved that Forbes was an outsider, loved the notion that he was proposing risky ideas! Dole's 60-second biographical ad was shown with Elizabeth and Bob talking about his war injury. Most of the focus group gagged. They were appalled. What does that have to do with the campaign? one asked. The others nodded. Who does this guy think he is? another inquired. They trashed Elizabeth, and one woman inaccurately said that she knew that the president of the Red Cross was a political appointment, so they knew how Elizabeth got that position. The members of the group also believed everything that was said about Dole in the Forbes negative ads. Some anti-Forbes ads were shown and the members didn't buy any of it. Bullets bounced off the guy.

Lacy found the second group, ten undecided voters, could be sold on some of the Forbes negatives, but they still liked him and found Dole wanting. Lacy returned to Washington stunned. He knew concentrated advertising could drill home a message, but he had never quite seen anything like it.

Reed and Lacy agreed there was no way they could spend several million dollars in Arizona to attempt to catch up. They didn't have the money. They would have to ride it out and see if their concentrated advertising paid off in Iowa, which was two weeks before Arizona.

"Got to get Forbes," Dole said. "Get Forbes."

That same day, January 17, about 10:30 A.M. Dole was in his Major-ity Leader's Office with Gingrich, Armey and the other Republican leaders. They were waiting for a call from Clinton to discuss where to go with the budget negotiations.

"You got to see *Time* magazine," Dole said to Armey. The previous week's issue of the magazine had a giant photo, covering nearly two inside pages, of their closed budget meetings with Clinton in the Oval Office. The photo showed Clinton talking at an easel with Magic Marker in hand like the professor. All the others—Dole, Gingrich, Armey, Panetta and the Democratic leaders—were seated around dutifully, seemingly spellbound and listening.

"Us getting taught by the master!" Armey exploded. He had seen how Clinton used photographs to manipulate people. The president had killed Newt with that picture of them together on Air Force One. At the beginning of the talks, Armey had insisted on personal assurances from both Clinton and Gore that if the White House photographer took pictures, none would be released. The picture had clearly been leaked from the White House to show the others in a subservient role.

As Armey was raging, Clinton called. Dole, Gingrich and Armey picked up phone extensions. After the most perfunctory greetings, Armey confronted Clinton.

"Mr. President," Armey said, "I'm sure that you have any number of people in that room, and you probably have somebody on the phone with us, and I'm sure somebody's taking notes."

Clinton voiced surprise at the accusation, and he assured Armey that he was on the phone alone in the Oval Office, and Panetta was in the room with him.

"Mr. President," Armey said, "I have to tell you how bitterly disappointed I am to have seen that picture in *Time*. You and the vice president both gave us your assurances that none of those pictures would be used."

"Armey's upset about a picture in *Time,*" Clinton said to Panetta. "What is it?"

"It's there," Armey snapped, "I just saw it a minute ago."

"Well, of course, you know, Dick, that's the White House photographers. You can't hold me responsible for that."

"Mr. President," Armey replied, "who am I supposed to hold responsible for it? It's your White House. You're the one that promised me it wouldn't be there."

To Armey, the photograph represented how Clinton had taken control. Armey thought if the year were a videotape, it would be of Republicans bringing the Contract through the House, lickety-split. In the Senate, it would start to bog down but still enough would pass and the tape would continue. Then the seven-year budget would get to the White House and the president would reach up and hit the pause button. With one stroke, bam!, Clinton had vetoed their work and put it in the dumper. Armey thought of the 1968 song from the pop charts, "MacArthur Park," and the line about working so hard and not being able to get the pieces back together again. He had resolved not to go back for negotiations with Clinton.

In the Oval Office, Clinton rolled his eyes as Armey continued. Armey would not let the issue of the photo go. After Armey finally stopped, Gingrich also voiced some anger about the photo. He was terribly frustrated by the process, but he finally relaxed. Gingrich and Clinton continued for some time talking about whether they could agree.

"I just don't think we can," Gingrich said. "There's no reason for us to come back up there."

Dole tried, but it was stalemate. He realized, without a doubt, that Clinton had stalled the Republican revolution.

Armey's performance had surprised Dole. Everyone exploded in politics, Dole knew, but Armey had really been rude.

"If I'd been the president," Dole said later, "and they were talking to me like that, I'd have hung up on them."

Clinton later berated McCurry for releasing the photo. "They have a right to be pissed about it," the president said. "Those are confidential meetings!"

Dole and Gingrich were appearing that same day with Jack Kemp to announce the findings of the Kemp Commission, a group the Republican leaders had set up earlier in the year to recommend changes in the tax reform.

Earlier on, Clinton and Dole had been speaking. "You're going to endorse the flat tax, aren't you, Bob?" Clinton had said encouragingly. Dole realized the president was in effect saying, "Drink the poison, Bob."

At the press conference, Dole split the baby. He said he could support a flat tax as long as it did not increase either the federal deficit or taxes on the middle class. Of course, he knew the flat taxes under consideration did both—which was why the flat tax was poison. Also, the rich would get dramatic tax reductions, and Dole knew that Clinton would love nothing more than for the Republicans to prove they were the party of the rich by endorsing it.

• • •

On Monday, January 22, both *Time* and *Newsweek* put Forbes on the cover of their magazines, a stunning twofer. Traditionally, the news magazines waited until after the New Hampshire primary—still a month away—before billboarding a primary candidate. Dal Col had been pushing reporters for both magazines, and when he saw the results, he went berserk with joy. *Newsweek* pictured Forbes tearing up the hated 1040 tax return under a giant headline: *RRRRip!* It was equivalent to millions of dollars of free advertising for the campaign.

Dal Col said to Forbes, who was taking his prominence coolly in stride, "Don't you understand, nobody half the time reads inside the magazine. You're on both covers!" Dal Col added that the public had to be feeling, "My God, he must be real. He must have arrived!"

Mari Will began putting together a long-term strategy, trying to block out the year ahead for Dole. The perfect kickoff would be for Dole to give the Republican response to Clinton's State of the Union speech. She lobbied very hard. To her amazement, some on the campaign didn't want Dole to do it. Someone suggested that Dole have some children or a family give the response to underscore the theme of protecting the future generations.

"Hel-looo!" Will said, "We're running for president. And it's our chance to be opposite Clinton."

Dole decided he would reply himself.

Will began preparing a ten-minute speech under the theme of what she called "While You Were Sleeping." As the voters were sleeping, the liberals had hijacked their major institutions. The schools were being run by the liberal teachers' union and the federal government. And the police couldn't arrest anyone without great difficulty, the courts couldn't convict anyone, the streets were a mess, kids weren't learning and the culture was debased. She crafted a strong values-laden speech that criticized the elite liberal establishment and held up Clinton as the embodiment of a pro-government, dying status quo. "While the president's words speak of change, his actions are a contradiction." The veto of the first balanced budget in a generation and the welfare reform plan proved it.

By noon on Tuesday, January 23, Dole's speech was done and ready —a world record for Dole. He practiced in his office several times on the TelePrompTer with Don Sipple, the former Wilson media adviser who had signed up with the Dole campaign. It was Sipple's first project with Dole. He was supposed to work on Dole's speaking habits—elevate his confidence level, his comfort level and his style of delivery. Dole's pace in reading the speech was crucial and Sipple tried to get him to slow down and use his body for punctuation. In the practice rounds it wasn't bad, though not yet smooth. Dole was having trouble getting the rhythm.

Gingrich stopped by Dole's office. He had just read Dole's text.

"Brilliant speech!" Gingrich said, booming in his best pep-rally self-confidence, "don't change a word, and you know I like to change everything."

Dole and the others laughed.

"Bob," Gingrich added dramatically, "no one will ever again say you don't have a vision."

Dole was up. He went back to practicing, but it was not that good. He felt like he was getting a cold, and he decided to go home about 5 P.M. to exercise and get some rest.

At the White House, Clinton was still fiddling with his speech. He had received the first draft six days earlier—"the fire hydrant draft," the speechwriters called it because figuratively they expected and encouraged everyone to urinate on it. Many did, including Clinton. The second draft contained the very Morrisesque line, "The era of big government is over." It was a declaration that Clinton was a different Democrat, a New Democrat, heading more and more in the Republican direction.

Dick Morris saw that his ideas were being used, and he backed off early in the process. The speech would present Clinton as touting traditional Republican objectives and values but saying he wanted to do it his way, with more heart and generosity. "It's going the way I want," Morris said. The speech was built around seven challenges that Clinton would make on issues ranging from families to smaller government.

Just before the State of the Union the night of January 23, Stephanopoulos and McCurry went to the basement map room of the White House residence to wait for Clinton to come down for the motorcade to the Capitol. They had obtained a copy of Dole's text and read it carefully.

On paper, McCurry thought Dole's speech the better. Reading them side by side, anyone would pick Dole's in a heartbeat, McCurry felt. But these were speeches, to be delivered, not read, and McCurry, who had been involved for years in preparing the Democratic responses to President Reagan's State of the Union speeches, knew it was not going to be a fair fight. Clinton had the communications skills, and he had the giant hall of the House of Representatives with a live audience as his stage. Dole would be in a small room staring into a camera.

Clinton arrived, aware that his aides had read the competition.

"What do you think?" Clinton asked.

Stephanopoulos and McCurry looked at each other.

"It's a good speech," Stephanopoulos said. "It's a very tough speech." Both McCurry and he thought it would be pretty effective. "But it's a primary speech, and you're giving a general election speech tonight to the whole country, and he's only talking to Iowa and New Hampshire."

Dole came back to the Capitol about 7 P.M. and took a Sudafed, the mild cold pill. He went down to the holding room in the Capitol to greet Clinton before their speeches.

"You'll excuse me," Dole said to Clinton, "I've got to run back and work on my response." Dole went back and began to practice his own speech.

In the House chamber, Clinton was announced and entered, shaking hands all along the way to the podium. The day before, Gingrich had been asked what he hoped Clinton would say in his speech. "Thank you and good night," Gingrich had replied, only half-joking. Upon taking the podium, Clinton turned to Gingrich, whose seat was directly behind, and handed him a piece of paper that said, "State of the Union . . . Thank you and good night." Gingrich burst out laughing.

Dole watched some of Clinton's speech from his own office. Clinton had the entire audience, which included the full Senate and full House, in his hand. Dole continued to practice, hitting his stride, even a new peak as he psyched himself up.

How much of Clinton's speech was left, he asked.

Clinton was at about five of 13 pages, one of Dole's aides reported.

Dole deflated. What? Why so long? He stopped practicing. He paced. He looked around, waited.

"This is getting past my bedtime," Dole joked about 10 P.M. As the time ticked by, Dole said maybe it would be past midnight before he had a chance to give his reply. Perhaps, he suggested mischievously, he should change his greeting from "Good evening" to "Good morning."

There was another 30 minutes of waiting for Clinton to finish.

Sipple wanted no one in Dole's eyeline so all the staff were sent out, leaving only the cameraman and director from ABC, which was providing the pool coverage. Sipple wanted to put a filter on the lens, but ABC controlled the situation and they had a rule against filters. Dole was going to stand up for the speech.

"Good evening," Dole finally began. "I'm Bob Dole, and I'm here to reply to the president's message on the state of the union."

The lighting was terrible, and Dole's face looked wrinkled, crinkly, dark. His voice was hurried, not steady. His nerves showed. A bit of cotton-mouth struck. Stiff and ill at ease, he nonetheless forged on. After several minutes he got better, but he was still shaky.

"President Clinton shares a view of America held by our country's elites," Dole said. "President Clinton may well be the rear guard of the welfare state."

"I've never gone in for dramatics, but I do believe we have reached a defining moment. It is as if we went to sleep in one America, and woke up in quite another. It is as though our government, our institutions and our culture have been hijacked by liberals and are careening dangerously off course."

"We will begin the unfunding of Big Brother."

Finally, he was done and said good night.

Mari Will ran into the room.

"Yes! Yes!" she declared. "Oh, boy, that was great."

Dole believed they would tell him the truth. "Yeeeeaaah," another senior staffer said. They all concurred.

Dole noticed a celebration in the outer office. He called Elizabeth.

"Oh, that was good!" Elizabeth said. She had just talked to her 94-year-old mother, a good critic, who also had liked it.

Dole called Scott Reed, who had watched it at his home in Annapolis.

"How did I do?" Dole inquired.

"I thought you did great!" Reed said. They still had to appeal to primary voters and the hosing of the liberals and the elites was perfect. "You were right on. You looked a little nervous at first, but halfway through it you got into feeling comfortable and into a rhythm and finished very strong."

Well, Dole thought to himself, the early returns are good. He went home to his Watergate apartment and slept well that night.

At about 5:30 A.M. the next morning, Charlie Black, chief strategist for Gramm, arose early and picked up a copy of *The Washington Post*. The banner headline read, "Clinton Embraces GOP Themes in Setting

Agenda." Beneath it was a very prominently displayed news analysis by David S. Broder, the dean of American political reporting. Black read: "President Clinton was longer and stronger." On the front-page portion of the analysis an independent pollster was quoted about Dole, "He seemed old and tired." A senior Republican said Dole "came across as having no soul," and another said it was "a pretty grim night for the GOP."

Black knew Broder was a powerful and generally cautious force in political reporting, and he had given a dramatic thumbs-down on Dole's performance. "Shit, man," Black thought to himself, "*there* is a feeding frenzy in the making. The chief blackbird just flew over to the next wire."

At the Watergate, Dole got up thinking, Jimminy, there's going to be a lot of nice stuff in the paper and on TV. He read the Broder article on his performance. God, that speech must have been awful, who gave it? he thought, trying to laugh it off.

The critique of his speech as bad television and bad performance art increased all day. Dole, flying off to campaign in Iowa, was glad he would not have to face his Republican colleagues in the Senate at their weekly policy lunch. Maybe he had let the party down, he thought. "There is nothing worse than trying to speak in an empty room," he said in Iowa.

But it had been a television event, and everyone had an opinion. Phil Gramm said, "Bob Dole cannot and will not beat Bill Clinton." Pat Buchanan, campaigning in New Hampshire, said, "I think for the last three months, we have been, quite frankly, getting our clocks cleaned by President Bill Clinton."

"Dole's response last night left me scratching my head," Rush Limbaugh said on his radio show. "Sure the words were there, but it was the overall energy and passion that disappointed me."

At the policy lunch of Republican senators, Jesse Helms stood up and declared, "That was the worst performance I've ever seen! And whoever did the lighting ought to be fired."

Many of the other Republican senators began pounding the tables in agreement like a scene out of the movie *Animal House*.

"You know," Dole said later, "I thought I'd done well but it turned out I didn't do well." It was that simple and that complicated. Dole's advisers may have thought that he had been better than he usually was. But they had failed to realize that he was not going to be measured against the former Bob Dole. He was going to be measured against Bill Clinton.

David Hume Kennerly, a Pulitzer Prize winner who had been President Ford's White House photographer, had been allowed to spend the entire week with Dole shooting pictures for *Newsweek*. The next week *Newsweek*'s cover blared "Doubts About Dole," with a most unflattering black and white photograph Kennerly had taken. Dole's face, which was half in shadow, had a crinkly, makeup-laden look. His eyes were dark, haunted and almost lost, as he clutched his good left hand to nervously cover half his mouth. The picture had been taken while Dole was wearing makeup for an MTV interview, but it seemed to be a still version—and a stark reminder—of the Dole many had seen replying to Clinton's State of the Union address.

When Dole later ran into Kennerly in a hotel lobby, he did a full U-turn to seek him out.

"Sure glad we let you spend all that time with us," Dole said. A smile was frozen on his face.

"I think the cover picture showed a lot of character," replied Kennerly. He had privately protested to the *Newsweek* editors about the use of such a hideous photograph.

"It made me look like I was dug up from the grave," replied Dole.

"Other than that," Kennerly said, "how'd you like it?"

Dole spun on his heel and walked away.

The day after the State of the Union speech, Clinton left for Kentucky to give two anti-crime speeches. En route on Air Force One, he called Gingrich. The Speaker had just publicly proposed a scaled-down version of a budget agreement. Instead of a seven-year plan, Gingrich had proposed a two-year plan with spending and tax cuts.

Clinton told Gingrich that he was intrigued by the possibility, but then Clinton went on at some length to explore the impact on Dole. What did Dole want? Where was his head now? "If we put that together," the president said, "I think it'll help Dole." A two-year agreement wouldn't hurt Dole in the Republican primaries, Clinton said, adding, "I think Dole will be able to do that."

After Clinton hung up, Mike McCurry asked about the sensitivity to Dole. "Why do you care so much about what Dole's position in the primaries is going to be?" McCurry inquired.

"Look at the bunch of nitwits they've got running," Clinton said, referring to the Republican field. "Dole's the only one that's got any capability to do the job. Something could happen to me. We could have a major crisis that goes bad on us or something bad could happen in

Bosnia and they might throw me out on my rear end." The news was full of new Whitewater allegations, long-missing files suddenly turning up in the White House residence, memos and notes surfacing that seemed to contradict statements that Hillary had made. He might need Dole's support on Bosnia or Whitewater, Clinton said. Or he might lose the presidency. "I want to have some confidence in the person I turn the keys over to."

Flying back that night, McCurry had a touchy task. He knew that Clinton detested the Washington culture, especially the hang-around crowd of former government officials and journalists who seemed to have lifetime tenure. William Safire was the very embodiment of two of those loathsome strains. Safire had been a speechwriter in the Nixon White House, and as a *New York Times* columnist for the last two decades was forever putting the heaviest positive spin on Nixon's legacy.

McCurry handed Clinton a large red professional boxing glove. It belonged to Safire.

Clinton looked at it in disgust. In his column, Safire had earlier in the month called Hillary a "congenital liar" on various Whitewater matters. McCurry had replied publicly that if Clinton were not the president, he would deliver a response "on the bridge of Mr. Safire's nose." Clinton himself had said, "When you're president, there are a few more constraints on you than if you're an ordinary citizen. If I were an ordinary citizen, I might give the article the response that it deserves."

This had created a big flap, generating lots of attention for Safire and his column. When Safire had appeared on NBC Television's *Meet the Press,* host Tim Russert had given Safire a pair of boxing gloves. Safire had then sent one of the gloves to McCurry with a note which said, "Dear Mike, Do you suppose the president would be goodnatured enough to sign my glove? Indelible ink pen enclosed."

"I can't do that," Clinton said, holding the glove and the pen. "I can't do that. I know I should. Do you think I should?"

"Mr. President," McCurry replied, "the guy's going to write a column two days a week for the rest of this year, and we're going to have to live with him." McCurry had to act as the conciliator. He knew Clinton's feelings about the Washington journalists, who had set themselves up as the moral arbiters of everything and everyone in politics. But Clinton needed to have the best possible relations with media heavies like Safire. "I think he's trying to reach out to you," McCurry added.

"I just can't play the game," the president said, shaking his head. He returned the glove unsigned. McCurry took it back to the White House, stashed it under his desk and wondered how to bridge the gap.

Clinton a number of times voiced fascination that while 60 percent of the public had opposed the deployment of U.S. troops to Bosnia, public approval of his foreign policy went up not down after he ordered the deployment anyway. He realized this was in part because there had been no combat casualties so far. At the same time, he saw that toughness and decisiveness were appreciated and respected even if people disagreed. He even likened it to telling your children they have to go to the dentist— they don't want to go, but they know you're right.

For months Morris had been obsessed with getting a budget deal. At first he had predicted that Clinton would get the deal on a specific date at the end of September. Then he had two dates in October by which it would happen. Next there were two dates in November, then one second before midnight December 31, then in early January.

Having failed, Morris turned to stealth. In an unusual step, on January 25, he wrote a memo to the other side, directly to the Dole campaign.

"Dole cannot win in either New Hampshire or Iowa *unless* there is a budget deal," he wrote, citing polling data he said he had gathered after the State of the Union address. He set out different scenarios, all of which showed that Dole gained support if he pushed for a budget deal.

In one such scenario, Gingrich balked at a deal but Dole supported one. According to Morris, 57 percent said they would be more likely to support Dole because of his position and 21 percent would be less likely. In other scenarios, Dole would only beat Forbes by a large amount if there was a budget deal. Without the deal he would run even with Forbes.

Morris wrote, "You might want to check this with your own pollster." He gave a copy to Paul Manafort, a Republican advising the Dole campaign who Morris knew from Republican circles.

Morris also gave a copy of the poll results to President Clinton, but deleted the reference to checking with "your own pollster."

Ann Devroy, the ever resourceful White House correspondent for *The Washington Post,* soon obtained a copy of the memo that had gone to the Dole campaign. Devroy called Mike McCurry for comment.

McCurry tracked down Morris, who accused George Stephanopoulos of leaking it to the *Post* in order to discredit Morris. Stephanopoulos had taken Clinton's copy of the memo from the White House, Morris alleged, and passed it to James Carville, the 1992 Clinton strategist, who in turn gave it to his wife, Mary Matalin, the former Bush campaign spokesperson. Matalin had seen it got leaked.

"I can prove it," Morris said, "because the memo I sent to the president had this sentence different from the one I sent Dole."

McCurry checked with Devroy, whose copy had the sentence about checking with "your own pollster," disproving Morris's allegation. McCurry, Panetta and Ickes went to see Clinton to outline what had happened. Stephanopoulos, the accused, stayed away.

Clinton got Morris on the phone.

"George did it," Morris alleged.

"Whenever something goes wrong around here you blame it on George," Clinton yelled. He really chewed Morris out. What an incredibly stupid, amateur stunt, Clinton said. He was furious.

Passing poll data to the Dole campaign made them look desperate for a budget deal, and it fed media accounts that Morris was playing both sides.

Ickes, who loathed Morris, took the opportunity to try to further inflame Clinton. Ickes had forced Morris to disclose his consulting fees, and they had included finder's fees of some $18,500 from Paul Manafort's firm—the same Paul Manafort who had received the poll data.

McCurry worried that this was the moment that Clinton's unstable political team might come unhinged. If the incident became a big story, everyone, including Clinton, might have to take sides.

Finally everyone, including Clinton, calmed down. The only way to defuse the issue, Clinton decided, was for McCurry to issue a public rebuke to Morris in Clinton's name. McCurry had to make clear that Clinton did not know about or authorize the sharing of poll data outside the campaign. Creating a little distance between Clinton and his increasingly famous consultant would not hurt.

Stephanopoulos felt it had been a very good day.

After Devroy's story ran on the front page, Morris wrote Stephanopoulos a note of apology and then called him to repeat the apology.

"Dick," Stephanopoulos said, "I'm going to work with you, we're professionals, and I'm going to do my job, but you know I essentially don't accept this." His hostility boiled over. The accusation of leaking to an opponent was perhaps the worst thing in politics—flagrant disloyalty and dishonesty.

After hanging up the phone, Stephanopoulos was reminded again just how small time Morris was. Morris had made three mistakes. One, why put the information to the Dole campaign on paper? Two, why risk anyone seeing how silly and slanted the poll questions were? Three, why accuse someone in the blind, out of panic, with no evidence?

Morris claimed that he was taking the efforts to undermine him as a tribute. Because so many people wanted to deprive the president of his advice, something must be working.

McCurry believed the episode underscored his fears that the whole White House and campaign operation would come undone at some point. There were a lot of people at the table, probably too many. And Ickes had launched a war on Morris, cutting the commission on all paid advertising and even insisting that Morris stay at a cheaper hotel than the Jefferson when he was in Washington on the campaign's expense account. Clinton obviously did not want to give either Morris or his White House staff the upper hand, but the day might come when he would have to choose.

Dole wondered about Morris. "Why would he send us that?" he asked. "It's too tricky for me, I guess. I never was a CIA guy."

He was equally uncomfortable with the close, longtime relationship his deputy Trent Lott had with Morris.

"Got this little thing from Morris," Lott once said to Dole, "maybe you'd like to see it."

Dole looked and Lott had a piece of paper filled with budget numbers reporting what the White House would accept on key issues such as Medicare.

"I don't make any promises," Lott told Dole. "I just receive information. I don't call. Now he calls me. Understand?"

"I don't understand anything," Dole replied.

23

Scott Reed thought he was finally going to get his old boss Jack Kemp to endorse Dole. "Quarterback's coming on board," Dole said. He needed some good news. The polls showed that Forbes was coming on dangerously strong. Nabbing Kemp, the big flat tax advocate, would take some of the wind out of Forbes's sails, Dole hoped.

Reed had found that nailing endorsements was tricky because Dole would not ask anyone for help outright. That meant Reed had to work out the logistics before the pledge was sealed in a face-to-face meeting between Dole and the endorser. Though Kemp had cautioned Reed that he was not yet committed to Dole, he had dropped enough hints so that Reed felt comfortable proceeding. His plan was that Kemp would announce the endorsement in New Hampshire, where Dole really needed help against Forbes. Without Kemp's knowledge, Reed arranged through Kemp's staff to clear Kemp's schedule for Thursday, February 1, later that week.

Kemp had asked to meet personally with Dole, repeating that he was still undecided about an endorsement. Reed set up a meeting for Tuesday night, January 30. That afternoon Kemp called and said he wanted to bring along Senator Robert Bennett, the Utah Republican who had already endorsed Dole.

Reed was delighted. This was a good omen. Bennett, 62, a tall, wealthy Mormon known for his calmness, was a confidant and friend of both Dole and Reed. That evening the four—Dole, Reed, Kemp and Bennett—met in Dole's office.

"Let me tell you what bothers me about your campaign," Kemp said, correcting himself intentionally, "your campaign team. They've criticized Steve Forbes for a flat tax." Kemp was probably the nation's best known advocate of a flat tax. "You can disagree with the flat tax, but you can't say it's going to destroy the home building industry or cause the collapse of the economy because I think the economy will boom. But put that aside, you're also attacking him for trying to privatize a portion of Social Security for young workers, which I support." Kemp also repeated his criticism of California's controversial Proposition 187 that would call for the suspension of government services to "suspected illegal aliens."

"I don't want children kicked out of public schools because their name might be Gonzalez or Fong," Kemp said. "Bob, let's reform the welfare state, not turn America into a police state."

Reed couldn't keep quiet. This was incredible. "You're not running for president," he said tersely. Senator Dole was the candidate.

But Kemp had more complaints. "The next thing I know you'll be attacking Steve for the gold standard." Kemp favored the gold standard. "What's left for Jack Kemp?" he added, laughing.

Dole and the others laughed also.

"Jack," Dole said, "I'm with you on the racial side. You have always wanted the Republicans to reach out to blacks and other minorities and not pull up the drawbridge. I have always tried to keep the party open."

Bennett said that he thought Forbes was damaging the flat tax by making too many extravagant claims about its impact. "If you eliminate the mortgage deduction overnight, you render about a trillion dollars worth of capital wealth moot," Bennett said.

Reed said that they wanted Kemp to come to New Hampshire on Thursday to make the endorsement. He defended their attacks on Forbes. Forbes had started the negative advertising, driving Dole's favorable ratings from 80 percent to 50 percent. "And we had to respond."

"You have to pull the anti–flat tax ad," Kemp insisted.

"We have," Reed said. "We pulled it today." Would Kemp come to New Hampshire?

Kemp said he was going to have Gingrich write him a letter saying he ought to continue his work on the tax commission and not endorse anyone.

"Jack, you don't need a letter," Dole said. "I mean, if that's what you want to do, that's what you ought to do." Kemp was always looking for a way out, Dole thought.

"I promised Steve Forbes I would not endorse you until I gave him a chance to talk to me," Kemp said to Dole, "and I have to honor that promise. I'm going to meet with him tomorrow night, then we'll talk again."

Dole thanked Kemp, who then left with Bennett.

Reed stayed behind with Dole. Time for Dole to stop personal attacks on Forbes, let the advertising and others level the criticism, Reed said. "The campaign's going to do the job on him," Reed said. "You don't need to talk about him anymore." Dole had to be positive. "Let the campaign do it. It doesn't look presidential. You've got to get back to why do you want to be president."

Dole agreed.

On Wednesday night, January 31, Forbes met with Kemp in Washington. Forbes was still looking for some reinforcement for his campaign, and he was worried that Kemp might go with Dole. Sitting on one of the blue sofas in Kemp's office at Empower America, Forbes did not invoke Kemp's earlier promise of support. He just said that he wanted Kemp's formal, public endorsement.

"You've got my undying support for the ideas," Kemp said.

"Jack," Forbes said, "these are all your ideas."

"Thank you," Kemp said, "and you answer questions about them better than I ever did on my best day."

Forbes waved off the compliment.

"I'm troubled by two or three things," Kemp continued. The Forbes campaign ads were not worthy of the Lincoln wing of the Republican Party, Kemp said. The harsh, negative advertising would make it harder to unite the party, which was splintering into factions like the Balkans.

"It's a necessary evil," Forbes replied. He was running on ideas, Kemp's ideas—tax cutting. Nothing in the ads was inaccurate, he said.

"Look," Kemp said, "if you're accusing Bob Dole of voting for a bicycle path in an appropriations bill for Florida, you know maybe I voted for it too. Who knows? I may have voted for my own pension plan at one time. I don't even know. I can't remember, but I voted for 1,000 appropriations bills."

Forbes tried not to get defensive. He was aware that Kemp identified with at least a part of Washington, and that he didn't like Forbes's implied criticism.

"I don't like calling politicians dinosaurs," Kemp said. "To me it's ad hominem, and it's not like you. You're a man of ideas."

Forbes insisted it was the reality of trying to get the nomination. His campaign also had to run the ads to keep other people from rising in the polls.

"Let me ask you a question," Kemp said. "What if the amigos"—Gingrich, several others from Congress and Kemp—"came to you, and you had won the nomination, and we say we think the party platform has to be a little broader than just a pure flat tax? We've got to get working men and women into this mix." Suppose they suggested that working people be allowed to deduct their payroll Social Security tax? "What would you tell us?" Kemp asked, smiling.

"I would tell you all that I got the nomination on the flat tax and that I was going to run on it," Forbes answered.

"I admire that," Kemp said, "but these are not impractical politicians you'd be talking to."

Forbes held his ground. Even if the legislative mill changed his plan, if he couldn't defend the flat tax and explain it, his campaign would be lost before it started, he said. And if he won the nomination, how the hell did he win millions of primary voters if his idea was so bad?

The session ended inconclusively.

About 9 P.M., after the meeting, Kemp and Reed spoke.

"I'm not ready to go," Kemp said.

"We need you now," Reed said. "We don't need you in two weeks, we don't need you in three weeks."

"Don't force me to do this," Kemp said, "you're trying to force me."

"Jack, I'm giving you friendly, sound advice. This is the time to do it. Any other time, it's not going to be important."

"Well, I'm not ready to do it," Kemp said. He said he had a commitment to attend the National Prayer Breakfast the next morning.

"You can miss the prayer breakfast," Reed said. He had a Federal Express plane chartered to take Kemp to New Hampshire. "We could go up at 8 A.M., put together an event?"

"This would be a real feather in your cap," Kemp said.

"I don't need a feather in my cap," Reed replied. "My cap's fine right now. This is to help you."

No, Kemp said, he wasn't going.

Reed reported to Dole that it was no go.

"Last time we're dealing with the Quarterback," Dole said harshly.

Without Kemp, the Dole campaign needed *something*. A *Boston Globe* poll just out showed that Forbes was 9 percentage points ahead of Dole in New Hampshire, 31 to 22, though Dole remained ahead in several other polls. Reed and Lacy had Governor Steve Merrill, the most popular politician in the state, cut a 30-second television ad attacking Forbes. "The Steve Forbes income tax plan increases the deficit and raises our taxes," Merrill said in the ad. "The typical New Hampshire household will pay $2,000 more in taxes." Lacy and his research department had got it wrong again. Because of the exemptions for adults and children in Forbes's plan, families with low incomes—the typical New Hampshire household mentioned in the ad—would actually pay much less tax. This was pointed out in the news media.

Reed was left again to wonder why the ads were so screwed up. "Our advertising has sucked," he said. "It has been wrong." He again, however, knew that pulling the ad would draw more attention to the screw-up. Merrill was calm and willing to stick to what he had said, and he cited the statistics that many people would pay higher taxes under the Forbes plan.

Dole also wondered about the ads. Why was the research so poor? "I don't think it's spectacular," he had said of even their best ads. He hadn't seen any that just knocked him off his feet. "We've got to do better," Dole said. "We need the world's best people." He thought he had made that request 50 times.

Kemp read about the flat tax ad. Instead of his endorsement, Dole was running an attack ad. He talked to Reed.

"Oh, man," Kemp said, "I'm glad I wasn't in New Hampshire because I would have said 'Pull the ad' in public." The ad again put Dole on the side of defending the status quo, opposing change and new ideas.

"We had to do it," Reed explained. "We were getting hammered by Forbes, and we had to take him on frontally."

"You guys have made a mistake," Kemp said. They ought to take the suggestion that Dick Morris had made in the leaked memo about the popularity of a budget deal.

Reed was growing increasingly worried. Every morning he and Lacy had a conference call with their media consultant Stuart Stevens and the pollster Bill McInturff. The call often lasted an hour or an hour and a half, and the pollsters were constantly asking: Now what ad do we have in rotation? It hit Reed. Why didn't the pollsters know what ads were on TV? How could they analyze the impact of the ads? Reed decided to act on his own without Lacy's knowledge. He contacted Tony Fabrizio, a pollster doing some work for the campaign and an attack specialist who had had a hand in the infamous 1988 Willie Horton ads that helped George Bush win the presidency.

"Go in and take a snapshot in New Hampshire for us," Reed told Fabrizio. He didn't trust the babble he was getting. "Don't tell anybody. I'll pay you as a consultant; no one will know it was paid for survey research so it doesn't cause alarm."

Reed had to face it. His team wasn't working. He did not have confidence in his own guys, and the realization made him sick. Fabrizio's results came back a few days later: Dole and Forbes were tied in New Hampshire 26 to 26.

Pat Buchanan was not getting on the radar screen enough, and he didn't have the money for much television advertising. He was running in single digits in Iowa polls. He decided to make a virtue of necessity and take Phil Gramm's strategy and try to beat him with it. They were fighting for the same hard-line social conservatives. For some time Gramm had been working his neighboring state of Louisiana, which had decided to get ahead of Iowa with the first caucus. Dole, Forbes and Alexander had declined to participate in Louisiana. Buchanan decided to take on Gramm there and began campaigning hard in search of attention and momentum.

On Tuesday, February 6, Republicans voted. Twenty-one delegates were up for grabs. In the worst-case scenario, Gramm figured he would get 15 of the 21. But when the voting was complete, Buchanan had won 13 and Gramm only 8. Though only some 5 percent of the registered Republicans had voted, and the margin of victory was only 2 percent or 1,000 votes, Gramm had been hit hard.

"Well, hell, I'm out of the race," Gramm said privately to an adviser. "Can we come back from this?" The newspapers used words like "devastating," "crushing" and "near-fatal."

Dole held his tongue on Forbes for a while. But soon he started bashing Forbes on the campaign trail as the rich guy trying to buy the presidency. Nelson Warfield tried to cool Dole down.

"Senator," Warfield said, "that was a great speech we gave on the issue, but what they're going to write about is the Forbes attack."

"Well, he deserves to be attacked," Dole snapped.

Warfield called his 911, campaign headquarters, knowing there was only so much police work he could manage alone on the campaign trail. "The only goddamn news we made was attacking Forbes," Warfield reported, "frequently in very class-conscious terms."

Governor Merrill talked to Dole about the importance of leaving Forbes to others. Mari Will was sent out to try to help redirect Dole to the positive. Warren Rudman phoned in, "Now, Bob, all I can say is just stay totally positive and let us take on Forbes."

The Dole campaign set up an operations center on the third floor of the Hotel Fort Des Moines in Iowa the weekend before the February 12 caucus vote. On the night before the vote, Reed was sitting around in the staff room throwing a fit about their failure to move off the defensive. "We have to do something," he yelled.

Mike Glassner, Dole's personal aide, opened an envelope he said had been handed to him by some man earlier in the day. It was a copy of a 26-page confidential polling memo done for Forbes months earlier that suggested a road map for attacking Dole, and it included some polling questions that were negative about Dole. "What do you like least about Bob Dole?" was one question. Forbes was currently generating a lot of press by attacking Dole for similar polling, and Reed was very worried that their campaign was looking too negative.

Reed was ecstatic. "Beep the King," he said, referring to John King, the chief political correspondent for the Associated Press. They invited King over. He was the favored avenue of tips and leaks because his stories disseminated at once on the national wire to all newspapers, radio and television stations. They got a couple of six-packs of beer and tried to figure out the meaning of the memo.

King soon had a 1,000-word exclusive story on the wire suggesting Forbes did exactly what the Dole campaign had done. Reed and Warfield pushed the story hard to the network reporters late into the night, figuring they had hit gold. But the story had no legs.

Forbes was furious and felt helpless against King's story about the old memo. To make what the Dole campaign was doing days before the caucuses the moral equivalent of a seven-month-old poll to gather information was outrageous, Forbes felt. But he had much bigger problems. He was in a freefall.

The final *Des Moines Register* poll had Dole at 28 percent, with Forbes at 16 and Buchanan at 11. Dole's Sunday overnight polling came in showing that Dole had nearly 35 percent, with Forbes, Buchanan and Alexander all at about 12 or 13 percent each.

The numbers were too good to pass to Dole, Reed concluded. But the staff was feeling cocky. They had killed Forbes. Buchanan and Alexander were going nowhere. Gramm, once thought formidable, seemed dead. No one had traction, and they were going to hit in the mid-30s or better.

Dole went to bed about 10:15 P.M. Sunday night and was up at 7 A.M. the day of the caucus. He made a number of campaign stops, and later in the afternoon I interviewed him for about 45 minutes. He was in a great mood. He knew Forbes was dropping. "He had money and message," Dole said, speaking of Forbes in the past tense as if he were gone. "And not a bad message," he said, adding with a twinkle, "but I think the message has been muzzled a little bit."

The television networks polled people as they were going into the caucus meetings, and right after 7 P.M. Iowa time, the first numbers appeared on the computers. The Associated Press story by John King hit the wires at 7:03 P.M. and began, "Bob Dole won a clear-cut victory. . . ."

Dole was riding up in the elevator at a school where he had dropped by for a precinct caucus meeting. King reached Warfield by cellular phone with the first numbers from the exit polls—35 percent for Dole, 19 for Buchanan and all the others less. Warfield repeated them to Dole.

Sounds pretty good, Dole said, and then he was very quiet. His first reaction was to call his sister Norma Jean, who was in the hospital, and tell her not to worry. He was at 35 percent.

Immediately, Warfield drafted a statement for Dole to issue. Dole edited it. "Please do include 'if these polls hold up,' " he said. They all went back to the Hotel Fort Des Moines and up to Dole's suite where there was lots of happiness, smiles, back slapping, even euphoria, though by this time he had dropped to 33 in the exit polls.

A pleased Elizabeth gave her husband a big kiss. She was proud of the way he had weathered the attacks. All the negative ads would have made her pretty livid, but he had been steady and had handled the criticism very well.

Lacy said these numbers were early and Dole's 33 percent would probably go down even more.

Dole nodded. He turned to the television but there were no results on TV yet.

Warfield phoned for more numbers. Dole had slipped down to 29 then 28, and Buchanan was rising to 20 then 21, then 22 and closing, all within an hour. Will watched as Dole's face grew darker and darker and darker. More and more tension. Fewer and fewer people were hanging around Dole's suite.

The Doles ordered dinner from room service.

Television was still offering no results, but Dole began surfing with the remote control. The other candidates were on the air criticizing Dole. At one point Lamar Alexander was on *Larry King Live,* and Dole hurriedly snapped him off. Lacy knew Dole well enough to see that he was in a minor rage, though visibly keeping the cap on his emotions.

Now the numbers showed Buchanan up to 23 percent and Dole at 27 percent, still dropping. John King's AP stories had pulled back from the "clear-cut victory" to "shaky."

Mari Will too could see Dole was upset and angry, was thinking and brooding. She knew that at such times he was capable of doing anything. She worried about what he was going to do next, what he was going to say.

"It's a win, Senator," she said, trying to lift his spirits.

Dole looked up. He was not going to let Will or anyone be happy about it. She realized they had to find a way to get him out of this funk. He was going to have to go downstairs to the ballroom and make a statement. She had reminded him many times that his face was an open book. He could wage the war of his emotions on his face for all to see. "Use your words to control your thoughts because otherwise everything that you're feeling is going to be on your face," she had told him. That's why Will was always careful to remove harsh words from written speeches because Dole's face would reflect and even amplify the harshness. Tonight he was going to have to put on a brave face before the television cameras. How could they loosen him up?

Earlier in the day, Dole had appeared on a radio show and the host had played the famous song, "You'll Never Walk Alone," from the musical *Carousel.* Dole had wept on hearing the song, which he had played 30 to 40 times a day when he was recovering from his war wounds. Will figured the song might soften him up a little bit if it was played as he walked to the podium to make his statement later that night. Better tears than anger. Elizabeth thought it was a good idea.

Warfield proposed they allow TV cameras in the suite to show Dole watching the results of his victory, which were now on television.

No, Dole said. He went into the bedroom with Elizabeth. "This may be bad news," he said, "because if Forbes continues to spend heavily, he may succeed." Though Buchanan was clearly the big winner of the night with a second-place finish, Dole was blaming Forbes for his own poor showing. Forbes wouldn't win, but the barrage could drive Dole down further in the coming primaries.

"Oh, come on," she said to her husband, "we've won. Come on. Let's go."

The vote stabilized with Dole at 26 percent and Buchanan at 23 percent. A win by less than 3,000 votes, no 10- or 15-point victory. They were separated by 3 percent. In 1988, Dole had beaten Bush 37 to 18, and Bush had gone on to win the nomination and the presidency.

Will wrote out some remarks making a reference to the song "You'll Never Walk Alone," and went over them with Dole. He finally agreed to go downstairs after 9 P.M. The master of ceremonies had worked the crowd up and they were cheering, "We want Bob! We want Bob!"

The song was playing as Dole walked on stage, and he kept his composure. If tension could be bottled, he would have kept a bottling plant busy all night. Stiffly, he read a five-minute speech. "Thank you, Iowa," he said, trying vainly to drum up enthusiasm. "It's twice in a row. We withstood a barrage of millions and millions and millions of dollars worth of negative advertising and came out on top." Loud cheers from the audience.

Afterwards Elizabeth told him, "A victory's a victory, you know, upward and onward and move on."

Scott Reed was astonished that the surge had come from Buchanan. The undecided Christian conservative voters apparently all had gone to Buchanan. They had expected a two-man race out of Iowa but not with him. Okay, Reed figured, it was going to be a race against Buchanan now. It could be worse. It was time to hunker down. They had planned a tight thematic schedule for Dole the next week before the New Hampshire primary, which should answer the criticism that Dole didn't have a message. Reed didn't want an out-of-control candidate wandering around New Hampshire, showing up at shopping malls, saying whatever came into his mind, as Dole often did.

On the plane that night for the flight to New Hampshire, Dole and Elizabeth sat in the front. There was a big competition among the rest to see who could sit in the back of the plane.

What did it mean? Dole asked himself. He had wanted to go into New Hampshire with a big head of steam, and now he wouldn't. In his view, Buchanan was never going to be the nominee. His base was not broad enough. Dole was worried about someone from the center like Lamar Alexander breaking through. Alexander had finished with 18 percent in Iowa, only 5 behind Dole.

Tom Synhorst, the genius of 1988, had predicted 45,000 to 65,000 votes for Dole. The actual vote for Dole had been only 25,000. Overall voter turnout had been much lower than expected, lower than 1988, and the negative advertising had no doubt turned many people off and kept them from the polls. But that wasn't a good enough explanation. What had happened? No one had a very good answer. What was with the crazy overnight polling showing Dole ahead 35 to 12? Again no good answer.

Dole asked for the speech Will had drafted for his address the next day to the New Hampshire legislature. He read it for about ten minutes.

"Any other speeches back there?" he said, throwing the draft over his shoulder. He was tired of getting the speeches so late, almost as he was walking to the podium, it seemed. This speech was too partisan to deliver to the legislature, which included lots of Democrats.

Mari Will was insulted, upset that he would treat her so badly.

On the plane Dole began to take the speech apart. What about that speech he had given to the legislature in one of the Dakotas? It was about trusting state legislatures. He wanted a copy of that now. Kerry Tymchuk, an aide in the Majority Leader's Office, was rousted out of bed at 1 A.M. A copy was finally faxed to Dole's hotel in New Hampshire at 4 A.M. and an alternative draft developed. That seemed to pacify Dole for a while. But he didn't sleep well.

Reed had been working to bring Don Sipple into a more central role in the campaign. Sipple had met with Dole several months earlier to get the chemistry straight, and it had been okay, but Sipple was a fifth wheel. Reed wanted Sipple to conceptualize a general election. But the Dole team, Sipple judged, clearly was not ready to frame the issues on the evening television news each day—a necessity for the coming general election. He deemed them tactical and defensive. They needed to find out what the country and the voters thought were Clinton's weaknesses, and begin systematically to underscore them. But this campaign didn't seem to have an overall strategy. Lacy was spending most of his time discussing individual television spots. Issues for the ads seemed to be selected from a Chinese restaurant menu, without any overall strategy.

"Let's not think of a spot," Sipple told the others, "let's think of a plan." They had to talk about all the spots and work backwards to make sure they had assembled the strongest possible case for Dole. Dole was coming off as old and stale and dull—not strong and fresh as Reagan had. In reply to his suggestions Sipple received blank stares, or was told by Lacy that decisions had already been made. Governor Merrill privately called Sipple "the campaign's mistress."

Finally, Sipple told Reed, "Until I have some responsibility or authority or I'm empowered to do something, I can't emotionally invest in this campaign. It's too maddening to me. I mean, you give them an idea, they screw it up. These are children."

Reed said he wanted some wins under his belt before he made any changes in the campaign team, and Iowa wasn't a real victory.

The day after Iowa, February 13, Sipple wrote a one-page memo to Reed. "I am very concerned that our campaign is making a strategic and tactical mistake vis-à-vis Buchanan. It is my view that Lamar is our problem. . . . The last plausible potential nominee is Lamar. We need to nail him and nail him in New Hampshire." Sipple had looked at the Iowa exit polling, which showed that Alexander had drawn from Dole's natural voter base. By contrast there was a limit to Buchanan's base. A two-front war on both Buchanan and Alexander would not be possible in the remaining week before the New Hampshire vote. "We've got 12 hours to make the right call," he said in the memo.

Reed took the memo to Lacy. "Is this right?" he asked. "Maybe he's right."

It took Lacy several days to agree, and even when he did, there was no negative ad ready to attack Alexander. It took another day to come up with one.

Dole had reached the same conclusion as Sipple about the real threat coming from Alexander, but he and Sipple weren't in direct contact. Dole's speech to the legislature the next day, Tuesday, February 13, was routine, some of it new and some old, as he mentioned his life story, his war wound and his values. Phil Gramm's campaign was leaking word that Gramm, after his fifth-place finish in Iowa with only 9 percent of the vote, was going to drop out the next day.

Gramm told his advisers that he realized why a candidate had to run at least twice before getting the Republican nomination. There was too much to learn in one try.

"I'm going to follow the philosophy of Gus in the novel *Lonesome Dove,*" Gramm told Charlie Black. "The best way to handle death is to ride away from it."

Gramm later told his staff, "People are either Greeks or Romans. Greeks look death in the face and go on. Romans are romantics and have to think there is hope." Amid the tears and doubts, Gramm said, "I'm one of the Greeks."

Nelson Warfield felt special malice for Gramm. More than any of the others, Warfield thought Gramm had been the assassin, gleefully lining up the crosshairs to squeeze off a round at Dole's head and heart.

The next day, after Gramm dropped out, Dole phoned Gramm. "You did a good job," he said, "gave it your best shot. I've been there. I remember back in '88 how I felt, and I just wanted to let you know that I'm thinking about you today." Dole continued to commiserate and attempt to console Gramm. As he talked about defeat, what it meant, how the loser was tested more than the winner, Dole suddenly broke down. His voice choked and his body started heaving.

Gramm was obviously touched, and he said something about possibly endorsing Dole.

"I'm not calling to solicit you," Dole said, still teared up. "I just want you to know I understand. I know it's really tough. Isn't much I can say."

24

The next days of campaigning in New Hampshire were difficult for Dole. The crowds were not big or loud. Dole knew they had out-of-state supporters traveling with them, packing the crowds, but looking out rally after rally he saw the same people. They were always in the same place. He even knew some names. There was Arnold, there was so-and-so, like they were part of the Dole group. "Where are the new people?" Dole wondered. It was disheartening.

The day of the New Hampshire vote, Tuesday, February 20, Dole and Elizabeth made their rounds of the polling places. Elizabeth felt he wasn't going to win. A cold rain started.

"A lot of people probably aren't going to get there," Dole said to her. The rain would keep them away. "A lot of our voters aren't going to go because it's pouring rain. If I were on my way home from work I think I'd go on home maybe, you know, thinking he's got it and don't worry about it."

He started asking his aides for weather forecasts.

In room 702 of the Holiday Inn in Manchester, Pat Buchanan was sitting on the bed, his head down and on the phone to his 27th radio show that day.

"Someone who is an out-of-the-closet homosexual and publicly declares himself to be so," Buchanan said into the phone, "and flaunts that lifestyle is someone clearly who has a political agenda. An agenda that is at odds with my agenda. And so someone like that really would not be in my cabinet."

Buchanan had his jacket off. He was wearing a fresh shirt and a new Brooks Brothers tie.

"They're afraid of me," he said. "Ha! Ha! I can win." He said that the exit polls showed a very close race. "A dead heat. That's why it's imperative every conservative traditionalist and populist realize this thing could be decided by 20 votes. Come on out to those polls! Get on out there! Bring a friend!"

An aide reported to Buchanan that he was at 26 percent, Dole 25.

Between phone calls, I asked Buchanan what he thought the old man would have made of this? What would Nixon have said?

"He would have loved it!" Buchanan said, joy flooding his face. An aide handed him the phone for the 28th radio interview.

"How are you doing?" Buchanan said in the receiver. "Ha! Ha! Ha! Ha! Listen, I do hear this thing is dead even. . . ."

About 6 P.M. Dole and Elizabeth went out to one last event, a small rally. Riding back in a Dodge minivan, Dole, as always, sat in the front seat because he could get in and out easier with his weak arm. Elizabeth and Nelson Warfield were in the back. The miserable, cold rain continued, not even New Hampshire's famous snow. Warfield called to get the latest exit poll numbers. Buchanan was narrowly ahead with 26 percent. Dole was second with 25 percent, and Lamar Alexander third with 22 percent but moving up fast, crowding Dole. Warfield reported the numbers to Dole.

Silence. No Republican had ever lost New Hampshire and then gone on to win the party nomination. Never.

Again from the back seat Warfield called on his cellular phone to get the most recent numbers. Buchanan still ahead and edging up a little. Dole second. Alexander third but moving up slightly, only some 900 votes behind Dole. He could overtake Dole.

"Looks like we could be third," Warfield said.

"If we're third, we're finished," Dole said.

The shadows from the streetlights played through the van windows on their faces as they passed through the wet streets in silence. Elizabeth was thinking hard, preparing.

About four blocks before they reached the hotel, Elizabeth leaned forward to her husband.

"Bob," she said gently, "after all you've done for your party, and your lifetime of public service, if the voters want to turn their backs on you, it doesn't matter." She said she was very, very proud of him. It was awesome running the Senate and running for president. He had done so much, done enough. "You're head and shoulders above them all."

Dole didn't even turn around from the front seat.

They arrived at the Holiday Inn and went up to Dole's 11th-floor suite where some of the New Hampshire elected officials were insisting that Dole was going to pull it out. They knew New Hampshire and didn't care what the exit polls said, he would win. Others were phoning individual precincts to get the numbers, trying to find victory.

Dole went to a back room with Mari Will.

"You know if I finish third," he said, "I will drop out."

"I think so, Senator," she said. She was going to suggest it. One of her fears, shared by Elizabeth, was that his whole reputation was at stake. He could not continue on when it was futile.

Dole went into the other room and sat down. It was bleak. Was it worth carrying on?

About 8:20 P.M., CBS called the New Hampshire race, declaring Buchanan the winner. Dole was soon holding a solid second, with Alexander falling back. Dole was not watching television but his staff was, having snuck off to other rooms on the 11th floor.

Mari Will entered Dole's suite.

"You're going to be second," she told him.

"Where did you get that?" he asked.

"It's on TV," she said, trying to pull him out of his gloom, "there's much more current estimates on TV. Let's put it on." They switched on the television.

Dole was indeed holding second place. He went across the hall to see Elizabeth.

"Keep in mind if we finish second we're still in it," Dole said.

New Hampshire had been so hard. Elizabeth had had a feeling of foreboding about the outcome for a long time.

"I beat Buchanan in Iowa," Dole said. "He beat me in New Hampshire. I can sort of live with that. We've traded." And in the process he seemed to be blowing up the other candidates—Gramm, perhaps Forbes and Alexander.

Will and Warfield found Reed. They all agreed Dole should go down-stairs to make his statement at once while he was still second. He could drop back to third. Will and Dole worked up some remarks, and Dole took the elevator down to the ballroom of the Holiday Inn where the crowd was too enthusiastic.

Dole calmed them with a final plea, "Hold it," then read his remarks. "You're looking at the nominee of the Republican Party right now," he declared, insisting bravely he eventually would win the nomination. The campaign now was a "battle for the heart and soul of the Republican Party," but he began to stumble and his pacing was all wrong, making it seem as if he was looking at the words for the first time. He tripped on a reference to the party of Lincoln, but read on, staring down at the text, pausing and hesitating. "In the next month we will decide if we are the party of fear or of hope," he said, "if we are a party that keeps people out or brings people in. And if we are angry about the present or optimistic about the future."

Tom Brokaw said on NBC, "This state has broken his heart now three times." Dole looked it.

At his victory party, an ecstatic Buchanan led his supporters singing "God Bless America." Fists and thumbs in the air, he said, "All the forces of the old order are going to rally against us. The establishment is coming together. You can hear them now. The fax machines and the phones are buzzing in Washington, D.C." He intended to take back the party, he said. "Do not wait for orders from headquarters. Mount up and ride to the sound of the guns!"

By the end of the night, Buchanan had beat Dole 28 percent to 27 percent, or by just over 2,000 votes. Alexander received 23 percent, and Forbes a meager 12 percent.

Elizabeth was upset, and she approached Reed. Why had Reed failed in helping to make Bob a better speaker? she asked. Why had he not put more effort and emphasis into it?

Reed said it wasn't easy. The senator had his ways.

But why was he getting his remarks at the last minute? Even at times on the way to the podium? "I don't think you need a different speech every time," Elizabeth said. Bob had such a strong speaking voice, one of the greatest speaking voices, full of passion and energy. In a one-on-one television interview, he was warm, humorous and established great rapport. She wanted to see that translated to his performance behind the microphone.

Reed knew she really wanted her husband to win. Elizabeth was extremely disciplined, more than anyone else in the campaign perhaps. She put in endless hours, making multiple stops at multiple cities day after day on the campaign trail, speaking and appearing for him. She often did more than Dole did. Obviously, the defeats in 1980 and 1988 had been awful for them. Traumatic would be an understatement, Reed thought. But Dole was not going to change, so why were they wasting their time?

About 1 A.M. Reed returned to his room and flipped on CNN. A rerun of Dole's remarks was on. Reed had been in the back of the ball-room talking to reporters, trying to say the defeat was a result of the Forbes negative advertising, and had not seen Dole's speech earlier. He couldn't believe what he was seeing on TV. Dole stared down and then looked up, clearly reading what should have come from the heart, not the cards. Will was an eloquent writer, but that was not the way Dole talked. He couldn't talk it if he didn't practice it.

The next morning Reed went to see Dole early, realizing this was the moment the campaign could implode.

"Senator," Reed said, "I watched on C-SPAN or CNN last night. We can't read speeches anymore. You've got to get up there, let it all hang out on why you want to be president, and here are my eight points." Reed had taken what Dole had read the night before and put the points on an index card. "Let's go through this." One point was "heart and soul of the Republican Party." That was all he would need as a memory aid. "Say what you want but say these eight things."

"You're right," Dole said. His eyes said he really meant it. He felt he never needed long text, but once they gave it to him there was no way to leaf through 20 pages to look for the key talking points. He didn't need to be perfect. He thought Eisenhower and Truman hadn't been the greatest speakers but they had been pretty good presidents. He was delighted to be unleashed from the bonds of a prepared text.

Afterwards, Reed talked to Elizabeth. She was still upset and still focused on the speaking.

"Do something about this," she said.

"You just missed my talk with him," Reed replied. "I hear you loud and clear." Reed said he had seen the speech late on television. He agreed, they had to do better to help him. It was a turning point, Reed hoped.

Reed had lists of what needed to be done—on a given day, that week, over the next three months. On the long-range list he put "Candidate Development." Dole would have to go to school, get into a routine of learning how to speak better and also how to deliver a prepared text on important occasions. Until then he would have to work off talking points.

Reed decided to travel with Dole for several days in advance of the next primaries. He couldn't send Dole off on his own or there would be no telling what might happen. If he were there he could help Dole develop his eight points, and they could change them at every stop. One point was "serious business," Dole's explanation of why selecting a president mattered, and how he would change the country. Another was the "contrast with Buchanan" on trade and jobs. Another was "contrast with Clinton" on taxes and welfare reform.

Reed wanted to demonstrate there was life in the Dole campaign. The day after New Hampshire, they put out 13 separate press releases. One announced the Dole organization in Oregon, another the 39th Florida state legislator to back Dole and another the endorsement of a famed race car driver.

Dole's New Hampshire loss was the lead TV news and made banner headlines in most newspapers. Brutal divisive fights in the upcoming Republican primaries were forecast. Dole was dented and nearly out, many said. Journalists started a drumbeat. What are you going to do? What changes are you going to make? How are you going to change your message? Change Dole? Change strategy? Change staff?

Warfield could find no market for their spin blaming the loss on negative advertising.

Privately, Dole almost felt better finishing second in New Hampshire than he did winning Iowa. He also thought he would still win the nomination, but he had decided to keep that conclusion to himself.

At the White House, most of Clinton's advisers were elated. Buchanan the extremist was the perfect foil for Clinton, and at minimum would set off a bloodletting in the Republican Party that would continue all year.

It was Clinton who disagreed. "Hey," Clinton said, "this isn't all good news. Because if Dole handles it right, he establishes his bona fides more as a moderate and beats back the extremists. Shows strength." Clinton said he thought Dole would win the nomination.

At a later evening meeting in the White House residence, Morris presented a detailed analysis of what would happen in the coming Republican primaries. In a rare show of uncertainty, he acknowledged that his scenario was speculative. Stepping through the primaries, he showed how Steve Forbes could resurface and win New York, a state that Morris knew well. Dole, however, could still recover, but he couldn't win the nomination before the California primary at the end of March. He added that Dole's probable success meant it was still important to obtain a budget deal, and he believed if Clinton-Gore and the Democratic Committee didn't launch new advertising with a massive buy by March 1, they could be in an impossible situation with all the focus and attention on the Republicans. In the ongoing competition for voter attention, Clinton had to have a forceful presence, and in the heat of the Republican primary battle, the only way would be paid advertising.

Clinton approved the media buys. Within ten days they would be on the air in 40 percent of the country.

The Delaware primary was four days off, Saturday, February 24. Dole wondered if he should campaign in Delaware, even though he had pledged he would not.

Delaware's effort to crowd in was sacrilege as far as New Hampshire was concerned. New Hampshire treated their first in the nation primary as almost a God-given right. Reed, Lacy and everyone else in the campaign said it was important to honor that pledge and leave it to the Dole campaign people in Delaware. The campaign's tracking poll of two days earlier showed he was ahead of Forbes. Dole finally agreed, but it made no sense to him. He had lots of friends in Delaware. "Well, New Hampshire's over," Dole said. "Why would it be breaking my faith now?"

The night before the Delaware primary, on the campaign plane, Dole reviewed the advertisements running in advance of the upcoming primaries in North and South Dakota. They had nothing about agriculture, his natural constituency, the key issue. Why? No one had a good answer and Dole was furious. Why wasn't someone who knew something about the Dakotas writing their ads? He wanted an agriculture ad right now.

About 9:30 P.M. Reed reached Lacy at home. Dole was being impossible, a bear. Can we do this?

Lacy said it could only be a radio spot and it would cost a fortune.

"Trust me," Reed said, "you don't want to . . . let's not worry about it, let's just get it done."

Lacy spent the next hour dialing and beeping the campaign advertising world. Someone was found. A script was thrown together and Dole recorded it over the phone. Lacy noted it was after midnight before they finished the goofy little radio spot on agriculture.

The next morning, Saturday, February 24, Reed told Dole that he was going to make some significant personnel changes.

Dole didn't ask who or when.

Reed left the campaign plane to fly back to Washington. For the first time he thought they could lose this whole thing. He didn't want to lose because of incompetence.

His plane stopped in Houston and he called in for the Delaware exit polls. Dole was running third, behind both Forbes and Buchanan. Reed was flabbergasted.

Warfield, alone with Dole, was getting the same exit polls.

Dole soaked in the results at first and then he started to talk about the campaign polling. Why was it always wrong? Finally Dole moved into second, but he still lost to Forbes 33 percent to 27 percent.

Late Saturday night, Dole was in a fury again, and he phoned Reed.

"What happened?" Dole asked sarcastically. "Thought we were going to do better than this. Do we even have a strategy for these states?"

Reed said he was going to take personal charge, take it into his hands.

Dole said he wanted action.

"Some changes," Reed promised, "and it's going to be swift and they're going to be big."

Who?

"I'm going to move Lacy out of his role," Reed said. Bill Lacy, Reed's personal godfather, and the godfather of the 1996 Dole campaign. Lacy was in charge of advertising and polling. Both were screwed up.

Fine, Dole said.

"I'm going to change pollsters too," Reed explained.

Dole was not upset at that prospect.

Warfield often sent in carefully interpreted dispatches from the field. From Dole's demeanor, body language, growls and eyes, it was possible to glean the larger meaning. Warfield called Reed. "You've a very short window," Warfield said, "in which, if you do not act, you will become part of the problem, and you too are at risk."

"I hear you," Reed replied.

Warfield said now that Dole had sanctioned action, he expected action. It was compulsory if Reed wanted to survive.

Reed told himself that all good teams make changes at halftime, whether it was football, basketball or politics. They had become a bureaucratic campaign overwhelmed by inertia. Worse, they weren't winning. An operation succeeds or fails, and they were on the verge of failing. Reed couldn't just stand back for fear of hurting somebody's feelings. They could not blow it for Dole, who had put his entire life into this.

On Sunday morning Reed checked in with Dole to review the plan of action.

"Do it," Dole said. "I want changes."

That Sunday afternoon, Lacy was in Annapolis driving to lunch with his wife when his car phone rang.

"We have a real problem," Reed said. He had a lump in the back of his neck, he was so tense. This was the hardest thing he ever had to do. "Dole's completely lost confidence in you. It's a problem."

Lacy was stunned. They agreed to meet at the headquarters in Washington. Lacy told his wife. "Nobody's ever said anything to me before today." He was in a daze over lunch.

At the office later that afternoon, Reed tried to be matter-of-fact with Lacy, but the lump was still in the back of his neck. Reed recounted how Dole had called him at home on Saturday night in a rage about Delaware and the inaccuracy of the polling.

Lacy pointed out that Bill McInturff, the pollster, had always warned that Dole was the functional incumbent, which meant he would get the percentage of the vote that showed up in the tracking poll. The big question mark was the undecided voters. Functional incumbents rarely received the vote of undecideds because they were known and had already been rejected. The question was, who else would receive the undecided support? In Delaware, the tracking showed Dole at 27, which was precisely what he had received in the final vote. Because the undecideds had gone to Forbes, he had leapt over Dole and received 33 percent.

Reed said that Dole had told him to make some changes and he wanted a new strategist. Period. Reed said he was acting on a direct order from Dole.

"I understand," Lacy replied; "if that's what Dole wants, I will go."

"You don't have to go," Reed said. "I don't think you should go. You can still be deputy chairman." Lacy could still collect his monthly consultant's fee and do other things for the campaign. But the new strategist would control polling and advertising.

"Look," Lacy said, "I'm not the least bit interested in staying under these circumstances." He said he would resign. "I think this is a terrible mistake, and I'd like to talk to Dole about it."

Okay, Reed said, Dole would be back in town on Tuesday. "I'll arrange for you to go see him."

"Let's get together tomorrow and talk about how we're going to manage the press on this," Lacy said. "I think you would do very well to do it on a primary day." His departure would get lost in the news of the primary, it would not affect the primary vote and it would not look like Dole panicked, Lacy said.

Reed said he agreed, and Lacy went back home.

"Beep the King," Reed told Warfield. He instructed Warfield to provide the story of the shake-up to John King of the Associated Press. Reed and Warfield expected that Lacy would try to get his own spin out to his press friends or even try to get to Dole. This was the campaign shake-up, chaos-in-the-campaign story that Dole had long feared. Removing the chief strategist and pollster could be a story that would spin out of control. They had to get their own interpretation on it.

Warfield felt Lacy had been a problem for months. Too often Dole would ask Warfield, Why is this wrong? Why can't we get better research? Well, Warfield had said, Bill Lacy's research department doesn't come up with it. Why is this messed up? Well, Warfield had answered, this was cleared by Bill.

Reed called Don Sipple, the former Wilson media consultant, whom Reed had kept waiting in the wings. He explained the changes.

"Will you take this on?" Reed asked. Sipple would be the new chief strategist to oversee the whole campaign message, the planning, advertising and polling.

"You know I will," Sipple replied.

Dole was on his campaign plane heading for Atlanta when John King's news story hit the wire about the campaign shake-up. Warfield went to brief Dole. He added that there was another news story about how Dole's campaign had compiled a 280-page vulnerability study on

Dole as part of the plan to protect themselves from attack and to show they were on the ball. Mary Anne Carter, head of campaign research for Lacy, had prepared the report. She and Lacy had proudly put this information about the self-investigation out to the press, including a description of how she had divided the project into 26 "mini-vulnerability studies."

"She's gone," Dole ordered, "get rid of her."

Lacy was at home asleep when the phone started ringing. It was his mother. He was an only child, and she was particularly distraught. The television was saying her son, who had devoted years to Dole, was being demoted. Lacy explained and calmed her down. He realized suddenly he had been hopelessly naive. He had intentionally let Reed handle virtually all the contact with Dole in phone calls and meetings over the last year. It was easier for Dole to have one contact point with the campaign, and Lacy knew that Dole didn't want a lot of people in his face. By taking himself out of the loop, Lacy realized, he had isolated himself from his candidate. He had never really had a personal relationship with Dole over the years, but the absence of any relationship at all had no doubt hurt. Lacy did not believe that Dole had said to get rid of him. Obviously Reed had decided to assert total control. Reed had not been in control of the advertising and the polling, and he had just now seized it. Lacy's father had recently bought a $20 million candy business in Kansas, and Lacy was planning to join the business after the election. Now he would just be there a little sooner. Lacy decided to keep quiet publicly. He still believed in Dole, still believed Dole was the right person to be president.

Sipple sat down with Stuart Stevens, who was doing the media advertising.

"This is how it's going to work," Sipple explained. "First thing we do, we're going to get rid of all this muck we've got on the air, and you and I are going to conceive of a good positive spot. We need to have Dole talking." Sipple felt that Dole had lost stature in the previous advertising by attacking others, and presenting himself as just one of the other candidates who wanted to be president—the old man in the pack of nine or ten at candidate forums. Advertising was about impressions and symbols.

The campaign advertising had been too literal as it picked at what Forbes may or may not have said about crime, or attacked Buchanan as extreme. Their ads seemed to rest on the premise that one line in an ad would win over some group or block of special interest voters.

Sipple wanted ads that would recapture Dole's stature as the senior Republican. They had to move quickly, using old footage of Dole talking about his values, what he wanted to do with welfare reform and taxes. All positive. The ad closed with the line, "Tested in war, proven in peace, Bob Dole embodies the strength of America. A man every American will be proud to call president."

There was not enough time to get Sipple's new ad on the air for the upcoming primaries on Tuesday in Arizona and the Dakotas. Reed was worried about those states. Polls showed Dole ahead of Forbes and Buchanan by several points in Arizona, but he was thought to have been ahead in New Hampshire and Delaware also. He was ahead by much more in the Dakotas, but suddenly everything seemed shaky. "If we lose South Dakota, we're fucked," Reed said.

On Monday, February 26, at 3 P.M., Senator Pete Domenici, the head of the Senate Budget Committee and one of Dole's closest friends in the Senate, called a meeting with nine other senators in his office—all Republicans who were supporting Dole. This wasn't the fax machines and phones buzzing that Buchanan had predicted. This was a gathering of the Republican establishment, in a panic.

Domenici said that he had spoken with Dole, who wanted their immediate help. It was time to rally around their leader. This was a big moment for Dole, for them, for the party and for the country. Domenici didn't have to pose the question on everyone's mind: What would happen to them and what would happen to the party if Buchanan or Forbes won the nomination? Two men who had never held elective office with views not a single sitting Republican senator could support?

Senator Judd Gregg, the New Hampshire Republican who had traveled with Dole in the first primary state, said that Dole needed a traveling companion. "You give him suggestions," Gregg said, "he takes them. He doesn't fight you. He's very approachable, but he just needs somebody traveling with him at all times."

Yeah, said Senator D'Amato, who was alarmed. "You gotta have somebody with him and make sure he stays on message," he said, "and when he says those stupid things, somebody that can say, 'Bob, you've done something wrong. That's stupid! Cut that out!' I can tell him and I have told him that."

Some senators said that D'Amato should then be the one to travel with Dole.

No way! No way! D'Amato shouted in his nasal voice. "I'm not going to be the one," said D'Amato, the chairman of the Whitewater committee, "and I'll tell you why not." He made the obvious point. "Whenever I show up, the press always wants to talk to me about Whitewater and that's a distraction, and I should stay off the campaign." Dole had to keep his distance from the investigation, not be seen as one of Clinton's inquisitors.

Ted Stevens, an Alaska Republican who was running for reelection, said he would cancel all his fund-raisers and accompany Dole. "There's nothing more important that I have to do," Stevens said.

Bob Bennett, the Utah Republican, remarked that he wasn't running this year and volunteered to travel with Dole.

The next morning around 11 A.M., Domenici, D'Amato and Bennett went to see Dole.

Dole was eating a bowl of soup, and he said he had to leave to get on his plane to campaign.

"You don't either have to leave," D'Amato said. "Stay right there! You can miss your plane. I'm telling ya this is too important. And Bob, you got to stay on message. You gotta hit Clinton." Dole started to balk. "It's more important than what you're doing," D'Amato insisted.

"Well," Dole responded, "I don't know about that."

The others told Dole that he was in trouble, and he needed someone with him at all times who had been a candidate, who knew the pitfalls and rhythms. They were not trying to take over the campaign or trying to replace anybody.

"I need help," Dole acknowledged. "I'm there on the campaign plane. I don't have any idea what's going on in the world. I'm just going from place to place." He described what it was like starting at 7 A.M. and getting back to his room at 8:30 P.M. Even though the media was all around, he barely saw a newscast.

The outside world was not the problem, they said. It was message and presentation.

"Yeah," Dole said, "I'm in trouble, but I've stopped reading the speeches. I have eight points."

"Well, Leader," Bennett said, taking a deep breath, "you know we think somebody ought to travel with you at all times. And I think I got elected."

Dole agreed at once. When could Bennett leave? They agreed to start on Friday.

After the meeting, Dole left for the airport. He reached Bill Lacy by phone.

"I'm very sorry that this had to be done," Dole said, "but changes had to be made." He said he wanted the two of them to remain friends, particularly after November. The friendship was what was really important. "This is just an election," Dole said.

"Of course," Lacy replied. He was beginning to feel that he had failed Dole miserably, not in the advertising or the polling but in communication. The facts had not been getting to Dole. "You need to understand, Senator, the following points," Lacy said. One was about the pollsters. "Somebody's been deceiving you," Lacy blurted out. "Somebody's misleading you about things. I don't know who it is, and I don't have any evidence except if they had told you what the pollsters had actually said, you would not have been surprised by New Hampshire or Delaware." As the functional incumbent, the percentages in the overnight tracking turned out to be what Dole received. That's what Bill McInturff had always said. Dole just didn't get any of the undecided vote. "Their numbers are right on." The new lead pollster, Tony Fabrizio, was the one who said Dole would win Iowa 35 percent to Buchanan's 14 percent.

Dole just made vague sounds in reply, but he didn't understand.

Second, Lacy said, the campaign had horrendous money problems, much, much worse than Dole thought. "You really need to get somebody in there that you have complete faith in who can get a handle on the money situation," Lacy said. "It's far worse than you know."

Dole mentioned a newspaper story about Lamar Alexander, who had not raised the maximum amount of money allowed. So Alexander was possibly in a position to raise the millions that would be needed for an advertising blitz. "Do you think there's any credibility to that?" Dole asked.

"Well, Senator," Lacy replied, "I mean, factually it's correct, but I don't think he can raise the money." Lacy didn't see how Alexander could convert his third-place finishes in Iowa and New Hampshire, and his fourth in Delaware into a bandwagon that would convince contributors.

Dole was unresponsive. Lacy felt that none of what he had said was registering, but then again new bombs could be falling or about to fall at 810—the campaign headquarters at 810 First Street Northeast.

"Just remember," Lacy said, "if you win Arizona, you're going to win South Carolina and you're going to be the nominee, and it was a strategy that the group that I led put together."

"I want you to come by and see me," Dole said in a very friendly way, "and talk about this." After the call, Dole thought maybe it had been unfair. Lacy was quiet, thoughtful, not seeking media attention, seemed to have no agenda beyond helping Dole.

Dole reported to Reed that it had been a very friendly chat. Lacy was not going to blow up in public. "He says you're spending too much money, though," Dole added. The subject of campaign expenditures was one Dole had raised with Reed repeatedly. "I don't want to start a fight here," Dole said, raising the money question again.

Reed acknowledged. He thought that at least Lacy had showed some balls, trying to blow the whistle. Reed nonetheless was relieved that no big public struggle with Lacy was on the horizon. The real struggle would be that night as the results from the three primaries, Arizona and the two Dakotas, came in.

Having lost two of the last three primaries, much was on the line. Dole went to his Watergate apartment that night. Elizabeth was campaigning for him out of town. The first Arizona exit polls showed him in third place, behind Forbes and Buchanan. Dole tuned in to ABC's *Nightline*. He rarely stayed up that late.

"It is still far too early to be drafting a funeral oration for Bob Dole's presidential ambitions," Ted Koppel said. "But the candidate is not looking well, politically speaking," Koppel added. "Yes, he won in North and South Dakota tonight, but that was not the prize of this primary election day. The prize was Arizona, with its 39 delegates, winner take all. Bob Dole did not win Arizona; he came in third."

"Devastating," ABC political correspondent Jeff Greenfield pronounced. "Dole has finished third tonight, he's fired top staff members, he faces a potentially serious money crunch, and he still hasn't explained why he should be president."

Forbes was the victor, but the second-place Buchanan had the momentum. "We've all been so wrong about the Buchanan candidacy," Koppel said, "and there is now the smell of genuine electric excitement about it."

Watching, Dole was very disturbed. "My God, it's worse than I thought," Dole said to himself. He felt roasted, toasted and buried. After *Nightline* ended at midnight, Dole watched CNN's Headline News with the latest returns scrolling across the bottom of the screen. He was still in third place at 2 A.M. when he finally fell asleep.

In the morning, Dole woke up to learn that the exit polls had been wrong. Forbes won with 33 percent, but Dole took second with 30 percent and Buchanan was third with 27 percent.

25

Suddenly two firsts in the Dakotas and a second looked a lot better for Bob Dole. "Boy, got a new life," he said to himself. It was the third time he'd come back from the brink of a third-place finish—New Hampshire, Delaware and now Arizona.

Later that day, Reed and Sipple had positive ads on the air in nine states. They were playing beat-the-clock to get to the South Carolina primary in three days. No one was running negative ads against Dole there, and Dole had not spent much time there so he was not overexposed. That meant little time for voters to develop doubts. But South Carolina was the first southern primary state, and Buchanan's message of social conservatism, pro-worker populism and isolationism might just register.

Thursday night, February 29, Reed watched the evening news. Most times Dole was shown out on the campaign trail with boom microphones in his face and all around him, stopping to make a few comments as he moved in and out of the van or a car. He looked like he was being mugged. He did not look like a president. Dole was too anxious to service the press. "They're fucking us," Reed shouted at the TV. Earlier, Reed had been banged hard in the cheek by a TV cameraman when he had been engulfed in the swarm. It was very dangerous.

"We've got to tighten this thing up a little more," Reed recommended to Dole later. "Wave, look like a president, get in the car and go. Get what we want out of that camera and move on."

The morning of Friday, March 1, the day before the South Carolina primary, Reed reviewed the polling showing Dole in the high 40s, even into the 50s. Dole had never had anything like that. Could it be true? Dole's favorable rating was in the 70 percent range. Maybe with their positive ad they could get a large portion of that 70 percent to the polls to actually vote. With so many disappointments, however, Reed held his breath. He lowballed the tracking poll numbers to Dole, saying they were ahead with only 38 or 39 percent.

Money was low, with only about $5 million left. Reed was tightening up on expenses. He was literally going around the office unplugging fax machines that didn't seem necessary.

Senator Bennett joined Dole that Friday for a New England swing. Junior Tuesday was coming up in four days: the five remaining New England states and Georgia, Colorado and Maryland. In Connecticut, Bennett frantically took notes as Dole spoke to a large crowd in a packed state office building. It was almost perfect. Dole stuck to his eight points. He was forceful, pounding the lectern occasionally, not reading. Bennett wondered what in the world he was doing on this trip.

"Great job," Bennett told Dole afterwards.

They flew on to Rhode Island and Dole's performance was a notch lower, but Bennett didn't say anything. Then next in Massachusetts, Dole went down a notch more. On Saturday, in Maine, Dole started to come apart. He hit the same points but started adding stuff about Senate procedure, wandering off. In Vermont, he unwound some more. Bennett could see that Dole was clearly bored. He could not deal with performing like a plug-in cassette tape. Bennett decided he had to say something.

About 3 P.M., they got on the plane to go to New York.

"Any exit poll numbers?" Dole asked about the South Carolina voting, which was still in progress.

Dole 42, Buchanan 29.

"Okay," Dole said, trying to be calm, cool. The numbers were higher than Reed had reported in the tracking poll. "Well, that's good," Dole said. "That's good." But the early exit polls had been high before. Dole said no more. It was a more conservative state where Buchanan might have hit pay dirt, or where Alexander might have caught fire. But in his innermost he thought he was going to win now.

Bennett decided not to give a fully candid performance review, but since Dole seemed to be feeling good, he decided to offer some fragments.

"By the way," Bennett said, "when you tell the story about growing up in Russell, Kansas, that is the emotional high point of what you do.

And when you do that, don't add any more after that. It detracts." His advice was simple. "No matter what happens, when you tell that story, you're through."

In New York, Dole did his eight points and told the story about growing up in Russell. The crowd was cheering, going crazy. He finished the story. He paused. "God bless America," he said, and he turned and sat down.

Less was more, Dole saw yet again. Something he had known for a long time, his entire life really. Hadn't he? Wasn't that the essence of his war wound? He had made more out of less.

Warfield watched Bennett's interaction with Dole. It was nice to have another body for Dole to talk to without Warfield having to absorb every single question. Bennett had explained to Warfield that he was aboard because there was no one around who would plainly tell Dole yes or no. Guess what? Warfield thought to himself. There was still no one who plainly could tell Dole yes or no.

Warfield received word that one of the networks had called South Carolina for Dole, and then all but NBC called it for him.

"Senator," Warfield said to Dole, "I think we might get a nice response from the cameramen back there." They were Dole's friends. "They'll cheer if I announce the race has been called."

"Yeah, sure, go ahead."

Warfield went up, took the intercom, and said, "I'm pleased to announce that according to the Associated Press, ABC, CBS and CNN, Bob Dole's the winner in South Carolina."

The cameramen, the crews, the staff went wild; an uproarious clatter erupted from the back of the plane.

"AAArrrggghhh," Dole said, throwing his thumb in the air.

The victory was sweet. Dole ended up with 45 percent, Buchanan with 29—a 16 percent edge. Forbes, with 13 percent, and Alexander, with 10, were in the dust.

"Now you've won," Bennett said, "you've won big and the bounce out will hit New England. You're going to carry all the places we've been in New England, and New York will fall into place."

"Yeah," Dole said.

Elizabeth gave him a big kiss.

"I'm so proud of you," she said. "Isn't it great?"

But Elizabeth felt they needed to focus on what was next—the eight states of Junior Tuesday in three days, then New York two days later, and then five days later Super Tuesday with the big southern states, Florida and Texas. There was very little time to sit back and relish the victory. Okay now, she said to herself, tomorrow we've got to do such-and-such. Where was that schedule?

"Why don't you sleep?" Bennett asked Dole.

"No," Dole said, "I'll sleep coming back." But he didn't.

From the stops in all those states and the response of the crowds, Bennett concluded that ordinary Republicans were still not in love with Dole. But the Republican officeholders who had come out in droves to support Dole had decided that any other candidate at the top of the ticket would jeopardize their own reelection and the party's stature. They effectively had said, "Holy cow, if I share the ticket with Steve Forbes, or particularly Pat Buchanan, it could be over. But Dole is respectable, not going to drag me down."

Reed thought that South Carolina was the shot that would be heard around the world. Finally, they had won big. But he told himself again, "You can't get emotional about this stuff. Emotion doesn't work in this business."

"I've got to say to you, Mr. Clinton," Dole said at a rally that night in South Carolina, "we are going to veto you in 1996."

When Dole received applause for a line, he tended to use it again, and he did so over the next several days. The talking points helped him sound more concise, and he was able essentially to hop from one applause line to another. He was animated and more direct. Many reporters noticed it and mentioned it in their stories. David Broder wrote, "Dole has appeared increasingly confident on the stump."

Over the weekend before Junior Tuesday, when eight states would hold their primaries, Reed spoke with Gaylord, Gingrich's top adviser.

"You got to say something good about Dole," Reed said. Time to deliver. "Is your guy going to vote?" Gingrich could vote in the Georgia primary, one of the eight Junior Tuesday states, on March 5.

"He's going to vote absentee Monday," Gaylord replied.

"Why don't you get him to say he's voted for Dole?" Reed pressed.

"Fine, that's easy."

In his Monday morning phone call with Dole, Reed reported, "By the way, Gingrich is going to vote for you today and say to reporters that he voted for you."

"Oh, great," Dole said. Big endorsement in the Speaker's home state. About 15 minutes later, Gaylord called Reed.

"Here's the Speaker," Gaylord said, "let him tell you what he did."

"Hey, congratulations," Gingrich said to the Dole campaign manager. "You guys are going to win. Marianne and I talked and we decided, you know, I ought to keep my vote to myself."

Oh, great, Reed thought.

Gingrich said he was doing everything possible to help Dole. He had led the public charge urging Lamar Alexander, whose best finishes had been thirds in Iowa and New Hampshire, to drop out of the race. But Gingrich said his own vote would remain secret, and he had already told reporters he was not going to reveal his choice.

After the call, Nelson Warfield called Reed from Atlanta to report that Dole, speaking from the platform, had just thanked Gingrich for voting for him.

"Aw, shit," Reed exclaimed, as his assistant burst into the room to say reporters were calling.

"I need you to help us on this," Reed said in an immediate call to Gaylord, who was on a plane with Gingrich, flying to New York.

Gaylord laughed and handed the phone to Gingrich.

Reed told the Speaker his problem. Dole always blurted out the news before it happened.

Gingrich burst into loud laughter. "I'll bail you out, fine. Let me just call Marianne and then we'll put out a statement." His office later faxed a statement saying Gingrich had voted for Dole.

The next day, Tuesday, March 5, the earliest exit polls showed that Dole might win all eight states. Reed called Bay Buchanan, Pat Buchanan's sister and his campaign chair. Reed and Bay had a good relationship going back several years.

"Let's get together," Reed said.

She went nuts and yelled, "We're going third party. Pat's not there, but I am. What you've done is outrageous." The personal assault on Pat in the negative Dole ads had been out of bounds, she said, the worst thing in American politics in 25 years.

"What's done is done," Reed replied.

What's done was unacceptable, she said, refusing to meet.

Reed felt she was a psycho, and he concluded that Buchanan himself was on a jihad and impossible to deal with.

Reed and Dole discussed the Buchanan factor. Dole still considered Buchanan a friend.

"We've got to ignore the guy," Reed said

They would get Buchanan the next Tuesday if they won those primaries, Dole thought. He had known Buchanan for decades, and he appreciated Buchanan's humor, loved watching him on CNN's *Crossfire* show. "I like his wit, and I like that smile he has," Dole said, "and he kind of laughs at himself, you know, that little laugh." Dole didn't personally like some of the things Buchanan said about him, but he sure appreciated the performance.

"Beltway Bob!" Dole said, repeating one of Buchanan's favorite names for Dole, "that's clever stuff. Busboy for corporate America! You've got to admire a guy like that. I mean, it doesn't irritate me. If somebody else would say that, I'd be all upset, but when Pat does it, I think, boy, that guy's smart."

If Buchanan were to run as a third-party candidate, Dole realized, that would hurt him. But he thought Buchanan was both smart enough and enough of a party man not to break with the Republicans. "Hopefully," Dole said, "he'll call some day and say, 'I'm ready to suit up.' "

Later in the day, Dole returned to the Majority Leader's Office in Washington. The exit polls now showed he was going to win all the primaries, 8 to 0, the five New England states, Georgia, Maryland and Colorado. In some cases, it was by more than a 2-to-1 margin. Though Buchanan had the most second-place finishes, Forbes was second in Connecticut, and Alexander was second in Rhode Island. The opposition was splitting the vote, and Dole was winning in all regions of the country.

Clinton had called and, about 3 P.M., Dole returned his call.

Clinton said that in the wake of a suicide bomb attack in Israel that had killed 14 people, he was immediately going to transfer sophisticated equipment to Israel for detecting explosives.

Dole said he agreed with the decision, and he apologized for the delay in getting back. "I've been running around trying to find out what's happening in all the primaries," he said.

Clinton said that Dole ought to win because he was the only one in the field who understood how it all worked down at the White House.

About 6 P.M., Dole, Gingrich, Reed, Sheila Burke and Joe Gaylord gathered in Dole's office. The Speaker had been pressing much of the day for such a get-together.

Gingrich said he wanted to help pull the party together—the Republican National Committee, the House majority, the Senate majority, the

Republican governors. He wanted to head up a task force, a strong policy group to lay out themes and issues, and to get personally engaged in the race.

Dole wasn't paying much attention, walking in and out. "Anything going on?" he asked several times. New exit polls? What was on television? He had to have some makeup for an upcoming television appearance.

Gingrich was focused. He said he wanted to come up with what the presidential campaign was going to be about, what Dole was going to run on. "We need to have a team effort," Gingrich said.

Dole wandered in. "Well, we haven't won the nomination yet, you know, don't take anything for granted."

Gingrich said he wanted to start working on the agenda.

"I appreciate that very much," Dole said, "the thing's not over yet, it's just beginning."

"Great," Reed said. "We've got a team effort. We've got all the governors, we've got all the senators. You will be a huge asset to control the 236 guys," a reference to the House Republicans. "The first thing we need to do is agree that there's going to be a presidential Dole message of this campaign for the party." The message could not be driven by the day-to-day activities in Congress, Reed said.

Gingrich said he agreed. He proposed a big meeting, strategic planning.

"Great," Reed said, "we'll talk about it later."

Dole didn't talk about it with Gingrich. He made it clear to Reed what he wanted. "There's not going to be any Contract with anybody," Dole said. "It's going to be what Bob Dole outlines for the campaign and for America." Dole realized Clinton wanted to tie him to Gingrich— "Have Newt and Bob in every picture." No more.

Later that evening, Dole went to the Holiday Inn near Capitol Hill. Up in his suite, the final results came in at about 9 P.M. It was indeed 8 to 0. Reed came to the suite to bring Dole to the victory rally downstairs.

Dole walked over to greet Reed.

"Congratulations," Dole said, and shook Reed's hand. Some of Dole's Senate colleagues had expressed private doubts about Reed early on, but there was nothing like victory to erase doubt. It was the most emotional Reed had ever seen Dole, except when he was talking about his war wound. He was obviously reaching out.

"Congratulations to you," Reed responded. "We're going to make it."

Elizabeth was smiling.

"We're going to make it now," Reed said confidently to her. They were heading over the top.

Elizabeth gave Reed a kiss.

At the victory celebration downstairs, Dole called Reed and some of the other senior campaign staff up on stage.

President Clinton spoke at a memorial service for the bombing victims at the Embassy of Israel that evening, and came back to the White House to learn that Dole was winning 8 to 0 and on the verge of being anointed.

"We're not ready for that," Clinton said, surprised and troubled. Two weeks ago, he noted, the conventional wisdom seemed to be that this race was going all the way through to California in three weeks, with bitter fighting and the Republicans torn asunder. If Dole was a lock, that would force a general election dynamic he didn't yet want. Clinton said he believed Gingrich wanted to have some achievements to put on the scoreboard before his House majority went running for reelection in the fall. Perhaps some welfare reform bill, a limited health care bill.

The next morning Clinton went over the prospects with Panetta.

"Did Dole have this locked up?" Clinton asked. What did it mean? He conveyed a lot of anxiety. Who knows? they finally agreed. How could they understand the Republicans? Republicans themselves didn't understand Republicans. Clinton pressed. What does this mean? How are we going to deal with this environment? What will the equation be? Clinton had thought that the next four to six weeks would be *the* optimum moment in 1996 to get some things done that he could point to in November. He hoped that the House Republicans would say, Screw the presidential campaign, we've got to save our own skins first, we need something we can take to the people. "We've got to think through how we handle all the issues," the president said.

Clinton had so many questions that Panetta was late to his own senior staff meeting.

The next day, Wednesday, March 6, Lamar Alexander, biting his lip, dropped out of the race. In a gracious exit, the 55-year-old former governor said he was endorsing Dole. "What the people in the Republican primaries have said is that they look to his experience not as a liability, but as an asset. They look at his maturity not as a liability, but as an asset." He ruled out the vice-presidency, adding, "I'm ready to take a nap rather than think about our future."

Senator Richard G. Lugar, the high-road candidate, also dropped out, praising and endorsing Dole. "I look forward to his presidency," Lugar said.

Following Gingrich's half-meeting with Dole the day before, Scott Reed knew some things needed to be clarified with the Speaker.

Reed first went back to Gaylord. Dole appreciated that Gingrich was willing to roll up his sleeves to help, Reed said. "This is great. We're not a bunch of insecure people. We're going to take advantage if the Speaker wants to." Gingrich's input would be invaluable, Reed added. "The first secret is, you don't get in front of Dole. If there's a perception created that Gingrich is running Dole's life, it won't work." The psychology was pretty simple, given Dole's experience over the last months, having to stand at Gingrich's side in all the budget machinations. They could not, and would not, name Gingrich to be chairman of anything or give him any title. Just in case Gaylord did not fully understand, Reed added, "He's not running the campaign, and he's not going to run the campaign, and the minute it looks like he is running the campaign, it's going to end."

Gaylord agreed. He later reported that Gingrich had received the message. Gingrich said to Reed, "Let's go to work. I'll act as your super-consultant."

George W. Bush, the Texas governor and son of former President Bush, planned to endorse Dole. But first he wanted Dole's assurance that Texas would get some help on Medicaid, the expensive federal-state health program for the poor. California and New York had been allowed to fund the program at lower levels, but in an earlier legislative move apparently aimed at Texas Senator Phil Gramm, Texas had not been allowed to do the same. That had cost the state about $1 billion. Bush finally made his pitch for the savings directly to Dole.

Dole said that the other Texas senator, Kay Bailey Hutchison, was on top of the situation, and Bush should talk to her. It was a "write-your-congressman" response that made Bush furious.

The story of Bush's intention to endorse Dole had leaked to the media, so Bush now had maximum leverage. If he were to pull back it would generate a big story, especially given the longtime rivalry between his father and Dole. The governor let it be known that he was reconsidering his support.

On March 5, Dole faxed a "Dear George" letter to the governor's office. Dole said that Sheila Burke, his chief of staff, had just "brought me up to speed on your request regarding Medicaid. Be assured, I am committed to working with you. . . . You can be certain of my support during any consideration on the Senate floor." It was an unusual assurance, it was almost a quid pro quo. The next day, March 6, Bush endorsed Dole in a large public ceremony at the governor's mansion in Austin, Texas, six days before the state's primary.

That same day just before the New York primary, Jack Kemp finally made his endorsement decision. He came out for Forbes, not Dole. Forbes declared that Kemp would be his "guru-in-chief." Scott Reed was furious. Dole joked about the fuel they had wasted keeping planes on the runway to bring Kemp for an endorsement that had never come. Yet he felt sorry for his campaign manager after so much wasted effort. The next day, Reed wrote a public letter to Kemp urging him to use his powerful influence as the new Forbes "guru-in-chief" to stop the negative television advertising against Dole.

"I can't believe you're doing this to me," Kemp said in a phone call to Reed in the afternoon. He could not stand by and let Dole supporters attack the flat tax.

"Now that you're the guru-in-chief," Reed said to his former boss.

"Fuck you," Kemp replied, "don't call me the guru-in-chief."

"Jack, you've blown this," Reed said, adding that the early exit polls were coming in showing Dole way ahead.

"I'm not in this for politics," Kemp replied. "I'm in this for policy."

"Your guy's ruining the flat tax. He's an absolute wrong messenger. Jack, everybody's shaking their head at you. Why did you do this?"

"This was the most difficult decision I made," Kemp insisted. "Newt Gingrich told me I was done with the party. I'm done."

Dole won the New York primary, taking all 93 delegates, in spite of Forbes's massive advertising.

A reporter asked Dole if he was ready to smile now.

"I smile," Dole replied, "but I'm not ready to declare anything." He didn't want to look like he was overconfident. He was thinking, "Now don't get out there too far and look like you're arrogant or something."

On March 12, Dole won all seven Super Tuesday states, putting him within striking distance of a lock on the nomination. Still Dole wasn't publicly claiming the nomination.

The next day, Mari Will went to see Dole. She said she wanted to make sure he was nominated, but she had decided at age 42 to devote most of her time to being a wife and mother.

Dole apologized to her for being so rough on the speech she had drafted for the New Hampshire legislature. "I didn't mean that," he said.

She accepted the apology.

"We're not through the woods yet," Dole said. He asked her to stay on as a senior consultant, and she agreed.

Will had some ideas on the vice-presidency. Dole needed to choose a running mate who would help him the most to become president, she said, but that calculation had to be made much later down the road. He should wait as long as possible.

Dole said he was insulted by the suggestion circulating that he was such a weak candidate that he had to pick a vice president right now.

Yes, Will agreed. It was pack journalism—the same flowering of thought that had held it was going to be such a hard nomination fight. Well, he was sweeping the field faster than Bush had in 1988. Go back to the Senate, confront Clinton there, be on your home turf, she advised. Then in the summer, when everything settles down, pick your running mate.

They discussed Colin Powell. Dole said he would love to have Powell on the ticket.

"If that's what it takes to win, then that's what you need to do," Will said. But a Powell selection would risk something with the party, particularly to talk about it right now with Buchanan still out there. He shouldn't do that now, she said. "Be very cold-eyed about the whole thing," she recommended, "and just hold off. Don't spend the nickel now. Spend it when it's time. Get the bounce when you need the bounce, and make sure you have exactly what it takes to win."

Steve Forbes told his campaign manager, Bill Dal Col, "Put together a scenario, don't worry about money, how do we win something?" Four big primaries were coming up in the Midwest. "Finishing second ain't going to cut it. Is there any realistic way in the remaining short period of time to open it up?"

The answer was no. Forbes could spend millions advertising in one of the states such as Michigan. He would have to be very negative. Dole would respond, and the media would portray it as a last desperate act for Forbes.

Forbes prided himself as a realistic businessman, and he saw now that he had a product, himself, that would not sell. His feelings were a combination of sadness and disappointment. "I genuinely thought I was going to do it," he said. But he had to focus on the logistics of dropping out. He planned to announce his withdrawal Thursday, March 14, in Washington. He made the calls, and gathered his family and key supporters in a Washington hotel. Kemp joined Forbes for the announcement. Forbes's daughters were in tears, and Kemp gathered the family together for a prayer. Good God, Forbes thought, everyone was going to break up before they got to the podium.

In his announcement, Forbes said, "We made our best effort, and it didn't work." He said he was "wholeheartedly" endorsing Dole, but defended his criticism of Dole during the primaries.

Later, he was asked on television about what was widely seen as a tepid endorsement. Forbes was shocked. He felt as if he were at his own funeral, and he just had "wholeheartedly" endorsed the guy who had turned him into a corpse, and they called that "tepid"?

Dole called Forbes later in the afternoon. Forbes was the one who had really gotten under his skin. Dole joked to himself that Forbes could have bought his skin for the $35 million. It would have been enough for a skin transplant.

"Congratulations, Senator," Forbes said in the phone call.

Dole thanked him for the endorsement, and asked for his help.

"If you feel that my campaigning for you would help, I'd be willing to do it," Forbes said. "If you feel that my not doing anything for you would help you, I'll do nothing."

Dole chuckled. He said that he didn't agree with Forbes on all the details about the flat tax, but some genuine tax reform was needed. He also added that he knew what it was like on Forbes's end, recalling 1988 when he lost to Bush.

Several days later, I spoke with Forbes at length. He said the presidential race had lifted the scales from his eyes about the Washington journalistic and political reporting community. It was a closed system, he said, that looked at itself as the personnel department—a screening and interviewing and background-checking operation for the presidency. If the chief political reporters didn't know a candidate, they were aghast at the candidate, not at themselves. When he had come within striking distance and had won some primaries in Delaware and Arizona, Forbes said, "I think they were genuinely, every cell in their body was outraged that this could be happening. And it wasn't put on. It came from the soul."

On March 19, Dole won the four midwestern primaries. By most counts made by the newspapers and networks, that gave him more than the required 996 delegates to ensure the nomination—over half the total of 1,990 delegates who would be going to the Republican Convention. Dole still made no declarations, saying it was on to California for the last key primary in a week. He brought along Dennis Shea, a policy expert from his Senate staff.

At one speech in California, Dole had to hold a microphone in his good left hand. The podium was slanted so his other atrophied hand could not keep the paper with his notes in place. So the notes were no use, and he had to ad-lib. Afterwards he didn't feel he had done very well. On the plane, he was testy and he went to Shea and said, "I don't like the way the podium was. You get ahold of Scott Reed and tell him I want the podium right!"

Jim Hooley, the chief of advance, who was in charge of making sure the podium was correct, said it was his fault. "I'll fix that, Senator."

"You told me you'd fix it last time!" Dole said. It was both an unprecedented outburst and as direct as he ever got.

On March 21, 1996, when Jean Houston visited the White House, she thought that Hillary seemed a little down. In her role as spirit lifter, Houston told some jokes and stories.

Maggie Williams, chief of staff to the First Lady, said later, "Oh, Hillary's ticking. She's had her 'Jean fix.' "

As Williams saw it, Hillary found Houston very smart and colorful, a vivid personality with a great gift for language. In these toughest of times, Hillary had 10 to 11 confidants, including Houston and Hillary's own mother. But Houston was the most dramatic.

That night the president and Hillary attended the Radio and Television Correspondents' Association dinner in Washington, where the crude radio personality Don Imus made jokes about Clinton's infidelity and Whitewater while the First Couple sat on the stage only a few feet away. It was a tasteless performance.

When the president and Hillary returned to the White House they went up to the solarium, where Houston was waiting. Clinton voiced disgust that things had gotten so out of hand, that Imus would feel free to make such jokes in front of them. He asked Houston if she wanted to see a replay of the Imus performance that was going to run on television.

"Nope," Houston said, "nor do you."

She and Hillary sat with Clinton while he watched his beloved University of Arkansas Razorbacks basketball team lose to the University of Massachusetts 79 to 63 in the NCAA Tournament. Clinton was not happy at the loss.

Houston was amazed at the change in the president over the 16 months she had known him. In their first meeting in December 1994, he was wounded and almost lost. But he was one of the fastest and deepest learners that she had ever encountered. He had been retrained by circumstance. He was no longer the Dauphin. "This is the king," Houston said. He had gone from bitterness to accommodation, and he was getting close to transcendence. He had fully become the president, she believed.

Houston thought she had partially helped Clinton undertake perhaps the most difficult task of his presidency. That was to put himself, his critics and his opponents in historical context—to see the woundings, the road of trials and his adversaries clearly. He had to absorb all of this to move to the next stage. When he understood the context, she found Clinton deepened and fortified. He was fast becoming wise. "He is the elder in the younger," she said.

Houston and Bateson asked to hold deeper reflective sessions with the president, but he never responded. Houston sensed his nervousness around her, and she was not sure the president liked her. So she asked Hillary whether he did.

"Oh, yes, yeah," Hillary replied.

"Sometimes he's uneasy," Houston said.

"Well, he's basically a very conservative man," Hillary said.

Houston wondered what might happen if her role as adviser and friend to the first couple became public.

"If I ever get caught," Houston asked Hillary, "what should I say?"

"Just tell the truth," Hillary replied, "just tell them you're my friend."

Elizabeth didn't think her husband was selling himself enough. She was out there selling the heck out of him, pulling out all the stops. He was too modest, she felt.

"Don't say *we*," she said, "say *I*, you know, about what *you've* done." She had been on him about this for years. His modesty was getting in the way of the necessary sale. He would acknowledge his habit, but then lapse into "we," or refer to himself in the now-famous third person, "Bob Dole." Elizabeth kept after him. He didn't change.

Dole later told me why he used "Bob Dole" instead of "I" or "me." "We were taught in our little family you don't go around saying, 'I did this.' And my mother felt very strongly about that, you don't run around bragging about yourself. People don't like it. And that's where you"—he said, not using "I"—"get into this third person all the time."

Elizabeth asked him about a scheduled stop in Russell, Kansas, the day before the California primary that was expected to give him way more than enough delegates by any count.

"You're going to Russell just before you go over the top," she said. The plan was for a big hometown celebration. "That's going to be interesting. Have you won or haven't you?"

"Everybody else says we've won, and I think we have won, but you know we are trying to have a little suspense for California," he said. He was still keeping his counsel.

Why not wait until after California to visit Russell for the celebration because then it would be certain?

"We've got to be practical," Dole told her, then provided an unusual list: "(a) We're on our way home from California and it makes a lot of sense to stop there now than have to go all the way back; (b) we're going to win California; and (c) everybody, except Bob Dole, says he's the nominee anyway." He thought it was pretty safe. "There's so much going on in the Senate I need to be back in the Senate."

On the plane heading into Russell, population 4,800, on March 25, someone on the staff asked Elizabeth if she would introduce the man who was to offer a special surprise for Bob. After Dole spoke, a baritone was going to sing her husband's favorite song, "You'll Never Walk Alone," at the end of the program.

"No," Elizabeth said. "If you have him stand there the whole time the man's singing that song, he is going to cry. It's going to bring the emotion. And that's not the way to end the program, to have three or four minutes of standing there listening to that song." And her husband would be stuck there, crying for all that time. "Look, don't do it that way." She arranged for the two of them to go out and greet people in the crowd as the song was being sung at the end.

Dole appeared before a crowd of about 3,000 in the Russell High School gym. A 20-minute speech had been prepared and the text handed out to reporters.

"At this moment," Dole said, "I wanted to be home, to come to this place." His voice broke, tears came to his eyes, and he put his hand to his mouth. After a few seconds he recovered, gave a thumb-up. "And see all my friends." The crowd broke into applause. "Some debts can never be repaid, but I have come to Russell to acknowledge mine." He spoke of war, crisis, deceased friends, teachers, memories and voices from the past.

Elizabeth liked it. The emotion showed that he was human, that he felt his past, that he was genuine, and it revealed the man's heart. She felt a great deal of warmth and love for him, just hoping that he would be able to go on. He made it through, and together they plunged into the crowd.

The baritone sang: "When you walk through a storm, Hold your head up high, And don't be afraid of the dark."

That evening before they left for Washington, Dole visited the graves of his parents.

The next day, March 26, he won California 66 percent to Buchanan's 19 percent. In the winner-take-all primary, Dole received all 165 delegates. Dole declared himself the Republican nominee.

That week, Colin Powell had spoken to the International Republican Institute in Washington, D.C. He hadn't mentioned Dole's name once, the nominee of Powell's new party. The next morning Reed had been flooded with calls from a number of Republicans wondering what was going on. Reed called Ken Duberstein, who said it was an oversight. Then several days later Duberstein called Reed back to say that Powell wanted to call Dole.

"What's the topic?" Reed asked.

"He's going to congratulate him for winning the nomination," Duberstein said.

Reed wondered if that might be the spark. He had talked with Dole several times about Powell as a potential running mate. Dole was obviously enchanted with the possibility.

"If this is something you want to do," Reed advised Dole, "it's going to be done by you. It's not going to be done by me to Duberstein or somebody to Armitage or these other guys. I mean, it's you to him. You've got to be thinking about developing a relationship." Reed knew that Powell had built his entire life and career on personal relationships—him to the boss, or him to his subordinates, or him to special journalist friends

—no intermediaries or press officers. Powell handled the important business in his life himself. Dole needed to do the same.

After several days, Powell finally reached Dole.

"I want to congratulate you," Powell said. "I knew the Bob Dole I know would pull through."

"I really appreciate it," Dole said. "I'm proud that you're a Republican, and I'd like to sit down and talk to you about maybe what you could do to help the effort. And also on defense and foreign policy matters."

Any time, Powell said.

Dole felt that Powell didn't want to be asked anything more. Not that Powell said he had to go, but it was something Dole could sense on the phone with people sometimes.

Clinton's weekly campaign meetings in the residence continued to focus on the advertising, which was still going unanswered since neither Dole nor the Republican National Committee were on the air in any significant way. Mark Penn, the pollster, had a sophisticated computer program that helped them make the decisions about which media markets to target. Some seven variables were included in the program: previous voting history in the market, cost of the advertising time, the estimated number of undecided or persuadable voters, the cumulative previous pro-Clinton advertising that had run over a given time period, the likely impact on congressional races, Senate races and the presidential electoral college. For instance, the program could calculate the most efficient way to use an additional $500,000 in their advertising budget, determining the "cost per persuadable voter" in each market.

In early March, the Clinton-Gore committee had advertised heavily in the most populous regions of Wisconsin, Illinois, Michigan (excluding Detroit), much of Ohio, northern Florida, Oregon and the non-coastal areas of California.

Morris talked of getting Clinton's support up so high in key states that they would have what he called a "condominium," or ruled territory, in those states. He believed that if they could use advertising to drive Clinton's approval rating high enough, Clinton couldn't lose it later. As Morris saw it, they would need 61 percent approval nationally in 1996 for a "condominium." Then the president would essentially own the election.

Clinton and most of the others disagreed, arguing that it was a nice goal, but presidential elections were incredibly volatile, and they often turned around suddenly. But in the spring confidence built as Clinton maintained a double-digit lead in the polls. Morris was almost obsessed with putting it away early. The others reminded him that there was only one day they had to win: November 5, 1996. There was a real danger in trying to win the election early.

Leon Panetta spent most days that spring in a series of meetings, whether around the conference table in his large West Wing office, in the Roosevelt Room down the hall or in the Oval Office. His team was quick in responding to the daily tactical skirmishes with Dole. Clinton and the White House seemed to be winning the war for the best daily sound bite.

Panetta had reached an uneasy equilibrium with Dick Morris. Morris's ability to undermine the chief of staff's chain of command—Panetta called it "free floating" or "backdooring"—had been minimized, and Morris seemed to have acquiesced, aware that the White House was now working to Clinton's benefit. Nonetheless Panetta thought too much attention was being paid to campaign polling, and he was baffled by the talk of "cost per persuadable voter" and a "condominium" to win the election early. It was very different from the world of politics he had known as a California congressman. Often in meetings he found himself wincing and at times wondering how previous presidents had been able to survive without the modern campaign consulting machinery. "My God," he thought once, "how did Abraham Lincoln possibly govern?"

The good news was that Clinton was less volatile and tended to explode less. The president more often rolled with screwups or criticism that would have set off a temper tantrum in the first two years of his presidency. Panetta found Clinton more comfortable with himself and his job. And oddly, the president's greatest strength had emerged from having the Republican Congress go haywire before his eyes.

One thing about Clinton hadn't changed. He continued to conduct a personal quest for information and ideas. "This guy is like a hungry lion who searches for every morsel of information he can get," Panetta said. Clinton was not going to be deprived of advice because some members of his staff didn't like or get along with the others such as Morris and Ickes, or Morris and Stephanopoulos. Panetta might be able to manage the government, but he knew now there was no way he could manage and control the information flow to Clinton, or the people the president spoke with or saw. No one was going to limit Clinton's exposure to a wide range of viewpoints, people or ideas. Clinton's personal outreach program, the late-night visitors and phone calls were going to continue. Clinton would determine what advice was bad.

As the president once put it to his chief of staff, "I'll make the decision whether somebody's an asshole."

By April, Clinton, Morris and the others had developed the beginning of their strategy to beat Dole. First, they would try to make Dole into what they called "Washington–Congress–status quo." Dole's campaign was trying to make Dole into this perfect embodiment of Russell, Kansas, and midwestern values, who went to war, risked his life and emerged full blown as the Republican presidential nominee. His 35 years as a Washington politician were being wiped away.

The Clinton-Gore plan was to fill in Dole's 35 years in Congress, show the inconsistencies in his voting record and behavior and his occasional extremism. Dole would be cast as a creature of Washington. Every effort would be made to suggest he was not a man for the future, and indirectly to remind voters of his age. In contrast, Clinton would be shown as the non-partisan presidential leader, speaking on larger national themes, acting tough on crime and fiscal matters, making government leaner and more efficient but not meaner. They wanted to show Dole as the legislator caught in the procedural morass of the Senate while Clinton acted presidential. Clinton wanted it to be an election between the head of Congress and the head of the nation.

Morris was in charge of the big picture, the thematic speeches and bully pulpit and the presidential schedule. Stephanopoulos was going to run the daily response and attack on Dole.

The Clinton strategy contained one more critical element. They would attempt to cast Gingrich as Dole's vice president until Dole selected his own. They were all taken with the idea of sticking Dole with Gingrich. "He doesn't get somebody else as vice president until he picks 'em," one of Clinton's team said.

As Clinton's strategists tried to figure every angle, every possible bump in the road, every possible downside in the upcoming campaign, a number of them quietly discussed the possible mirror image of Dole's problem with Gingrich. It was the First Lady. If for some reason the Dole campaign was able to suggest that Hillary was vice president or co-president or had some hidden hand in the Clinton presidency, they could be in significant trouble. Fortunately, Hillary seemed to recognize this herself, and she was fading more and more into the background.

Gore had his own analysis of one of their greatest vulnerabilities— the Whitewater scandal. In substance, he found it small and unfair. But the threat was not so much from what already had been revealed or even what might be in the future. Gore believed in the political axiom that whoever controls the agenda will control the outcome. He was astounded that the Republicans and the scandal machinery in Washington had been able to batter Clinton on Whitewater for three years already. He was worried that these people might be able to keep Whitewater front and center with a constant pounding, new revelations or seemingly new revelations. They could weaken the president. The attacks went to the very foundation of trust on which the presidency rested.

Privately, Gore had taken to delivering a withering attack on Whitewater independent counsel Kenneth Starr as the latest example of unfettered investigation, cynicism and character assassination. He cited Starr's partisan background, and Starr's decision to maintain his million-dollar-a-year private law practice while investigating the sitting president. Many of Starr's private clients were well-financed opponents of the president, including two tobacco companies and several private conservative foundations. At one point before being appointed independent counsel, Starr had assisted in legal research on Paula Corbin Jones's sexual harassment suit against Clinton. Gore said it was a blatant, unfair, outrageous and even intolerable conflict.

Gore was worried, but he did not attack Starr publicly.

The Dole campaign strategy was, not surprisingly, to focus on Clinton and make the 1996 decision a referendum on the incumbent. Scott Reed wanted to make Clinton accountable for what he had not done and emphasize the broken promises. In 1992, Clinton had promised to cut middle-class taxes. Instead, he had raised the gas tax 4.3 cents a gallon for everyone. He had pledged to end welfare as the nation knew it, and then he blocked welfare reform. He had finally agreed to balance the federal budget in seven years, and then had vetoed the Republican plan and cleverly stiffed them on any compromise. Reed wanted to keep it simple, and the bumper sticker was going to essentially say, "Do we want Bill Clinton for four more years?" It didn't need to be cute, saying, "Bill and Hillary." It just had to say, "Bill Clinton." Clinton was not trusted. In Clinton's best days, still 40 percent or more of the public said in polls that they disapproved of his handling of the presidency.

Reed wanted to present Dole as the candidate of sensible, conservative reform—less government, less spending, less taxes, real change. The plan was to turn Clinton's obvious speaking mastery against him with the theme that Clinton was a talker, Dole was a doer. But the centerpiece of the Dole strategy was even simpler: Dole's a conservative, Clinton's a liberal.

As super-consultant, Gingrich was helping Reed to formulate a strategy. "It's election day," Gingrich said, starting one meeting with Reed. "What do we want the people to be walking into the booth thinking? And then let's work backwards."

Answering his own question, Gingrich said, "We are the reform party." Much of the campaign would have to be built around that message. He also insisted they address what could screw it up for Dole and cause him to lose. The Speaker wanted to get those things right out on the table. They were age, inarticulateness and lack of a clear direction.

Reed also was planning their strategy around the nuts and bolts of winning the necessary 270 electoral votes. Since the South would probably remain solid-Republican, Dole could count on 73 electoral votes from those 12 states. Another dozen states with 165 electoral votes had gone Republican in all but one of the last seven presidential contests. That could give Dole a total of 238 electoral votes. The election would then turn on the battleground states. Reed initially identified eight: New Jersey, Michigan, Ohio, Illinois, California, New Hampshire, Connecticut and Florida. Those were the states where Dole would be camping out. All eight had Republican governors who would be mobilized like never before, Reed hoped.

For Dole personally, it was even simpler. "Once Clinton's perceived as a liberal, the election's over," he said. But Dole's problem was that Clinton had staked out firm, centrist ground. "He's not perceived as liberal," Dole said in an interview April 20, "and he's been on kind of a roll. He's had a six-month sabbatical."

He added, "Bob Dole needs to have an agenda. It's got to resonate. It's got to make sense. It's got to be credible. It's got to be real. You've got to be able to touch it, and feel it, and apply it to your kids or your family, your business or your farm. And that's what I've got to do."

On April 3, Commerce Secretary Ronald H. Brown and 32 others traveling with him during a trade mission were killed when their plane crashed into a mountain in Croatia. Clinton spent days consoling the families and the nation, speaking at funerals and memorial services. In death Brown was hailed and praised endlessly for his personal and political skills. He had, however, been under investigation by an independent counsel for various financial dealings in a protracted inquiry very much like the Whitewater investigation that was still haunting the Clintons.

Back at the White House, after all the Brown ceremonies, Clinton was physically a wreck and emotionally drained. He let loose his anger at the media. "How they vilified him, tried to destroy him, and now they write all these glorified things about him now that he's dead," Clinton said, alternating between rage and resignation. "Why didn't they write any of that while he was alive? They're going to just kick the shit out of you until you pass from the scene and then they'll write nice stories about you." Brown had been "under a cloud," in the newspaper parlance. "What was the cloud that he was under?" Clinton asked. "What really was it? How significant was it, and how do you put it into some historical context?"

"You just get brutalized," he finally said poignantly, "and you might as well just understand that's part of the deal."

On Sunday, April 14, Clinton watched some of the Masters Golf Tournament on television. An avid golfer, Clinton loved to tune in, especially for the last holes of the last day, the height of golf drama. The 1996 Masters was like no other. Greg Norman, the Australian "Shark," rated the best golfer in the world, had started the fourth and final 18-hole round with a six-stroke lead, making him virtually unbeatable. No one in the history of the famous tournament had ever been defeated with such a lead, and going back to 1910 when records were first kept, no one had ever squandered such a big lead in any major golf tournament. In the final round, Norman came apart, playing more like a Sunday hacker on a number of the last holes, putting two balls in the water on shots that any pro should have been able to play safely. He lost by five strokes to Nick Faldo.

Clinton was leaving for a trip to Korea, Japan and Russia that night. When Mike McCurry came on Air Force One, he immediately asked Clinton, "Did you get a chance to watch any of the Masters today?"

"Yes," Clinton said, snapping his fingers. He lit into McCurry. "That's going to be our new *theme* for the campaign, that we're not going to allow ourselves to be Greg Normanized."

"You think we're going to blow a six-stroke lead?" McCurry said, laughing. "Is that what you're trying to say?"

"Yes," Clinton said. "I'm going to make a tape of those four holes and make it mandatory viewing for every campaign worker." He laughed but then turned serious again. He meant it. He absolutely hated it when anyone was quoted about how far they had come since 1994. He wanted people to be very hungry and focused. Overconfidence could kill them. He knew about the volatility of the game—both golf and politics.

On Friday, April 19, Dole asked his closest friend, Bob Ellsworth, to come to his office. Ellsworth, only three years younger than Dole, had first been elected to Congress from another Kansas district in 1960, the same year as Dole. A tall, congenial, people-smart political operator, Ellsworth had been a strategist in Nixon's successful 1968 election, later served as Deputy Secretary of Defense, and had been the best man at Bob and Elizabeth's wedding. Dole trusted Ellsworth more than anyone. Ellsworth had acted as a personal political adviser to Dole for 36 years. He had been among a handful of men involved in Nixon's selection of his running mate, Maryland Governor Spiro T. Agnew, in 1968.

Dole told Ellsworth that he was about to begin the search for his own running mate, and he wanted Ellsworth to act as his overall coordinator. "I don't want anybody else to know," Dole said. It was an advantage to have four months before the August convention when he expected to announce his decision. He wanted Ellsworth to come up with a list of possible vice presidents, and then to sit down privately with Scott Reed. They would have to find some lawyers to do exhaustive background checks, look at the candidates' FBI files, then make an evaluation and recommendation.

Dole said that he did not want a public spectacle in the process. He did not want possible candidates dragged in for public tryouts. "I'm looking for somebody that I really know," Dole said, carefully adding, "or that I would know by convention time." He wanted a running-mate relationship that would be marked by total candor, someone he could sit with, that both could let their hair down. Something along the model of what appeared to be the Clinton-Gore relationship, he said. His goal was not to please any interest group. On a scale of 1 to 10, he wanted the best. "I'm going to find a 10," he said. "This is a big one, would change everything."

As Ellsworth got up to leave, Dole said, "What I want is that when this is announced, most everyone who thinks about these things is going to know that we've really thought about it and it's somebody who can do it. Won't be any doubt."

Afterwards, Dole spoke with Reed. "This is going to be my decision,"

Dole said. "This is the most important decision I'll make in this campaign. It should be mine, and I don't want a big committee flopping around with a different story in the paper every week about candidate A, B or C."

In the next to last of my Saturday discussions with Dole, April 20, I mentioned that Clinton harbored two lingering resentments against him. Dole leaned forward, eager to know what they were.

First, I said, Clinton had not forgotten that in early 1993 Dole had wasted no time telling the new president that he would not get a single Republican vote for his first economic plan if it included tax increases.

Dole voiced amazement that Clinton could have been so naive. "He beat Bush because of taxes partly, and he should have understood the last thing you could expect from Bob Dole or anybody else was to go out and say, you know, we just got beat because somebody broke their no-tax pledge, so we're going to try to square all that by voting for a $265 billion tax increase."

"What's the other area?" Dole asked.

I said it was Dole's aggressive call for a Whitewater independent counsel back in early 1994, the day Clinton's mother had died.

Dole said that Clinton had never raised the issue with him. He looked troubled. "I remember talking to him about his mother," Dole recalled. "I told him it was tough to lose your mother. I told him I still find myself trying to call my mother on the telephone." Dole's mother Bina had died 13 years earlier.

As Dole sat in his chair, he stiffened, and continued, "I want to pick up the receiver and dial 483-4274." At the recollection of his mother's phone number, he broke down. Tears came to his eyes. He put his hand to his mouth briefly.

In a second or two, he recovered. He was sure he hadn't attacked Clinton on such a vulnerable day. "That's not something Bob Dole would do," he said. He squinted his eyes. He was thinking hard. "I just wouldn't do that," he said. "I'm very sensitive to that." Later Dole said, "Maybe I owe him an apology."

All weekend, Dole was haunted by what he might have done. He had an aide dig out the transcripts of his television appearances in January 1994. They reviewed them, and they found that Bob Dole had used cruel words.

On Monday, April 22, Dole dispatched a personal letter to Clinton.

"Dear Mr. President:

"This letter is written not as a Senator or as a presidential candidate, but as an individual whose parents instilled in him a sense of common courtesy." He cited the events and transcripts. "In hindsight, I can see that, after learning of your mother's passing, it might have been the better part of valor to have cancelled the interviews or refused to answer certain questions." He recounted how he had once publicly praised Clinton's mother for her perseverance after Clinton's father had died. "Those words were true then, and they are true now. I look forward to the campaign ahead, and only wish that Bina Dole and Virginia Kelley were here to experience it with us."

Later that week, Dole was at the White House for an anti-terrorism bill signing ceremony. Clinton took him aside into a corridor so they could speak alone. The president thanked him for the letter. He said he had read it twice. He was touched and appreciated it very much.

"Mothers are important," Dole said.

Emotion rose up in both men. They looked at each other for an instant, then moved back to business. Soon they agreed on a budget for the rest of the year. It was not the comprehensive seven-year deal both had envisioned and worked on for months. But it was a start.

26

Bob Ellsworth set up a confidential structure to assist Dole in selecting his vice-presidential running mate. First, Ellsworth planned to hire a senior New York lawyer, bound by a permanent attorney-client privilege, to conduct the background checks of those seriously under consideration. That would get it out of Washington, and he hoped to protect the names and information from surfacing in the media. Second, Ellsworth asked Ann McLaughlin, the former Labor Secretary in the Reagan administration and the 54-year-old ex-wife of television political talk show host John McLaughlin, to help him review prospective candidates for what Ellsworth called "political suitability." McLaughlin agreed to take the job, and Ellsworth swore her to secrecy about all phases of the process.

Ellsworth and Scott Reed initially worked up a list of 15 possible running mates. Ellsworth realized it was too long, and contained some clunkers and too many Republican governors as well. Dole had told Ellsworth that there were many Republicans who had helped him through the primaries. "I do owe a lot to some of these guys," Dole said, adding that the political debt would be a factor in his decision if all else were equal. Dole also said that he did not want to pick someone who would alienate conservatives. "Don't give me someone who would send up the conservatives," he said.

By the end of June, Ellsworth hoped to have the list reduced to five or six whom Dole would approach to see if they would agree to be considered. Those interested then would be interviewed and their backgrounds would be checked by the New York law firm. Ellsworth and Reed agreed to conduct polling in late July and early August before the Republican convention to determine the possible impact of the various potential running mates.

"To see who would help the most," Reed said.

No, Ellsworth said. "We've got to get someone that would harm the least." Vice-presidential candidates normally did not help. It was a matter of inflicting the smallest damage, he said. Ellsworth believed that a brilliant pick could be found occasionally, such as John Kennedy's decision in 1960 to select Senator Lyndon Johnson. Johnson helped carry some key southern states, including his home state of Texas. But such an opportunity for a politically adroit move was rare. They had to search. The goal would be to give Dole two or three candidates that he could consider ten days before the San Diego convention, which was to begin on August 11. Then Dole would have time to make his decision unless circumstance, opportunity or necessity forced him to choose earlier.

Secrecy was the key, Ellsworth felt, to give Dole the maximum maneuvering room. He told Reed and McLaughlin that their discussions, thoughts, ideas and information had to be kept private. "As far as we are concerned the structure doesn't even exist," he said.

At the top of the list of 15 was Colin Powell. Much would hinge on Powell's actions and attitude before the selection process got under way. Would he make campaign appearances with Dole in late spring? Would he go out on his own for Dole? Would he help develop campaign positions on national security and defense issues? Dole planned to set up a private meeting with Powell soon.

On paper the most qualified governor on the list was perhaps Pete Wilson, but he was damaged goods in his own state, and his fumbled try for the Republican nomination made his selection almost impossible. No one could argue that most of the other governors would be manifestly ready to step into the presidency, which was Dole's first requirement. None ranked an obvious "10" on Dole's scale. But there was one remote, sleeper possibility—Tom Ridge, 50, the Republican governor of Pennsylvania. Ridge had graduated from Harvard and served as an Army sergeant in Vietnam. He had Washington experience as a member of the House of Representatives for ten years, and was a pro-choice Roman Catholic with a tough-on-crime reputation.

The Senate offered two possibilities—Senator Richard Lugar, 64, the

Indiana Republican who had been mayor of Indianapolis and had extensive foreign policy experience. Though Lugar had done poorly in his own bid for the Republican nomination, he had not embarrassed himself. The other was Senator Connie Mack III, the 55-year-old Florida Republican who had won reelection in 1994 with 71 percent of the vote.

Three other real prospects—men who could be credibly presented as ready for the presidency—had made their names in the Republican foreign policy establishment. Dick Cheney, the former Wyoming congressman and Bush Secretary of Defense, who decided not to seek the Republican nomination in 1996, was widely admired in the party for his cool leadership. He had strong conservative credentials, and had served as President Ford's White House chief of staff at the age of 34. Cheney had suffered three heart attacks but in 1988 had undergone a successful quadruple coronary bypass operation.

Another was Donald H. Rumsfeld, 63, who had one of the strongest résumés: former Illinois congressman, NATO ambassador, Ford's White House chief of staff and later his Secretary of Defense, and then for eight years chief executive officer of the drug company G. D. Searle. Dole had known Rumsfeld since the early 1960s, when they had both been in the House of Representatives.

The third was James A. Baker III, the former Treasury Secretary and Secretary of State. Baker, 66, had been Reagan's first-term White House chief of staff. He had managed Reagan's 1984 reelection, Bush's successful 1988 presidential campaign and Bush's unsuccessful 1992 reelection effort. Though Baker was often suspected in Republican conservative circles of being a moderate, his identification with Reagan was probably sufficient to immunize him. No one was Baker's match in terms of combined heavyweight government and presidential campaign experience. His tenure at the center of the Reagan and Bush administrations had convinced him he would know what to do as president, and he had told associates he would love to be president some day. Baker had written Dole a note saying he was ready to do anything to help him win.

Rumsfeld and Baker offered real possibilities as somewhat younger versions of Dole with many of Dole's strengths. They were experienced, solid and knowledgeable about Washington. Both had accomplished records in foreign and domestic policy and were intimately familiar with the White House and presidential power.

Dole believed that he alone would have to make the decision on his running mate. Reed, Ellsworth, Elizabeth and many others might help, but he would have to consider all the factors, give them appropriate weight in his own mind and then decide. The big decisions required solitary work, he had come to realize more and more.

Months earlier a seed had been planted, something that had nagged at Dole since the Republican primaries when he was being beaten up as this creature from Washington, "Beltway Bob." Buchanan, Forbes and Alexander regularly had aimed their most pointed attacks at his longtime service in the Senate. Dole knew that people didn't like Washington, and his opponents had effectively wrapped the entire political culture of the capital around his neck. As he started winning the primaries, he dismissed the problem. But over the Easter break he had eight days of rest in Florida, a record for him. The negative interpretations of his total identity with the Senate gnawed at him. He was pretty sure that 90 percent of the people in the country didn't know what the title majority leader meant. To them, it meant just another politician making deals, raising their taxes, spending more money. That was what Washington conjured up out there. That's what he conjured up out there.

In Florida, Dole had time to walk and sit in the sun, look around, think. He thought about his late parents. He thought about the frustrations of average people. He thought about his mail, the nasty letters, many of which had a common theme, "You're like everybody else. You're like all the rest of 'em." He had to be different, but he wasn't. He had to break through the Washington noise and expectations, many of them of his own making.

Dole decided he would quit the Senate completely, not just give up the Majority Leader's Office, but resign his Senate seat. He then had to live with the decision and work through it. He wanted to feel good about it, so he discussed it with no one for weeks, including Elizabeth or Scott Reed. "You can't have everybody else make up your mind," he told himself. Politics was too much of that. "Some things are so important that they shouldn't be made by a committee." He found he was sleeping well and having no second thoughts.

The last full week of April, after Dole had returned from Florida, Mark Helprin, 48, the novelist and an occasional contributing editorial writer for *The Wall Street Journal,* paid a visit to him. Three months earlier, Helprin had written an adoring column in the *Journal* praising Dole as "a conservative of both heart and mind, of conviction and of practical effect." Helprin had urged that Dole, "a master of legislative tactics," adopt the strategy of sending Clinton bill after bill to balance the budget, thus forcing the president to veto everything. In his meeting with Dole, Helprin noted that Dole's current strategy was obviously not working, as the White House and Democrats tied the Senate and Dole into knots.

"One thing you ought to do is get out of here," Helprin said two minutes into their discussion. "Leave this place."

"I've been thinking, and I've decided to do it," said Dole, who had the hardest time keeping secrets. He still hadn't discussed it with Elizabeth or Reed. "Will you help me put together a statement?"

Helprin agreed, and Dole pledged him to secrecy and then outlined what he wanted to say.

Two days later Dole asked Reed to his Majority Leader's Office, and the two sat in green stuffed chairs.

"I'm going to get out of here," Dole said. "I mean resign." Just stepping aside as leader wouldn't get them anything, he said.

Reed was at first shocked, then amazed, and quickly pleased. It would be the ultimate way to get away from the shackles of the friggin' Senate, Reed said. The best way to get in sync with the Senate staff was to eliminate it.

Dole said he was convinced that if he didn't give up anything, his campaign wouldn't mean anything. He could hang on, farm out the Senate power to the other Republicans in the leadership. "But I'm still Bob Dole, Washington senator," he said disparagingly of himself.

Reed had received dozens of memos and a great deal of phoned-in advice about Dole's need to get away from the Senate. Republicans also were saying that the talk among the money people was real bad, that many were saying that Dole was another Bush, who in 1992 didn't get it, wouldn't engage the real-life issues, wouldn't get out from behind the shield of Washington.

"Have you talked to anyone else about this?" Reed asked.

"No," Dole replied. "I can't." Only Mark Helprin, the writer, who was working on a statement.

Dole waited another week before telling Elizabeth.

"I've decided the only way to do this is just a clean break," Dole finally told his wife. Maybe it was unfair to her, but he felt that he had to make the decision before trying it out on Elizabeth. If he didn't feel pretty firmly about it, she or somebody else might dissuade him.

"Give up the leadership," she said.

The whole Senate, Dole said, resign, a clean break.

Elizabeth said she thought there might be some value in still being a senator, that it maybe would make a difference to people.

No, he said, he wanted to chuck the power, the trappings, the comfort and the security.

"Let me think about that," she replied.

Dole had spent lots of time on the decision, and he felt she was entitled to think about it for a while also.

Elizabeth consulted confidentially with her brother, and soon had a three- or four-page memo for her husband discussing the possible downsides. Some would say it was politics, even desperation. He had already said he could do both jobs—lead the Senate and run for president—though she had from the beginning raised questions about it, the memo noted. If he resigned, it would be a big deal and he could not just get up there in public and wing it. He would need a carefully crafted and practiced speech with a TelePrompTer.

Dole and Reed referred to it as their "secret project" on the phone over the next several weeks. Helprin kept sending in new drafts of the announcement. Dole worried about what would happen to his staff in the Majority Leader's Office and his regular Senate office, 40 to 50 people who would lose their jobs. Most really needed them, he knew.

"Senator," Reed said, "your staff, your colleagues, we love them. They love you. This is about you. They're going to love you a lot more if you get elected president."

Dole was taking a serious pounding because he couldn't move legislation through the Senate. The Clinton White House was winning the daily tactical skirmishes on everything from health care to the minimum wage.

Sitting through Republican leadership meetings and listening to his colleagues try to get bills and votes scheduled, Dole thought, "Boy, two more weeks and I'm out of here. Free at last."

After considering an earlier date for the announcement, Dole set it for Wednesday, May 15.

On Monday, two days before, Elizabeth called. She was going out to campaign for him.

"Are you sure this is it?"

"This is it," Dole said. "I feel good about it. I don't have any second thoughts. I'm not looking back."

Was he certain?

"Listen," he said, "I've thought about this day after day."

Okay, she said. His instincts were as good as anybody's in politics.

She left him a private message. It was the single-spaced text of a speech she occasionally gave about her religious convictions. She yellow-highlighted important passages on the fifth page.

Dole read his wife's words, "I've had to learn that dependence is a good thing. That when I've used up my own resources, when I can't control things and make them come out my way, I'm willing to trust God with the outcome."

In her near-perfect penmanship, Elizabeth wrote at the bottom: "Bob, I believe God has prepared you for such a time as this! Pray for strength, wisdom, and discernment—and trust God with the outcome. I love you so much, E. See you 10:30 p.m. Tues."

That Tuesday night, the media was reporting that Dole would announce he was giving up some of his responsibilities in the Senate. Reporters staked out the front of his campaign headquarters. Dole entered through the basement so he could practice his speech with the TelePrompTer. The element of surprise was what would make it. Reed didn't trust anyone. Reed had learned how to run the TelePrompTer himself, and threw everyone out of the room while Dole practiced. Dole ran through the speech, now in its 15th draft, several times. He eliminated any mention of Clinton or even the message of his own presidential campaign. This had to be personal.

The next morning before the announcement, set for 3 P.M., Reed looked at five newspapers. They all had somewhat different stories about Dole giving up the Senate leadership in some form, but none had the story about Dole resigning from the Senate. When Dole came over, Reed showed him the newspapers. "We got them totally confused," Reed said.

At 9:41 A.M., Tim Russert of NBC went live to report that Dole would resign from the Senate entirely.

Dole saw Gingrich on television saying that Dole was not going to resign from the Senate.

"Oh," Dole said, "I'd better get Newt on the phone."

He reached Gingrich. "I wanted to get to you earlier but I just hadn't. I've been over here working on my speech and practicing on the TelePrompTer and getting ready." Dole said he was going to resign completely.

"That's more than I would have counseled you to do," Gingrich said. Later he came to realize it was a bold and necessary move.

About 12:30 P.M., Dole called Clinton.

"Mr. President," Dole said, "you may have heard rumors, but at three o'clock today I'm going to sort of pull the plug and leave the Senate." He noted how legislation was tied in knots. "If I'm going to be a candidate, I've got to get out and work at it."

"I'm surprised," Clinton replied. He was appreciative but formal, thanking Dole for his service of so many years.

Dole called former President Ford, 82, and explained what he was doing.

"You're giving up the Senate?" Ford asked, somewhat baffled.

"Yep."

"Giving up the Senate?"

Dole said yes.

Ford said such a move hadn't occurred to him. "Well, whatever you decide, I'm proud of you, and I'm 100 percent behind you."

Dole reached former President Bush on a golf course in New Jersey.

"You may have heard rumors," Dole said.

Bush said he hadn't heard anything.

Dole told Bush what he was about to do.

Bush seemed to hesitate a second, then got it. "I agree with you totally," Bush said sincerely. "Well, I'm playing golf with Quayle and I'll pass it on."

Dole's last call was to Nancy Reagan. Dole asked about President Reagan, but she ignored his question, making it clear that she did not want to talk about her husband's condition.

Dole said he felt he owed it to the party and everyone else to be a full-time candidate.

Nancy said she agreed, and said she was very pleased to be informed.

Dole met privately with the Senate Republicans and then at 3 P.M. went to the Hart Senate Office Building for the announcement, covered live on all four networks. Reed had hoped to have the dome of the Capitol showing through a window as Dole's backdrop, but the Republican leadership packed in behind him. Gingrich's face was present at even the closest camera angles.

"My time to leave this office has come," Dole said, "and I will seek the presidency with nothing to fall back on but the judgment of the people, and nowhere to go but the White House or home." He said he would resign within four weeks, by June 11. "And I will then stand before you without office or authority, a private citizen, a Kansan, an American, just a man." His voice broke and he held back tears. He looked down and then back up, slowly shifting his head between the two TelePrompTer

screens. "But I will be the same man I was when I walked into the room."
He regained his composure.

"I trust in the hard way, for little has come to me except in the hard
way, which is good because we have a hard task ahead of us. . . .

"This is where I touch the ground, and it is in touching the ground in
moments of difficulty that I've always found my strength. I have been
there before, I have done it the hard way, and I will do it the hard way
once again." He was speaking more slowly now, and his voice was strong.

"I have absolute confidence in the victory that to some may seem
unattainable."

The election was 174 days away.

AFTERWORD

Writing in the spring of 1997—three months into the second Clinton term—I realize how vastly I underestimated the significance of money in the recent presidential election. As new information emerges almost daily about the fund-raising frenzy by Clinton and the Democratic National Committee, it is clear that money, and what it was able to buy, played a much more central role in the president's reelection than I initially thought. The money then in 1995 and 1996 paid for the Democrats' unprecedented television advertising campaign, an artful, all-out media blitz that cost upwards of $85 million, according to Dick Morris, the president's former chief political strategist. These two ingredients, money and advertising, were the keys to the Clinton victory.

If I were writing the script for a movie about the Clinton victory, I would begin with a scene depicted in this book (pp. 51–52): the December 27, 1994, White House breakfast between Clinton and Terry McAuliffe, the Democrats' chief fund-raiser. That morning, McAuliffe did something unusual in American politics. He issued a guarantee. He promised he could raise the necessary money if Clinton would grant a favor: regular access for large campaign donors. "Sir, I need to get people to see you," McAuliffe said. Clinton agreed at once. Access became the campaign obsession. Thus were launched a thousand fund-raising events in the White House under the guise of routine presidential outreach. Playing on Clinton's natural gregariousness, DNC fund-raisers arranged for a continuous and incessant stream of donors or future donors to meet with the president at the White House. These meetings included informal coffees, Oval Office meetings with Clinton, state dinners, receptions, parties, movies, rides on Air Force One and sleepovers in the Lincoln Bedroom.

A second key scene in the movie (depicted in pp. 236–239 here) would be when Clinton and his campaign team realized they could skirt the donor and spending limits imposed on a presidential campaign. Federal campaign finance laws created after Watergate set a $1,000 limit on individual contributions to presidential campaigns and an aggregate spending limit of some $40 million. The Democratic National Committee, which Clinton controlled as head of the party, was not subject to the federal limits. Unlimited soft money from individuals and corporations— the so-called high-dollar contributions of $25,000 to $100,000 or more —was perfectly legal, if given to the DNC.

In the late summer of 1995, Clinton authorized an initial $10 million fund-raising drive for a DNC "media fund" to pay for a series of pro-Clinton television spots. The special fund-raising never stopped until the election, with the DNC providing tens of millions more just for television advertising.

"We created the first fully advertised presidency in U.S. history," Morris later wrote in his book with pride. These ads, mostly thirty-second spots, were brutally effective. They were deceptive enough to be appalling, depicting Dole and the Republicans as anxious to "cut" Medicare by $270 billion when in fact the Republican plan called for a reduction in the rapid rate of Medicare growth. Clinton himself was proposing a Medicare growth reduction of half that amount. But the ads were also truthful enough to strike a chord with voters anxious about health care and their retirement. In the ads Clinton cast himself as the protector of programs such as Medicare, Medicaid (the health insurance program for the poor), education and the environment. These four issues—Medicare, Medicaid, education and the environment—became the cornerstone of Clinton's campaign.

Clinton met one night most weeks with his campaign team in White House strategy sessions, personally editing the television scripts, honing his message, determining precisely what he wanted to say in the television ads. This intense involvement put Clinton through a process of what I would call "self-hearing." He developed, heard and retained his own message. The ads reflected precisely what he wanted to say, stating the reasons he wanted to continue to be president. So, in the daily routine of being president, he began to echo his campaign message. Chaos, multiple and inconsistent daily messages had marred the first two years of his presidency. Clinton had been talking too much on too many issues. The new campaign message imposed a needed discipline. As president, he began using the same language that was appearing in the DNC-financed television ads. For the first time in the Clinton White House there was consistency.

Clinton's television ads pierced into the soul of middle America and the homes of people who often did not read political coverage in their daily newspapers or watch the evening television news. The ads were carefully calibrated to appear in media markets rich with undecided or persuadable voters. The same ads or variations on them often appeared hundreds of times in key markets. Clinton's poll numbers began to move up in these markets. This gave the president more confidence. He stuck to his themes. By moving to the center more, he neutralized the Republicans on their issues such as crime and a balanced budget. He never claimed to be tougher on crime than the Republicans or to be one to balance the budget faster. He would, however, tackle these problems in his own reasonable way. With those issues somewhat off the table, Clinton portrayed himself as the government's mature protector. House Speaker Gingrich embodied radical extremism. As the Senate leader, Dole was Gingrich's partner. The television ads almost always pictured Gingrich and Dole together, and the narrator referred to them as almost one person —"Gingrich-Dole."

The Clinton television advertising ran for six months, from the fall of 1995 to the spring of 1996, while Dole and the Republicans engaged in bloody primary fights. The Republicans spent tens of millions of dollars on television attacking each other, including nearly $20 million Steve Forbes paid to portray Dole as an aging, big-spending career politician and Washington insider. The Republican primary battles gave Clinton the opening he needed. In retrospect, I would argue that Clinton won the 1996 election in late 1995 and early 1996. He found his message, stuck to it and brought it into the homes of millions.

Dole also lost the election of 1996. The economy's strength, the relative absence of turmoil overseas and Newt Gingrich's unpopularity made it an uphill battle for Dole, perhaps an impossible one.

After he had locked up the Republican nomination, Dole attempted to present himself as the seasoned, can-do master of Washington and politics. But he faltered almost weekly. In my extensive interviews with Dole, I found a basic decency in him. But that decency did not surface enough in the campaign.

Dole is not a natural executive; he is rarely decisive or crisp. He often seemed disoriented in his campaigning or message. The first fiasco of the summer of 1996 was his declaration that tobacco was not necessarily addictive. It looked like he was pandering to the tobacco states. When Dole fought with *Today* show anchor Katie Couric over the question of tobacco addiction, an issue apparently settled by most experts, he seemed old, out-of-touch and threatening. Scott Reed called it "tobacco gulch," and Dole couldn't get out of it. Dole's statements hurt him especially with women, and with the press.

Knowing he would have to present an economic plan of his own, Dole finally proposed a 15 percent tax cut over three years, but he never got behind it with conviction. He talked and danced around the issue, betraying his doubts about his own program. He next selected Jack Kemp as his running mate. Kemp went over well initially with the Republican faithful. It seemed that Kemp, a former congressman, former Bush cabinet officer and former presidential candidate from 1988, had sufficient stature and seasoning. But Kemp faltered in the television debate with Vice President Gore, throwing out old sound bites from previous campaigns and speeches. He seemed unprepared for the debate and the vice-presidency.

Dole never mastered television. On the air, he frequently seemed uncomfortable, uncertain. He did not naturally hold convincing eye contact with the camera. He was out of Clinton's league.

Dole's last-minute effort to get Ross Perot to drop out of the race leaked to the media, and it looked like the desperation effort it was.

Dole also never had a fixed and trusted inner circle of advisers to lend his campaign order and consistency. For all his decades in politics, Dole was a strangely isolated man. He had hundreds if not thousands of friends. None were really close. I talked to those closest to him. "Dole didn't know how to have a relationship with anybody," one of them said, echoing a thought expressed privately by many others.

Dole was 73, running against a sitting president age 50. Though the polling never showed that the age issue was a big factor, I believe it was very significant. In the United States, the smallest and most inconsequential business would ordinarily not think of making someone at age 73 the chief executive officer. There would have to be an overwhelming reason. Dole did not provide one.

• • •

Clinton won the election by mastering most of the political fundamentals. I believe there are ten such fundamentals for a winning presidential campaign. They are:

1. A political base. That is a large, substantial block of voters or supporters. Clinton had a base by virtue of being president. He worked assiduously to prevent a primary challenger from within the Democratic Party and he succeeded. So there was no competition to the left of him in the '96 race.

2. Money. Clinton, Gore and the DNC raised more than $180 million, the key, as I have said, to the victory.

3. Political communications skills. Here Clinton has no equal. I have seen him maintain eye contact continuously for an hour-long interview, even through the bottom of a glass as he was finishing his soft drink.

4. Status as an outsider or anti-Washington. Though the president, Clinton always was at war with the Washington culture and the city's permanent establishment. He reflected the national mood against Washington and was able to present himself as someone intent on altering the relationship between the citizens and their government. Dole, in contrast, was seen as the symbol of Washington. He lived at the Watergate apartment complex and had been in the city for 35 years.

5. A message for the 1990s. Clinton set himself up as the restraining force on Gingrich-Dole Republicanism. He was the protector of Medicare, Medicaid, education and the environment.

6. Focus and discipline. In 1995 I wrote in an afterword to *The Agenda* on the first two years of Clinton administration economic policy making that to win reelection, Clinton would have to face an issue, crisis or moment, and demonstrate that he would be willing to risk his presidency to prove his commitment and conviction. "Then might he find some higher ground and win reelection in 1996." Such a moment or crisis never came. But Clinton was able to convert his own reelection into the all-consuming issue. No one brought more singlemindedness to the job of reelection than Clinton. The high ground, though it was not as lofty as the public might have liked, was winning. Holding a sober course that was a mix of Republican and Democratic ideas was enough. Though the concept was exceedingly modest, Clinton brought clear and convincing energy to the task. It spilled over; the permanent "up" and the condition of having always to be "on" came through. Clinton demonstrated the classic passion, the so-called fire in the belly that must be present to win.

7. A game plan and organization. Clinton essentially turned his campaign over to Dick Morris, who had clear theories and tactics for winning. Morris did not always win and Clinton ratified and approved each step. The dovetailing of the campaign and presidential messages was almost seamless.

8. Proven executive experience. Clinton had been president for nearly four years when people voted. He had clearly improved and learned, grown into the office. In contrast, the disarray in the Dole campaign must have given many voters pause.

9. The texture or feel of a president. This is more than image or charisma, it includes demeanor, humor and conviction. Here Dole was in the ballpark. Dole was always a plausible president. But less so than Clinton. This notion encompasses the stewardship role of the president as someone who will take care of the nation. Here Clinton's basic message as the sober protector reinforced the feeling he was able to convey.

10. Be perceived as a truth teller. This is Clinton's greatest weakness. Dole also had the problem. Dole flip-flopped and seemed to cut and trim on enough issues—abortion and assault weapons—to make voters feel he was not talking straight. Dole could look and sound shifty. In contrast, Clinton was smooth when he was shifty.

It is on this last issue—truth telling—that the Clinton presidency will likely endure or falter.

The question of straight talk is at the core of all the Clinton scandals. Whatever the poison in the current political atmosphere, Clinton would not have been subjected to a prolonged independent counsel investigation on the Whitewater land deal, which was made in 1978 even before he was Arkansas governor, if he and his wife had told the full and total truth early on. They had the chance in the 1992 campaign, and they didn't, issuing a misleading report. But the deal was screwy, questionable if not sleazy. Then in 1993 they again had the opportunity to put it behind them, release all the documents, answer all the questions and probably be forced to apologize for getting entangled with a crowd that included James and Susan McDougal, their Whitewater partners.

But apology or contrition is not the Clinton style. Partial disclosure, legalistic justifications and defensiveness are habits they have brought to the White House. They continue to practice partial disclosure in truth telling, probably because it has worked in the past. The approach got the Clintons to the White House.

Clinton went through his first term as president and the first months of his second without being really tested. In the primary roles of the presidency—managing the economy, foreign and defense policy—he had not faced a genuine, full-scale crisis.

As president, Clinton had not had to deal with a stock market crash, a recession, urban riots, massive terrorism, foreign disaster or a war. Though the peacekeeping missions in Haiti, Somalia and Bosnia often turned violent, Clinton did not even have the equivalent of the 1991 Gulf War of his predecessor George Bush.

Most of Clinton's tests have involved political or personal scandal —allegations of marital infidelity, draft dodging, the Whitewater land investment, the discovery of raw summaries of nearly 900 FBI files in the White House, and the escalating campaign fund-raising controversy. No one had really seen how he functioned as a leader in a national or international emergency.

Among a few friends and aides, Clinton complained, often bitterly, that the scandals, investigations and questions eroded his legitimacy as president. He was right. The suspicions created a nagging undercurrent of distrust that worked against his credibility and authority. Clinton blamed partisan Republicans, the media and the climate of investigative zeal that grew out of Vietnam and Watergate. He was partly right.

But Clinton was also responsible. Faced with inconsistencies, criticism or doubts, his reflexive instinct often seemed to be to reveal only a small portion of the truth. Partial, often misleading, disclosure became the order of the day. Outright denial was another strategy.

"The Lincoln Bedroom was never sold," Clinton said on February 25, 1997. "That was one more false story we have had to endure." But Clinton's own handwriting was on the back of a 1995 memo from Terry McAuliffe putting a price tag on the use of the Lincoln Bedroom. Clinton wrote that he wanted to start the "overnights" for the donors who had given $100,000 or $50,000. Two days later Clinton was asked, "Can you really say the White House was not used as a fundraising tool?"

"Absolutely," Clinton declared in the face of irrefutable evidence that the lure of the White House was used for thousands of potential or actual large donors.

The Justice Department set up a special task force to investigate the campaign fund-raising, and the FBI developed evidence from sensitive national security wiretaps and communications intercepts that the People's Republic of China planned to funnel up to $2 million to influence the 1996 elections. This was the most serious part of the inquiry and threatened to keep the spotlight on fund-raising abuses for months if not years to come.

Vice President Gore's personal involvement in making fund-raising calls and assembling the most formidable money network in American politics almost guaranteed that the controversy would last as Gore and others geared up for the 2000 presidential campaign.

For their own survival, the Clintons now need to break the cycle of evasion. At this point the scandals pale significantly when compared to Watergate, which was the active subversion of government by Nixon. Watergate was a massive effort to use power to be reelected and seek vengeance on political enemies. Nixon was forced to resign because the Republicans in his own party, typified by Senator Barry Goldwater, rebelled when the final batch of secret tape recordings was revealed. Too many crimes, too many lies, Goldwater said.

Nixon had a dozen key witnesses who testified to their own corruption and to the crimes of the president. Nixon had piles of documents and dozens of tape recordings that showed his guilt.

Interestingly and significantly, there are no witnesses from Clinton's White House years who are known at this point to provide incriminating testimony alleging that the president or his wife committed crimes. The Clintons and their lawyers ought to find comfort in that. Without credible human witnesses or tape recordings, the Clintons should not be in legal trouble. But the suspicion of them is very deep, and the only way to end the investigations of independent counsels and congressional inquiries is full disclosure and, if necessary, apology.

For months after the Watergate break-in on June 17, 1972, perhaps even up to a year afterwards, Nixon probably could have come clean, even admitted technical violations of law, and humbly apologized. Watergate would then have gone away. Americans are forgiving.

But Nixon persisted in the cover-up and in his misreading of evidence, public sentiment and history. In the end, he lost the most vital element of the presidency: He lost moral authority.

President Clinton has a strong, decent, caring side. When he loses his temper and rages, he often directs his fire at himself. He is not small like Nixon. He ought to capitalize on his capacity for larger purposes, and his obvious ability to define the next stage of good for the country. But he needs to clear the decks and put the scandals behind him. That will require rigorous introspection and self-investigation. The daily dance of justification, denial and technical defense is insufficient.

Clinton and Dole agreed to meet after the election. The afternoon of Friday, December 20, Dole went to the Oval Office to see the president alone for nearly an hour. Clinton didn't seem in a hurry.

Dole sat in one of the two gold chairs, the one normally used by Gore or a head of state. He wished Clinton success, and noted that not only had the president won, but the election had not been close, with Clinton getting 49 percent, Dole 41 and Perot 8. "Wasn't embarrassing, but it wasn't close," Dole said of his defeat.

Clinton said that after Dole had resigned from the Senate, the Republican Congress had been great in the last months, passing a limited health care reform bill and raising the minimum wage.

"I noted that," Dole replied.

Clinton said he was very appreciative of the Republican leadership in those last months.

"Yeah," Dole replied somewhat acidly. He knew the Republicans had to deliver on some legislation to save their own skins. "They gave you everything you wanted—and then some."

Though Clinton had won 379 electoral votes compared to 159 for Dole, the president voiced disappointment that he had lost Georgia and Colorado, even expressed concern about losing Montana.

"Those Medicare ads," Dole said, "you know, they were killers. We weren't going to take people off the Medicare rolls. And my name is not Gingrich-Dole, the way it was in all the ads."

Clinton indicated that he had to do what he had to do.

Dole understood, but he said the Medicare ads were particularly lethal to him in Florida, a traditionally Republican state that Clinton had won.

"We had a thousand things going in Florida," Clinton said ominously.

Knowing Clinton, Dole figured it was probably an exaggeration, but Dole was struck by how little he knew about what had hit him in Florida and elsewhere. Dole realized that Clinton had it mapped out and planned.

"I hope you're going to stay active," Clinton said.

Dole said he intended to do some things but to wait a while.

"You've got such credibility in the disability community," Clinton noted, and there was much to be done.

"I intend to do some of those things," Dole added, noting that he and Elizabeth planned to stay in Washington.

At one point, Clinton got around to complaining about the millions of dollars in legal bills he faced from the various Whitewater and other investigations.

"You're going to be a young man when you leave this White House," Dole said. "You can go out and make millions of dollars. Don't worry about it."

Dole had always been opposed to the independent counsel law that required the appointment of a lawyer to investigate possible wrongdoing by a president or his cabinet members. He had always said that it was pretty sad if the country couldn't put faith in the attorneys in the Justice Department. In contrast, Clinton had supported the new law and signed it.

"You were right and I was wrong on the independent counsel," Clinton said.

Nearly three months later, on March 10, 1997, I went to do a final interview with Dole, who was still keeping a suite of offices on the tenth floor of his old campaign headquarters building. He was in his traditional white shirt and a subdued necktie. For more than two and a half hours we reviewed the campaign, what had happened and why. There were no tears, no self-pity, no blame for others. There was a new serenity about Dole. His response after his defeat had been to appear on television comedy shows, the *Late Show with David Letterman*, *Saturday Night Live* and the *Tonight* show with Jay Leno. He had also appeared in a couple of humorous commercial ads, giving most of his fees to charities.

Why this response to defeat?

"Well, your instincts are to run out on a Wednesday, you know, and justify everything. You know, it wasn't our fault, da-da, da-di-da. It was my responsibility for winning or losing, and we lost, and I assumed all the experts would comment on it without my help." He acknowledged that in some form he had known for days or even weeks before November 5 that he would lose. "It just seemed to me that the thing for me to do was not to rush out and growl."

Why the Letterman show, of all things, as his post-election debut?

"It occurred to me this would be the way to kick it off and demonstrate that there is life after defeat. There's a lot of people—thirty-eight million I think—out there looking for something other than a poor loser."

Why did he lose?

"I think I've always said it in shorthand that Clinton elected a Republican Congress and a Republican Congress reelected Clinton, because I think there were fears out there of some of the excesses and people were frightened." He was referring to Gingrich, the Contract With America, the talk of a Republican revolution. "And I was part of it," he added. "I'm not saying I'm blameless."

Dole noted how the good economy no doubt helped Clinton. The president and his team were expert in polls. "I'm a poll watcher too, but I'm a novice compared to these people. He's good at it."

Dole had been defeated in the 1988 New Hampshire primary by Bush in large part because of a celebrated television ad calling Dole "Senator Straddle." He noted the parallel between the 1988 defeat and the most recent loss. "It was all about TV ads again!" He was following the un-folding campaign finance scandal. "It's mind-boggling to somebody who follows it every day and you sort of, for a while you want to leap out and say something. But I've gotten over that, too."

What did he really think of Clinton? "He's sort of a likable rogue," Dole said. "This is a guy who's always on the edge. He's just always on the edge, and maybe you never slip off that edge, but, boy, you can't always be on the edge."

Dole added, "He's always pushing the envelope. Go as far as you can. 'Nobody's going to catch me. I didn't do anything wrong.' And it doesn't look like that's what happened. Somebody did something wrong."

Dole looked up. He didn't wince or shake his head. He just stared straight ahead.

ACKNOWLEDGMENTS

I am more than fortunate to have the trust and support of two of the strongest media companies, Simon & Schuster and *The Washington Post*. They gave me the time and permitted me the independence to report and write a book about a presidential campaign as it was evolving.

Alice Mayhew, vice president and editorial director at Simon & Schuster, came up with the idea for this book in August 1994. She monitored progress, prodded me, insisted that I focus attention on the Clinton White House once again, asked questions, repeated them patiently when they weren't answered and then in the finishing stretch devoted weekends and nights to helping me complete it on time. Citizen Mayhew, as I sometimes think of her, may love politics as much as Bill Clinton or Bob Dole. For 23 years and eight books she has been my editor. I salute and thank my dear friend.

Carolyn K. Reidy, president and publisher at Simon & Schuster, went the extra 10,000 miles on this book, performing a sort of publishing miracle to get it out and into bookstores less than a month after completion of its final chapter.

At *The Washington Post*, Leonard Downie, Jr., the executive editor, Robert G. Kaiser, the managing editor, and Steve Luxenberg, an assistant managing editor, again allowed me to work largely untethered while providing me a professional home. These bosses and friends are the best in American journalism. I owe special gratitude to Steve Luxenberg, now the Outlook editor of the *Post,* who over long lunches forced me to think more deeply about this project. He helped with editing and provided much wise counsel.

There is no way to work at *The Washington Post* and not feel, and often hear, the presence of its owners, Katharine Graham and Don Graham. Their generosity and flexibility about my professional wanderings were once again tested, and they once again did what is hardest for them: they left me alone. They are the best friends, benefactors and protectors a journalist could have.

There are dozens of people at the *Post* whose careful attentions, often under considerable time pressure, have made all the difference to this book. Jennifer Belton, director of news research, oversees a library and photo library of the finest caliber. I owe a special thanks to Melody Blake and her news research staff, who delivered the answers to questions large and small, sometimes even before they were asked: Alice Crites, Richard Drezen, Ruth Leonard, Bob Lyford, Roland Matifas, Heming Nelson, Richard Ploch, Bobbye Pratt, Robert Thomason and Mary Lou White.

Olwen Price worked tirelessly and with zeal, and her contribution was, once again, gracious and invaluable. She was a blessing to this project.

Joe Elbert and his talented photo staff at the *Post* provided most of the pictures in this book. They are the pros operating at the top of photojournalism.

Jon Newcomb, the chairman of Simon & Schuster, encouraged this project from the start. Also at Simon & Schuster I thank vice president and associate publisher Michele Martin, vice president and deputy general counsel Eric Rayman, publicity director Victoria Meyer, assistant publicity director Pamela Duevel, vice president and director of art Jackie Seow, jacket designer Michael Accordino, copyediting director Marcia Peterson, production manager Jim Thiel, copy supervisor Steve Messina, designers Amy Hill and Edith Fowler and editorial assistant Lisa Weisman.

Ann Adelman brought patience and wisdom to Washington, along with her dictionary, and copyedited the manuscript with a knowing and graceful touch. She did a month's work in a week, and I am grateful.

In preparation for my own reporting, I and my assistant, Karen Alexander, read and often studied hundreds of newspaper and magazine articles. *The Washington Post, The Wall Street Journal, The New York Times,* the *Los Angeles Times* and other daily newspapers have covered the White House and the presidential primaries with admirable skill and vigor. There is no way to write a book about a presidential campaign and not realize the immense debt of gratitude I owe to those who write the first draft of history each day. This book is based almost exclusively on my own reporting, and therefore is my take on the candidates and the process. But with so much that has been reported before by others, any book on a presidential campaign is, in the end, in part derivative.

The Hotline, The Daily Briefing on American Politics, a 20- to 30-page summary of political news coverage in the newspapers, magazines, radio and television, is an amazing, comprehensive and sophisticated barometer. We waited for it each day, and we used it all the time. Special thanks to its founder and executive publisher, Doug Bailey.

David Maraniss, my colleague at the Post, provided special encouragement. His wonderful biography of President Clinton, First in His Class, and the series he and Michael Weisskopf wrote for the Post about the federal budget negotiations were valuable resources, as was all the rest of his coverage of Clinton and Dole. The Post has an extraordinary team of political reporters. David S. Broder is the dean for a reason. He both knows the most and explains the most. The work of several others stands out. Ann Devroy and Dan Balz could put out their own newspaper many days, and it seems they often do. The Post columnists, especially my friend Richard Cohen, provided regular insight. Richard always had a string of questions and shared his endless knowledge and curiosity about politics with me. I also owe much to Post writers Charles R. Babcock, Tom Edsall, Ruth Marcus, Sue Schmidt, Kevin Merida, John Harris, Ed Walsh, Glenn Frankel, Helen Dewar, Walter Pincus, Al Kamen, Blaine Harden, William F. Powers, Jr., George Lardner, Serge Kovaleski, Dale Russakoff, John Yang, Eric Pianin, Dan Morgan, Michael Dobbs, Lou Cannon, John Pomfret and dozens of others. Special thanks to all the senior editors at the Post, especially Michael Getler, Tom Wilkinson, Steve Coll, Wendy Ross and David Von Drehle. The editors on the exceptional national staff of the Post were more than generous; special appreciation to Karen DeYoung, Bill Hamilton, Bob Barnes, Marilyn Thompson and Maralee Schwartz.

Newsweek, U.S. News & World Report and Time magazine cover politics with depth and skill. Each week I counted on and used them. The New Republic and The Weekly Standard provided fresh and provocative ideas. The Almanac of American Politics 1996 by Michael Barone and Grant Ujifusa is the bible, and I relied on it. Richard Ben Cramer wrote the definitive story of the 1988 presidential race, What It Takes. His profile of Bob Dole in that book has stood the test of time, and was of great help to us. Jake H. Thompson's biography of Dole was of much use. So too were the works of Theodore H. White, the godfather of campaign reporting. Carl Bernstein, my friend and former colleague, helped in dozens of ways with thoughts and advice. Richard E. Snyder, the former head of Simon & Schuster, as always, provided me with immense support in both my work and my life. Special gratitude to Benjamin C. Bradlee and Sally Quinn.

Politics is now television. Many friends at the networks assisted me, foremost among them Jim Wooten of ABC. He is a living and walking encyclopedia, and the most thoughtful reporter who knows the difference between a passing examination and a larger effort aimed at understanding. Special thanks to Barbara Cochran at CBS. I have deep appreciation for the team at NBC, especially Tim Russert, Colette Rhoney, Lisa Myers and Tom Brokaw. At CNN, Bernie Shaw, Judy Woodruff and Larry King were very kind and sharing, as was Jim Lehrer at PBS.

Robert B. Barnett was again my agent, counselor and friend. He is also one of the most prudent and skilled lawyers. Because of his association with President and Mrs. Clinton, he did not read the manuscript until it was finished.

The backbone of this work consists of the hundreds of people who were willing to be sources. Whether candidates speaking on the record, staff or friends speaking on background, they gave me extraordinary amounts of time. I have tried to be as careful as possible, and those closest to the events will recognize what I have described.

One of those sources gently warned me not to exploit these people, reminding me that often the closer a reporter moves toward the real emotions and doubts of the inside story, the greater the chance the story will be misunderstood. Compression and reduction of people or events to a sound bite of a few sentences or even a headline of merely a few words inevitably will take place. Candidates and their staffs, friends and family fear these simplifications the most. The emphasis often is on the negative. So the candidates and the campaign apparatus move to shield themselves, and the central questions of character are too often dodged. Who are these people who seek the presidency? What do they truly stand for? What are their values? How do they deal with people close to them? How do they make decisions? What ground do they hold? What ground will they give?

I hope I have tried to answer some of those questions without exploiting or misusing the information I was given.

• • •

Rosa Criollo again cared for and nurtured us at home so well and with love.

Tali, my daughter, who is now about to start her junior year at the University of California at Berkeley, helped with her ideas, love and a thorough, perceptive read of the page proofs of the entire book.

The spouse of any writer bears a burden. Elsa Walsh, my wife and closest, dearest friend, bears that with unusual grace. My work is intrusive and demanding. Selflessly she interrupted her own writing to participate almost daily in my work as wise counselor, tough editor and voice of reason. Friends regularly note that I am lucky and she is a saint. They are right.

INDEX